The Future of Project Management

The Future of Project Management:

Adapting to Modern Needs

Edited by

Igor Vrečko and Brigita Gajšek

Cambridge Scholars Publishing

The Future of Project Management: Adapting to Modern Needs

Edited by Igor Vrečko and Brigita Gajšek

This book first published 2024

Cambridge Scholars Publishing

Lady Stephenson Library, Newcastle upon Tyne, NE6 2PA, UK

British Library Cataloguing in Publication Data
A catalogue record for this book is available from the British Library

ISBN (10): 1-5275-5373-6
ISBN (13): 978-1-5275-5373-6

TABLE OF CONTENTS

FOREWORD

Welcome to the pioneering volume of the "Researching Challenges in the World of Projects" series. This remarkable initiative emerges from the fervour and diligence of the Slovenian Project Management Association, an organisation deeply committed to elevating project management theory and practice. Born from a desire to span the chasm that often exists between the theoretical models and the practical realities of project management, this series is designed to serve as a valuable platform for practitioners, researchers, and enthusiasts alike. The rich tapestry of the series presents the dynamic nature of project management and acknowledges its many nuances, reflecting the constant evolution that characterises the discipline.

The inaugural volume of this series, "Project Management: Adapting to Future Needs," presents itself as a unique compilation of profound and insightful research. Our contributors have endeavoured to dissect, analyse, and address the multifaceted challenges that continue to shape the fabric of modern project management. Embarking on this exploration, we engage with intricate problems, unprecedented scenarios, and novel solutions that resonate with the unique demands of the contemporary world. As a scientific monograph, it presents diverse perspectives, stretching across different domains and disciplines, capturing the essence of a rapidly transforming field and relentlessly pushing boundaries. Our contributors have meticulously collected and synthesised knowledge from various corners of project management, threading together a narrative that both comprehends the rapid pace of change and anticipates the multifaceted needs of the future. This monograph, we believe, not only highlights these challenges but also inspires us to rethink, reimagine, and redefine our strategies and approaches to tackle them successfully.

In this anthology, we journey across the intricate terrains of project management, starting with a comprehensive review of the existing literature that sets the stage for subsequent discussions. It draws attention to the rapidly changing methodologies and tools redefining project management over the past decade. The intersection of technology and project management forms a significant portion of our narrative. From exploring the capabilities of artificial intelligence and machine learning to adopting sophisticated information and communication technologies, the monograph navigates the transformative power of technological advancements in project management. The exploration of building information modelling (BIM) as a tool for optimisation illuminates one such innovation. Also woven into the narrative is an examination of the implications of data analytics in enhancing reporting and decision-making processes within project environments. This signifies the broader drive towards digital transformation and highlights the potential for technology-enhanced strategies in project management. A prominent aspect of the current project management landscape lies in its growing complexity and diversity. This volume delves into the multifaceted nature of international development projects and the nuances of open innovation projects that can present challenges and opportunities. The need for hybrid approaches to project management in today's volatile, uncertain, complex, and ambiguous (VUCA) world is also reflected on. The discourse includes the merits of integrating agile principles into traditional project management methodologies, underscoring the necessity of adaptive approaches in achieving project success. The educational aspects of project management also receive much-needed attention. The development of new learning paradigms and the role of project managers in multimedia production offer unique insights into the ongoing evolution of project management pedagogy. Sustainability also figures prominently in our discussions as the significance of environmental consciousness in project management continues to gain traction. With a greater understanding of projects' global impact, sustainable project management principles are becoming increasingly important. This monograph also recognises the generational shift occurring in the workforce. As newer generations with distinct values and expectations enter the labour market, project management must evolve to accommodate these changes.

The Slovenian Project Management Association is deeply honoured and privileged to present this inaugural monograph, a profound testament to the unwavering dedication and collaborative endeavours of an incredibly diverse group of contributors. As we embark on this momentous journey together, we are filled with immense pride and excitement for the future it heralds. With great anticipation, we extend our heartfelt hope that this monograph becomes a luminous beacon, guiding project management practitioners and researchers alike towards a sustainable, adaptive, and innovative future. It is our ardent desire that these pages ignite a spark within you, propelling you towards new frontiers of knowledge and empowering you to navigate the ever-evolving landscape of project management with confidence and finesse. Indeed, the journey has just begun, and the path stretching out before us is filled with infinite possibilities and untold discoveries. Within these meticulously crafted chapters, you will find profound insights and inspiration to fuel your intellectual pursuits and practical endeavours.

As we traverse uncharted territories together, let us seize every opportunity to learn, grow, and evolve. Let this monograph be the catalyst that propels us towards a future where project management becomes a transformative force, creating sustainable value and fostering innovation across all sectors of society.

In closing, we express our deepest gratitude to all the contributors whose unwavering dedication and tireless efforts have made this monograph a reality. We sincerely appreciate our readers, whose thirst for knowledge and unwavering support inspires us to continually push the boundaries of excellence. Together, let us embark on this intellectual odyssey with open minds and hearts, knowing that through our collective pursuit of knowledge, we can shape a brighter and more prosperous future for project management and the world.

Welcome to a world where the only constant is change—the world of projects.

ZPM
Slovenian project
management association

Prof. Igor Vrečko, PhD
President of the Slovenian Project Management Association

I

THE CHALLENGES OF MODERN PROJECT MANAGEMENT: A LITERATURE REVIEW

BRIGITA GAJŠEK AND SIMONA ŠINKO

1.1 Project Management in the 21st Century

Projects are the economic engine of the 21st century, the era of the project economy. This is not about introducing change overnight but about slow change, with increased time spent working on projects at the expense of reducing time spent on so-called regular, standardised and normalised work. Industries, particularly information technology, manufacturing and construction, are becoming project-orientated. The Project Management Institute (PMI), one of the world's leading authorities on project management, defines the project economy as a "fundamental paradigm shift" in which companies create value for stakeholders through the successful completion of projects. These deliver new infrastructure, products, services, software, and better living conditions, enable economic growth and contribute tangibly to the GDP, in Germany's case by more than 41% (Nieto-Rodriguez 2021). Today, projects deliver financial and social value. They are a means of organisational flexibility, which depends on project team members' project management skills.

The expansion of project work gave impetus to developing the profiles of project managers and leaders and the corresponding competencies. It also began grouping project management experts under professional associations' auspices. The International Project Management Association (IPMA) and PMI are the most influential international associations. Over the years, both have developed international networks based on national associations and chapters. The standards, the Individual Competence Baseline (ICB) and *A Guide to the Project Management Body of Knowledge* (the PMBOK Guide) define the processes in the project life cycle, tools and methods for the work on projects and a list of competencies for project managers.

While business is concerned with delivering projects successfully and productively, a supportive environment for employers and their project managers is prepared and has a built-in mechanism for continuous improvement. International project management associations act as partners with the knowledge and mechanisms to further educate the workforce and grow a new generation of project management experts (PMI 2021). The work of the associations also includes education, research and development dimensions. Nevertheless, not everything runs smoothly. Problems arise in the field of the labour market. The increasing number of projects is reflected in the increased number of jobs requiring very well-developed project management skills. Due to economic growth, this phenomenon can be observed mainly in emerging and developing countries. However, developed countries are no exception, as the number of people retiring is increasing (PMI 2021). According to PMI forecasts, 77 million project management employees are expected to retire by 2030, and 25 million new project professionals will be needed. This requires 2.3 million project managers and change makers per year. PMI studies (PMI 2017; PMI 2021) show that project managers are important contributors to productivity. A talent shortage in the profession can potentially cause risks to the GDP of almost 204 billion EUR over ten years in the 11 countries studied. In response to the staff shortage, an offer of above-average salaries and the opportunity for lifelong training is being developed. The additional training pays off for employees and employers. Employees who are certified by international project management associations report higher average salaries than those without certification. Employers save through better utilisation of resources and a higher percentage of completed projects.

In addition to the term project economy, the terms 'projectification' (Jensen et al. 2016) and 'project society' (Händeler 2011; Lundin et al. 2015) are also frequently used, even in fields that are not traditionally project-orientated, such as scientific research, politics and art—neither private nor social life are exceptions. However, it is not just a matter of creating new terminology. Among other things, the structure of staff in the organisation is also changing. Whereas in the past, most employees were tied to regular work and departments with long-term, stable contracts, today, there are more and more project employees and project managers with temporary contracts (Hodgson & Cicmil 2006). A paradigm shift occurs (Schoper & Ingason 2019), regardless of what it is called and who writes about it. One must search the records under various keywords to understand the phenomenon described. Scholars, researchers and practitioners must do much to clarify the shift and standardise the terminology in the coming years.

An increasing number of projects requires organisational adaptation or formalisation of the approach to managing projects within an organisation. Practice and science confirm that it is insufficient to change from one organisational form to another. The organisation must also master continuous improvement. Is there a best practice that makes sense to approach in small steps? An answer to this question has been attempted for many years by developing maturity models for project management, measuring the maturity level and analysing the results (Kerzner 2019). In this way, the developers wanted to give companies a tool to help them discover their gaps and plan the next steps in developing project management to a more mature stage. The timeliness of the topic and the eagerness to find solutions were reflected in more than 30 project management maturity models, between which it is easy to find overlaps and differences. None of them is suitable for all organisations. Of course, the challenging choice between maturity models is not the only way for an organisation to improve its project management tools, methodology and organisational alignment. There is also the classical approach of learning from one's and others' successes and failures and implementing a continuous improvement mechanism. A more efficient and faster way is based on the project management maturity model, which is also an excellent basis for maturing programme and portfolio management. Adapting the project management maturity assessment can transform a "portfolio of projects into strategic business outcomes that meet strategic business objectives" (Kerzner 2019). Currently, it cannot be claimed that there is a consensus on what project management maturity is. However, there is agreement that planning, reviewing and analysing to improve the project delivery system and its supporting environment must be done frequently to mature. Business operations in the era of the project economy require a shift to a certain level of project management maturity through minor or destructive improvements that, in extreme cases, may exceed employee acceptance and block the improvement process. Kerzner (2019) writes about the costs associated with maturing and improving using organisational change management. The project management office should do the most to reduce these costs, but awareness and application of these lessons in practice are low.

31 October 2020 was the opening day of Berlin Brandenburg Airport, a project with nine years of delays and costs that have risen from 2.83 to 7.3 billion EUR. The project was part of a political strategy to make Berlin more accessible and establish the city as a new world centre (Lopez 2019). The

privatisation of the airport was unsuccessful, leaving a group of politicians with questionable project management and construction skills in charge of the project (Larsson Castro et al. 2020). Berlin Airport and similar examples show the dividing line between public and private projects. It seems that the PMBOK theory and project management standards are practised to a lesser extent in the public sector. It cannot be denied that there are differences in the maturity of project management in the private sector depending on the industry. Cook-Davies and Arzymanow noted in 2002 that industries with a long tradition, such as the petrochemical and defence industries, have more mature project management than industries that have only recently adopted project management. Engineering-based industries also perform better than those that have only recently adopted project management, such as financial services or pharmaceutical research and development.

Project management has evolved differently in different environments. There are many versions of project management models. Each alternative acts as a shell within which project portfolios are managed in a specific ecosystem. There is excellent potential for exploring the differences and similarities between differently classified industries and companies, with maturity models providing a good basis for research. Grant and Pennypacker (2006) suggest examining and comparing project management maturity between companies that rely primarily on internal projects and companies that typically use external project support. They are interested in "a clear relationship between project management maturity and successful project delivery, which could be determined by performance indicators," as Kerzner (2019) suggested. In general, it is expected that a company that has reached a certain level of maturity in project management will maintain or improve the achieved level. Mullaly (2006) has shown that the level of maturity achieved can also decrease by one or several levels in successive years. The retirement of senior project managers and acquiring the necessary skills by novice project managers can lower the maturity levels of private or public organisations.

Project management is now a mature discipline recognised as an enabler of strategic change and economic growth. There are standards for project management at project, programme, portfolio and organisational levels. The supporting professional environment for project management professionals and novices is functioning, and maturity assessment models are available. On the other hand, companies perceive project management differently, on a continuum from a fad to a strategic enabler. Project management is considered necessary but not fully utilised as an organisational capability. Given the transition to the project economy/projectification/project society, companies will likely become more interested in using project management as a competitive advantage. Interest in examples of best practices will increase depending on the type of industry and organisation. We also expect to see increased interest in project organisation, project programmes and portfolios, project managers' skills, digitalisation, automation, artificial intelligence in project management, knowledge management about project management and linking project management to strategic objectives. To facilitate engagement with the challenges of modern project management, we have examined the below articles in three eminent scientific journals regarding project management from 2015 to the first half of 2022. We are interested in the characteristics of scientific publications and trends to predict current research topics better. We believe that textbooks and project management standards are insufficient to support projectification and the increasing understanding by organisations and new entrants of lessons learned, benchmarking and other things that could help establish a project delivery ecosystem more quickly and achieve strategic and customer goals as expected.

1.2 Methodology

The quantitative approach of a bibliometric analysis was applied to summarise the scientific efforts in project management described in three scientific journals from January 2015 to July 2022. Two selected journals, the *International Journal of Project Management* (IJPM) and the *Project Management Journal* (PMJ), are affiliated with international project management associations. The third, the *International Journal of Managing Projects in Business* (IJMPB), is independent but focuses exclusively on project management. All three journals publish articles in management research and are ranked in the JCR—Serials Impact Factor of Journal Citation Reports (Table 1.1). The impact factor of all three journals decreased slightly in 2020, but IJPM remained in the first quarter.

The IJPM is published by the Association for Project Management and the IPMA. It claims to be: "The leading journal for the field of project management and organisation studies where its mission is to publish leading edge innovative research that significantly advances the field of project management" and organisation. IPMA is a federation of the leading project management associations in 71 countries. They are available in most European countries and are spreading to Asia and America, with tremendous growth and demand.

Table 1.1 *Serials Impact Factor from Journal Citation Reports*

Year	IJPM			PMJ			IJMPB		
	JCR IF	Q	Ranking	JCR IF	Q	Ranking	JCR IF	Q	Ranking
2020	7.17	1	38/226	3.57	3	126/226	2.63	3	164/226
2019	6.61	1	12/226	2.50	2	112/226	1.98	3	146/226
2018	4.69	1	30/217	2.04	3	121/217	1.60	3	106/147
2017	4.32	1	26/210	1.95	2	101/210	1.32	3	152/210
2016	4.03	1	21/194	2.71	2	52/194			
2015	2.88	1	29/192	1.76	2	77/192			

PMJ is the scholar and research journal of the PMI and contains the latest research, theories, techniques and applications in project management. PMJ's mission is to influence thinking about the need for using project management and its impact by publishing cutting-edge research that advances theory and evidence-based practice. PMI members are organised into over 300 PMI Chapters in approximately 100 countries. PMI Chapters are volunteer-led communities that enable members to interact with other project management professionals, develop their skills and make a difference in their local communities.

The IJMPB strives to promote the theory, research and practice of all aspects of project management. It seeks high-quality empirical and theoretical research to advance the understanding of project management and stimulate the publication of new knowledge in project management using multidisciplinary approaches entrenched in the social sciences.

Table 1.2 *Distribution of articles between journals*

Journal	JCR Ranking	Quarter	Number of articles	Share [%]
IJPM	38/226	Q1	534	54.16
PMJ	126/226	Q3	249	25.25
IJMPB	164/226	Q3	203	20.59
		Sum	986	100

Articles were selected from the *Web of Science* in July 2022 via a keyword search using "project management." Only articles in English were considered. The search results include 986 articles for further analysis. Five hundred and thirty-four (54.16%) articles are published in the highest ranked IJPM, 249 (25.25%) in PMJ and 203 (20.59%) in IJMPB (Table 1.2).

Bibliometrix 4.0 by R-Studio Biblioshiny is a network analysis software tool for visualising the dynamics and structures of science. It was used for an in-depth study of the intellectual structures of the research field of project management.

1.3 Results

The world is facing an increase in the number of projects launched per unit of time, the phenomenon of projectification and the challenges of the project economy era. It seems that individuals' business and personal lives during working hours are increasingly permeated with project activities. In the past, the experience of undertaking projects and building a project environment was scarce and scattered across different cultures; today, there are enough data for real studies for the first time. It would be expected that intensive project work at the practice level would be followed by intensive academic research.

Table 1.3 contains the descriptive data on the scientific literature studied, published in three central and eminent journals in project management. The average number of authors in an article is 2.83; 1,907 authors wrote 986 scientific articles, of which 90 (9.12%) were written by a single author.

Table 1.3 *The descriptive data on studied scientific articles*

Query area		Result
Documents by document type	Scientific Article	964
	Review Article	16
	Editorial Materials	5
	Reprints	1
Number of international scientific journals		3
Annual growth rate for the number of published articles		-15.85%
Authors		1,907
Authors of single-authored documents		90
Co-authors per document		2.83
Author's keywords (DE)		960
Document average age		3.93

The annual growth rate for the number of articles published is 15.85%. This percentage shows that the number of articles on project management in the three central, eminent journals in project management is declining on average. A similar conclusion can be drawn from the average age of the articles, which is 3.93 years. The percentage is even lower as we only considered published articles from the first half of 2022.

Figure 1.1 provides more detailed insight into publishing project management articles for individual journals. IJPM had the largest decline in the number of publications. With 123 articles published in 2015 and 51 articles in 2021, the journal saw a 46.5% decline. The IJMPB did not publish any articles on project management in 2015 and 2016. Within the observed period, the journal published the most articles in 2020, with a sudden decrease after that year. The number of articles published in PMJ fluctuates steadily.

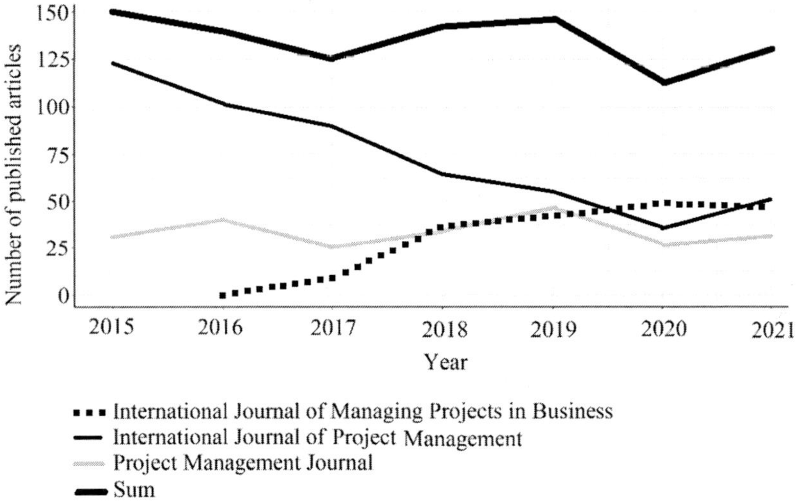

Figure 1.1 *The dynamics of publishing scientific articles*

One thousand nine hundred seven authors contributed to the articles selected for analysis. Table 1.4 shows 16 authors who contributed to eight or more articles during 2015–2022. The three most prolific authors are Müeller, who contributed to 23 (2.33%) articles; Aaltonen, who contributed to 15 (1.52%); and Anderson, who contributed to 12 (1.22%) articles. Three of the six most prolific authors published articles on project management each year. Müller, as the most prolific author, made the largest contribution in 2018 when he published five articles, which is also the highest number of published articles per author per year.

Table 1.4 *The* m*ost prolific authors*

Author	Year								N. of articles	[%]*
	2015	2016	2017	2018	2019	2020	2021	2022		
Müller	4	3	1	5	4	2	3	1	23	2.33
Aaltonen	2	1	2	1	3	3	2	1	15	1.52
Andersen	1		2	3	4	1	1		12	1.22
Martinsuo		1	1	2	4	2	1		11	1.12
Sankaran	2		1	3	2	1	2		11	1.12
van der Hoorn	3	3	1	1	1	1	1		11	1.12
Ahola		1	2	1	1	3	2		10	1.01
Aubry	1	2		4			2	1	10	1.01
Zhu				2	3	2	2	1	10	1.01
Gemünden	1	3	1	2	1	1			9	0.91
Geraldi		1	1	1	2	3	1		9	0.91
Kock		2	1	2	2	2			9	0.91
Whitty	3	1	1		1	2	1		9	0.91
Brunet		2		1	2		2	1	8	0.81
Davies	1	2		1	2	1	1		8	0.81
Yu				2	1	2	2	1	8	0.81

* Percentage is calculated based on 986 included articles

The co-authorship analysis helped us understand the structure of scientific contributions in project management (Figure 1.2, Table 1.5). It shows the presence of four collaborative Clusters with more than three article writers and measures the extent of joint publications between authors contributing to the advancement of knowledge in project management. Each node in Figure 1.2 represents one author. The size of the node represents the number of contributions by the author. The thickness of the connecting line shows the number of publications jointly authored by the authors.

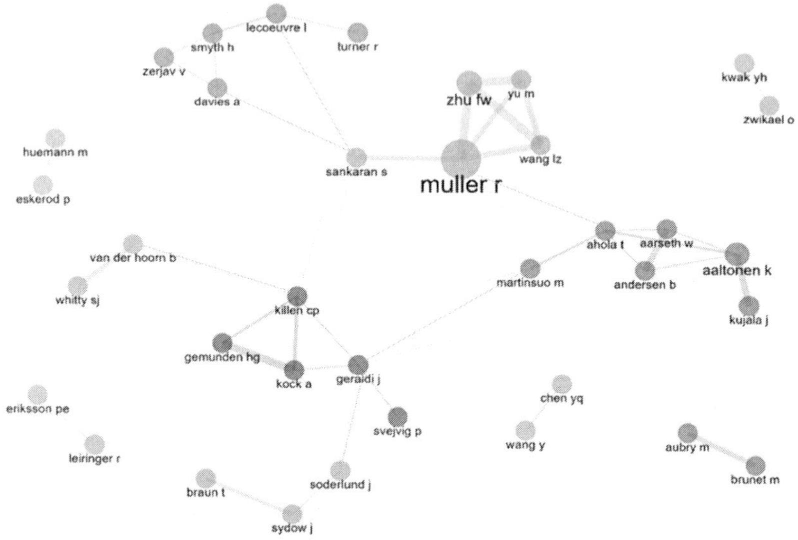

Figure 1.2 *Co-authorship analysis of authors*

The most prolific and collaborative author is Müller, and the most prolific Cluster is Cluster 1 (Figure 1.2, Table 1.5), which includes researchers from Norway, China and Australia. Three other clusters are the groups of equally productive authors. The Cluster 2 brings together six authors from Finland and Norway, the Cluster 3 and Cluster 4 five, and the smaller Cluster 5 three. The Cluster 3 includes researchers from the United Kingdom. In each cluster mentioned, two authors are linked by joint publications with authors from two other clusters. Müller, Sankaran, Ahola, Martinsuo, Killen and Geraldi connect the project management research community through publications with authors from other clusters. In addition to the interconnected clusters, ten researchers work in five pairs that are not meaningfully connected to the rest of the research community through joint publications.

The authors' countries were also analysed (Tables 1.5 and 1.6). Table 1.5 shows the countries from which the corresponding authors came who contributed ten or more articles. If we add up the contributions of corresponding authors from the European Union in Table 1.5, the European Union is in the lead with 290 (29.4%) articles. If we look at each country individually, China is in the lead with 154 (15.62%) articles, followed by Australia with 107 (10.85%) articles and the United Kingdom with 97 (9.84%) articles.

Table 1.5 *The* d*istribution of authors and countries by Clusters*

Cluster	Authors within the cluster
Cluster 1	Müller R. (Norway), Sankaran S. (Australia), Zhu F.W. (China), Yu M. (China), Wang, Y (China)
Cluster 2	Aaltonen K. (Finland), Andersen B. (Norway), Martinsuo M. (Finland), Ahola T. (Finland), Aarseth W. (Norway), Kujala J. (Finland)
Cluster 3	Davies A. (UK), Turner R. (UK), Zerjav V. (UK), Lecoeuvre L. (independent), Smyth H. (UK)
Cluster 4	Gemünden H.G. (Germany), Geraldi J. (Denmark), Kock A. (Germany), Killen C.P. (Australia), Svejvig P. (Denmark)
Cluster 5	Sydow J. (Germany), Braun T. (Germany), Söderlund J. (Norway)
Cluster 6	Aubry M. (Canada), Brunet, M. (Canada)
Cluster 7	Chen Y.Q. (China), Wang Y. (China)
Cluster 8	Huemann M. (USA), Eskerod P. (Austria)
Cluster 9	Zwikael O. (Australia), Kwak Y.H. (USA)
Cluster 10	Leringer R. (Hong Kong), Eriksson P.E. (Sweden)
Cluster 11	van der Hoorn B. (Australia), Whitty S.J. (Australia)

Figure 1.3 shows a world map with countries from which the authors of the studied articles originate. The authors are active in 56 different countries around the world. We were interested in the countries without active authors. These countries are:

- Europe: Albania, Andorra, Belarus, Bosnia and Herzegovina, Bulgaria, Croatia, Iceland, Kosovo, Latvia, Lithuania, Luxembourg, Malta, Moldova, Monaco, Montenegro, Northern Macedonia, San Marino, Slovakia;
- Asia: Afghanistan, Armenia, Azerbaijan, Bangladesh, Bhutan, Brunei, Cambodia, Georgia, Iraq, Kazakhstan, Kuwait, Kyrgyzstan, Laos, Lebanon, Maldives, Mongolia, Myanmar, Nepal, North Korea (Dem. People's Republic), Oman, Philippines, Sri Lanka, Palestine, Syria, Tajikistan, Timor-Leste, Turkmenistan, United Arab. Emirates, Uzbekistan, Yemen.

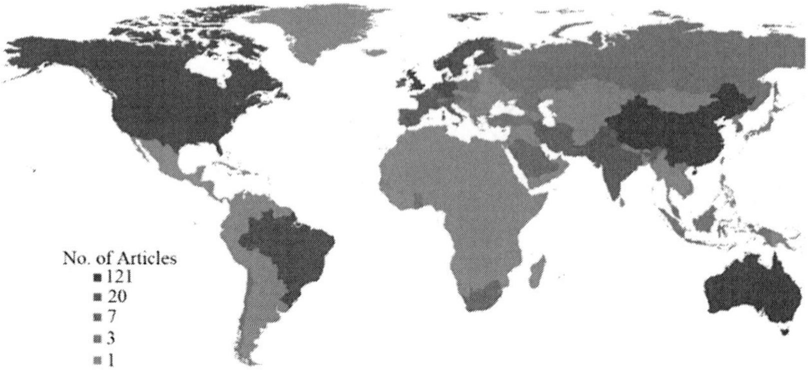

Figure 1.3 *Countries with publications*

The authors associated with the countries of North America are active in Canada, Haiti and the US. The authors associated with South America are active in Brazil, Chile, Colombia and Peru. Authors associated with Australia are active in Australia and New Zealand, and authors associated with Africa are active in Angola, Egypt, Ethiopia, Ghana, Senegal and South Africa. The distribution of articles by year for each country separately is shown in Table 1.6.

Müller, who works for the Norwegian Business School, published articles with co-authors from 11 countries, and 12 articles (52%) were published with co-authors from China. Sankaran, who works for the University of Technology Sydney, published articles with co-authors from seven countries, five (45%) with co-authors from Norway. Figure 1.4 shows the international collaboration in publishing joint articles based on authors' publications linking the clusters identified in Figure 1.2. The associated researchers collaborate to a greater extent with Norwegian and Australian researchers, with Müller and Sankaran leading the way. This type of collaboration is also of interest to researchers from India, China, South Africa and Japan.

Sankaran from the University of Technology Sydney, Müller from the BI Norwegian Business School and Drouin from the Université du Québec à Montréal explored collaboration in project management research. They conducted collaborative research under the PMI umbrella involving researchers from nine countries: Australia, Canada, China, India, Lithuania, South Africa, Norway, Sweden and the Netherlands.

Table 1.6 *Articles per corresponding author's country*

Country	Articles per country							N. of CA**	Share [%]*
	2015	2016	2017	2018	2019	2020	2021		
China	19	24	18	13	9	12	20	154	15.6
Australia	20	19	17	13	19	12	14	107	10.8
UK	22	16	13	13	13	15	18	97	9.8
Canada	9	12	3	9	6	8	8	64	6.5
USA	20	10	14	12	14	2	10	60	6.1
Norway	8	8	6	15	14	6	5	54	5.5
Finland	2	5	4	7	9	5	5	41	4.2
Sweden	4	3	6	5	5	5	2	38	3.9
Brazil	3	6	4	4	5	6	6	37	3.8
Netherlands	6	8	6	5	8	2	2	37	3.8
Germany	3	7	3	8	10	3	5	35	3.5
Denmark	2	3	1	3	3	3	6	23	2.3
France	5	2	4	2	4	0	1	20	2.0
Spain	3	1	2	0	2	4	2	16	1.6
Italy	3	0	3	0	1	2	2	15	1.5
Pakistan	1	0	2	2	3	2	4	14	1.4
S. Korea	4	1	0	2	2	0	1	13	1.3
Belgium	2	0	2	0	2	0	1	12	1.2
India	1	3	1	2	2	2	2	12	1.2
Iran	1	1	0	3	0	3	1	12	1.2
Ireland	0	2	3	3	2	1	1	12	1.2
S. Africa	0	1	1	1	1	1	1	11	1.1
Austria	1	0	1	1	0	1	2	10	1.0

* Percentage is calculated based on 986 included articles
** Number of corresponding authors

Sankaran and Müller as researchers from developed countries working with researchers in emerging and developing countries. We could not understand whether this collaboration resulted from the desire to be mentored by a renowned top researcher or to work with a prestigious institution. The authors (Sankaran et al. 2021) found that collaboration with a renowned top researcher is often more important than belonging to a prestigious institution.

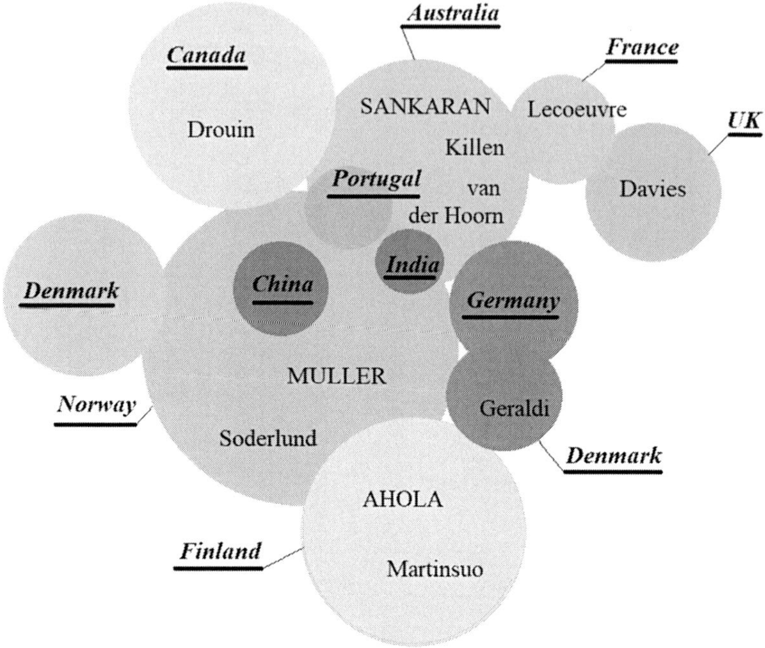

Figure 1.4 *International cooperation of authors who link the clusters*

1.3.1 Keywords analysis

Keyword analysis is a tool for studying trending topics, and scholars are focusing on this area (Song et al. 2019). Figure 1.5 shows four clusters of authors' keywords in four rows based on the 20 most frequently used words.

From the first line (Cluster 1, Figure 1.5), it can be seen that researchers are exploring the agile approach and SCRUM framework in their desire for flexibility and comparing it with traditional project management and its tools.

The second line (Cluster 2, Figure 1.5) describes a strong research stream in project management for infrastructure projects and construction. Contractors for such projects are mostly selected through public tenders. The main challenge is to evaluate the projects and select the most favourable and trustworthy contractor to implement the project within the limits and wishes set out at the beginning. The second challenge is implementing the project, which also brings many interesting research challenges.

The third line (Cluster 3, Figure 1.5) deals with project control as an important phase in the project's life cycle that requires accountability. Investors usually hire agents to carry out control and delegate decision-making powers to them. Agency theory assumes that the interests of the agents may differ from the interests of the investors and refers to these as principal-agent problems (Kopp 2021). The words in Cluster 3 summarise this area of research within project management very well.

The fourth line (Cluster 4, Figure 1.5) refers to the modern challenges of project organisations, multinational companies or firms where the number of projects is increasing. In the face of global change, more and more companies are affected by this problem. The PMI (Ross & Shaltry 2006) define a project portfolio as "A collection of projects, programmes and other work that is grouped to facilitate the effective management of that work to meet strategic business objectives. The projects or programmes of the portfolio may not necessarily be interdependent or directly related." A portfolio can be managed at either a functional or organisational level. In either case, it requires the implementation of a complex adaptive system.

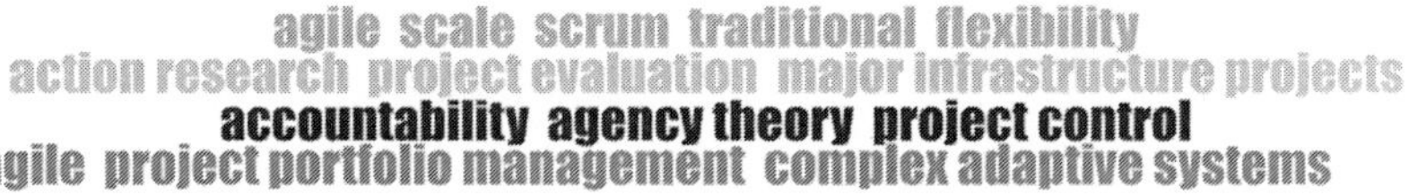

Figure 1.5 *Authors' keywords cloud*

Figure 1.6 sums up the dynamics of the authors' keywords. The analysis revealed several groups of keywords that appeared and were used more frequently in a given period. The perceived relevance of the keyword groups (marked in Figure 1.6 with A, B, C, D, E) in the period between 2015 and 2021 is as follows:

- 2015 (keyword group A): absorptive capacity, knowledge management, managerial practices, R&D project management;
- 2016 (keyword group B): 5D BIM, cash flow analysis, financial decision-making, project financing;
- 2017 (keyword group C): active leadership, stakeholder management, community leaders, disaster recovery projects, case study, Japanese culture;
- 2019 (keyword group D): accelerating projects, benefits management, project value creation, project success and case study;

- 2020-2021 (keyword group E): open innovation, organisational capabilities, project capabilities, project capability-building, event structure analysis, ESA.

After project management matured from a methodological-technical perspective, the research focused on project success and types of capability (organisational, personal, project).

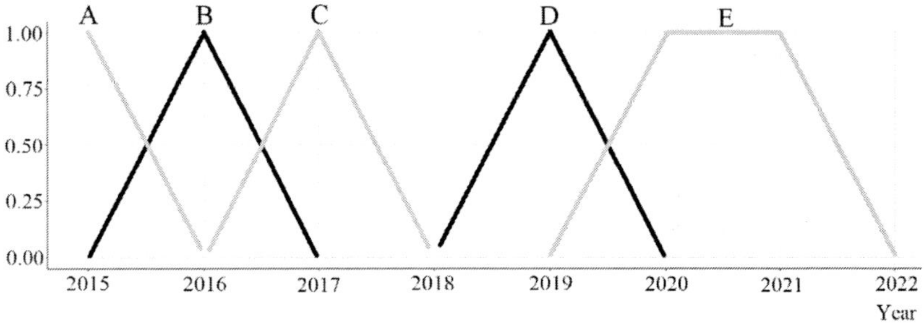

Figure 1.6 *Keywords dynamics*

1.3.2 Titles analysis

The most frequently used phrase in the titles of the 986 articles analysed is "project management" (Figure 1.7). It occurs in 166 (16.84%) titles, as seen in Table 1.7. The second most common phrase is "project managers," which occurs in 52 (5.27%) titles of articles.

Figure 1.7 *Most frequently used phrases (bigrams) in articles' titles*

The phrase "construction projects" is the third most commonly used. It was used in 49 (4.97%) titles in its plural form and 20 (2.03%) titles in its singular form, "construction project." When we combine the two phrases "construction projects" and "construction project" into one, "construction project" becomes the second most common phrase, occurring in 69 (7%) titles. The analysis of the titles shows that in the period studied between 2015 and 2022, project management was often studied using examples from the construction industry.

Other phrases among the ten most frequent bigrams appearing in the titles are "project success," "project teams," "infrastructure projects," "project performance," "development projects," and "project governance." These phrases define the researched topics (primarily) in construction.

Table 1.7 *Most relevant phrases (bigrams) in articles' titles*

Phrase (bigram)	Occurrence	Share [%]*
Project management	166	16.84
Project managers	52	5.27
Construction projects	49	4.97
Project success	44	4.46
Project teams	30	3.04
Infrastructure projects	29	2.94
Project performance	28	2.84
Development projects	27	2.74
Project governance	22	2.23
Construction project	20	2.03

*Percentage is calculated based on 986 included articles

The co-occurrence network is shown in Figure 1.8. Each circle graphically illustrates a phrase. Its size depends on the frequency of occurrence of the phrase in the titles. The more frequently the phrase occurs in the titles, the larger the circle is. If a line connects two circles, the phrases appear together in one or more titles. The more often they appear together in the titles, the thicker the line is. R-Studio Biblioshiny's Bibliometrix 4.0 has identified seven clusters of phrases.

The largest Cluster in Figure 1.8 evolves around the central phrase "project management." The phrase "project management" is often associated with 15 other phrases, among which "project managers", "project success," and "project performance" stand out. In relation to "project managers," research was conducted on "emotional intelligence," "mediating role," and "project success." In addition, "project success" was frequently mentioned in connection with "project governance," "knowledge sharing," "project managers," "mediating role," and "construction projects."

In the second largest Cluster, in terms of the number of related phrases, the most frequently associated phrase, "development projects," is in the middle of the Cluster, associated with information systems, systems development, development project, software development, product development and project team.

Figure 1.8 *Co-occurrence network connectivity visualisation for phrases in articles' titles*

The next cluster consists of six equally frequent phrases that refer to the success of partnership projects, with a focus on public-private infrastructure projects. It is linked to the other phrase clusters by the phrases "development projects," "project management," and "mediating role."

An analysis of the trigrams in the titles of the articles was carried out to sharpen the insight into the most common topics of the published articles. The phrase "project portfolio management" is the most frequently used trigram in ten titles. It appeared in ten (1.01%) titles from 2016 to 2020. This phrase has been around for a long time and therefore has probably not reached a mature stage in its development. Similarly, "product development projects" appear yearly in at least one title. "Critical success factor" and "project risk management" appeared in eight (0.81%) titles each in the period from 2016 to 2019.

The trigrams "software development projects," "construction project management" (2017–2021), "information system projects" (2016–2017) and "project management research" (2015–2018) are similarly common. They each appeared in seven (0.7%) titles. These groups include the most recent title, "software development projects," which refers not only to this type of project but also to software development projects to support project work.

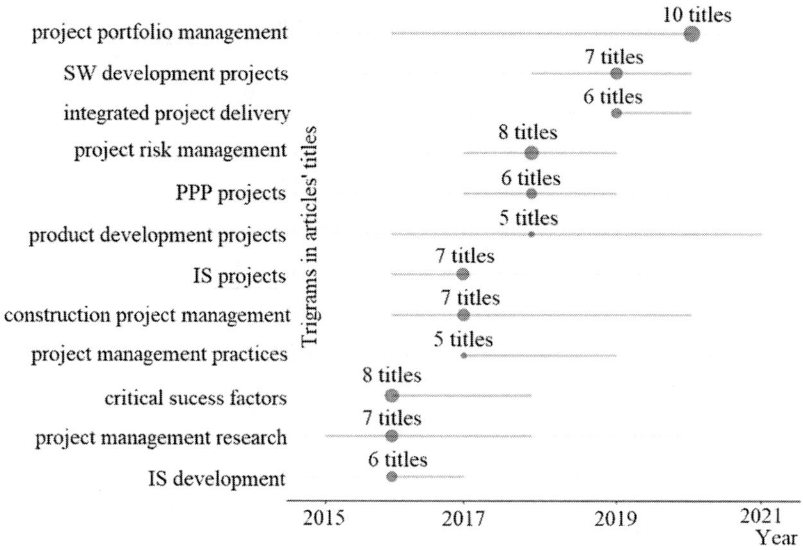

Figure 1.9 *Occurrence of the trigrams in articles' titles in the 2015-2021 interval*

Three pairs of connected trigrams were discovered (Figure 1.10). Among them, the most frequent link is between "public-private partnership projects" and "critical success factors" in 2017. Slightly less frequent is a link between "information systems development" and "systems development projects" in the titles of articles in 2016.

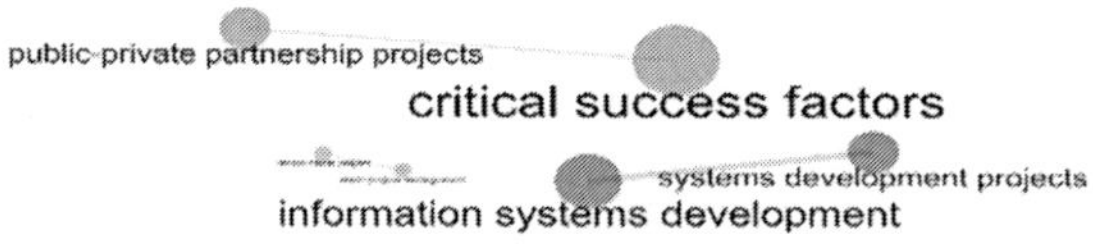

Figure 1.10 *Co-occurrence network connectivity visualisation for trigrams in articles' titles*

Figure 1.11 shows the word cloud based on keywords plus. Keywords plus are words or phrases frequently occurring in the titles of references in the article but not in the article's title (Garfield & Sher 1993). Management is the most frequently used word. It is part of the phrase "project management," and conversely, the practice and theory of "project management" is often based on the skills of "management." The phrase "construction projects" follows as the second most frequently used phrase as a logical continuation of the findings from the previous sections of the analysis, which have already established that many articles deal with topics from construction projects. With few exceptions, most other words in Figure 1.11 occur only once. Exceptions are "dynamic," "capabilities," "strategies," "organisation," "explanation," "challenges," "emergence," "knowledge, "inference," "implement," and "adoption."

Figure 1.11 *Frequently occurring keywords plus in articles' titles of references*

1.3.3 Abstracts analysis

The analysis of the phrases in the titles of the articles showed that the phrase "project management" is the most frequently used bigram. The same was seen in the analysis of the abstracts (Figure 1.12), which revealed that "project management" occurs in 884 (89.66%) abstracts analysed. The phrase "project managers" follows in 365 (37.02%) abstracts, and the phrase "project success" appears in 237 (24.04%) abstracts. Other phrases among the ten most frequently used bigrams in abstracts include "project performance," "construction projects," "project governance," "project team(s)," "project complexity," and "risk management." An analysis of the abstracts yields comparable results to the analysis of the titles. Eight out of ten phrases listed in Table 1.8 for abstracts are the same as in Table 1.7 for the titles. The most frequently used bigrams in both tables are "project management" and "project managers." The abstract analysis adds two frequently used bigrams to the title analysis results, "project complexity" and "risk management."

Figure 1.12 *Frequently used bigrams in articles' abstracts*

Table 1.8 *Bigrams' occurrence frequency in articles' abstracts*

Phrase	Occurrence	Share* [%]
Project management	884	89.66
Project managers	365	37.02
Project success	237	24.04
Project performance	167	16.94
Construction projects	142	14.40
Project governance	105	10.65
Project team	104	10.55
Project teams	87	8.82
Project complexity	86	8.72
Risk management	86	8.72

* Percentage is calculated based on 986 articles included

The pairs and frequencies of co-occurrence of bigrams in article abstracts are shown in Figure 1.13. The analysis included 50 frequently used bigrams in abstracts and analysed their co-occurrence. Bigrams that have no connection with the articles' content contributions are "factor analysis," "semi-structured interviews," "management literature," and "equation modelling." These four bigrams are frequently mentioned in abstracts to explain the research methodology used.

The largest Cluster (Figure 1.13) consists of 33 (71%) out of 46 bigrams that are contextually linked to the key phrase "project management." Within the blue Cluster, there are significantly more observed co-occurrences than we defined in the title analysis (Figure 1.8); as in the abstract, the authors often place the discussed topic in the context of project management in general and capture attractive terms. In any case, the same conclusions apply to the analysis of the abstracts as to the analysis of the titles, with the difference that now the set of phrases co-occurring with the phrase "project management" has been expanded.

One of the clusters (Figure 1.13) contains six phrases around the central phrase "project team(s)." The articles address the challenges of building a project-based organisation and managing/sharing/transferring knowledge. This also explains the co-occurrence of the phrases "project teams" and "knowledge sharing" in the results of the title analysis of the articles in Figure 1.8.

From the perspective of sectors, only the construction sector is mentioned. This does not mean that project management is not researched in other sectors, but only that the construction industry is in articles mentioned most often.

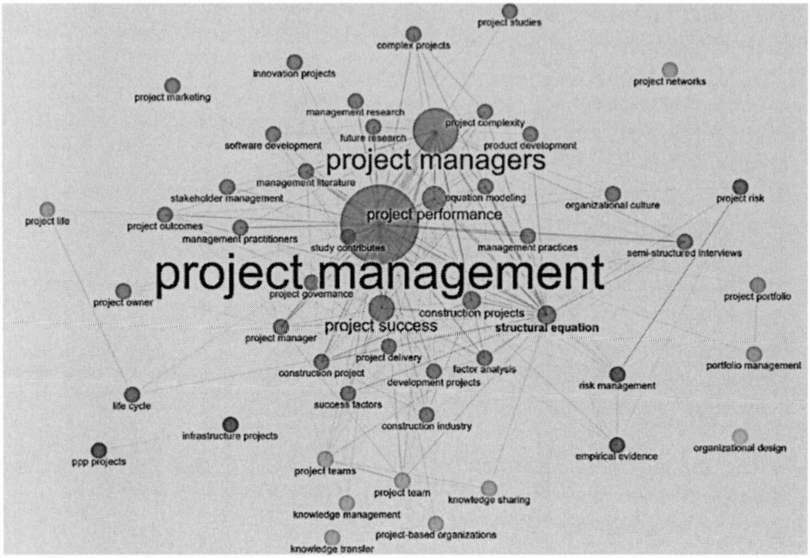

Figure 1.13 *Co-occurrence network connectivity visualisation for phrases in articles' abstracts*

"Project management literature" is the most frequently used trigram (Figure 1.14). It was used in 46 (4.67%) abstracts (Table 1.9). It is followed by "project management practices" in 38 (3.85%) abstracts and "structural equation model" in 34 (3.45%) articles. The first and third trigrams represent the methodological approach to studying project management issues. Among them, the trigrams "social network analysis" and "top management support" stand out as they were not discovered in previous analyses.

Figure 1.14 *Most frequently used trigrams in articles' abstracts*

Comparing the list of trigrams used in the titles of the articles (Figure 1.9) with the list of trigrams used in the articles' abstracts (Table 1.9), only "project risk management" and "project management research" are among the ten most frequently used trigrams in both lists.

Table 1.9 *Most frequently used trigrams in articles' abstracts*

Phrase	Methodological approach	Occurrence	Share* [%]*
Project management literature	yes	46	4.67
Project management practices	no	38	3.85
Structural equation modelling	yes	34	3.45
Project management research	yes	27	2.74
Project management practitioners	yes	25	2.54
Project life cycle	no	24	2.43
Project management PM	no	22	2.23
Project risk management	no	21	2.13
Systematic literature review	yes	18	1.83
Critical success factors	no	16	1.62

* Percentage is calculated based on 986 included articles

1.3.4 Trending topics and thematic analysis

In thematic analysis, bigram clusters are formed from the titles of the articles. Clusters group bigrams that refer to the same topic and are characterised by density and centrality. These two characteristics define the degree of relevance and development of the topics. Density is a measure of cohesion between nodes, and centrality represents the degree of correlation between different topics (Esfahani et al. 2019). The upper right quadrant represents the driving themes, the upper left quadrant represents the very specific themes, the lower right quadrant represents the basic themes, and the lower left quadrant represents the emerging or disappearing themes.

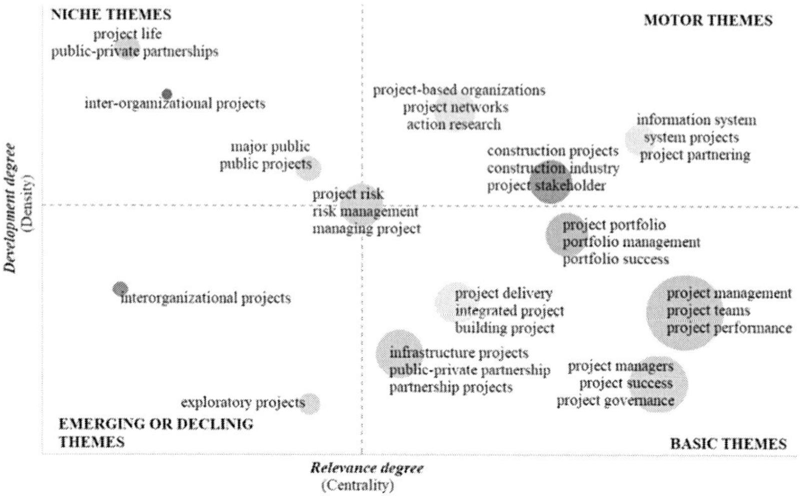

Figure 1.15 *Density and centrality of project management themes from the article's titles*

The thematic map of project management from the titles of the articles (Figure 1.15) was derived from 97 bigrams divided into 17 themes. Table 1.10 shows the links between themes and bigrams. Particularly relevant topics in project management are placed in the right quadrants, namely project-based organisation, information systems, construction projects, project portfolio, project delivery, infrastructure projects, project managers and project management. The project-based organisation, information systems and construction projects are motor themes; the rest are basic. Project management is the most central among motor and basic themes, with 36 bigrams. Project life, inter-organisational projects and the major public are highly developed and isolated themes.

Table 1.10 *Themes and corresponding bigrams from the articles' titles*

Theme	Corresponding bigrams from articles' titles
Infrastructure projects	infrastructure projects, public-private partnerships, partnership projects, comparative analysis, major infrastructure, PPP projects
Project managers	project managers, project success, project governance, mediating role, empirical investigation, emotional intelligence,

	transformational leadership, project benefits, agile project, citizenship behaviour, impact project
Project-based organisation	project-based organisation (s), project networks, action research, knowledge transfer, Chinese construction, collaborative research, public sector, research project
Project management	project management, project team(s), project performance, development projects, project complexity, project manager, success factors, knowledge sharing, software development, innovation projects, development projects, product development, complex projects, information systems, international development, management practices, critical success, management research, systems development, network analysis, organisational design, social capital, innovation project, management office, moderating role, social network, software projects, governance mechanism, knowledge management, managerial control, moderating effect, organisational project, shared leadership, top management
Construction projects	construction projects, construction industry, project stakeholders, engineering projects, influencing factors, relationship quality, stakeholder management, structured literature
Project risk	project risk, risk management, managing project, project portfolios, exploratory study, international project
Project control	project control
Major public	major public, public project
Safety-critical projects	safety-critical projects
Project delivery	project delivery, integrated delivery, building projects, capital project
Project life	project life, public-private partnerships
Inter-organisational projects	inter-organisational projects
Project portfolio	project portfolio, portfolio management, portfolio success, project selection
Information system	information system, system projects, project partnering

Horizontal leadership	horizontal leadership
Exploratory projects	exploratory projects
Interorganisational projects	interorganisational projects

The thematic map of project management from the articles' abstracts (Figure 1.16) was derived from 99 bigrams and divided into five themes (Figure 1.16). From the analysis of the articles' abstracts, theme project management is more developed and approximately the same relevant as reported from the thematic map of project management from the articles' titles. Opposite, the themes of construction projects are less developed and have approximately the same relevance. Theme risk management lies between niche and declining themes, as in the analysis of the titles. Themes related to the project portfolio appear as emerging themes with the potential to develop further.

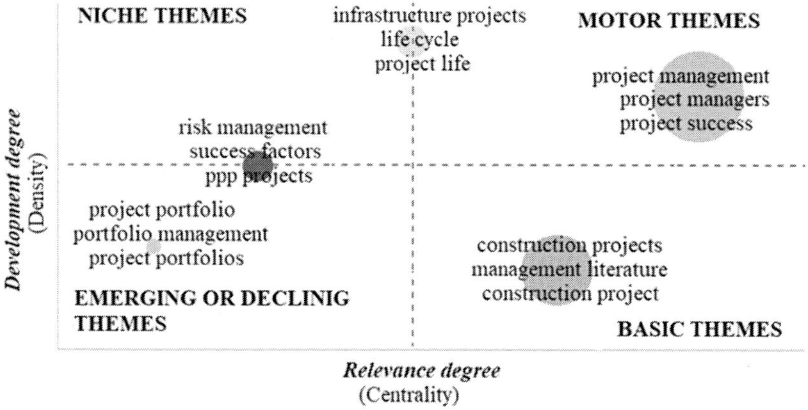

Figure 1.16 *Density and centrality of project management themes from the article's abstracts*

The analysis based on bigrams in the articles' abstracts produced fewer themes than the analysis by title, namely five of the previous 17 (Table 1.10). Let us look at grouping topics into larger thematic clusters (bold text in Table 1.11 represent subthemes). The relevance and maturity of the parent themes change according to the average score for the underlying themes. The abstract analysis should give a more detailed insight into the development and relevance of the project management themes.

Table 1.11 *Themes and corresponding bigrams from the articles' abstracts*

Theme	Corresponding bigrams from articles' abstracts
Infrastructure projects	infrastructure projects, life cycle, **project life**, project studies, public sector, dynamic capabilities, project capabilities, project organising
Project management	project management, project managers, project success, project performance, project governance, project team(s), project complexity, **project manager**, knowledge sharing, structural equation, future research, study contributes, project-based organisations, factor analysis, project outcomes, equation modelling, development projects, software development, empirical evidence, knowledge transfer, management research, product development, innovation projects, management practitioners, knowledge management, organisational culture, project marketing, project owner, transformational leadership, customer satisfaction, development project, information technology, management pm, project level, social capital, knowledge integration, top management, emotional intelligence, **information systems**, international development, management support, action research, agile project, benefits management, governance mechanisms, management approaches, questionnaire survey, regression analysis, moderating role, organisational performance, project uncertainty
Construction projects	construction projects, management practices, **project delivery**, construction project, management literature, construction industry, complex projects, semi-structured interviews, stakeholder management, project networks, social network, change management, empirical research, supply chain, content analysis, project alliance, project context, project stakeholders, resource allocation, traditional project, empirical data, project practitioners, **project control**, project implementation, project organisations, systematic literature, lived experience, management practice
Risk management	risk management, success factors, PPP projects, **project risk**, **international projects**, success criteria,

	critical success, project portfolio, portfolio management, organisational design, project portfolios
Project portfolio	project portfolio, portfolio management, organisational design, project portfolios

1.3.5 Most cited and most used articles

The ten most cited articles were published in IJPM between 2015 and 2017 (Table 1.12). Two of these are literature reviews. Thirty authors, an average of three per article, come from ten countries, of which 11 are from Europe, four from the Americas, nine from Asia, five from Australia and one from Africa. Half of the articles were written in international co-authorship.

Table 1.12 *Ten most used articles between 22.1.2022 and 21.7.2022*

Authors	Title	Journal	Publishing year	Citations
Müller, R Drouin, N Sankaran, S	Modelling Organisational Project Management	PMJ	2019	16
Willumsen, P Oehmen, J Stingl, V Geraldi, J	Value creation through project risk management	IJPM	2019	39
Mok, KY Shen, GQ Yang, J	Stakeholder management studies in mega construction projects: A review and future directions	IJPM	2015	278
Imam, H Zaheer, MK	Shared leadership and project success: The roles of knowledge sharing, cohesion and trust in the team	IJPM	2021	15

Pavez, I Gomez, H Laulie, L Gonzalez, VA	Project team resilience: The effect of group potency and interpersonal trust	IJPM	2021	3
Zhou, QW Deng, XP Hwang, BG Yu, M	System dynamics approach of knowledge transfer from projects to the project-based organisation	IJMPB	2022	1
Fuller, J Hutter, K Kroger, N	Crowdsourcing as a service - from pilot projects to sustainable innovation routines	IJPM	2021	8
Martens, ML Carvalho, MM	Key factors of sustainability in project management context: A survey exploring the project managers' perspective	IJPM	2017	151
Derakhshan, R Turner, R Mancini, M	Project governance and stakeholders: a literature review	IJPM	2019	68
Todorovic, ML Petrovic, DC Mihic, MM; Obradovic, VL Bushuyev, SD	Project success analysis framework: A knowledge-based approach in project management	IJPM	2015	115

In addition, 198 (20% of 986) of the most frequently cited articles and 198 (20% of 986) of the most frequently used articles were examined for the occurrence of phrases in the titles of the articles (Table 1.12). Table 1.13 shows the distribution by year of publication and by journal. Eighty-four of the most cited articles were published between the beginning of 2015 and the end of 2017. No most-cited article was published after the end of 2019. In contrast to the most-cited articles, the most-used articles are from recent years. Fifty-four per cent of the most cited articles were published from the beginning of 2019 to the end of 2021.

One hundred and eighty-one (74.5%) of the most cited articles and 122 (67.4%) of the most used articles were published in IJPM. The fewest articles on both lists were published in IJMPB.

Table 1.13 *Basic data about 198 most used and 198 most cited articles*

		198 (20%) of the most used articles	198 (20%) of the most cited articles
Year of publication	2015	19	59
	2016	17	56
	2017	27	52
	2018	27	21
	2019	31	10
	2020	28	-
	2021	49	-
	Sum	198	198
Journal	IJMPB	32	3
	IJPM	122	181
	PMJ	44	14
	Sum	198	198

Sixty-one (30.81%) articles were recognised as frequently cited and frequently used. The terms “complex,” “project management,” and “risk” are most often used phrases in their titles, followed by “construction,” “success,” and “stakeholder.”

The terms “construction,” “success,” and “project management” appear most frequently in the titles of both groups (Table 1.14). In the most frequently cited articles, the words “risk,” “stakeholder,” and “complex” in the title follow before the listed phrases in order of frequency of use. The most frequently used words in the group are “team” and “knowledge.” Articles with the words “team,” “knowledge,” “agile,” “leadership,” “portfolio,” and “governance” in the title are more often found among the most used than among the most cited articles. Conversely, articles with the phrases “risk,” “stakeholder,” “complex,” “governance,” “PPP,” “trust,” and “benefit” in the title are more often among the most cited than among the most used. In the first half of 2022, interest in articles with the words “construction,” success,” “project management,” “team,” and “knowledge” was higher, followed by “risk,” “leadership,” “stakeholder,” and “complex” in the title.

Table 1.15 *Occurrence of phrases in 20% of the most used and cited articles*

Phrase	Occurrence in 198 (20%) of most used articles' titles	Occurrence in 198 (20%) of most cited articles' titles	Occurrence in the most used and the most cited 61 articles' titles	Occurrence in 986 selected articles
Construction	35	34	6	97
Success	31	32	6	86
Project management	30	34	8	155
Team	27	12	4	79
Knowledge	21	8	4	49
Risk	19	23	7	72
Leadership	17	6	2	38
Stakeholder	16	20	6	50
Complex	14	20	9	59
Relationship	13	12	3	41
Governance	11	19	4	53
Portfolio	10	6	1	33
Practice	8	8		51
Project manager	8	6	3	45
International	7	5		23
Project-based organisation	7	2		21
PPP	6	11	1	25
Trust	6	10	2	24
Process	6	7		30
Benefit	5	13	3	25
Decision	5	4		27
Uncertainty	4	8	3	20
Software	3	2		23

"Modelling" appeared in three articles' titles (Qazi et al. 2016; Yang et al. 2016; Qureshi and Kang 2015) among 986 articles. All three articles are between 20% of the most cited and 20% of the most used.

"BIM" appeared in two of the 986 titles analysed and "artificial" in one. All three articles are on the list of 20% of the most cited articles.

"Multicultural" appeared in one out of 986 titles analysed. The same article is in 20% of the most cited articles in the first half of 2022.

1.4 Discussion

Project management today is different from what it was ten years ago. The most striking difference is the increased number of projects and the spread of projects to areas where it did not seem possible. Suddenly, most people in developed and developing countries seem involved in at least one project. The use of information and communication technologies and social networks supports project work. In addition to technical skills, project managers are also developing soft skills. But that is far from all.

Due to the ageing population and retirement, involving young people in project work is necessary. In underdeveloped countries where the average age of the population is lower due to development activities, projects are just starting with people who are novices in project management. Older, experienced project managers are in the minority there. The need for project management skills is increasing. Learning the basics of project management from existing literature and standards is not difficult. However, these are no longer sufficient to manage the complex world of projects that require 7 x 24 x 365 work, trillion-dollar budgets and a multicultural composition.

Software support for project work is expected to be actively developed in the coming years. This will include technologies such as artificial intelligence, speech recognition, mixed reality and more. Project management information systems (PMIS) are in full swing. However, the next stage of development in terms of connecting PMIS with social networks and other enterprise software solutions is already on the horizon. However, this is not the only prospect for the future.

In this chapter, the search for scientific publications only considered articles in three renowned journals of project management, even though researchers use a variety of channels such as conference papers, book chapters, blogs and films to disseminate their research findings in addition to scientific journal articles. Why the limitation to articles? Publishing scientific journal articles usually takes time. The results are made available to the public only after a delay. On the other hand, most scientists decide to publish in a journal only after the research has been fully completed and the results have been processed to a high quality. All articles are also peer-reviewed.

Despite the worldwide increase in the number of projects carried out per unit of time, the phenomenon of projectification and the era of the project economy, the number of scientific articles on project management is declining with an annual growth rate of -15.85%. A slight decrease in published articles can be observed in three central and important PMJs. This is not an isolated case. We have not investigated the causes, but it would be useful to mention that a few days to a few years can pass between submitting and publishing an article. Another explanation is offered by Geraldi and Söderlund (2018). They believe that academic research and management practice in the field of projects is rapidly diversifying, which can lead to a segregation of the field. While the number of articles on projects and the project environment is increasing, publications are spread across journals from different academic fields. The growth trend in the number of articles is, therefore, not directly visible in the central scientific journals of the field.

Researchers work in interconnected formal or informal research groups, referred to as Clusters in the previous chapter. In project management, a research network enables the international transfer of new knowledge between individual research groups. Clusters include examples of grouping around experienced researchers, with young researchers coming from the same country or mostly from countries with low-level development or lower GDP. They also include PhD students who gained experience in research and co-authored publications. The lead researchers usually establish links between the Clusters. Joint activities lead to publications in prestigious journals. Two of the most prolific authors practice and investigate this topical form of collaboration in project management research based on their own experiences within their Cluster with an international team of researchers (Sankaran et al. 2021).

The analysis of the number of articles by individual countries showed that countries with published articles in the three journals analysed have a higher average GDP per capita than countries without published articles ($p=0.000$; $p<0.050$). Countries without published articles have an average GDP per capita of 9,276.52 EUR (Table 1.16). This is, on average, 22,944.11 EUR less than countries with published articles (Table 1.17). The growth in the number of projects stimulates interest in projects. Consequently, the resulting challenges and questions trigger research. In both developed and developing countries, the number of articles on project management has grown steadily on a cumulative basis. In order to maintain steady growth in regions with lower GDP, higher productivity levels of project management organisation experts are crucial for their future. Countries with lower GDP per capita should encourage their citizens to acquire project management skills, as it has been proven that project management experts achieve higher project productivity levels.

Table 1.16 *Average GDP Per Capita for countries without published articles in EUR*

Countries without authors	Average GDP Per Capita	St. dev	Min GDP Per capita	Max GDP Per capita
Europe	35,604.24	45,737.21	4,986.60	173,688.20
Asia	5,647.97	7,100.83	516.70	31,722.70
Australia	5,248.39	3,750.10	1,514.60	14,243.90
Africa	2,329.25	2,617.28	236.80	13,306.70
North America	9,753.69	6,473.36	2,090.80	28,239.40
South America	9,753.69	6,473.36	2,090.80	28,239.40
Together	9,276.52	20,716.23	236.80	173,688.20

Table 1.17 *Average GDP Per Capita for countries with published articles in EUR*

Countries with authors	Average GDP Per Capita	St. dev	Min GDP Per capita	Max GDP Per capita
Europe	46,477.00	35,242.30	4,835.60	169,049.20
Asia	21,978.73	22,017.04	1,537.90	72,794.00
Australia	54,367.90	5,566.20	48,801.70	59,934.10
Africa	3,000.72	1,997.56	944.00	6,994.20
North America	41,051.20	28,622.81	1,814.70	69,287.50
South America	9,211.25	4,238.61	6,131.20	16,502.80
Together	32,220.33	31,805.42	944.00	169,049.20

Regarding content, the question "What does the use of the agile approach bring that the traditional waterfall approach does not?" is still open. Agile versus traditional, there is no conclusion yet. There is enormous room for innovation on the continuum between the two extremes.

It is evident from the literature review that the research is the most intensive in construction content. Recalling the Australian Opera House and Berlin Airport, construction industry projects are often associated with corruption, contractor vested interests, lagging resource use transparency, extra work annexes, and much more. They often combine a large number of subcontractors with different profiles and interests. Budgets are large but limited and often involve public money. It is a production subject to unpredictable weather fluctuations and poorly supported by computer information. Perhaps the reason for the phenomenon of many articles is precisely this exposure to the public and the use of public money.

The research has shown that the keywords differ considerably between the different periods. The content of publications is influenced more than ever by national and global events. Finally, the content of publications is determined by the strategic goals of countries and communities. For example, in 2017, a frequent link was observed between "public-private partnership projects" and "critical success factors." At the time, the European Court of Auditors (2018) concluded that while "public-private partnerships (PPPs) have the potential to achieve faster policy implementation and ensure good maintenance standards, the projects audited were not always managed effectively and did not offer value for money." One and a half billion euros were spent ineffectively, of which 0.4 billion were EU funds. Few member states had consolidated experience and expertise in implementing successful PPP projects. Developments in practice were followed by research. Large investments in infrastructure trigger construction projects that the public wants to see carried out sensibly. This means that the associated problems must be solved in the academic field. Finally, we are in a period of extraordinary efforts that better connect research and development with the real sector.

In the first half of 2022, the greatest interest was in articles with the following words: "construction", "success", "project management", "team" and "knowledge", followed by "risk", "leadership", "stakeholder" and "complex" in the title. There is a general interest in developing good knowledge management practices related to project content and work. Training project staff is in the interest of project management associations and other stakeholders already involved in the project economy. The digitalisation of this knowledge is necessary so artificial intelligence can be used as a decision-making tool. Articles on the topic of artificial intelligence project management are rare. Even if there is interest, it cannot be traced through an overview of citations and the use of existing articles. The situation is similar to other topics such as social networks, digital, maturity, simulation, competencies and multicultural. These words do not appear in the title or abstract of the articles analysed. They could be found in journals from other fields, or the time is not yet ripe for discussion. The academic dialogue revolves around the terms: "success", "risks", "knowledge", "construction" and "team" in project management.

1.5 Conclusion

Research of publications in eminent journals on project management revealed a very modest number of publications on artificial intelligence, automation, digitalisation, human resource management and other topics that affect how projects are delivered. Engaging with new, emerging, pilot and similar project management topics is extremely important for benchmarking, young people just entering the labour market, planning development strategies in practice, and rapid scientific progress. The dynamic environment of projects, the technologies available, the people and the problems solved by the projects require rapid publication of relevant works that follow developments in practice and research as closely as possible. The challenges of project management and related areas are increasing, and the solutions require a high level of coordinated action between researchers and practitioners.

References

Esfahani, Hossein and Tavasoli, Keyvan and Jabbarzadeh, Armin. "Big data and social media: A scientometrics analysis." *International Journal of Data and Network Science*, No. 3(3) (2019): 145–164. https://doi.org/10.5267/j.ijdns.2019.2.007.

European Court of Auditors. Public Private Partnerships in the EU: Widespread shortcomings and limited benefits. Luxembourg: EU Publication Office. 2018. Accessed 21 July 2021. https://www.eca.europa.eu/Lists/ECADocuments/SR18_09/SR_PPP_EN.pdf.

Garfield, Eugene and Sher, H. Irving. "KeyWords Plus™Algorithmic Derivative Indexing." *Journal of the American Society for Information Science*, No. 44(5) (1993): 298-299.

Geraldi, Joana and Söderlund, Jonas. "Project studies: What it is, where it is going." *International Journal of Project Management*, 36(1) (2018): 55-70. https://doi.org/10.1016/j.ijproman.2017.06.004.

Grant, Kevin P. and Pennypacker, James S. "Project management maturity: an assessment of project management capabilities among and between selected industries." *IEEE Transactions on Engineering Management*, 53(1) (2006): 59-68. https://doi.org/10.1109/TEM.2005.861802

Händeler, E. 2011. "Projekte aus Kondratieff-Perspektive. Die Kultur der Zusammenarbeit bestimmt die nächste Stufe des Wohlstands." In Exit Matters – Auf dem Weg in die Projektgesellschaft, edited by Ladwig,

Desiree and Kunze, Jürgen and Hartmann, Michael, 219-232. Frankfurt: Peter Lang Internationaler Verlag der Wissenschaften.

Hodgson, Damian Edward and Cicmil, Svetlana. 2006. *Making Projects Critical*. New York: Palgrave Macmillan.

Jensen, Anders and Thuesen, Christian and Geraldi, Joana. "The projectification of everything: projects as a human condition." *Project Management Journal*, No. 47(3) (2016): 21–34. https://doi.org/10.1177/875697281604700303.

Junping, Qiu and Rongyingm, Zhao and Siluom Yang and Ke Dong. "Author distribution of literature information: Lotka's law." Informetrics, (2017): 145–183. https://doi:https://doi.org/10.1007/978-981-10-4032-0_6.

Kerzner, Harold. 2019. *Using the project management maturity model: strategic planning for project management*. John Wiley & Sons.

Kopp, M. Carol. 2021. "Agency theory: Definition, Examples of Relationships, and Disputes." Accessed 10 November 2021. https://www.investopedia.com/terms/a/agencytheory.asphttps://www.investopedia.com/terms/a/agencytheory.asp.

Larsson Castro, Sara and Lundblad, Lovisa and Nilsson, Gabriella and Pang, Xiaopeng. 2020. "Case study Berlin Brandenburg Airport. ACE225 - Project Management in Construction." Accessed 10 November 2021. https://chalmers.instructure.com/files/648907/download?download_frd=1.

Lopez, Julyssa. 2019. "Berlin's 'cursed' Brandenburg Airport finally nears completion." Accessed 10 November 2021. https://edition.cnn.com/travel/article/berlin-brandenburg-airport-opening-date/index.html.

Lundin, Rolf. A. and Arvidsson, Niklas and Brady, Tim and Ekstedt, Eskil and Midler, Cristophe and Sydow, Jorg. 2015. Managing and Working in Project Society. Cambridge University Press.

Mullaly, Mark. "Longitudinal Analysis of Project Management Maturity." Project Management Journal, No. 37(3) (2006): 62-73. https://doi.org/10.1177/875697280603700307.

Nieto-Rodriguez, Antonio. 2021. "The Project Economy Has Arrived." Accessed 10 November 2021. https://hbr.org/2021/11/the-project-economy-has-arrived.

PMI. 2017. "Project Management Job Growth and Talent Gap 2017-2027." Accessed 10 November 2021. https://www.pmi.org/-/media/pmi/documents/public/pdf/learning/job-growth-report.pdf.

PMI. 2021. "Talent Gap: Ten-Year Employment Trends, Costs, and Global Implications." Accessed 11 November 2021. https://www.pmi.org/-/media/pmi/documents/public/pdf/learning/career-central/talent-gap-report-2021-finalfinal.pdf?v=a7ff5855-2b86-4578-9b7f-3dbe26d0402d&sc_lang_temp=en.

Qazi, Abroon and Quigley, John and Dickson, Alex and Kirytopoulos, Konstantinos. "Project Complexity and Risk Management (ProCRiM): Towards modelling project complexity driven risk paths in construction projects." *International Journal of Project Management*, No. 34(7) (2016): 1183–1198. https://doi.org/10.1016/j.ijproman.2016.05.008.

Qureshi, Sheheryar Mohsin and Kang, Chang Wook. "Analysing the organisational factors of project complexity using structural equation modelling." *International Journal of Project Management*, No. 33(1) (2015): 165–176. https://doi.org/10.1016/j.ijproman.2014.04.006.

Ross, David W. and Shaltry, Paul E. 2006. "The new PMI standard for portfolio management." Paper presented at PMI® Global Congress 2006—EMEA, Madrid, Spain. Newtown Square, PA: Project Management Institute.

Sankaran, Shankar and Müller, Ralf and Drouin, Nathalie. "Investigating collaboration in project management research: Using action research as a meta-methodology." *International Journal of Managing Projects in Business*, No. 14(1) (2021): 205–230. https://doi/10.1108/IJMPB-01-2020-0033.

Schoper, Yvonne and Ingason, Helgi Thor. "Projectification and the impact on societies." *International Journal of Managing Projects in Business*, No. 12(3) (2019): 517-521. https://doi/10.1108/IJMPB-09-2019-288.

Song, Yu and Chen, Xieling and Hao, Tianyong and Liu, Zhinan and Lan, Zixin. "Exploring two decades of research on classroom dialogue by using bibliometric analysis." *Computers in Education*, No. 137 (2019): 12–31. https://doi.org/10.1016/j.compedu.2019.04.002.

Yang, Rebecca J. and Zou, Patrick X.W. and Wang, Jiayuan. "Modelling stakeholder-associated risk networks in green building projects." *International Journal of Project Management*, No. 34 (2016): 66–81. http://dx.doi.org/10.1016/j.ijproman.2015.09.010.

Brigita Gajšek holds a teaching position at the University of Maribor, Faculty of Logistics. She is vice president of the Slovenian Project Management Society. She consults Slovenian production companies in intralogistics and digitalisation of business processes. Her research interests include digital maturity, industry 4.0/logistics 4.0, renewal of business processes, project management and ergonomics.

Simona Šinko is an assistant at the Faculty of Logistics, University of Maribor, Slovenia. She is writing her doctoral dissertation about personal transport mode choices. Her research interest is intralogistics. Her bibliography consists of 12 original scientific papers, 15 conference papers and five scientific chapters in monographs.

II

Assessing PM Knowledge in Large Pre-Trained AI Language Models – Results from Polling Experiments

Helge Nuhn, Alfred Oswald, Agnetha Flore and Rüdiger Lang

2.1 Digital Transformation and Artificial Intelligence

Digital Transformation seems to be ubiquitous, and it is radically changing humans' lives. Artificial Intelligence (AI) and Machine Learning (ML) are two very effective drivers of this transformation.

Following Vial (2019), we understand Digital Transformation to be an ongoing, far-reaching process of change in all areas of society and business, driven by the emergence of increasingly powerful digital technologies, with their nature being that they scale easily, and cost effectively and therefore have cause large and rapid impacts. Digital Transformation increases the interconnectedness of technical, social, and natural domains. This creates highly volatile dynamics with great potential for surprise: small changes can have enormous effects. Complex systems are emerging that need to be mastered (Oswald & Müller 2019).

For this chapter, we align with several Artificial Intelligence (AI) definitions:

- "Artificial intelligence leverages computers and machines to mimic the problem-solving and decision-making capabilities of the human mind." (IBM 2022)
- "AI is computer programming that learns and adapts." (Pichai 2022).
- "Through AI, machines can analyze images, comprehend speech, interact in natural ways, and make predictions using data." (Microsoft 2022a)

- "AI complements and strengthens human abilities in seeing, hearing, analyzing, deciding and acting." (Microsoft 2022b).

Machine learning is the part of the field of artificial intelligence in which large amounts of data are usually used to train AI systems so that they learn to solve complex tasks. Our definition and scope do not cover "strong AI" in a sense that we envision an intelligence that is hard to differentiate from human intelligence. Also, we are agnostic to which underlying techniques help achieve this sort of intelligent behavior. However, most impressive recent advances in capabilities of such systems have been achieved using deep neural networks or similar approaches like the transformer principle (Vaswani et al. 2017). Such advances are the source of inspiration for the propositions that we make in this chapter. Finally, autonomy is not a necessary precondition for an AI system to follow into our definition. But the systems we talk about are either easily accessible, very close to the action – imminent – or even self-starting – proactive – in nature. They will be parts of human autonomy teaming as discussed by O'Neill et al. (2020) and others.

Our perspective onto AI integrates the three different views onto AI according to Peeters et al. (2021):

- technology-centric perspective,
- the human-centric perspective,
- and collective-intelligence perspective.

Each of these perspectives is based on different beliefs and is not complete on its own. The technology-centric perspective emphasizes the technical side of AI technology and believes that technological innovations help cope with handicaps of our growth-oriented societies. The human-centric perspective sees an essential difference between the intelligence and cognitive capabilities of humans and the technical, "inhuman" capabilities of an AI. The collective-intelligence perspective emphasizes the interweaving of human intelligence and artificial intelligence to better master our existence. AI brings further complexity to this existence, however, with appropriate handling, it can help regulate complexity.

The advances in the field of AI, as far as they are close to implementations that are or may become useful for business or the broader public, can be charted in three areas described below.

First, recent advances in fields of video and image recognition, segmentation, manipulation, and generation have resulted in stunning IT capabilities like generating (moving) pictures based upon very little input information like text prompts (Liu et al. 2021), other artists' work (Härkönen et al. 2020; Abdal et al. 2020) or mere sketches (Ghosh et al. 2019).

Second, there is a lot of research studying autonomous agents that act in environments that require cognitive understanding, tactical as well as strategic understanding and finally finesse in execution (OpenAI 2019). Such examples include AI systems that drive cars autonomously, win strategy games designed to be played by humans in teams like Dota 3, or board strategy games like Go.

Third, a long-time existing field of scientific research that has benefitted greatly from the development of capable AI algorithmics is text analysis, classification, manipulation, or generation. In this field we see how the precision of text summarization algorithms that find the essence of a document has increased tremendously. So much, that it is being employed in business use cases in marketing contexts already, e.g., copywriting for advertorials. Likewise, techniques for machine generated translations of texts have reached more than acceptable performance, which is affecting our daily lives, e.g., through better product descriptions. Other types of models exist, that aim at filling in blanks in texts, finding specific passages within texts given a particular input or at answering specific questions accurately. They make use of very complex underlying AI structures like deep neural networks and specific paradigms (attention bias, transformer approaches as opposed to encoder or decoder approaches, only) that result in models with astonishing performance which are easy to handle. In this sense, they are easily pre-trainable with extensive computational power, highly performant about execution speeds and finally rather easy to fine-tune, given the existence of use case-relevant data to train on.

While all these technological advances are astounding and fascinating at the same time, the sheer number of different perspectives onto AI makes it a hard to answer seemingly superficial questions like "Will AI be useful for teams working together in the future?" or "What will the merits of AI be in the future of the project management discipline?". Many useful use case scenarios beg for categorization before the corresponding research agendas can be set and pursued. Our chapter aims at ordering the potential use of AI systems from top to bottom, starting with general functionalities that these systems may provide from a societal perspective, before we narrow our perspective onto the use of AI systems in the project management domain. We then present a framework of project management organizational functions or dynamics that are at work at any point in time within a project organization. This framework will be juxtaposed with various functions that AI research is exploring now. Selecting the field of natural language processing (NLP) along with its current research approaches and successes, we propose several potential use cases per project management organizational mode. Finally, to dive deep into one of these categories we set out to explore the current capabilities of state-of-the-art NLP models by means of an experiment that lets AI models answer project management-specific questions. We present and discuss the result and close with remarks on the importance of and potential further necessary actions to research useful AI application within organizations and projects specifically.

2.2 AI from a societal perspective

AI systems with Machine Learning capabilities are based on completely different principles than "classical" software.

"Classical" software systems are largely "hardwired" systems, so their capabilities to learn are non-existent. AI/ML systems, on the other hand, have an architecture whose system parameters self-organize based on training data. State-of-the-Art AI/ML systems can currently have anywhere from several 100 million parameters up to several billion parameters and are thus able to model, for example, images or texts in themselves, i.e., to incorporate representations of the data. They build representation models of the selected reality. Models and selected data depend very much on the values, beliefs and principles of the authors who create these models and select the data. AI/ML systems are "socialized" by this and thus carry this socialization into a potentially large application context (Christian 2020).

The AI/ML representation models are not perfect, they deliver probability statements based on the data. Not unlike human intelligence, the representation models incorporate uncertainty.

AI/ML systems only represent the values, beliefs, mental biases, or prejudices they perceive in the data. The ability to detect correlations within the data and associated abstractions and biases is already very much beyond our mental capabilities today. This means that AI/ML models detect hidden values, beliefs, mental biases, or prejudices, that we have not perceived so far. AI/ML systems, if used incompetently, can pass on these biases in a non-transparent way, contributing to a stabilization of biases and prejudices, or, if used competently, they can help reveal our hidden values, beliefs, mental biases, and prejudices. Our own ability to develop meta-competence is therefore decisive in determining the extent to which AI/ML systems help the digital transformation to become a real social transformation and not just degenerate into more technology (Oswald 2022).

Based on the outlined essential difference between AI/ML systems and "classical" software systems, significant consequences for society arise (Kissinger et al. 2021):

Artificial intelligence systems already recognize patterns in our reality that were (previously) closed to our intelligence. AI successfully trains chess strategies that no human has used before, or finds effective medicines that have remained undiscovered, or helps discover principles of physics and mathematics, etc. Used with meta-competence, AI systems can also make social patterns of the past and present visible and help support a transformation of our organizations and societies oriented towards freedom, equality, and justice.

AI will significantly change our view of physical reality and has the potential to transform our social reality. This happens in two ways: the development of AI drives the integration of different disciplines such as psychology, social sciences, natural sciences, computer science, mathematics as well as philosophy. And in addition, AI systems lead to new insights and applications in the respective disciplines. This can be seen very quickly for everyone in the (revolutionary) findings published every week by (DeepMind 2022) or the AI community (DeepAI 2022).

Social systems (like teams, organizations, or societies) will develop substantially differently depending on whether ML/AI is used and to what extent and in what quality.

The ability of AI systems to recognize patterns very quickly to physical reality in large data sets of videos and images, text, audio data, numbers, takes quantity and quality of scientific knowledge to a new level. Physical technology innovations, some of them revolutionary in nature, are becoming available faster and faster. On the one hand, this greatly increases the competitiveness of societies and organizations that have mastered these techniques and, on the other hand, leads to a corresponding dependence for societies or parts of societies that do not have these capabilities. A new type of "stratification" of society(ies) along individual ML/AI competences will result. Since AI systems are already being used to a large extent in (autonomous) weapon systems today without regulation, this also entails power over life and death (Kissinger et al. 2021).

The application of AI systems and other physical technologies possibly discovered with the help of AI can result in social technologies, for good or for bad. "For good" means that our individual, team, organizational, and societal meta-competence will be strengthened, enhancing freedom, equality, and justice. "For evil" means that AI systems and other physical technologies are used to authoritatively enforce certain behavior.

This results in the following fundamental demands on the social design of the Digital Transformation:

- A balanced general education includes technological knowledge of AI systems, related social impact, and ethic requirements.
- Models and data must be designed, implemented, and operationalized transparently for society.
- Creators of AI systems must be able to self-critically question their own values, beliefs, and principles. They must recognize the values, beliefs and principles contained in the models and data and make them explicitly transparent.
- Builders of AI systems must have proven systemic thinking to be able to assess the consequences of AI systems on society. Systemic thinking is oriented towards acting in the common good.

Since projects are shaping the future, the above requirements are also direct requirements for all project stakeholders, but especially for the project managers and core team members of an innovative project.

2.3 AI in projects

Projects are forms of temporary organizations for reaching specific goals (Lundin & Söderholm 1995). They are suitable organizational vessels for creating novel products, research results or induce organizational change for example. Therefore, projects challenge those working in them with constantly new situations, whether they are completely new to one of them, a couple of them, or even the entire organization. AI systems will become part of these dynamics, adding another type of agents that interact with humans in newly forming and ever-adapting social networks.

In addition, especially when projects are directed at creating product innovation or introduce new customer services, the projects themselves are exposed to increasing market dynamism and pressure. These increased pressures may have led to employing projects as forms of organizing within companies in the first place, there is also consensus about the fact, that we currently live in a phase of 'projectification' where increasingly more projects are spawned and working within projects becomes the new normal.

Projects are an important means of shaping the future; accordingly, the digital transformation will be shaped quite significantly by projects. AI, infusing society and work environments, will lead to three central changes for project management:

- The innovation process will change substantially, as one or more AI systems (AI agents) will significantly expand and change the R&D search space alone or in collaboration with humans (Vasilescu 2021).
- Project management must consider that tasks will be distributed between humans and AI, working either in isolation or as a team. Decision-making processes will change considerably in this composition (Puranam 2021).
- AI systems and solutions will be part of an increasing number of project solutions and AI will thus become a core competence in project work. At the same time, the impact of AI-based project solutions on stakeholders, society and nature must be considered.

Based on the above-mentioned fundamental demands for the social design of Digital Transformation and these three key changes in project management, additional AI competencies emerge for project leaders, project members, and other stakeholders.

There is considerable debate among practitioners as well as academics on what makes a good project manager (Chipulu et al. 2013). This debate may partly not be settled because of the high diversity of skills and capabilities that are typically asked for in a project manager. The demanded skills vary with the parameters of the project, whether it be small or large, have many teams involved or just a few people.

Some skills are so basic to successful project management and agreed upon by professional associations like the IPMA that competence catalogues have been developed that help assess what level of proficiency a project manager has. These are basis for assessments, which in turn make use of Q&A catalogues.

Because of the individual character of projects and the different parameters of projects as well as the individual skills and capabilities that a project manager may or may not have, there will likely be a mismatch between these in each individual case. This gap will naturally be smaller for highly experienced project managers and smaller for others. Our proposition is, that AI applications may come in helpful at this point.

Therefore, it is important to look at the capabilities of AI algorithms, models, and systems. We base our work upon a framework that gives an overview over certain use cases in the process of managing a project by the help of AI-approaches (Nuhn 2021). The original framework foresaw a life-cycle approach to projects as a foundation. It divided a project into distinct modes of action like 'vision and goal formulation', 'organizing', 'planning', 'value-creation and communication' as well as 'termination'. Project management research has acknowledged that environmental changes or changes in requirements, happen more quickly and more abruptly than before. While prior works on theories of project management have suggested phases to be overlapping, we take the approach further and differentiate not into phases but into modes of action that a project team can find itself be in, interchanging between modes continuously and rapidly at any given point in time. This approach is in line with previous works by Oswald and Müller (2019, 2018, 2017) as well as Tuczek et al. (2021) that mention various functions that agile teams need to display to remain effective.

A vision and goal formulation mode of action is essential for any team to establish a common understanding of the desired outputs and outcomes for which the team is joining their forces. They are (among other concepts) guiding principles that help make work efficient, by reducing the need for communication and coordination. However, human verbal communication, only, either by spoken language or written words, is an imperfect mode of sharing mental models like visions and goals. It has a very low bandwidth. Enhancing and supporting human communication by sketches, diagrams, images, or pictures helps develop shared mental models more quickly and more reliably. Potential AI-enhanced systems may support this process by e.g., generating pictorial representations of spoken words, summarize positions that people apparently have regarding strategic questions, or assess risks associated with uttered propositions.

Organizing is an important task for any organization as the name already suggests. It helps define processes and structures that facilitate teams' joint efforts, channel, direct and synergize them. Experience as well as creativity is necessary to devise the most functional organizational designs of a team. For agile purposes, it may well be that all team members, with their individual backgrounds and experiences, have diverging ideas of how to organize. Coordinating the process of organizing more complex problems may pose a challenge for such teams. Common command-and-control structures have centralized decision-making but may lack processes that allow superior solutions to be implemented, e.g., due to power dynamics, perceived competence, or authority, etc. In this case, AI systems may be of strong support if they are considered neutral agents, impartial and not suspected as being instruments of power dynamics, and a believable source of additional information or advice for better decision-making regarding organization and governance. For example, an AI system could make alternative team design suggestions, assess personality fit between people foreseen to be working together or even only check for availability issues for the coordination of joint meetings.

Based on the vision and goal, planning is essential for individual as well as team progress. It is noteworthy, that plans may either explicit or implicit. Furthermore, plans may vary in detail, which affects the effectiveness of its functions: information, and coordination. Therefore, plans reflect mental models as well as of underlying assumptions, values, experiences, skills, and capabilities. Project workers and project managers may be capable of judging plans of action regarding such latent constructs as mental models or product visions. It is a challenging problem especially when teams initially form, with team members that barely know each other and are of different professional or educational backgrounds. AI systems have proven to be of good use to find patterns in data that are not visible to the human eye. Given the access to the project teams' communication, work, results and so forth, they may give cues to where discrepancies occur between team members' explicitly or implicitly stated plans and give warnings when such discrepancies are discovered.

Projects strive to create value and are driven by humans and their communication. They share, receive and process novel information constantly, which either helps following a set plan or helps update a planned course of action. Such events are called interventions and they lead to more changes than just changes of plans but may even cause the entire configuration of a project to change. Especially in larger teams, this can easily lead to information or communication overloads within the social system. Especially quickly moving agile teams or companies in agile transition argue that information routing and regulation is a major challenge. AI systems may help assess the degree of useful communication and assist in fine tuning the organizations metabolism. Furthermore, such systems may offer useful services in checking for resonance and receptiveness of messages passed on within the system, so that intended outcomes of communication are produced. For example, content and tone of conversations might be surveilled, to check for potential clashes between two or more members of a team.

Termination mode of action is entered either for individuals as they disengage from a team's mission – maybe only temporally – or for the entire team that dissolves when the team's purpose has been achieved or is collectively not considered worthwhile any longer.

All the mentioned use cases here are of different degrees of intelligence. Some may have less or more intelligence required or built-in depending on the specific design of the system. Also, some of these foreseen functionalities may not be achieved by a single algorithm by itself, but potentially by a combination of different functionalities together.

The IPMA Individual Competence Baseline (IPMA 2015) distinguishes three major competence areas "perspective", "people" and "practice", which are subdivided into further competence elements, indicated in the brackets below. In the following, we list some examples of the three competence areas. These examples reflect our current state of knowledge in terms of both number and design. - The list is therefore to be understood as living and will evolve and expand in the future.

Perspective (strategy; governance, structures, and processes; compliance, standards, and regulations; power and interest; culture and values):

- Analyse and compare artefacts (images, videos, speech, text, spreadsheets, etc.) to identify target hierarchies and/or values and belief systems of different teams or organizations to display conflicts between these.
- Analyse artefacts and derive related social networks to propose changes to project organizations and related governance structures.
- Analyse conflicts and assess compliance with external or self-set rules and guidelines regarding communication.
- Generate descriptions of vision/goal and mission and value and belief systems of organizations, create comparisons between them and give advice for improvements.

People (self-reflection and self-management; personal integrity and reliability; personal communication; relationships and engagement; leadership; teamwork; conflict and crises; negotiation; results orientation):

- Analysis of team meetings, emails or chat flows based on the written or spoken word to improve communication and leadership behaviour, e.g., point out communication that runs in cycles, or is not focused, or show mental blockades, or is building a team collective mind etc.
- Review effectiveness of self-organization of teams by deriving competing values and goals in meetings or communication artefacts.
- Derivation of risks and transformational hints from verbal and textual statements (meetings, documents, emails or chats) of stakeholders.
- Support brainstorming processes by giving creative-enhancing impulses into meetings by word clustering or similar word and document analysis.

Practices (project design; requirements and objectives; scope; time; organization and information; quality; finance; resources, procurement; plan and control; risk and opportunity; stakeholders, change and transformation):

- Create summaries of various lengths of project visions, project charters, progress, and the like, combining textual descriptions of project endeavours.
- Filter tasks and / or status information out of project email communication.
- Generate goal or target hierarchies from analyses of written or verbal communication.
- Create work breakdown structures, organizational charts, graphical depictions of planned approaches (one-page summaries) from textual descriptions, sketches, tables in conjunction with available text of vision and goal formulations.
- Create time-plans (tables with dates, GANTT charts, milestone lists, etc.) that rely upon conventional knowledge of typical lengths of phases or work package (i.e., workshop series typically last weeks, not hours, workshops last hours not, months), but also on several textual inputs (project charters, work package descriptions) allow for real-time regulation.
- Verification of contract documents and their compliance.
- Generation of contract documents based on a predefined contract skeleton.
- Generate or process project contract descriptions, requirements, etc.
- Analysis of texts of any form about potential risks.
- Translation of texts into graphical representations (e.g., target-hierarchy, planning diagrams, etc.) and the other way around (e.g., formulate texts that describe graphs or diagrams, like organizational charts, visual process models, etc.).
- Translation of textual requirements into effort and cost estimates.
- Summarization of the core results of the temporary organization in various lengths and depths of detail, e.g., for a final project report.
- Create qualitative reviews of vision, goal, target, deliverable attainment, or changes over time.

Obviously, text and spoken words play a central role in all the above use cases. If AI systems will play an increasingly important role in PM, this requires appropriate artificial intelligence in text processing (Neural Language Processing (NLP)) in both project management and project-specific task domains.

2.4 Study aim and methodology

The aim of our study is to determine the maturity of AI systems available in terms of their NLP capabilities in the context of project management by means of PM knowledge questions asked and answers given by the AI. The result of this study in turn aims at the overall goal of obtaining AI-induced management support for daily work of project teams.

To approach this goal, we have made use of existing question catalogs available in the context of IPMA or on the internet. We posed the questions to an AI model and recorded the corresponding answers in three test runs by pre-trained NLP models and evaluated the answers afterwards with a panel of experts. This procedure will be described in more detail later.

We have used a question catalog from the German Association for Project Management (GPM), which contains questions for different levels of certification in project management as examination questions. This questionnaire comprises 215 questions, which are divided into 28 categories:

1. Strategy
2. Results orientation
3. Governance, structures and processes
4. Project design
5. Compliance, standards and regulations
6. Requirements and goals
7. Power and interests
8. Scope of services and deliverables
9. Culture and values
10. Process and deadlines
11. Self-reflection and self-management
12. Organization, information, and documentation
13. Personal integrity and reliability
14. Quality
15. Personal communication
16. Costs and financing
17. Relationship and commitment
18. Resources
19. Leadership
20. Procurement
21. Teamwork
22. Planning and control
23. Conflicts and crises
24. Opportunities and risks
25. Versatility
26. Stakeholders
27. Negotiations
28. Change and transformation.

To give you an impression of the questions, here are just two examples (see also chapter 'Discussion'):

- Name the five project management phases DIN 69901:2009!
- How can the project manager prevail in a staff/line organization?

To achieve the study objective, it was necessary to choose an evaluation method that could be used to assess the quality of the responses to the GPM questionnaire by the pre-trained NLP models. We decided to use a maturity model as the evaluation method.

A maturity model can be understood as a tool that can be used to measure the abstract quality "maturity". This quality can be described by a quantitative vector in an n-dimensional maturity space. The individual dimensions are divided into arbitrary but fixed scales, the maturity levels. Simpson (1989) describes maturity as a state of completeness, perfection, or completion (Simpson & Weiner 1989). Based on maturity models, clearly defined problem-solving areas are to be optimized or they are used to evaluate and assess certain quality characteristics (Uebernickel et al. 2015). Accordingly, maturity models are used to describe a logical, desired development path for objects of a class, in successive stages. This starts in the initial stage and ends in complete maturity (Becker et al. 2008). Maturity models are thus descriptive, determinative, and comparative (Poeppelbuss & Röglinger 2011). From the above, the typification of maturity models, into optimization models and assessment models, follows. Maturity models are a recognized tool that are used in strategy development both as a basis of planning, as well as for its evaluation. Thereby maturity levels (i.e. competence, capability, level of complexity) are measured within several dimensions with respect to a selected domain (Flore 2020).

For our study, we used the maturity model to assess the area of "comprehensibility and correctness of the answer given by the AI language algorithm". Six levels of maturity were defined for the evaluation:

- Level 0: Unrecognizable output
- Level 1: Linguistically acceptable
- Level 2: Linguistically acceptable, content far off-topic
- Level 3: Linguistically acceptable, content not far off-topic
- Level 4: Objective, formally correct in content
- Level 5: Acceptable, convincing answer, coherent in content - according to classic mindset
- Level 6: Acceptable, convincing answer, coherent in content - according to agile mindset.

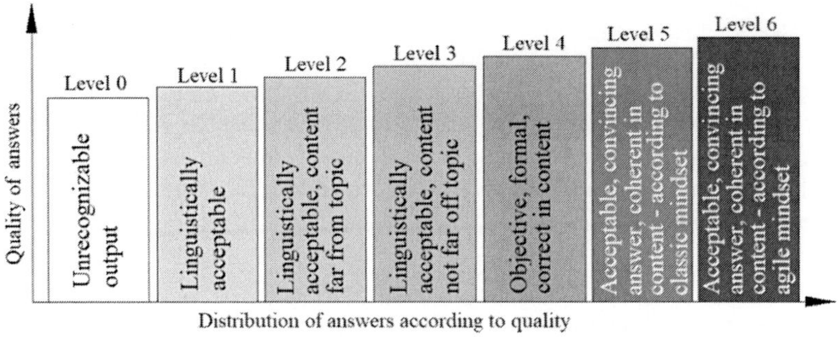

Figure 2.1 *Maturity levels for distribution the quality of responses by AI*

With this maturity model, an evaluation scheme was introduced to test the existing AI/NLP models for their project management capabilities.

We conducted the study using different AI-NLP models. We used Google's Colab service[1] as a runtime environment for our experiments, therefore using Python 3.6. For the first experiments we made use of the HappyTransformer[2] package, which is a façade layer for the Hugging Face[3] library and models. The NLP language models we used were GPT-NEO as provided by EleutherAI[4] in a 125 million parameter model for pre-evaluation and a 1.3 billion parameter model for actual answer generation. GPT-NEO was previously trained on a dataset called The Pile, a meta-dataset that contains 22 unique datasets itself (Gao et al. 2020). We also used a German BERT language model called bert-base-german-cased, available through the HappyTramsformer package.

Finally, to obtain access to state-of-the-art language models we were able to sign up with openAI and used the infamous GPT-3 model to obtain another set of generated answers to our questions.

While the Pile has roughly 800 GB of underlying data, the BERT model bert-base-german-cased was only trained on 12 GB of data. The Pile contains books, papers, github repositories, websites, and chat logs. The German BERTmodel was primarily trained on Wikipedia pages. GPT-3 was trained on a filtered CommonCrawl, several sets of book data as well as the entire Wikipedia, presumably adding up to 2 TB of data, or 499 billion tokens[5].

---

[1] https://colab.research.google.com/
[2] https://happytransformer.com/
[3] https://huggingface.co/
[4] https://www.eleuther.ai/
[5] https://lambdalabs.com/blog/demystifying-gpt-3/

As a data base for conducting our study, we sought questions from the project management field. The pre-evaluation question catalog included 48 questions and was a mix of questions of Wideman[6] and SVR Technologies[7]. The evaluation question catalog contained 215 questions and answers and came from the German Association for Project Management (GPM).

For our study we did three evaluation runs with different NLP models:

1. GPT-NEO,
2. GPT-3,
3. GPT-NEO with PMBOK training.

These evaluation runs were carried out with the GPM questionnaire, for which we also had sample solutions. Before conducting the evaluations, we translated them into English with the help of Amazon's AWS service. A native English speaker checked the quality of the translation.

We reduced this very extensive test catalog to our needs, so that only 56 pairs of questions and answers remained. For this purpose, we selected two questions per category listed above. In the expert panel, we discussed the questions and their importance and prioritized them. The two most important questions were included in the evaluation set of 56 questions for our evaluation runs.

A panel of four experts evaluated the answers from the three evaluation runs using the maturity model presented. The assigned maturity levels were then evaluated, and the results are presented in the next section of the chapter.

For the comparison and evaluation of the maturity levels by the expert panel, the minimum, maximum, mean, median and standard deviation of an evaluation run were determined for the mean across the four rater ratings per question. Furthermore, the Fleiss' Kappa was calculated for the inter-rater reliability measurement (Fleiss 1971).

The Fleiss' Kappa (1971) developed by Fleiss is based in its origins on the kappa statistic of Cohen (1960) and the weighted kappa statistic of Cohen (1968). Both kappa statistics are designed to measure the degree of agreement between two raters. Both kappa and weighted kappa include a correction for the degree of agreement that can be expected from chance alone. Kappa is useful when all disagreements can be considered equally severe, and weighted kappa is useful when the relative severity of different types of disagreements can be indicated. The use of kappa and weighted

---

[6] http://www.maxwideman.com/papers/questions/questions.pdf

[7] https://svrtechnologies.com/63-best-project-management-questions-and-answers-pdf/

kappa is limited to the case where the number of raters is two and where the same two raters rate each issue. Generalizations are therefore necessary for the case where there are more than two raters and the raters who rate one subject are not necessarily the same as those who rate another. Fleiss extended the kappa statistic in his studies to the case where there are more than two raters (n raters). Therefore, it was the appropriate choice for our study in this case.

To validate our approach and maturity model, we have done a pre-evaluation. We did the first pre-evaluation with a test question catalog of Wideman[8] and SVR Technologies[9]. This test catalog contained 49 German questions and were performed with both GPT-NEO and the German BERT bert-base-german-cased. The answers to the German questions were very poor so we excluded the results from the overall analysis. We then had the German questions translated and saw an improvement of the provided answers as provided by GPT-NEO. The decision was made to only continue with English questions.

2.5 Results

Table 2.1 summarizes the results of four independent assessing experts, averaged over 56 questions. Shown are the minimum, maximum, average, median and standard deviation for the assessments of the four experts. In addition, we calculated Fleiss Kappa for inter-rater reliability- measurements (Fleiss 1971).

The best results were achieved using GPT-3 as language model. The poorest were produced by GPT-NEO trained with the PMBOK content, while original GPT-NEO model ranked in the middle.

GPT-3 shows a remarkable average of averages of 4.29, representing a quality level corresponding to a qualitative assessment being "objective, formally correct". Even the minimum value ø min for GPT-3 with 3.68 was higher than any maximum value ø max of all other tests. The poor result of the test GPT-NEO with PMBOK training is demonstrated by an average value ø average of 1.34 and a maximum value ø max of 1.54.

The standard deviation indicates that the assessing experts were in most cases only one or two maturity levels apart from one another, indicating rather acceptable convergent validity of the maturity model.

---

[8] http://www.maxwideman.com/papers/questions/questions.pdf

[9] https://svrtechnologies.com/63-best-project-management-questions-and-answers-pdf/

Inter-rater agreement was classified as fair or poor. However, Fleiss' Kappa is generating more conservative scores with increasing number of rating categories.

Table 2.1 *Evaluation results, best averaged assessing results in boldface*

	GPT-NEO	GPT-3	GPT-NEO with PMBOK Training
ø min	1.29	3.68	0.77
ø max	2.20	4.66	1.95
ø average value	1.76	4.29	1.34
ø median	1.79	4.25	1.32
ø standard deviation	0.91	0.98	1.18
ø Fleiss Kapa - Inter Rater Reliability	0.34 Fair	0.29 Fair	0.19 Poor

Figure 2.2 graphically demonstrates the locality, spread and skewness groups of the numerical data through their quartiles for our four tests. The boxplot is based on the data of the average values for each question as rated by the four experts. It shows again the clear superiority of the GPT-3 language model, whereas the results for the GPT-NEO model were substantially lower and even decreased by training.

The results of GPT-NEO trained with PMBOK shows a wide range of values, having an outlier at 4.0. Values of lower and higher quartiles are within 0.8 and 1.8. The values for GPT-NEO show a low variety with a concentration within 1.5 and 2.2. The values for GPT-3 demonstrate again the good results with values of the lower and higher quartile between 3.8 and 4.9 but demonstrates one outlier on the lower side.

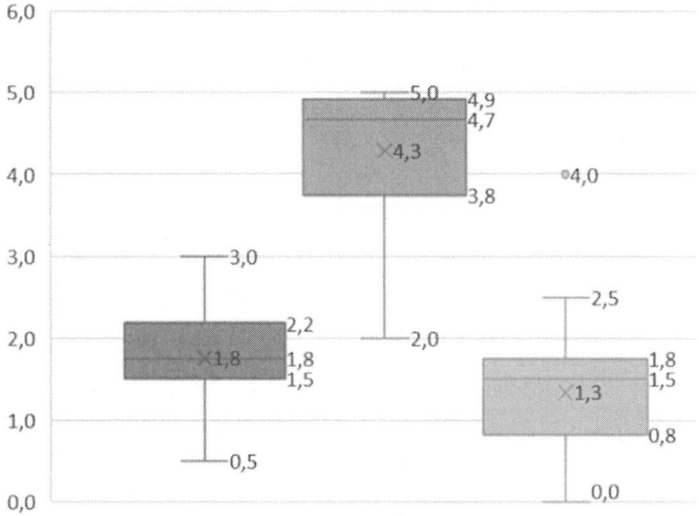

Figure 2.2 *Boxplot of analysis factors for the 4 tests*

Table 2.2 summarises typical classifications according to the maturity model.

Looking at the answers, we found that the quality was reduced due to some general findings.

The answers partially contained counter questions but not answers, contained special unreadable characters, and seemed to copy content directly from websites, blogs, chats etc. The copied content was mainly copied as answers without adapting them to the questions. Also, the use of colloquial language or the non-existing length limit of the answers didn't help to improve the quality.

A bad answer was usually also accompanied by strings containing special characters that could not be explained by ASCII to UTF-8 conversions or similar encoding incompatibilities. This problem could be traced back to formatting problems that already happened during the AWS-based translation. While this is a minor problem to fix for technically skilled users of the models, it did influence the experts' assessments. It led to systematically lower assessments as was discussed retrospectively between the experts. Notice for example the strings like 'â€' or '*â€*™' in Table 2.2.

Table 2.2 *Examples of the location of question-answer in the maturity model*

	Level	Question	Answer AI	Average value in the maturity model
0	Unrecognizable output	Outline an Eisenhower matrix!	A Guide to the Project Management Body of Knowledge (PMBOKÂ® Guide) â€” Fourth Edition Â©2008 Project Team, Inc., 14 Campus Blvd., Newtown Square, PA 19073-3299 USA HAPTER 4 - PR	0.00
1	Linguistically acceptable	What is Effort Management in a project?	By Keith P. Houlihan September 28th, 2011 Share: TwitterFacebookLinkedInPinterest Project Management is a very broad term that covers a variety of activities that are needed to complete a particular project. This	1.00
2	Linguistically acceptable, content far off-topic	What does quality management mean? How is it operated in the project?	What is the role of quality control and quality assurance? It is a project management process, and it focuses on the quality of the work, not on how it is done. Quality management is not about performance, but about what is right and necessary.	2.50
3	Linguistically acceptable, content not far off-topic	Name at least four relevant laws and regulations regarding occupational safety!	The Occupational Safety and Health Administration (OSHA) is a federal agency responsible for regulating workplace safety. Some relevant laws and regulations include:	3.33

			-The Occupational Safety and Health Act of 1970 -The Hazard Communication Standard -The Personal Protective Equipment Standard	
4	Objective, formally correct in content	What is Lean Management?	Lean management is the process of achieving the lowest operating cost for the most efficient production in the shortest possible time. The concept of Lean management has gained a lot of attention for several years and has evolved in several stages through the years.	4.25
5	Acceptable, convincing answer, coherent in content - according to classic mindset	What are the tasks of personnel development in projects?	The tasks of personnel development in projects are to identify the skills and knowledge needed for project success, develop training and education programs to meet those needs, and provide the necessary resources to support learning.	5.00
6	Acceptable, convincing answer, coherent in content - according to agile mindset.	For no AI system a question-answer pair could be located here.		

The best results are obtained with the AI system GPT-3. The average value with respect to our six levels of maturity was 4.29, which means that most of the questions were graded as “Objective, formal, correct in content”. Looking at the number of questions graded with level 4 or higher confirms this ranking. For 42 out of 56 questions GPT-3 provided a satisfying answer. Additionally, the high average value for median (=4.25) confirms the finding, too. The average value for the standard deviation of all results was acceptable with a value of 0.98.

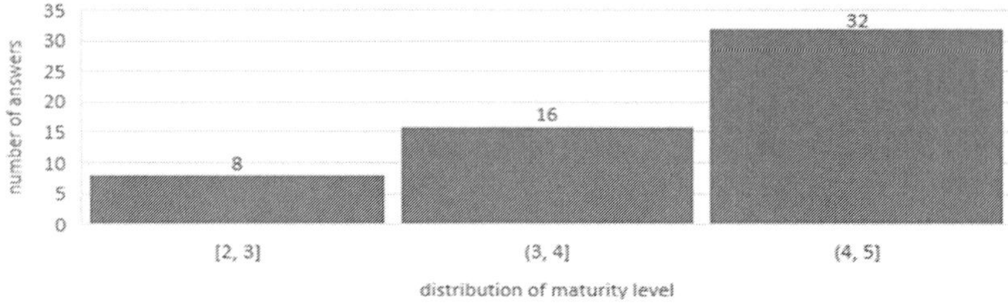

Figure 2.3 *Distribution of medians – GPT-3*

To further illustrate the quality of the answers we present two examples for answers with relatively poor (i.e. less than or equal to 3.33) and two with good quality (i.e., =5.00), Table 2.3.

Table 2.3 *Selected examples of answers for GPT-3*

Question	Answer AI	Average value of maturity model	Comment concerning ranking
Name at least four relevant laws and regulations regarding occupa-tional safety!	The Occupational Safety and Health Administration (OSHA) is a federal agency responsible for regulating workplace safety. Some relevant laws and regulations include (1) The Occupational Safety and Health Act of 1970, (2) The Hazard Communication Standard, (3) The Personal Protective Equipment Standard, (4) The Bloodborne	3.33	One of the results with poorer quality but still good quality in comparison to the answer of GPT-NEO

Name at least three PM standards.	ISO 9001, ISO 14001, ISO 45001	3.33	One of the results with poorer quality but still good quality in comparison to the answer of GPT-NEO
What are the tasks of personnel develop-ment in projects?	The tasks of personnel development in projects are to identify the skills and knowledge needed for project success, develop training and education programs to meet those needs, and provide the necessary resources to support learning.	5.00	Example of a very good result
What are the steps of resource planning?	The steps of resource planning are as follows: (1) Define the project scope and objectives, (2) Identify the resources required to complete the project, (3) Estimate the costs of the resources required, (4) Allocate the resources to the project, (5) Monitor and control the resources used throughout the project.	5.00	Example of a very good result

The worst results were obtained with GPT-NEO additionally trained with the PMBOK. The results were very poor, even worse than the results for the evaluation with GPT-NEO without additional training. The average value with respect to our six levels of maturity was 1.34, which means that many questions were graded only as "linguistically acceptable". Only one answer was of level 4 "Objective, formal, correct in content" and no answer of level 3 "Linguistically acceptable, content not far off topic". For 18 out of 56 questions the average value of the expert assessment was below or equal the level 1. Additionally, the low average value for median (=1.32) and the average value for the standard deviation of all results of 1,18 in Table 2.4 are in accordance with the our findings in Figure 2.4.

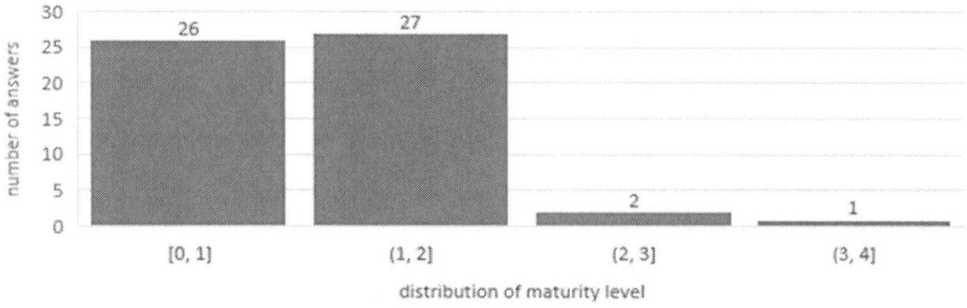

Figure 2.4 *Distribution of medians for GPT-NEO with PMBOK text training*

To further illustrate the poor quality of the answers we present two examples for answers with poor (<1.00) and two with better (>2.00) quality.

Table 2.4 *Selected examples – GPT-NEO with PMBOK text training*

Question	Answer AI	Average value of maturity model	Comment
Outline an Eisenhower matrix!	A Guide to the Project Management Body of Knowledge (PMBOKÂ® Guide) â€" Fourth Edition Â©2008 Project Team, Inc., 14 Campus Blvd., Newtown Square, PA 19073-3299 USA HAPTER 4 - PR	0	The lowest rated answer, full of special characters
Which escalation levels after Glasl are there in conflicts?	[1] Exercise.1.3.4.5.2.6. Scope Changes. The Scope Change exercise will affect the following: â€¢ The scope of the project (i.e. project scope) that	0.25	The second lowest rated answer, sems to be copied from somewhere.
What does quality management mean? How is it operated in the project?	What is the role of quality control and quality assurance? It is a project management process, and it focuses on the quality of the work, not on how it is done. Quality management is not about performance, but about what is right and necessary.	2.50	The second best rated answer

What is project management?	Project management is the process of managing and working with teams as they develop, implement, and deliver projects. It is a process in which teams work in a coordinated manner to manage their projects and make decisions. Project managers are often referred to as project managers	4.00	Best rated answer

The results of GPT-NEO with PMBOK text training show the following: The answers were often copied content from the PMBOK guide but often did not fit the question. In many cases the AI system did not respond with complete phrases but with words without overall meaning. Also, special characters with no relation to the questions was provided by the AI. The training with the content of the PMBOK guide did not show a positive but a negative effect on the quality of the answers.

2.6 Discussion and outlook

In this chapter, we argue that AI technologies will continue to shape societies, business and specifically project management. Among the diverse types of AI approaches, natural language processing use cases are deemed to be the most promising. We presented several use cases that are within reach of implementation, judging from current advances in algorithms and models shown within other research fields, especially computer science.

We have taken a closer look at existing pre-trained language models and developed the research question of how much project management-relevant knowledge is implicitly contained within these models. The results of this experiment gave us several insights.

For one, German language models, or language models that are not pre-trained with and result in English texts, are quite rare. As a major part of scientific research in the field is published in English journals and textbooks, this is straight-forward. It leads to substantially less published and maintained language models and according to our experiment results to significantly lower performance. At first thought, this could mean drastic negative consequences for companies that do not operate their business in English language. With AI advances undergoing technological diffusion within the upcoming years, businesses that communicate internally and externally could profit from AI language models heavily, not only within their project operations, and therefore build up competitive advantages much quicker than companies that do not have access to such technologies.

However, with recent advances also in the field of machine translation, which has become much more context- and concept-aware, such negative consequences could be rendered irrelevant.

For another, state of the art language models incorporate surprisingly solid knowledge regarding project management. Acknowledging that our prompting method was quite naïve, it is astounding how close the AI-generated answers were to the actual expected answers as they would have been asked for in actual tests. Arguably, if the tests were administered in text-only format, a test taker with access to the language model could have benefited greatly from AI-generated proposals for answers, even if they had only taken them as frameworks or templates for their own final answers to the questions.

Thirdly, the text corpora make a huge difference regarding the model performance. Seemingly, models that are trained on textbooks or the entire Wikipedia are much more reliable in this more professionally aspiring context than those that were also trained on data that includes internal discussion boards, forums in social media and such. While this seems intuitive it begs the question of how in the future such models should be trained, and what training strategies exist, what difference they make as well as ultimately, what level of expertise on a subject matter can be expected from a language model. Does it for example give answers on a level of expertise of a bachelor's degree holder, a master's degree holder or a seasoned expert in the field? Furthermore, we will probably need standardized tests, not only for humans, but for AI language models themselves, as a method of quality assurance and measurement of the level of expertise.

Obviously, our approach has some severe shortcomings that need to be addressed in follow-up research. But due to the novelty and only recent feasibility of the approaches we have taken, there are no gold standards available to our knowledge that would have made our research more robust. Most importantly, it is a naïve approach to examine language models that were trained on entirely different text corpora. Also, our additional training was very rustic, as we simply fed raw and un-preprocessed text data into an AI system without any further parameter-tuning or tests for optimal settings. However, it is interesting to study project management related implicit knowledge of models in very distinct case constellations: rather colloquial training texts like web conversations on the one hand, Wikipedia and textbooks on the other. For the future, scholars need to develop both ratings for the suitability of both learning texts as well as pre-trained models for specific purposes, like management or project management. Also, training guidelines need to be established that define what data sets are permissible, and how they should be (pre)processed for and during training.

Expert assessments should be based on more broadly accepted maturity models than the one that we introduced as we went through our research. Therefore, we believe that research into knowledge-bearing pre-trained models deserve the attention of trans-disciplinary teams in the future that apply the best methodologies for their respective fields.

The authors of this chapter are embarked on different research projects that aim at the mitigation of such limitations of the given research. For example, research is conducted into the possibilities and boundaries of classifying texts in emails about cultural and individual differences that may lead to conflict or misunderstandings. Secondly, extant language models are used to assess whether they are also able to extract project specific tasks out of email conversations, like the necessity to change plans, processes, or structures. A third research stream is directed at the core of the language models and how they reflect upon written reality that is contained within the texts that they were pre-trained with. For example, the structures of social, or psychological constructs like e.g., the Big Five personality traits should be identifiable within the structures of such language models. If these representations could be recovered in reliable ways, then the development of hypotheses regarding latent constructs, their development as well as their validation could be assisted tremendously by such language models.

Finally, another research stream shall be directed at the potentials of generative General AI models with regard to their ability to create graphical representations of text prompts, like organizational charts or GANTT charts from input text like emails.

This research is only covering small and very distinct parts of the potential entire uncharted territory of the interface between AI language models and business or management challenges. Researchers interested in this field greatly need an encompassing research agenda that takes all potentials and unknowns into consideration and makes suggestions about methods and the nature of research teams that should tackle such agendas. To our view, it should first encompass the systematic assessment of implicit and explicit knowledge of AI language models, dependent on which data they were trained with, in specific domains like management or project management. Second, ways to test language models of unknown origin about their understanding of a certain domain. Third, researchers need to come up with strategies and approaches that allow the creation of datasets for complex use cases like management or project management. This should include ideas on how to devise broadly acceptable ways of collecting data about projects in many different companies without giving away sensitive information of the organizations. Fourth, the domain needs standardized data sets, training texts and data challenges or benchmarks with respective performance indicators that allow for comparison and evaluation of AI models in general.

References

Abdal, Rameen and Peihao Zhu, Niloy Mitra, and Peter Wonka. „StyleFlow: Attribute-conditioned Exploration of StyleGAN-Generated Images using Conditional Continuous Normalizing Flows.“ (2020).

Becker, Jörg, Knackstedt and Ralf, and Poeppelbuss Jens. Dokumentationsqualität von Reifegradmodellentwicklungen. Arbeitsbericht Des Instituts Für Wirtschaftsinformatik, No. 121 (2008): 1–50. Retrieved from http://www.ifib-consult.de/publikationsdateien/2009.pdf

Chipulu, Maxwell and Neoh, Jay and Ojiako, Udechukwu and Williams, Terry. “A Multidimensional Analysis of Project Manager Competences,” IEEE Transactions on Engineering Management. No. 60, Art. no. 3 (Aug. 2013). doi: 10.1109/tem.2012.2215330.

Christian, Brian. 2020. The Alignment Problem: Machine Learning and Human Values. W. W. Norton & Company, kindle edition.

DeepAI (2021) deepai.org

DeepMind (2021) deepmind.com

Fleiss, Joseph L. "Measuring nominal scale agreement among many raters." Psychological Bulletin, No. 76(5) (1971): 378-382

Flore, Agnetha 2020. Reifegradmodell für Smart Grids: Bewertung der Migrationspfade anhand von zwei Fallstudien; https://www.shaker.de/de/content/catalogue/ index.asp?lang=de&ID=8&ISBN=978-3-8440-7749-0&search=yes

Gao, Leo and Biderman, Stella and Black, Sid and Golding, Laurence and Hoppe, Traiv and Foster, Charles and Phang, Jason and He, Horace and Anish, Thite and Nabeshima, Noa and Presser, Shawn and Leahy, Connor. (2020). The Pile: An 800GB Dataset of Diverse Text for Language Modeling. arXiv Preprint arXiv:2101.00027.

Ghosh, Arnab and Zhang, Richard and Dokania, Puneet K. and Wang, Oliver and Efros, Alexei A. and Torr, Philip H.S. and Shechtman, Eli. 2019. „Interactive Sketch & Fill: Multiclass Sketch-to-Image Translation.“ arXiv Preprint arXiv:1909.11081.

Härkönen, Erik and Hertzmann, Aaron and Lehtinen, Jaakko and Sylvain Paris. 2020. „GANSpace: Discovering Interpretable GAN Controls.“ arXiv:2004.02546

IBM (2022) Artificial Intelligence, Retrieved from

https://www.ibm.com/cloud/learn/what-is-artificial-intelligence

IPMA (2015) Individual Competence Baseline for Project Management, Version 4.0: IPMA International Project Management Association

Kissinger, Henry A. and Schmidt, Eric and Huttenlocher, Daniel. (2021) The Age of AI: And Our Human Future: Little, Brown and Company, kindle edition

Pengfei Liu and Weizhe Yuan and Jinlan Fu and Zhengbao Jiang and Hiroaki Hayashi and Graham Neubig. (2021). Pre-train, prompt, and predict: A systematic survey of prompting methods in natural language processing. arXiv Preprint arXiv:2107.13586.

Lundin, Rolf A., and Söderholm, Anders. „A theory of the temporary organization." 11 (1995): 437-455.

Microsoft (2022a) Artificial Intelligence Architecture. Retrieved from https://docs.microsoft.com/en-us/azure/architecture/data-guide/big-data/ai-overview

Microsoft (2022b) Künstliche Intelligenz. Retrieved from https://news.microsoft.com/de-at/microsoft-erklart-was-ist-kunstliche-intelligenz-definition-funktionen-von-ki/

Nuhn, Helge. (2021) Organizing for temporality and supporting AI systems – a framework for applied AI and organization research, Lecture Notes in Informatics, GI e.V

OpenAI, Berner, Christopher and Brockman, Greg and Chan, Brooke and Cheung, Vicki and Dębiak, Przemysław and Dennison, Christy and Farhi, David and Fischer, Quirin and Hashme, Shariq and Hesse, Chris and Józefowicz, Rafal and Gray, Scott and Olsson, Catherine and Pachocki, Jakub and Petrov, Michael and Pinto, Henrique and Raiman, Jonathan and Salimans, Tim and Schlatter, Jeremy and Schneider, Jonas and Sidor, Szymon and Sutskever, Ilya and Tang, Jie and Wolski, Filip and Zhang, Susan and. 2019. „Dota 2 with Large Scale Deep Reinforcement Learning." ArXiv Preprint arXiv:1912.06680

Oswald, Alfred., Müller, Wolfram. 2019. Management 4.0 – Handbock for Agile Practices, Release 3.0. BoD.

Oswald, Alfred. 2022. "The Whole – More than the Sum of Its Parts! Self-Organization – The Universal Principle!" In: Ding Ronggui, Wagner Reinhard, Bodea Constanta Nicoleta (editors). Research on Project, Programme and Portfolio Management – Projects as an Arena for Self-Organizing: Lecture Notes in Management and Industrial Engineering, Springer Nature

Peeters, Marieke M. M. and van Diggelen, Jurriaan and van den Bosch, Karel and Bronkhorst, Adelbert and Neerincx, Mark A. and Schraagen, Jan Maarten and Raaijmakers, Stephan. (2021) Hybrid Collective

Intelligence in a Human-AI Society, in AI & Society Journal, March 2021
Pichai, Sundar. 2022 AI at Google: our principles. Retrieved from https://www.blog.google/technology/ai/ai-principles/
Poeppelbuss, Jens, & Röglinger, Maximilian. (2011). What makes a useful maturity model? A framework of general design principles for maturity models and its demonstration in business process management. ECIS, 1–12. Retrieved from http://aisel.aisnet.org/ecis2011/28/
Puranam, Phanish. 2021. Human – AI collaborative decisionmaking as an organization design problem, Journal of Organization Design (2021) 10:75–80
Simpson, John and Weiner, Edmund. 1989. The Oxford English Dictionary.
Hoffmann, Christian Pieter and Lennerts, Silke and Schmitz, Christian and Stölzle, Wolfgang and Uebernickel, Falk. 2015. Das St. Galler Business-Innovation-Modell. Business Innovation: das St. Galler Modell. St. Gallen. https://doi.org/10.1007/978-3-658-07167-7
Vasilescu, Dragos-Christian and Filzmoser, Michael. 2021. Machine invention systems: a (r)evolution of the invention process?, Journal AI & Society, January 2021
Vial, Gregory. 2019. Understanding digital transformation: A review and a research agenda. J. Strateg. Inf. Syst., 28, 118–144.

Helge F. R. Nuhn is professor for Digital Business Engineering at the technical-oriented distance-education university Wilhelm Büchner Hochschulein Darmstadt, Germany and Vice President for Digitalization, Accreditation and Quality Management. He studied Information Systems at the Technical University Darmstadt and pursued a consulting career for 15 years, helping client world-wide deal with project management, agility and digitalization. Nuhn obtained his PhD from EBS University for Economic and Law, Wiesbaden, Germany, in organizational theory, especially on temporary organizations. He is head of the Special Interest Groupe "Agile Management" of the German IPMA-member organization GPM Deutsche Gesellschaft für Projekt management e.V. He has researched artificial intelligence for several years and insisted early that the real value of artificial intelligence system in project management will stem from natural language processing capabilities.

Alfred Oswald is Managing Director at IFST-Institute for Social Technologies GmbH in Germany, a Consulting Institute for Agile and Fluid Organizations. He earned his doctorate in Theoretical Physics at RWTH Aachen University. He is member of the leadership team of the professional group for Agile Management at GPM (German Association for Project Management e.V.). He is co-author of many articles and books in the context of self-organization and management, like 'Die Collective Mind Methode' and 'Project Management at the Edge of Chaos' and is co-editor of the handbook 'Management 4.0, Handbook for Agile Practices'. Currently, he is particularly interested in exploring the Collective Intelligence of humans and Artificial Intelligence in Project Management.

Agnetha Flore has been working at the Center for Digital Innovations Lower Saxony as Managing Director since 2021. She holds a degree in business administration and a doctorate in business informatics. From 2019 to 2022 she was a lecturer for agile project management at the Informatik & Business School Oldenburg and since 2023 she is a tutor for project management at the Wilhelm Büchner Hochschule. Flore already has 23 publications, one of which is a book, and three of them book chapters.

Rüdiger Lang is a business expert in digitalization with years of experience in the insurance sectors. He is principal at a major digitalization business consultancy and an AI entrepreneur in the education sector. Lang holds a degree in information technology, computer science and mathematics. His research interests lie in artificial intelligence and agile organizations.

III

Active BIM in Optimization-Supported Construction Project Management: Achievements, Challenges and Applications

Mario Galić and Uroš Klanšek

3.1 Active BIM

Quality decision-making is one of the main needs of contemporary construction project management in challenging market economy conditions and competition between companies. In principle, construction project management refers to directing and coordinating human and material resources over the life of a construction project by applying contemporary management techniques to reach pre-defined objectives of scope, time, cost, quality and participation satisfaction. Therefore, preparing reasoned bases for appropriate decision-making is much of the focus of project leaders. The necessity for achieving the highest quality and most effective decisions in managing large systems of human and material resources incites the usage of optimization models in the construction industry. Building information modelling (BIM), as an evolving concept in the construction business, is increasingly taking on the role of a decision-support tool since it enables a wider set of valuable data available in one place than conventional techniques.

Namely, BIM aims to deliver an object-orientated, data-rich, intelligent and parametric representation of various physical and functional characteristics transformed into a multi-dimensional digital model. Providing the continuous flow of numerical analyses of input data, their computer modelling, and quantitative proof of feasible outputs throughout the project's life cycle can be set among the main advantages of BIM. However, most BIM-based tools are highly user-dependent and characterised by discrete synthetic data modelling and transfer into virtual reality. They often include a 3D geometrical model with other visualized information, i.e., dimensions. Such an approach can be recognised in the literature as passive BIM since it includes no feature for output data synthesis. In this perspective, it is important to recollect and underline a well-known postulate that regardless of the model's nature, e.g., a physical, numerical or digital model, the model is just as efficient and good as the input parameters.

In the case of BIM, this postulate arguably forces not just the quality of the model's output but projects the overall success. In the case of passive BIM, input parameters are most often manually added to the model and are neither necessarily completely analysed nor optimal and might even result in an infeasible solution. Changes in some input parameters that usually occur during a project's life cycle, but mostly in its construction phase, must be repeatedly modelled and transferred back to the BIM model, which tends to be time-consuming and significantly increases the possibility of data overlaps and errors. Decision-support models developed with such an approach, at their best, ensure feasible solutions for project managers.

Indeed, the synthesis of structural output data, such as optimal project scheduling, building site workspace planning, risk assignment control in construction processes, constructability review, safety and health control, etc., also requires the employment of other tools, which should be appropriately backed by user's expert knowledge and computer skills. In the context of optimization-supported construction project management, BIM can provide digitally structured and transferable input parameters, whilst optimization search algorithms can resolve the synthesis of output data necessary for efficient decision-making. From the viewpoint of an exact mathematical understanding, BIM, as a concept, does not represent an optimization approach until at least one of the available optimization methods is engaged.

So, a clear difference exists between the solution found by a manually performed trial-and-error procedure and the one found by an employed optimization algorithm. An active BIM is a dynamic system integrating optimization algorithms and BIM to achieve two-way data enrichment. In this way, the added value of active BIM is the provision of semi-automated data transfer between models and phases. On the other hand, it is necessary to emphasise that active BIM heavily relies on utilised software packages and, even more importantly, on their mutual compatibility. To reach an active BIM environment with a dynamic data exchange, all engaged software needs to be compatible and, most commonly, object-orientated.

Enthusiasm for BIM was shown by the AEC professionals and in academia from 2005 to 2015. This has subsided due to numerous challenges that have not been bridged. The technologies required and brought by BIM recovered and prioritised some everlasting industry issues. Those challenges and issues have the same root and can be traced to the necessity of the industry's continuous reengineering. However, the main BIM challenges are reported in the literature and can be structured into four interrelated domains, i.e., conceptual, educational, traditional and contractual. The anticipated and required interoperability of BIM data transfer among different BIM digital environments still has not been reached in some crucial cases, which burdens BIM's conceptual applicability.

Besides its technological root, this issue can be categorised as directly related to the second domain of the issues above, i.e. educational drawbacks. Globally academia favours BIM and adopts it in curriculums, but the new generations of practitioners, colloquially called the BIM generation, still cannot push the entire AEC industry towards BIM. Hence, the gap between experienced practitioners and newcomers is increasing. This issue has a common root with the third domain of the BIM issue, the traditionalism of the industry. It is common knowledge that the construction industry hardly adopts new technologies and methodologies, especially fast-track ones such as BIM. Lastly, the domain of the BIM issues lies in legislation and contracting in the AEC industry. The traditional and still the most common design-bid-build contracting of construction projects interferes with reaching BIM's full potential. It is anticipated that the design-and-build type of contracting would allow the exploitation of BIM's benefits for the sake of overall project success.

Nevertheless, the BIM paradigm represents one of the most progressive developments influencing the construction industry's future. This chapter is thus devoted to the active BIM approach to developing optimization-supported models for efficient decision-making in construction projects where special emphasis is placed on achievements, challenges and applications. After a brief introduction to active BIM, the chapter presents the optimization platform for the development of such models (i.e., formulation, classification, solution methods, and modelling tools), related achievements from the perspective of construction project management (i.e., construction site layout planning, project scheduling, and special applications), recent in-house developed applications, a discussion of open challenges, conclusions and proposals for further research.

3.2 Optimization Platform for Active BIM

3.2.1 General Optimization Problem Formulation

The optimization field covers various methods developed to deliver optimal solutions for decision-making tasks. In doing so, the potential of optimization to determine the best solution without testing all possible solutions stems from the employment of advanced computational approaches. Optimization comes to the fore only after iterative numerical calculations, which follow clearly defined logical procedures or search algorithms implemented in computer equipment, and after the required processing time. Although optimization problems vary from one to another, they all may be covered by the following general formulation: minimise $f(\boldsymbol{x})$, subject to $\boldsymbol{h}(\boldsymbol{x}) = \boldsymbol{0}$ and $\boldsymbol{g}(\boldsymbol{x}) \leq \boldsymbol{0}$, where $f(\boldsymbol{x})$ stands for the objective function of decision variables $\boldsymbol{x}$ that determine the solution whilst $\boldsymbol{h}(\boldsymbol{x}) = \boldsymbol{0}$ and $\boldsymbol{g}(\boldsymbol{x}) \leq \boldsymbol{0}$ represent the set of equality and inequality conditions that need to be fulfilled by each alternative solution.

In the formulation above, the objective function expresses the criterion for selecting the optimal solution from the available alternatives. Equality and inequality conditions establish the restricted space of alternative solutions, i.e., the feasible region. The optimal solution is identified among the available alternatives as to the one that shows the extreme value of the objective function. So, the objective function may also be maximised over the feasible region if that adjusts more conveniently to the nature of the optimization criterion. It should be emphasised that decision variables' optimal values must be identified between their lower and upper bounds, i.e., $\boldsymbol{x}^{LO} \leq \boldsymbol{x} \leq \boldsymbol{x}^{UP}$.

3.2.2 Optimization Problem Classification

Specific optimization problems may be defined in different formulations. For instance, optimization tasks can be addressed simultaneously by a single criterion or multiple criteria. Moreover, optimization problems may include equality and inequality constraints and bounds on decision variables, or they can be without them. The latter class is called unbounded optimization problems. The variable $\boldsymbol{x}$ in the optimization problem may be either stated as continuous or as an integer. Discrete decisions can be optimally taken based on binary 0–1 variables. Optimization problems can be further divided into groups according to the form of functions $f(\boldsymbol{x})$, $\boldsymbol{h}(\boldsymbol{x})$ and $\boldsymbol{g}(\boldsymbol{x})$; see the classification in Figure 3.1.

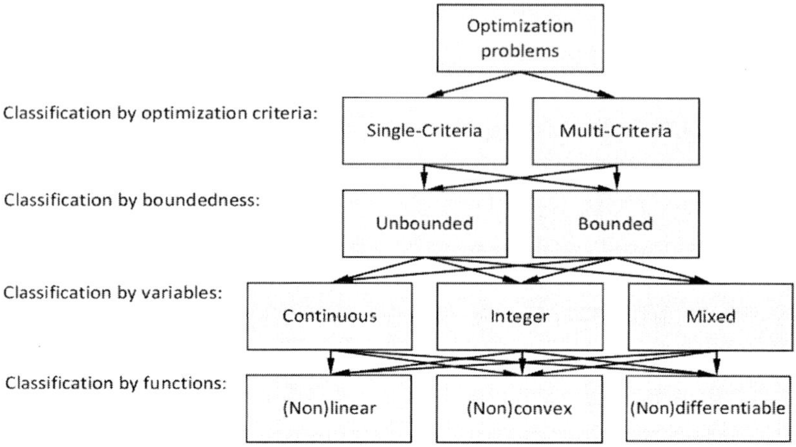

Figure 3.1 *Optimization problem classification*

Optimization problems in which the constraint functions $\boldsymbol{h}(\boldsymbol{x})$ and $\boldsymbol{g}(\boldsymbol{x})$ take a linear form can be classified as linearly bounded. However, when all functions $f(\boldsymbol{x})$, $\boldsymbol{h}(\boldsymbol{x})$ and $\boldsymbol{g}(\boldsymbol{x})$ are linear and vector $\boldsymbol{x}$ contains only continuous variables, the optimization problem can be identified as the linear programming (LP) task. If the task also comprises variables that can take an integer or binary 0–1 value, then it is a mixed-integer linear programming (MILP) optimization problem. As soon as the problem formulation with continuous variables includes nonlinear smooth differentiable functions, it may be classified as a nonlinear programming (NLP) task. Still, if the formulation covers integer or binary 0–1 variables, the optimization task determines a mixed-integer nonlinear programming (MINLP) problem. Mathematical programming problems may contain continuous and differentiable functions, which can be nonlinear and nonconvex. When optimization problem formulation shows discontinuous and non-differentiable expressions, heuristic approaches usually handle it.

3.2.3 Optimization Methods

Currently, no such method could be argued to be generally capable of solving all kinds of optimization problems. Furthermore, there is no method for which it can be claimed that it generally, without assumptions, ensures the global optimal solution. Thus, selecting an effective method for solving a particular optimization problem in construction operations needs to be executed thoughtfully to gain worthy results. Before selecting a solving method, the optimization problem should be classified as shown in the previous subsection. Approaches to solving single-criteria optimization problems can be roughly divided into two main classes, heuristic and mathematical programming methods.

Generally speaking, most heuristic methods have demonstrated the capability to cope with a wide spectrum of project management tasks in the construction industry. Their vital benefits are that most show fairly rapid convergence, and many confront optimization tasks that contain non-differentiable functions. Be that as it may, heuristic approaches have proven appropriate for solving a diversity of optimization problems in the construction industry, and the most often applied ones are perhaps: ant colony optimization, ACO (Colorni et al. 1991); differential evolution, DE (Storn & Price 1997); genetic algorithm, GA (Holland 1975; Goldberg 1989); harmony search, HS (Geem et al. 2001); neural networks, NN (Rumelhart et al., 1986); particle swarm optimization, PSO (Kennedy & Eberhart 1995); simulated annealing algorithm, SAA (Kirkpatrick et al. 1983); and tabu search, TS (Glover 1977). Yet, due to the complexity of optimization problems in construction and the perceived drawbacks of heuristic methods, meta- and hyper-heuristic algorithms seem more promising in terms of their problem-dependent effectiveness.

Being extensions of heuristic techniques, meta- and hyper-heuristic approaches predominantly represent bio-inspired search algorithms such as the African vulture optimization algorithm, AVOA (Abdollahzadeh et al. 2021) artificial bee colony, ABC (Karaboga & Basturk 2007); artificial butterfly optimization, ABO (Qi et al. 2017); artificial lizard search optimization, ALSO (Kumar et al. 2021); artificial plant optimization, APO (Cui & Cai 2013); bacterial foraging optimization, BFO (Passino 2002); bat algorithm, BA (Yang 2010); beetle antennae search, BAS (Jiang & Li 2017); bird mating optimiser, BMO (Askarzadeh 2014); cat swarm optimization, CSO (Chu et al. 2006); crow search algorithm, CSA (Askarzadeh 2016); cuckoo search, CS (Yang & Deb 2009); dolphin echolocation optimization, DEO (Kaveh & Farhoudi 2013); eagle perching optimiser, EPO (Khan et al. 2018); firefly algorithm, FA (Yang 2009); flower pollination algorithm, FPA (Yang et al. 2014); glowworm swarm optimization, GSO (Kaipa & Ghose 2009); grey wolf optimiser, GWO (Mirjalili et al. 2014); Harris hawk optimization, HHO (Heidari et al. 2019); jellyfish search, JS (Chou & Truong 2021); prey-predator algorithm, PPA (Tilahun et al. 2015); self-adaptive fruit fly optimiser, SFFO (Sang et al. 2019); social spider optimization, SSO (Cuevas et al. 2013); spider monkey optimization algorithm, SMOA (Bansal et al. 2014); symbiotic organisms search, SOS (Cheng & Prayogo 2014); whale optimization algorithm, WOA

(Mirjalili & Lewis 2016); wolf search algorithm, WSA (Fong et al. 2015) among others.

Extensions of heuristic approaches have been inspired by physics phenomena too. Nowadays, several efficient physics-based metaheuristic algorithms are available for solving optimization problems in construction processes, for instance, the arithmetic optimization algorithm, AOA (Abualigah et al. 2021); the big-bang big-crunch algorithm, BB-BC (Erol & Eksin 2006); the charged system search algorithm, CSS (Kaveh & Talatahari 2010); colliding bodies optimization, CBO (Kaveh & Mahdavi 2014); the galaxy-based search algorithm, GbSA (Shah-Hosseini 2011); the gravitational search algorithm, GSA (Rashedi et al. 2009); the galactic swarm optimization algorithm, GSOA (Muthiah-Nakarajan & Noel 2016); inclined planes system optimization, IPO (Mozaffari et al. 2016); etc. Suitable alternatives are also nature-inspired algorithms like the farmland fertility algorithm, FFA (Shayanfar & Gharehchopogh 2018); the intelligent water drops algorithm, IWD (Shah-Hosseini 2009); the water cycle algorithm, WCA (Eskandar et al. 2012); and the water evaporation optimization algorithm, WEO (Kaveh & Bakhshpoori 2016). There are also some other encouraging metaheuristic algorithms worth to be mentioned here, in particular, biogeography-based optimization, BBO (Simon 2008); the league championship algorithm, LCA (Kashan 2014); teaching-learning-based optimization, TLBO (Rao et al. 2011); and the vibrating particles system, VPS (Kaveh & Ghazaan 2017).

Notwithstanding their broad serviceability, heuristic algorithms may commonly assure at most that the solution found after terminating the search procedure is near-optimal, which simultaneously strengthens the significance of post-optimization analysis. On the other hand, the main advantage of mathematical programming methods is that they are rigorously anticipated to deliver the exact optimal solution even though the search procedure might need longer computational time in certain instances. In this way, mathematical programming approaches have also been extensively acknowledged as beneficial tools for optimising the construction process. Mathematical programming encompasses LP, NLP, MILP, and MINLP optimization methods.

LP can be recognised as the most mature field of mathematical programming. LP algorithms can solve optimization tasks formulated with linear expressions containing continuous variables. The latter assumptions that need to be fulfilled in optimization problem formulation can certainly reduce the applicability range of LP, though, in cases where this approach can be used, it, as a rule, provides exceptional quality solutions. The most established LP optimization method is a famous simplex algorithm, SA

(Dantzig 1963). Even so, it is necessary to stress that the interior point method, IP (Karmarkar 1984), is frequently proven to be a better choice for solving large-scale LP optimization problems.

The NLP approach should be used to achieve a solution when it comes to an optimization problem with continuous variables but with nonlinear functions. The said approach can be more widely used than LP since most optimization problems in construction project management contain at least some actual nonlinearity that needs to be covered in model formulation. However, at the moment, there is no universal optimization method that can equally well cope with just every NLP task. Therefore, an appropriate method for solving a particular NLP optimization problem should be chosen by considering its size and classification, as shown in the previous subsection. Nowadays, there are numerous highly-effective search algorithms from which a suitable one can be chosen to solve a determined NLP task optimally. Among NLP optimization algorithms, the augmented lagrangian approach, AL (Powell 1969; Hestenes 1969), the generalised reduced gradient method, GRG (Abadie & Carpentier 1969), and successive quadratic programming, SQP (Powell 1978), stand out in terms of frequency of use.

MILP supplements the LP approach with an ability to address discrete variables simultaneously with continuous ones. In this way, MILP can solve optimization problems formulated with linear functions that may include continuous, integer and binary 0–1 variables. However, it should be noted that any constrained integer variable may also be expressed employing a combination of a binary 0–1 decision variable and an integer parameter. A conventional approach for executing MILP optimization searches is the branch and bound method, BB (Land & Doig 1960), even though the cutting plane method, CP (Gomory 1958), as well as the branch and cut method, BC (Padberg & Rinaldi 1987), can be applied in various instances equally effectively.

Optimization problems containing discrete variables and nonlinear terms need to be handled by applying the MINLP approach. MINLP problems represent the most difficult group in the optimization field. However, they occur very frequently in the construction industry. Large-scale and nonconvex tasks can be quite challenging for all existing methods when they must be solved optimally. Whilst highly effective exact solutions may be anticipated from state-of-the-art MINLP techniques, it must be pointed out here that the area of nonlinear (discrete) optimization is the most demanding and has not so far attained the level of development compared to linear (smooth) optimization. Despite all that, several powerful search algorithms are at hand for solving MINLP optimization problems in construction projects, such as the augmented penalty/outer-approximation/equality-relaxation algorithm, AP/OA/ER (Viswanathan & Grossmann 1990), the branch and reduce method, BR (Ryoo & Sahinidis 1996), the extended cutting plane method, ECP (Westerlund & Pettersson 1995), the feasibility technique, FT (Mawengkang & Murtagh 1986), generalised Benders decomposition, GBD (Geoffrion 1972), the hybrid algorithm, HA (Bonami et al. 2008), the mixed-integer alpha BB algorithm, MIαBB (Adjiman et al. 2000), the nonlinear branch and bound method, NBB (Beale 1977), sequential linear discrete programming, SLDP (Olsen & Vanderplaats 1989), among others.

3.2.4 Modelling Tools for Optimization

As presented above, optimization methods are included in various software developed for their effective use in the computer-aided solution of optimization problems. The purpose of modelling tools for optimization is to present optimization problems in forms that can be recognised and then processed by a computer. The essence of the interaction between the user, the modelling tool and the optimization algorithm is given in Figure 3.2.

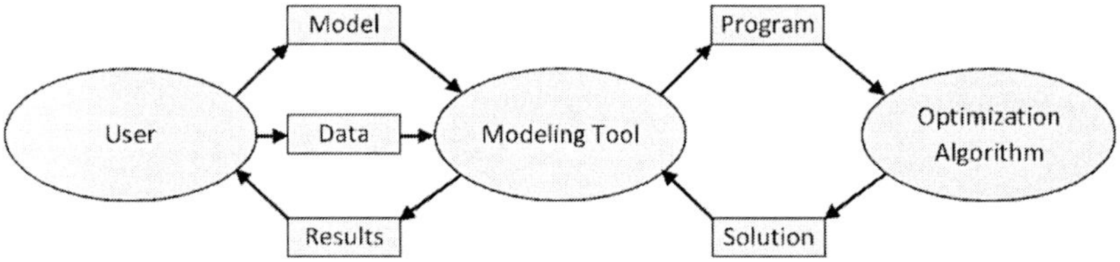

Figure 3.2 *Interaction between the user, modelling tool and optimization algorithm*

At this point, a user-defined general mathematical formulation of the optimization problem and its data are translated by a modelling tool into a syntax readable by a computer. The modelling tool generates a programme and forwards it to the optimization algorithm chosen to solve the problem as soon as the solution process is started. After the optimization algorithm completes its iterative search procedure and finds the optimal solution, the latter is sent back to the modelling tool, which presents the optimization results to the user through computer statements, reports, etc.

A wide range of modelling tools adequate for solving optimization problems is commercially available. Syntaxes of modern algebraic modelling languages are commonly adjustable and permit large-scale optimization models to be determined compactly using indexing. Hence, algebraic modelling languages like Advanced Interactive Multidimensional Modelling System, AIMMS (2021); Mathematical Programming Language, AMPL (2021); General Algebraic Modelling System, GAMS (2021); Linear-Integer-Nonlinear-Global-Optimization, LINGO (2021); Literate Programming Language, LPL (2021); Mathematical Programming Language, MPL (2021); Optimization Programming Language, OPL (2021); User Interface for Mathematical Programming, UIMP (2021) and others, can be employed for onerous and one-of-a-kind optimization tasks which may require several revisions before an accurate model is entrenched. These may be found especially serviceable when several optimization conditions of the same kind pursue the same pattern. In such cases, the algebraic modelling language is enabled to jointly formulate all the conditions of the same group whilst simultaneously addressing the variables of each type. This approach hastens various model management tasks like converting the data into model parameters, adjusting the model, accessing the data and examining the results.

A well-liked alternative to algebraic modelling languages is spreadsheets. Spreadsheets are broadly used in construction project management for computations and data analysis. Thus, it also appears natural for them to be employed as an optimization modelling environment. Indeed, Microsoft's Excel supported with add-ons, for instance, Evolver (2021), Solver (2021), or What'sBest (2021), may be mentioned here as commercial spreadsheet software commonly used for optimization modelling. Spreadsheet-based optimization can also be performed by applying Google Sheets with add-ons like OpenSolver (2021). Spreadsheets are user-friendly tools for optimization modelling within a more widely known software framework. Even so, the optimization model created using spreadsheet software is not so transparent compared to the one formed in the code of algebraic modelling language. Furthermore, optimization model generation via cells is proved to be time-consuming. Therefore, spreadsheets are suitable for establishing small- and medium-sized models with the same quantity of entries.

Interactive computer languages for numeric and symbolic computations are slightly less applied in managing construction projects but still useful for optimization modelling. Programs like Mathematica (2021) and MATLAB (2021) may be mentioned here as examples of interactive computer languages often employed in optimization modelling despite not being primarily designed for that. The software provides an interactive surrounding for generating and structuring the data, developing the model, and resolving the optimization task, including the representation of output results in graphical forms and printouts.

In addition to the aforementioned modelling tools, there is also a possibility for executing the optimization over internet-based services. The Network-Enabled Optimization System NEOS (2021) can be cited as among the popular optimization servers. The server allows access to several state-of-the-art solvers that cover various optimization categories and run on distributed high-performance machines. Its website complements the server, showcases the optimization case studies, presents the optimization information and resources, and provides background information. An advantage of employing such servers is that large-scale problems can be optimally solved on a high-performance online machine, which reduces the need for a powerful computer from the end user. The following section reveals the developments in optimization-supported active BIM systems useful in construction project management.

3.3 Achievements of Active BIM in Construction Project Management

3.3.1 Construction Site Layout Planning

One of the critical tasks in managing a construction project is construction site layout planning or CSLP. CSLP aims to arrange temporary facilities on a construction site to minimise the time workers and production resources should travel. Computer-aided design (CAD) based solutions came before active BIM methods in this industry. For instance, Osman et al. (2003) suggested a CSLP technique that combines the powerful search and optimization features of GA with the highly sophisticated graphical capabilities of CAD platforms. GA was utilised in this case from within the CAD system to locate temporary facilities on the construction site in the best possible locations.

The study by Khalafallah and El-Rayes (2011), who presented a practical automated system developed to optimise multiple conflicting planning objectives and provide all realistic optimal tradeoff solutions between them, was another accomplishment with CAD as the foundation. Four significant modules of their system were implemented and integrated: (1) a comprehensive and detailed multi-objective optimization engine that incorporates and optimises construction work zone safety, construction-related aviation safety, construction-related airport security, and all relevant site layout costs; (2) a relational database that incorporates planning data and stores all the generated optimal solutions; (3) an input/output module to make it easier to specify planning and optimization parameters as well as retrieve optimal construction site layout solutions; and (4) to enable the visualisation of the created ideal site layout plans and a visualisation module that interacts with external CAD software is also included.

An automated approach for developing dynamic construction site layout models using data from BIM was proposed in the study by Kumar and Cheng (2015). An optimization framework that considers on-site employees' and equipment's real travel patterns was developed using the A* algorithm in conjunction with GA. Their methodology optimises facility proportions and considers internal storage within newly constructed buildings to handle the space constraint on site. In order to create the best tower crane layout plan possible, Wang et al. (2015) proposed an integrated strategy combining BIM and FA. At the start, BIM is used to deliver the mathematical model inputs. The best locations for tower cranes and supply positions are then determined using the FA. Finally, BIM-based simulation assesses and evaluates the ideal tower crane layout design.

The development and implementation of a component-level system that can generate site layouts automatically were reported by Akanmu et al. (2016). BIM, GA, and a radio frequency identification (RFID) system that may provide real-time object locations are all integrated into the system. Marzouk and Abubakr (2016) presented a framework for selecting the types and placements of tower cranes at construction sites. The framework takes into account three primary models: an analytical hierarchy process (AHP) based decision-making model is used to choose the type of tower crane, followed by a GA-based optimization model for selecting the appropriate number and position of tower cranes, and finally, a 4D BIM to simulate tower crane operations. By utilising the data provided by BIM and project schedules, a framework for determining travel frequencies at various construction project phases was proposed by Hammad et al. (2016). Later, to enhance CSLP, the calculated frequencies are integrated as parameters in a MILP-based optimization model.

After utilising BIM technology and an enhanced A* algorithm, Tan et al. (2017) reported minimising the lift route for the offshore oil and gas platform (OOGP) module during disassembly. To represent OOGP models, the industrial foundation class (IFC) was employed. The OOGP components were explicitly represented by the IfcBuildingElementProxy entity, and data from IfcBuildingElementProxy was automatically extracted to determine the location and dimension of each OOGP module. The lift path and removal order of various modules with the shortest lift path distance were determined for a certain module configuration on the removal vessel. The A* algorithm, widely used in 2D contexts and customised to the 3D environment, was applied to determine the lift path distance. The layout plan of the removal vessel was then optimised using the GA technique by minimising the total lift route distance.

Tan et al. (2018) built a web system that integrates BIM and geographic information system (GIS) to deconstruct topsides for several offshore platforms effectively. The formulation of the lift planning optimization problem followed this work. BIM provided the specific information needed for planning the module layout on vessels, whilst GIS contained the maintenance and analysis of geospatial data for the scheduling of vessel transit. In order to optimise the module layout, three heuristic algorithms, i.e., GA, PSO and FA, were used and compared to determine the module configuration with the shortest overall lift time. In contrast, the graph search technique was combined with a newly created schedule clash detecting programme to find the transport plan with the shortest sailing time for the vessel. The suggested optimization algorithms and techniques were integrated into a developed BIM/GIS-based web system.

The CSLP formulation was developed by Singh et al. (2019) as an optimization task involving reducing transportation costs on a construction site with related constraints. With the use of BIM to model travel distances, the optimization model was given greater realism. GA was employed to optimise the objective function. Thus, all site constraints for travel paths captured in the BIM are included in the combined model, adding further realism to the CSLP modelling.

The dynamic construction material planning optimization model was put forth by Cheng and Chang (2019) to examine the optimization of material layout from the standpoint of dynamic task scheduling. Task float times were analysed to account for the changes in 3D travel distances among material supply and demand sites concurrently with changes in task schedules to ensure the observations were consistent with real-time conditions. These factors included schedule advancement and evolution, dynamic material requirements and storage site and area changes. The quantity take-off, building materials, quantity analysis, BIM and scheduling processes were combined to create dynamic material requirements data for construction layout planning. Second, the optimised construction site material layout plan was created using the SOS algorithm. Finally, a construction project was employed to implement the suggested paradigm.

3.3.2 Project Scheduling

The core of managing a construction project is scheduling. However, project scheduling problems (PSP) in the construction industry, particularly those with resource constraints, are usually difficult to optimise. Because PSPs are often considered difficult to solve optimally, several algorithms have been developed to deal with them, mostly focusing on heuristics and metaheuristic methods. The basic PSP goal is to identify an activity schedule that demonstrates the shortest project duration, whilst numerous practical applications also contain other costs- or resource-related goals. In addition, the development of optimization-based BIM tools created specifically for construction project scheduling is discussed.

In order to create the time-cost integrated schedule for the construction project, Feng et al. (2010) demonstrated a scheduling system that utilises a multi-dimensional (MD) CAD model, object sequencing matrix (OSM), and GA. To test the viability of the suggested approach, a computer implementation known as the MD CAD model-based project scheduling system (MD PSS) was created. The authors described the methodology for using GA to assist with crews' assignments and improve the construction sequence in six main sections. The suggested approach takes into account productivity, workspace and resource limits.

By researching workspace conflict analysis for a bridge model, Moon et al. (2012) proposed configuration methodologies of active BIM features that enable practical control constraints by optimising schedule overlap connected to its space models. By combining an efficient analysis algorithm with the BIM, their study creates the functionalities of an active BIM system so that managers may directly examine practical requirements and enhance passive BIM operation settings. The work mentioned above makes use of fuzzy and GA techniques as functions for assisting active BIM operations.

A virtual reality (VR) system for the construction stage was presented in the study by Kim et al. (2013), which can enhance the value of BIM in construction projects. Analysing progress, sequencing failures and risks in the proposed VR method enable integrated construction data management. The research proposed a fuzzy analysis and a straightforward GA-based optimization paradigm coupled with BIM functionalities. The system can be actively used as an efficient decision-making tool for a building project since it visually depicts intricate data and numerical information.

After developing a GA procedure for a schedule that reduces the simultaneous interference level of the scheduled workspace, Moon et al. (2014) implemented an active simulation system based on BIM. The impact factor of workspace interference, which takes schedule overlap and adjacency into account, was examined in order to complete this task. A location-constraint GA-based optimization approach that can reduce workspace interference is provided based on the impact factor. Integrating with 4D CAD, the GA visibly simulates the execution schedule's optimization level relating to the original plan. This created a 4D CAD system that can examine workspace interference by a GA.

By obtaining sufficient data from a project's BIM, Faghihi et al. (2014) demonstrated an innovative method for creating construction sequencing for installing construction elements. As a result, a computer application was created that can automatically deduce a structurally (statically) stable construction sequence utilising the GA concept. In their article, the phrase "structurally stable sequencing" referred to the order of erection sequencing in which the structure maintains stable local and global behaviour throughout the installation procedure.

In order to improve a project's operational performance, Moon et al. (2015) created a systematic methodology and computer system for an optimal construction schedule simulation that minimises overlapping operations. Their research focuses on locating tasks that overlap, using fuzzy theory and assessing the risks associated with schedule overlap issues. The GA principle is used to minimise the overlap of risky activities. In a BIM-based 4D CAD environment, the best schedule is visualized. The suggested 4D CAD system includes a scheduling simulator and fuzzy and GA analysis tools.

In their 2015 study, Wang and Song (2015) investigated the automatic generation of construction progress within the IFC file of 3D design and provided an ontological constraint principle and an automated approach based on GA-based progress scheduling. The authors provided evidence that the recommended technique can generate building progress automatically by constraining relationships between various components during construction. Additionally, the created progress schedule improves the efficiency of the progress generation process by defining the selection operator because GA can execute optimization.

By thoroughly integrating BIM product models with work package data, process simulations and the PSO algorithm, Liu et al. (2015) presented a BIM-based integrated scheduling approach that automatically generates optimised activity-level construction schedules for building projects under resource restrictions. The suggested system, however, has some drawbacks: simulation must be manually set up; durations and productivity are dependent on the manager's experience; weather considerations are ignored; etc. The development of a panelised construction system as an Autodesk Revit add-on tool was detailed.

To resolve the time-cost-quality tradeoff problem and guarantee an optimum schedule, GA was used in the Xu and Wei (2015) research. The graphic converter transformed objects based on the BIM model from BIM to the data in the table. Whilst Microsoft Project provided the scheduling results, structured query language was employed to calculate quantities.

Faghihi et al. (2016) presented graphical correlations between pre-defined schedule optimization objectives using their previously described construction schedule-generating algorithm. Construction schedules are created as the first step of the process using resource data and the project's BIM as input. The procedure then moves on to the GA-based optimization of all created construction schedules in compliance with the added job site movement target and time and cost objectives. The last phase is creating a 3D space as a 3D solution cloud point containing all the developed and computed construction schedules. These 3D construction schedules display three Pareto fronts and a solution's cloud of points.

De Soto et al. (2017) presented a method for project scheduling that incorporates the TS algorithm for determining optimal schedules, which can be tailored to address specific objectives such as duration, costs and resource utilisation. Additionally, this methodology incorporates 4D models for project visualisation, allowing for examining the optimised schedule to ensure compliance with sequencing and constructability requirements. Through this visualisation process, further adjustments to the schedule can be made.

A new approach named the BIM-IGA-based ASPO method was developed by Wang et al. (2018) to address the assembly sequence planning and optimization (ASPO) problem in precast concrete buildings. The aforementioned approach uses BIM for parametric modelling, an improved GA (IGA) for finding the best assembly sequence, and BIM yet again for visual simulation to validate the assembly process. IGA is also utilised to achieve the dynamic adjustment of assembly sequence throughout the construction process. IGA is enhanced in coding mode, crossover operation and mutation operation.

Ahmadian Fard Fini et al. (2018) proposed an innovative framework for optimising hiring and firing decisions within construction projects. This framework considers organisational human resource strategies, labour rights and technical and managerial constraints. Workforce planning is a vital aspect of achieving successful completion of construction projects. The framework utilises data from the BIM, project performance database and legal and contractual documents to establish the model parameters and decision-making criteria. Then, a dynamic programming technique determines the optimal duration and type of employment for workers with varying skills, skill levels and multi-skilling capabilities.

Volk et al. (2018) proposed an innovative approach for planning deconstruction projects utilising ResourceApp. The system can recreate a

3D building model by recording the building using Microsoft Kinect and automatically recognising building elements. The system then requires user input on parameters and general information about the building to generate an inventory of building materials and equipment. Additionally, the system generates deconstruction-related activities and uses an optimization model formulated in MATLAB to minimise the duration of the deconstruction project whilst considering resource limitations. The optimization model is set as a MILP task, which is optimally solved by employing the BC search of the CPLEX solver. The final results are exported to MS Excel and given as a Gantt schedule.

Ma and Zhang (2019) showed an overlapping optimization method that determines an appropriate overlapping strategy with precise overlap rates and creates the necessary duration at the lowest cost to effectively handle the concurrency-based time-cost tradeoff problem. The method uses an overlapping strategy matrix to show how the linkages between the various activities are interdependent. Then, using overlapping and crashing, this method employs the GA to compute an overlapping strategy with exact overlap rates. The authors then put forth a combined framework of GA and BIM to demonstrate the viability of theoretical research in actual practice. The study has value for practitioners since the suggested method allows for establishing a compressed schedule that meets the restricted budget within the contract duration. It is also meaningful to the research community because the offered method may expeditiously compute the optimal scheduling strategy with precise overlap rates, crashing degrees and resources.

He et al. (2019) proposed a 5D construction duration-cost optimization model that combines GA and BIM techniques. The suggested approach analyzes the characteristics of changing construction duration and cost and subsequently improves the GA's genetic mechanism and data processing methods to align with these characteristics. The feasibility of the model was demonstrated through its application in a practical engineering project, utilising BIM technology in conjunction with GA. This approach not only allows for rapid determination of optimal construction duration and cost decisions based on historical data and project demands but also enables visualisation of the construction process and dynamic scheduling of the project.

Based on the manufacturing process model and GA, the automated optimization framework discussed in the paper by Xu et al. (2020) was designed to establish an ideal schedule for prefabricated component production. An extraction and segmentation technique based on IFC was suggested for prefabricated component production. The position and geometric information of the prefabricated components were adapted during this procedure and output in the retrieved IFC file. The GA was then used to investigate and recreate each production process and completion time. Finally, the automatic optimization solution was developed by connecting the production scheduling database and the computational environment.

Wang et al. (2020) introduced an integrated solution for construction schedules that allows for fluent data flow from the BIM to the resource-constrained project scheduling problem (RCPSP) model. A work package-based information model was presented as part of this method to capture all RCPSP-required data. The proposed information model was then formed by applying a semi-automatic method that integrates multi-source data, whereas an adaptive data transmission technique was employed to assist a created multi-mode RCPSP model. The given study introduced a novel integrated strategy for formalising a construction information model employing a semi-automatic data integration approach, which covered the information demand whilst facilitating fluid data flow in the RCPSP-solving process.

The main objective of ElMenshawy and Marzouk's (2021) research was to develop a model for automatic schedule generation using BIM and to handle the time-cost tradeoff problem from the numerous scenarios available to the user. A model was created that used quantities exported from a BIM platform to set construction activities, calculate each activity's duration, and apply logic/sequence to connect the activities. To gain the best solutions whilst keeping project duration and cost in mind, a multi-objective optimization was accomplished by nondominated sorting GA (NSGA-II).

Nusen et al. (2021) presented a systematic BIM-based multi-objective GA technique for renovation project construction planning and scheduling. The results presented multiple options for various circumstances for future examination. Depending on the strategies based on the Pareto front data provided, the construction process may benefit from relevant information for better decision-making. BIM and multi-objective GA collaborated using standard spreadsheet files with.xls,.xlsx, and.csv extensions. Standard file formats are simple to read, edit and share, which is useful when sending model results, and the receiver only has standard spreadsheet tools like Microsoft Excel, Google Sheets, Smartsheet or Numbers.

3.3.3 Special Applications

The literature review revealed several special optimization-based active BIM applications that are useful for project management in construction. Specifically, Said and El-Rayes (2014) created an automated multi-objective construction logistics optimization system called AMCLOS. The system used MS Visual Studio C++ and consisted of five principal modules, including one for reading input data from the project's BIM IFC file and the component for importing a schedule from MS Project. The BIM geometry attributes were linked to activities within a relational database model. The construction logistics planning module was created to develop the model and optimise the solution using a GA. A user interface component was also created to help users navigate the AMCLOS system and transmit data across modules. The solution was designed to reduce overall logistical costs and project schedule criticality.

Marzouk and Abdelkader (2020) developed a BIM to assess various project alternatives' environmental and economic impacts. The model calculates direct and indirect emissions and primary energy during the project life cycle. A hybrid fuzzy multi-objective NSGA-II problem was formulated to model the uncertainties related to the quantification of the judging attributes and, as a result, to identify the most sustainable materials by minimising the objective functions: project duration, project life cycle cost and total project primary energy. Finally, the technique for order of preference by similarity to the ideal solution (TOPSIS) was employed to choose the most sustainable material from a collection of Pareto optimal alternatives for each construction component.

Wu and de Soto suggested a spatiotemporal model of lifting task scheduling for tower cranes (2020). A decision-support model with a TS is set to find the optimal lifting task scheduling for the least total time, and alternative solution structures in the scenarios of single and multiple tower crane(s) are created. In addition to the no-load and loaded lifting processes, the pre-and post-lifting processes, primarily caused by material preparation and transfer times, are integrated into the lifting task time model. In order to show the element information of the lifting operations and complex relations between lifting tasks intuitively and effectively, a lifting task scheduling display technique with normal- and fine-level schemes is introduced by combining the hue and value of colour with 4D simulation.

Yu et al. (2021) developed a system combining BIM and optimization models to optimise the cost and duration of large-span spatial steel structure projects. In this context, a PSO technique was utilised to provide Pareto-optimal solutions. The system retrieves the optimal solution for the steel structure project from the BIM-based model to simulate the construction process. To demonstrate the effectiveness of the suggested BIM-based time-cost optimization model in real-world scenarios, the authors conducted a case study on an airport terminal building with a large-span spatial steel structure.

Chen et al. (2021) suggested a BIM-based camera placement optimization methodology; construction cameras were deployed to facilitate autonomous job site monitoring. The framework considers changes in dynamic impediments and working spaces at various construction phases. The data image serves as a data mediator between the three modules (the BIM module, the mathematical module, and the GA-based optimization module), showing the discrete and optimised output of the construction site.

In response to the needs of the AEC industry and to identify current gaps in knowledge on active BIM applications for construction project management, in-house research activities were also performed, and the following section briefly presents the outcomes.

3.4 Recent In-House Developed Active BIM Applications for Construction Project Management

3.4.1 Optimal Simultaneous Positioning of Work Facilities and Tower Crane on Construction Sites

An in-house developed active BIM application intended to support construction project management represents a system for optimal simultaneous positioning of work facilities and tower cranes on building sites with repetitive operations (Dasović et al. 2019). In this particular system, the construction-ready BIM enrichment begins with exporting input parameters necessary for optimization, i.e., 3D building coordinates, construction site perimeter, relevant segments of the building with repetitive work, and the feasible region. A script of input parameters was transferred from the BIM to a document with a compatible extension to the optimization model to assure a dynamic linkage between the BIM and the optimization model.

At this point, a spreadsheet was employed to accomplish that. The optimization model was developed for the simultaneous positioning of work facilities and tower cranes to minimise the total duration of operation cycles. Depending on the classification of the optimization problem and its size, the user can select both the optimization tool and the solving algorithm. The optimization is followed by post-optimal analysis and solution entry into the BIM. The proposed system application was demonstrated using an actual construction site of a multi-story residential building in Osijek, Croatia. See Figure 3.3.

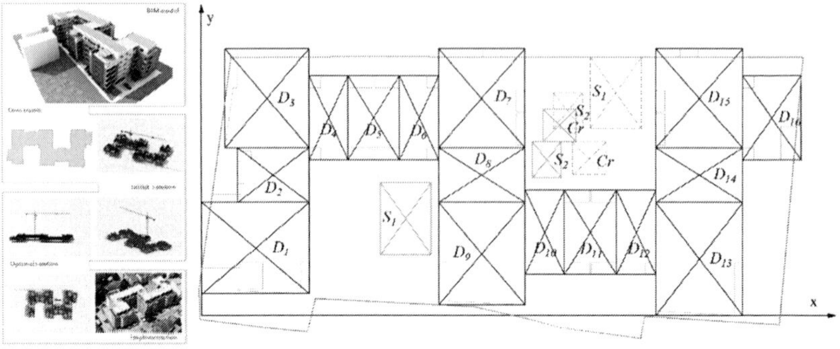

Figure 3.3 *Application of active BIM system for optimal simultaneous positioning of work facilities and tower crane on construction site*

The BIM was created with the Allplan (2018) software. The input parameters for optimization, provided by the BIM, were: (i) coordinates, materials, and required quantities of demand points; (ii) coordinates of feasible tower crane positions; and (iii) the number and type of available tower cranes. The NLP model was computer-generated using Microsoft Excel, where the optimization procedure was done employing the GRG method of the Solver (2018) add-in. After running and converging the GRG algorithm, the suggested system provided output results at the minimum total duration of supply cycles in the form of optimal position coordinates for work facilities and tower cranes. Finally, the local position coordinates were transformed into the global ones according to the Croatian reference coordinate system for map projection HTRS96/TM (2018).

In further developing the technique, it makes sense to involve a dynamic crane in the active BIM since visualising the crane's operation may aid in resolving eventual clashes and might enhance the solution. Additionally, it would be meaningful to modify the active BIM system in a way as to enable solving optimization problems with several tower cranes.

3.4.2 Optimal Positioning of Temporary Storages and Optimal Supply Chain Routes of Masonry Blocks on Construction Sites

A BIM-supported optimization model based on the theory of the transportation problem was successfully applied to solving the temporary storage locations and transportation routes of masonry blocks and mortar on the construction site (Galić 2019). Using the same 3D BIM model in the previous case study, input data were gained and transferred into a Microsoft Excel document, where the optimization model was set. The solution approach, from the 3D BIM model to optimal locations fixed for placing block pallets on a certain story level, is shown in Figure 3.4.

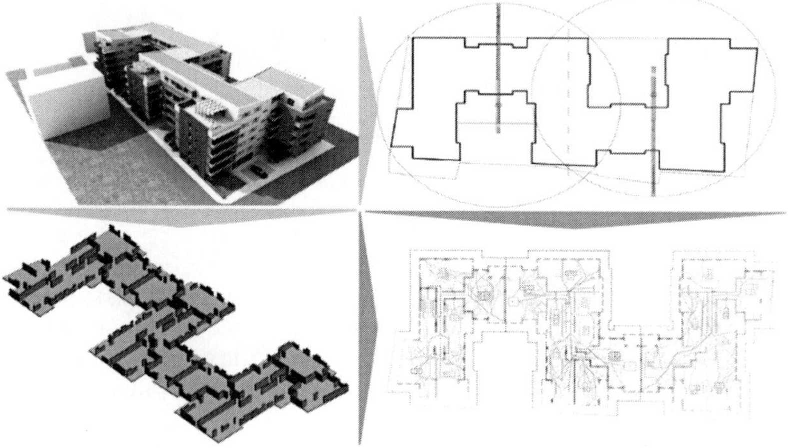

Figure 3.4 *Optimal positioning of temporary storage and optimal supply chain routes of masonry blocks on a construction site*

The optimization goal was to locate temporary storage (meeting points) of masonry blocks on the construction site for optimal supply chain delivery and transfer of blocks and mortar. In the post-optimal analysis, the question arose about how to apply the obtained results on-site, i.e., how to explain the new working routine to the workers. The first step is to set the starting point of the material transfer, in this case, the position of the block pallets and meeting points for the mortar. Since pallets are placed in their positions by a crane, marking the locations where the crane operator should place them is suggested. Thus, the worker who places the pallets knows exactly where they should be placed. The mortar checkpoints must be marked as well. It is advised to form teams of workers and to assign a certain work zone to each team respectively. Once the pallets have been temporarily placed, it is proposed to mark the pallets by zones so that workers can distinguish which pallets are in their work zone.

Post-optimization should strive for such a pallet arrangement, in which the shortest distance between the pallet and the wall will also be optimal. In that way, the workers will use the closest starting points to transport the material. When planning, it is vital to include in the project documentation a presentation of the location of the starting points of materials and a graphical presentation of the WBS structure so that the site manager can control the process of transporting materials. It is also recommended to give solutions to transport problems to provide the site manager with all the information for the best preparation for transporting materials in this way.

3.4.3 Optimization of Storage Facilities and Work Groups for Masonry Works on Construction Sites

In continuing the work on active BIM, using the same BIM model as in the previous two examples, an active BIM approach was applied to solve the optimization of construction storage facilities regarding masonry work groups (Galić 2019). The optimization model consists of two-step mathematical modules for decision-making of material supply planning and scheduling and simultaneously storage facility planning and utilisation, presented in Figure 3.5. The first module determines the quantities and deadlines for the supply order and is also an input data source for optimising the work dynamics in the second module. In the second module, under the constraints of permitted consumption of materials from the first module, a schedule is set, i.e., the duration of activities, the number of working groups for a particular activity, and the links among activities are established, to minimise the total duration of the execution. Both modules can operate separately, independent of one or the other. However, for full harmonisation of the supply and material consumption systems, it is vital to harmonise the decisions in both modules.

The model proved to be a successful tool for solving the problem of cramped, confined storage areas on construction sites in relation to the work dynamics. The output, i.e., storage facility utilisation and time plan, specify exactly how many working groups work on which wall and when. The plan is harmonised with the supply chain and storage restrictions, meaning there will be no downtime due to a shortage of materials if the planned amount of materials is delivered to the construction site in time per the supply order and storage plan.

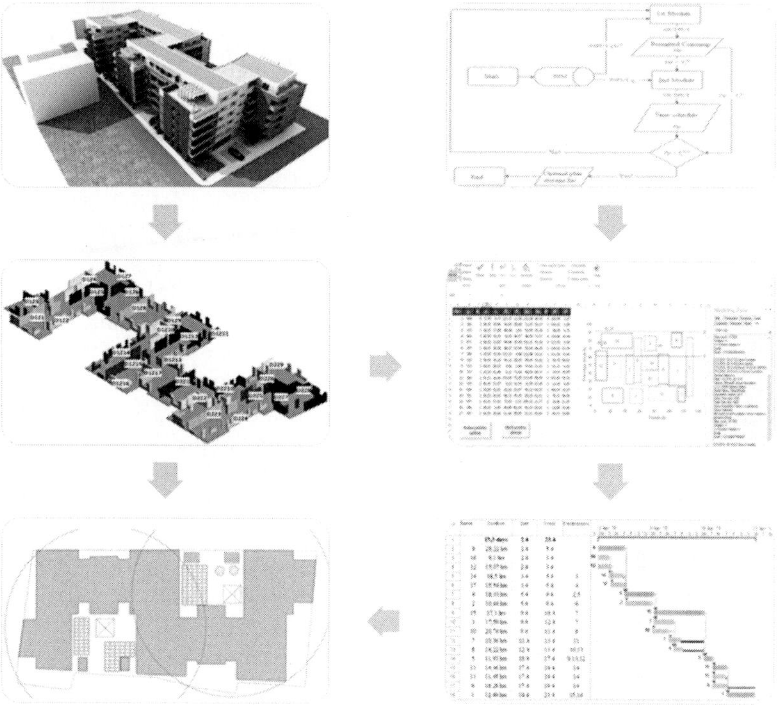

Figure 3.5 *Active BIM approach for optimization of storage facilities and work groups for masonry works on construction site*

The model's main advantage is its adaptability, meaning that low-effort changes can be applied at every stage of the work. As the work progresses, the amount of input parameters decreases, which results in a better solution. The presented model can also be applied to all materials that may appear on the construction site. The model can be further improved by introducing several types of materials (works) simultaneously, but the tool for solving this problem should be considered because, in that case, the number of variables increases many times over. As for the main disadvantage of the model, it is important to admit its relatively complex process of generating or changing the input parameters because the use and modification of the model require work on the computer with optimization modelling language OML since Microsoft Solver Foundation Solver was applied for modelling and solving the problem. Another drawback is the impact of the number of input parameters on the computation duration and the optimization result.

Sections 3.3 and 3.4 presented the achievements of other authors and the in-house contributions to the development of active BIM in construction projects. The next section discusses the open challenges found in that area.

3.5 Open Challenges of Active BIM in Construction Projects

3.5.1 Industry 4.0, Construction 4.0 and BIM

The world is witnessing the fourth industrial revolution (4IR). Despite its natural and logical analogy following the third revolution, which is still developing in most parts of the world, the 4IR has a fuzzy start. It will probably have a fuzzy transition towards the fifth revolution compared to previous industrial revolutions with clean-cut transitions (Begić & Galić 2021). It will be perhaps the first revolution aiming to provide a significant difference in green energy with a saving energy consumption agenda, but in terms of production digitalisation and automation, which theoretically could be adopted worldwide simultaneously. As well, 4IR has a reported exponential pace in developed industries forced by the revolution drivers, i.a., Digital Twin Construction (DTC), BIM, the Internet of Things (IoT), Big Data (BD), and Additive Manufacturing (AM)/3D printing. The premise and the anticipation from the 4IR can be extracted from a definition of "a fusion of technologies that are blurring the lines between the physical, digital, and biological spheres" (Schwab 2017).

The construction industry is known for its specifics that can probably be traced back to the pioneer construction projects, technologies and methodologies, i.e. traditionalism, sluggish acceptance of new technologies, and lagged benefits, but with a significant impact on the economy and society. Due to the aforementioned specifics, the construction industry is on the verge of its domain of a 4IR, known in the literature as Construction 4.0. Even though Construction 4.0 adopts most of the generally stated 4IR drivers and benefits, it aims to solve the construction industry's everlasting issues pointed out in the famous Egan's report from 1998 (Construction Task Force 1998), which were summarised more recently by Sawhney et al. (2020), i.e., productivity, sustainability, fragmented communication and responsibility, quality assurance, overall image, project cost and duration overruns, work environments and safety, model prediction and accuracy, focus on investors.

However, the euphoria from the early stages of Construction 4.0, induced by the prospects of new technologies and the concept of cyber-physical systems for construction, has subsided due to the numerous drawbacks and challenges that must be bridged. Perhaps the best example of such a "reality strike" is the current issues with and regarding the main Construction 4.0 driver, i.e., BIM. Even though BIM has a long path until its current high development stage and the fact is that there are significant efforts in developing legal frameworks, adjusting contracting, and standardisation of BIM (ISO 19650), there are recent reports worldwide that BIM is underachieving in the construction phase due to numerous reasons, illustratively suggested in Figure 3.6.

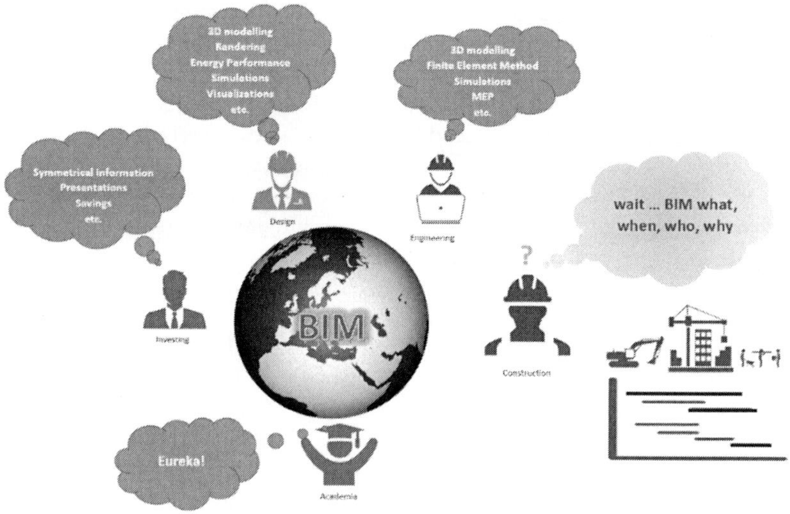

Figure 3.6 *Illustration of generalised perceptions and expectations from BIM among participants in the AEC industry*

Active BIM challenges can be directly connected to the main drawbacks, whilst perhaps interoperability is the most pointed single lack of BIM. BIM interoperability was concisely defined by Shehzad et al. (2021) as the information exchange capability of two or more organisational units or networks. As such, the authors accept the common understanding that interoperability is mainly a technological issue but can also arise as a semantic, legal and organisational issue. Based on this, the authors deployed a BIM interoperability adoption model (BIAM) for AEC organisations, consisting of four segments, i.e., technical, organisational, legal and semantic. Following this perspective, recently reported BIM drawbacks presented in the next subsections are structured into four interrelated domains, i.e., conceptual, educational, traditional and contractual.

3.5.2 Concept-Related BIM Challenges

The anticipated and required interoperability of BIM data transfer among different BIM digital environments has still not been reached in some crucial cases, which burdens BIM's conceptual applicability. A comprehensive study done by Ozturk (2020) proved the current BIM implementation and adoption difficulties throughout the project life cycle. It highlighted issues, i.e., data sharing, integration inefficiencies, lack of collaborative design, construction, operation and facility management and barriers to communication in project and construction management. Furthermore, the results of the study indicated that the interoperability research should be expanded from the commonly researched areas (i.e., architectural design, BIM model, IFC, and BIM) to knowledge-integrated, ontology-based, IT-based, collaborative, automated, well-visualized and sustainable outcomes throughout the project life cycle.

One of the critical interoperability issues concerning the model and data exchange is related to the data transfer from architectural design to structural analysis (Vilutiene et al. 2019). In this context, Wu et al. (2021) presented a study on interoperability between architectural design and structural analysis. The authors stated that the data exchange between architectural and structural analysis software is not fully interoperable yet, and presented a data-driven method to use invariant signatures for solving practical tasks in BIM applications. The proposed method was used, and the results showed successfully generated structural analysis input files with high accuracy. Ren and Zhang (2021) recently published a six-step research methodology that addresses the BIM interoperability problems between architectural design and structural analysis. The said work resulted in a new framework for dealing with BIM interoperability in the AEC domain from the technical and process dimensions viewpoint.

De Gaetani et al. (2020) studied interoperability problems using several BIM tools in real-life applications. The findings outlined three main challenges and suggested directions for BIM development, i.e., the usage of specialised software add-ins for debugging the conflicts of the IFC files or Gantt charts in collaborative work; the use of software tools from the same vendor for each stakeholder; and active encouragement and support for the development of tools in a neutral file format covered by standardisation.

Farghaly et al. (2018) presented international data-based taxonomy of required data for an effective application of BIM for asset management. In the same paper, the authors present an appropriate Revit plug-in enabling the creation of the required parameters. In the same period, Arayici et al. (2018) pointed out that the performance-based design requires a holistic design approach that entails multiple stakeholders interacting with a life cycle perspective, considering neighbourhood-level aspects and using various BIM applications. Addressing this interoperability issue, the authors used integrated process modelling, applying an information delivery manual (IDM) for energy-efficient design development by bringing energy databases, simulation and collective knowledge exploration through an integrated supply chain.

In a comprehensive study presented by Jin et al. (2019), the significant frequency of interoperability issues related to the application of BIM in building energy performance analyses was underlined. A similar study conducted by Sušnik et al. (2021) presented two methods addressing BIM's interoperability issue for energy and acoustic evaluation. One method is focused on exporting data from the BIM authoring tool into the analysis tool, whilst the second shows how exporting can be completely avoided, leaving the user to choose the method based on his needs and previous knowledge.

3.5.3 Education-Related BIM Challenges

Globally, academia favours BIM and, in some form, mostly adopted it in curriculums, but the new generations of practitioners, colloquially called the BIM generation, still cannot push the entire AEC industry towards BIM. Hence, the gap between experienced practitioners and newcomers still exists. BIM has changed construction project stakeholder definitions and requirements by creating new BIM roles (Akintola et al. 2017). Also, simultaneously there is an unsavoury combination of current reports of an increasing mismatch of BIM-related required skills and knowledge in construction along with a global shortage of skilled workers and high demand, which is putting a time-lag stamp on BIM adoption (Brucker Juričić et al. 2021). Considering new knowledge-related requirements and shortages, it is logical first to turn the spotlight toward the education systems.

Comparing education efforts and challenges in industries that perhaps reached further in BIM implementation, i.e., Australia, UK and USA, Hamma-adama and Kouider (2019) concluded that despite the similarity in the availability of technology infrastructure, hardware, and software (BIM tools) the availability of experts differs, which is connected with BIM courses and programs, where the USA takes the lead. Further, the authors recommend mandating BIM to accelerate adoption and alleviate education and training challenges. In further research on a similar topic, Casasayas et al. (2021) report that Australian universities are failing to prepare students for BIM-related roles, despite the galloping adoption of BIM in academia and industry. The authors recommend a stronger involvement and influence of professional associations on the curriculum and compact collaboration with BIM research departments, prioritising BIM as a requirement in the university reaccreditation process. In a review of BIM adoption in higher education of AEC disciplines, Wang et al. (2020), besides the innovative educational approaches, stress the importance of continuous educational innovation to bridge the gap between the higher education and AEC industry needs regarding the technical and managerial digitalisation capabilities.

A study of BIM adoption in Chinese curriculums presented by Li et al. (2020) revealed significant growth of BIM-related programs in the last six years, but more than 50% of analysed papers indicate that the current BIM education is still insufficient for the AEC industry. The same study revealed the unbalanced distribution between BIM research and education. In the Chinese AEC industry context, Wu et al. (2021) suggested that organisations should stimulate BIM training and post-graduate education on recently initiated BIM-related courses available in various universities as career-boosting opportunities.

A comprehensive study done by Olowa et al. (2020) on existing approaches to BIM for construction education, besides exposing different techniques applied in BIM courses, defined current challenges from this perspective. The two main directions that the authors underlined aim at the specific university microenvironments, including the pilot programmes, associated contextual and intervening conditions, and the mechanisms by which different approaches respond to perceived industry needs. Multi-disciplinary BIM courses on all educational levels are highlighted by Ghaffarianhoseini et al. (2017) as the main driver that might help the industry transition and smoother BIM adoption in the industry.

An interesting study by Jin et al. (2019) on students' perceptions of BIM in Australia, China and the UK revealed the flip side of the academic view on the BIM medal. Videlicet, the results, with negligible differences among countries, showed that students are critical or have less positive thinking and anticipations from BIM movements, especially in later construction project phases. Perhaps, this challenge inter alia seems like the most important one for the future. The perception of new-coming specialists and practitioners should have a clear view and proven benefits of technology, which must be prioritised. Olatunji (2019) suggested a step in that direction, concluding that students' motivation is highest if they develop their software skills on real-time case study problems. Our experience in mentoring students' master theses dealing with active BIM, i.e., Babić (2017), Čorak (2018), and Dasović (2018), confirms the above statement.

3.5.4 Traditionalism- and Contracting-Related BIM Challenges

Lastly, the domain of BIM issues lies in the legislation or contracts in the AEC industry. The traditional and still the most common design-bid-build contracting of construction projects interferes with reaching BIM's full potential. It is anticipated that the design-and-build type of contracting would allow the exploitation of BIM's benefits for the sake of overall project success. Also, it is common knowledge that the construction industry hardly adopts new technologies and methodologies, especially fast-track ones such as BIM.

A comprehensive literature review presented by Manderson et al. (2015) identified the main challenges of BIM implementation, i.e., compensation and consideration, contract conditions, data security, intellectual property, information and communications technology, protocol process and responsibilities, interoperability, legislation and judicial precedence, professional liability, public sector agencies and risk allocation. In addition to the challenges, Fan et al. (2018) stress the incompatibility issue of traditional procurement systems with BIM. The main challenges identified can be summarised into a few suggested directions for changes, i.e., adopting and pushing collaborative procurement tools, equal and fair distribution of risks and responsibilities among project participants, recognition of BIM as a legally relevant contract document, open standards for usage and the inclusion of BIM specific processes in the contract mechanisms.

Browsing the recent relevant literature on legal and contracting issues in the BIM environment, two main outputs stand out, i.e., blockchain and smart contract. According to Nawari and Ravindran (2019), blockchain is "the creation of a digital distributed consensus among decentralised nodes, enabling transparency of data and ensuring no single actor can claim authority over the entire network." As a certain safety net for BIM-induced roles in construction projects, blockchain applications turned to the financial sector and resulted in more technological innovation of automatically executable contracts, i.e., smart contracts.

Blockchain as a potential solution to the open legal and contracting issues was elaborated by Liu et al. (2019). The authors underline that the innovative blockchain-enhanced transactions in the BIM process have the potential to solve, i.e., technical, financial, legal, intellectual property and cyber security challenges that hinder the use of BIM for sustainable building design. However, the BIM and blockchain integration became a challenge of information redundancy.

In a study addressing the problem mentioned earlier, presented by Xue and Lu (2020), the authors proposed a novel semantic differential transaction (SDT) approach. The authors concluded that SDT is effective and efficient for blockchain BIM systems with less than 0.02% BIM file size in near real-time. Regarding cyber-securing, the collaborative design upon which BIM starts and develops, Tao et al. (2021) proposed a distributed common data environment as a framework for leveraging blockchain and interplanetary file systems. The approach was successfully verified in real-world project scenarios, resulting in positive practitioner feedback.

A study on BIM-based interoperability from a legal and contracting perspective, presented by Abd Jamil and Fathi (2020), highlighted the importance of BIM-based contract documents to critically formalise participants' redress and mitigation strategies into a contractual framework designed for a design-bid procurement system. Also, the mentioned study confirmed the issue of subcontractors' legal-, work- and organisation-breakdown structure in a BIM environment regarding as-build feedback quality.

3.6 Conclusions and Proposals for Further Research

The transition of the AEC industry towards the 4IR, i.e., Construction 4.0, has been a rougher road than anticipated. There are and will continue to be many challenges that must be overcome. The reasons may be found in a few overlapping and interconnected facts. Perhaps the first one is the usual early, baseless enthusiasm and optimism which can be traced to the early phases of revolutions. On the other hand, the high expectations can only justify just a small portion of the sluggishness of the transition, whilst the main reasons require a thorough analysis.

This study revealed that BIM, as the main driver of Constructions 4.0, although with clear and verified overall benefits to the AEC industry, has its rough path. Conceptual challenges are arising faster than the answers and solutions. Solutions for educational issues and gaps are lagged and late, whilst legal issues and drawbacks are in a fuzzy state of traditional procurement systems, digital ownership questions and modern cyber security systems.

Interoperability is perhaps the main term in browsing the recently reported BIM challenges and issues. Data transfer, late and asymmetrical information among the BIM environment participants are still the main issues. Different software usage in the same BIM project still generates communication and information interpretation problems. Solutions are mainly suggested in the direction of clearer global guidelines, standardisation of software add-ins, IFC development, user-friendliness of standard software and information regarding the energy characteristics of a building.

As for the educational challenges, it is hard not to notice a common late start of serious BIM-related courses worldwide as one of the main sources of the problems. Even the most developed AEC industries, such as those of Australia, China, the UK and the USA, report a late start and there is only recent significant improvement in this area. Most authors advocate multi-disciplinary BIM curriculums and courses employing standard software on real-time case study problems, long-life education courses for post-graduates and practitioners, and stronger back-to-back collaboration among universities, research institutes and professional associations.

The aforementioned late start, along with challenges and issues, caused students reluctance regarding BIM; hence the students developed doubts and less positive expectations from and for BIM. Education usually is and must be the first step in reengineering what BIM needs. The lack of required knowledge, skills and specialities will generate most future problems and challenges. Active BIM applied to real-time case studies was proven convenient and motivating for students in adopting simultaneous new knowledge regarding optimization and BIM.

As a digital data storage and exchange environment, BIM requires a clear contract arranging responsibilities, risks and security among stakeholders. Blockchain and smart contracts are proven as a potential way of solving the issues. Cyber security with high-level utilisation of large online databases is found to be a critical issue not just for Construction 4.0 and Industry 4.0 but for society in general. The secure protocols and communication process has to be robust. On the other hand, the procurement process in construction projects incorporating BIM still provides headaches and pushes practitioners and academia to the limit. Traditional design-bid-build contracting does not fit the BIM concept, whilst design-and-build does fit but requires adjustments according to the BIM roles and hierarchy.

Active BIM has real potential for educational purposes in combining and teaching courses in construction management, project scheduling, cost analysis, optimization and BIM simultaneously. A commonly strict mathematical optimization approach by active BIM can be presented and visualized; scenario simulations can be applied for multi-criteria and multi-variant decision-making. Interoperability between optimization and BIM software can be used to learn more about programming languages, modelling, etc. It should be noted that the optimization-based active BIM can be achieved using currently available software and possesses a significant potential for improving construction operations. However, for wider usage of the said approach in construction, it is necessary to address the fundamental challenges of BIM highlighted in the chapter.

Acknowledgements

The authors acknowledge the financial support from the Slovenian Research Agency (research core funding No. P2-0129). The authors would like to acknowledge that this research was developed within the framework of the international bilateral Croatian-Slovenian project (No. BI-HR/23-24-024) "Digital Transformation of Construction Projects Induced by Synergy of Optimization Methods and BIM with Premise of More Efficient and Safer Construction".

References

Abadie, Jean; and Carpentier, Jean Pierre. 1969. "Generalization of the Wolfe reduced gradient method to the case of nonlinear constraints." Optimization, 37-47.

Abd Jamil, Ahmad Huzaimi; and Fathi, Mohamad Syazli. 2020. "Enhancing BIM-based information interoperability: dispute resolution from legal and contractual perspectives". Journal of Construction Engineering and Management, No. 146(7): 05020007. https://doi.org/10.1061/(ASCE)CO.1943-7862.0001868

Abdollahzadeh, Benyamin; Gharehchopogh, Farhad Soleimanian; and Mirjalili, Seyedali. 2021. "African vultures optimization algorithm: a new nature-inspired metaheuristic algorithm for global optimization problems". Computers and Industrial Engineering, No. 158: 107408. https://doi.org/10.1016/j.cie.2021.107408

Abualigah, Laith; Diabat, Ali; Mirjalili, Seyedali; Abd Elaziz, Mohamed; and Gandomi, Amir H. 2021. "The arithmetic optimization algorithm". Computer Methods in Applied Mechanics and Engineering, No. 376: 113609. https://doi.org/10.1016/j.cma.2020.113609

Adjiman, Claire S.; Androulakis, Ioannis P.; and Floudas, Christodoulos A. 2000. "Global optimization of mixed-integer nonlinear problems". AIChE Journal, No. 46(9): 1769-1797. https://doi.org/10.1002/aic.690460908

Ahmadian Fard Fini, Alireza; Akbarnezhad, Ali; Rashidi, Taha H.; and Waller, S. Travis. 2018. "Dynamic programming approach toward optimization of workforce planning decisions". Journal of Construction Engineering and Management, No. 144(2): 04017113. https://doi.org/10.1061/(ASCE)CO.1943-7862.0001434

AIMMS. 2021. "AIMMS Development". Accessed July 7, 2021. https://www.aimms.com

Akanmu, Abiola; Olatunji, Oluwole; Love, Peter E. D.; Nguyen, Duy; and Matthews, Jane. 2016. "Auto-generated site layout: an integrated approach to real-time sensing of temporary facilities in infrastructure projects". Structure and Infrastructure Engineering, No. 12(10): 1243-1255. https://doi.org/10.1080/15732479.2015.1110601

Akintola, Adeyemi; Venkatachalam, Senthilkumar; and Root, David. 2017. "New BIM roles' legitimacy and changing power dynamics on BIM-enabled projects". Journal of Construction Engineering and Management, No. 143(9): 04017066. https://doi.org/10.1061/(ASCE)CO.1943-7862.0001366

AMPL. 2021. "About AMPL". Accessed July 7, 2021. https://ampl.com

Arayici, Yusuf; Fernando, Terrence; Munoz, Victor; and Bassanino, May. 2018. "Interoperability specification development for integrated BIM use in performance-based design". Automation in Construction, No. 85: 167-181. https://doi.org/10.1016/j.autcon.2017.10.018

Askarzadeh, Alireza. 2014. "Bird mating optimizer: an optimization algorithm inspired by bird mating strategies". Communications in Nonlinear Science and Numerical Simulation, No. 19(4): 1213-1228. https://doi.org/10.1016/j.cnsns.2013.08.027

Askarzadeh, Alireza. 2016. "A novel metaheuristic method for solving constrained engineering optimization problems: crow search algorithm". Computers and Structures, No. 169: 1-12. https://doi.org/10.1016/j.compstruc.2016.03.001

Babić, Aron. 2017. "Application of transportation problem for solving internal transport of materials in masonry works at multi-storey constructions". Master thesis, Josip Juraj Strossmayer University of Osijek.

Bansal, Jagdish Chand; Sharma, Harish; Jadon, Shimpi Singh; and Clerc, Maurice. 2014. "Spider monkey optimization algorithm for numerical optimization". Memetic Computing, No. 6: 31-47. https://doi.org/10.1007/s12293-013-0128-0

Beale, E. M. L. 1977. "Integer programming". In The State of the Art in Numerical Analysis, London: Academic Press.

Begić, Hana; and Galić, Mario. 2021. "A systematic review of Construction 4.0 in the context of the BIM 4.0 premise". Buildings, No. 11(8): 337. https://doi.org/10.3390/buildings11080337

Bonami, Pierre; Biegler, Lorenz T.; Conn, Andrew R.; Cornuéjols, Gérard; Grossmann, Ignacio E.; Laird, Carl D.; Lee, Jon; Lodi, Andrea; Margot, François; Sawaya, Nicolas; and Wächter, Andreas. 2008. "An algorithmic framework for convex mixed integer nonlinear programs". Discrete Optimization, No. 5(2): 186-204. https://doi.org/10.1016/j.disopt.2006.10.011

Brucker Juričić, Belinda; Galić, Mario; and Marenjak, Saša. 2021. "Review of the construction labour demand and shortages in the EU". Buildings, No. 11(1): 17. https://doi.org/10.3390/buildings11010017

Casasayas, Oskar; Hosseini, M. Reza; Edwards, D. J.; Shuchi, Sarah; and Chowdhury, Mahmuda. 2021. "Integrating BIM in higher education programs: barriers and remedial solutions in Australia". Journal of Architectural Engineering, No. 27(1): 05020010. https://doi.org/10.1061/(ASCE)AE.1943-5568.0000444

Chen, Xinyang; Zhu, Yifan; Chen, Hainan; Ouyang, Yewei; Luo, Xiaowei; and Wu, Xiaoling. 2021. "BIM-based optimization of camera placement for indoor construction monitoring considering the construction schedule". Automation in Construction, No. 130: 103825. https://doi.org/10.1016/j.autcon.2021.103825

Cheng, Min-Yuan; and Chang, Nai-Wen. 2019. "Dynamic construction material layout planning optimization model by integrating 4D BIM". Engineering with Computers, No. 35(2): 703-720. https://doi.org/10.1007/s00366-018-0628-0

Cheng, Min-Yuan; and Prayogo, Doddy. 2014. "Symbiotic organisms search: a new metaheuristic optimization algorithm". Computers and Structures, No. 139: 98-112. https://doi.org/10.1016/j.compstruc.2014.03.007

Chou, Jui-Sheng; and Truong, Dinh-Nhat. 2021. "A novel metaheuristic optimizer inspired by behavior of jellyfish in ocean". Applied Mathematics and Computation, No. 389: 125535. https://doi.org/10.1016/j.amc.2020.125535

Chu, Shu-Chuan; Tsai, Pei-wei; and Pan, Jeng-Shyang. "Cat swarm optimization". In Pacific Rim international conference on artificial intelligence, edited by Yang, Quiang; and Webb, Geoff, 854-858. (Berlin, Heidelberg: Springer, 2006). https://doi.org/10.1007/978-3-540-36668-3_94

Colorni, Alberto; Dorigo, Marco; and Maniezzo, Vittorio. "Distributed optimization by ant colonies". In Toward a Practice of Autonomous Systems Proceedings of the First European Conference on Artificial Life, edited by Varela, Francisco J.; and Bourgine, Paul, 134-142. (Amsterdam: Elsevier Publishing, 1991).

Construction Task Force. 1998. "Rethinking Construction – The Egan Report". London: Department of trade and industry.

Čorak, Marko. 2018. "Optimization of deposit areas for execution of masonry work on construction site". Master thesis, Josip Juraj Strossmayer University of Osijek.

Cuevas, Erik; Cienfuegos, Miguel; Zaldívar, Daniel; and Pérez-Cisneros, Marco. 2013. "A swarm optimization algorithm inspired in the behavior of the social-spider". Expert Systems with Applications, No. 40(16): 6374-6384. https://doi.org/10.1016/j.eswa.2013.05.041

Cui, Zhihua; and Cai, Xingjuan. 2013. "Artificial plant optimization algorithm". In Swarm Intelligence and Bio-Inspired Computation, edited by Yang, Xin-She; Cui, Zhihua; Xiao, Renbin; Gandomi, Amir Hossein; and Karamanoglu, Mehmet, 351-365. (Amsterdam: Elsevier, 2013). https://doi.org/10.1016/B978-0-12-405163-8.00016-8

Dantzig, George B. 1963. "Linear programming and extensions". Princeton, New Jersey: Princeton University Press.

Dasović, Borna. 2018. "Optimal locations of tower crane and material deposit areas for masonry works on construction site". Master thesis, Josip Juraj Strossmayer University of Osijek.

Dasović, Borna; Galić, Mario; and Klanšek, Uroš. 2019. "Active BIM approach to optimize work facilities and tower crane locations on construction sites with repetitive operations". Buildings, No. 9(1): 21. https://doi.org/10.3390/buildings9010021

De Gaetani, Carlo Iapige; Mert, Mertkan; and Migliaccio, Federica. 2020. "Interoperability analyses of BIM platforms for construction management". Applied Sciences, No. 10(13): 4437. https://doi.org/10.3390/app10134437

de Soto, Borja García; Rosarius, Anton; Rieger, Jochen; Chen, Qian; and Adey, Bryan T. 2017. "Using a tabu-search algorithm and 4D models to improve construction project schedules". Procedia Engineering, No. 196: 698-705. https://doi.org/10.1016/j.proeng.2017.07.236

Državna geodetska uprava. 2018. Accessed November 26, 2018. https://dgu.gov.hr/proizvodi-i-usluge/podjela-na-listove-karata-i-katastarskih-planova-rh-u-htrs96-tm-projekcijskom-koordinatnom-referentom-sustavu/podjela-na-listove-mjerila-1-5-000-5k/5240

ElMenshawy, Mohamed; and Marzouk, Mohamed. 2021. "Automated BIM schedule generation approach for solving time–cost trade-off problems". Engineering, Construction and Architectural Management, No. 28(10): 3346-3367. https://doi.org/10.1108/ECAM-08-2020-0652

Erol, Osman K.; and Eksin, Ibrahim. 2006. "A new optimization method: big bang–big crunch". Advances in Engineering Software, No. 37(2): 106-111. https://doi.org/10.1016/j.advengsoft.2005.04.005

Eskandar, Hadi; Sadollah, Ali; Bahreininejad, Ardeshir; and Hamdi, Mohd. 2012. "Water cycle algorithm – a novel metaheuristic optimization method for solving constrained engineering optimization problems". Computers and Structures, No. 110-111: 151-166. https://doi.org/10.1016/j.compstruc.2012.07.010

Faghihi, Vahid; Reinschmidt, Kenneth F.; and Kang, Julian H. 2014. "Construction scheduling using genetic algorithm based on building information model". Expert Systems with Applications, No. 41(16): 7565-7578. https://doi.org/10.1016/j.eswa.2014.05.047

Faghihi, Vahid; Reinschmidt, Kenneth F.; and Kang, Julian H. 2016. "Objective-driven and Pareto front analysis: optimizing time, cost, and job-site movements". Automation in Construction, No. 69: 79-88. https://doi.org/10.1016/j.autcon.2016.06.003

Fan, Su-Ling; Lee, Cen-Ying; Chong, Heap-Yih; Skibniewski, Miroslaw J. 2018. "A critical review of legal issues and solutions associated with building information modelling". Technological and Economic Development of Economy, No. 24(5): 2098-2130. https://doi.org/10.3846/tede.2018.5695

Farghaly, Karim; Abanda, Fonbeyin Henry; Vidalakis, Christos; and Wood, Graham. 2018. "Taxonomy for BIM and asset management semantic interoperability". Journal of Management in Engineering, No. 34(4): 04018012. https://doi.org/10.1061/(ASCE)ME.1943-5479.0000610

Feng, Chung-Wei; Chen, Yi-Jao; and Huang, Jiun-Ru. 2010. "Using the MD CAD model to develop the time–cost integrated schedule for construction projects". Automation in Construction, No. 19(3): 347-356. https://doi.org/10.1016/j.autcon.2009.12.009

Fong, Simon; Deb, Suash; and Yang, Xin-She. 2015. "A heuristic optimization method inspired by wolf preying behavior". Neural Computing and Applications, No. 26(7): 1725-1738. https://doi.org/10.1007/s00521-015-1836-9

Frontline Solvers. 2021. "Solver". Accessed July 13, 2021. https://www.solver.com

Galić, Mario. 2019. "Active BIM: how data (pl.) become information (pl.)". Accessed July 13, 2021. https://prezi.com/view/zgWwklHRZA16Ot3V7sGj/

GAMS. 2021. "GAMS – the modeling language". Accessed July 13, 2021. https://www.gams.com

Geem, Zong Woo; Kim, Joong Hoon; and Loganathan, G. V. 2001. "A new heuristic optimization algorithm: harmony search". Simulation, No. 76(2): 60-68. https://doi.org/10.1177/003754970107600201

Geoffrion, Arthur M. 1972. "Generalized Benders decomposition". Journal of Optimization Theory and Applications, No. 10(4): 237-260. https://doi.org/10.1007/BF00934810

Ghaffarianhoseini, Ali; Tookey, John; Ghaffarianhoseini, Amirhosein; Naismith, Nicola; Azhar, Salman; Efimova, Olia; and Raahemifar, Kaamran. 2017. "Building information modelling (BIM) uptake: clear benefits, understanding its implementation, risks and challenges". Renewable and Sustainable Energy Reviews, No. 75: 1046-1053. https://doi.org/10.1016/j.rser.2016.11.083

Glover, Fred. 1977. "Heuristics for integer programming using surrogate constraints". Decision Sciences, No. 8(1): 156-166. https://doi.org/10.1111/j.1540-5915.1977.tb01074.x

Golberg, David E. 1989. "Genetic algorithms in search, optimization, and machine learning". USA: Addison-Wesley.

Gomory, Ralph E. 1958. "Outline of an algorithm for integer solutions to linear programs". Bulletin of the American Mathematical Society, No. 64(5): 275-278. https://doi.org/10.1007/978-3-540-68279-0_4

Hamma-adama, Mansur; and Kouider, Tahar. 2019. "Comparative analysis of BIM adoption efforts by developed countries as precedent for new adopter countries". Current Journal of Applied Science and Technology, No. 36(2): CJAST.49779. https://doi.org/10.9734/cjast/2019/v36i230224

Hammad, Ahmed W. A.; Akbarnezhad, Ali; Rey, David; and Waller, S. Travis. 2016. "A computational method for estimating travel frequencies in site layout planning". Journal of Construction Engineering and Management, No. 142(5): 04015102. https://doi.org/10.1061/(ASCE)CO.1943-7862.0001086

He, Wei; Shi, Yichao; and Kong, Dewei. 2019. "Construction of a 5D duration and cost optimisation model based on genetic algorithm and BIM". Journal of Engineering, Design and Technology, No. 17(5): 929-942. https://doi.org/10.1108/JEDT-12-2018-0214

Heidari, Ali Asghar; Mirjalili, Seyedali; Faris, Hossam; Aljarah, Ibrahim; Mafarja, Majdi; and Chen, Huiling. 2019. "Harris hawks optimization: algorithm and applications". Future Generation Computer Systems, No. 97: 849-872. https://doi.org/10.1016/j.future.2019.02.028

Hestenes, Magnus R. 1969. "Multiplier and gradient methods". Journal of Optimization Theory and Applications, No. 4(5): 303-320. https://doi.org/10.1007/BF00927673

Holland, John H. 1992. "Adaptation in natural and artificial systems: an introductory analysis with applications to biology, control, and artificial intelligence". USA: The MIT Press.

Hürlimann, Tony. 2021. "Mathematical modeling using LPL". Accessed July 13, 2021. https://lpl.unifr.ch/lpl/index.html#lpl

IBM. 2021. "Optimization programming language (OPL)". Accessed July 13, 2021. https://www.ibm.com/docs/en/icos/20.1.0?topic=opl-optimisation-programming-language

ISO 19650. 2018. "BIM – building information modelling". Series 1-5, 2018-2020.

Jiang, Xiangyuan; and Li, Shuai. 2017. "Beetle antennae search without parameter tuning (BAS-WPT) for multi-objective optimization". arXiv preprint arXiv:1711.02395. https://doi.org/10.48550/arXiv.1711.02395

Jin, Ruoyu; Zhong, Botao; Ma, Ling; Hashemi, Arman; and Ding, Licyun. 2019. "Integrating BIM with building performance analysis in project life-cycle". Automation in Construction, No. 106: 102861. https://doi.org/10.1016/j.autcon.2019.102861

Jin, Ruoyu; Zou, Patrick Xiaowei; Li, Bo; Piroozfar, Poorang; and Painting, Noel. 2019. "Comparisons of students' perceptions on BIM practice among Australia, China and UK". Engineering, Construction and Architectural Management, No. 26(9): 1899-1923. https://doi.org/10.1108/ECAM-07-2018-0275

Kaipa, Krishnanand N.; and Ghose, Debasish. 2009. "Glowworm swarm optimization for simultaneous capture of multiple local optima of multimodal functions". Swarm Intelligence, No. 3(2): 87-124. https://doi.org/10.1007/s11721-008-0021-5

Karaboga, Dervis; and Basturk, Bahriye. 2007. "A powerful and efficient algorithm for numerical function optimization: artificial bee colony (ABC) algorithm". Journal of Global Optimization, No. 39(3): 459-471. https://doi.org/10.1007/s10898-007-9149-x

Karmarkar, Narendra K. 1984. "A new polynomial-time algorithm for linear programming". In STOC '84: Proceedings of the sixteenth annual ACM symposium on Theory of computing, 302-311. USA: The Association for Computing Machinery, inc. https://doi.org/10.1145/800057.808695

Kashan, Ali Husseinzadeh. 2014. "League championship algorithm (LCA): an algorithm for global optimization inspired by sports championships". Applied Soft Computing, No. 16: 171-200. https://doi.org/10.1016/j.asoc.2013.12.005

Kaveh, Ali; and Bakhshpoori, Taha. 2016. "Water evaporation optimization: a novel physically inspired optimization algorithm". Computers and Structures, No. 167: 69-85. https://doi.org/10.1016/j.compstruc.2016.01.008

Kaveh, Ali; and Farhoudi, Neda. 2013. "A new optimization method: dolphin echolocation". Advances in Engineering Software, No. 59: 53-70. https://doi.org/10.1016/j.advengsoft.2013.03.004

Kaveh, Ali; and Ghazaan, Majid Ilchi. 2017. "Vibrating particles system algorithm for truss optimization with multiple natural frequency constraints". Acta Mechanica, No. 228(1): 307-322. https://doi.org/10.1007/s00707-016-1725-z

Kaveh, Ali; and Mahdavi, Vahid Reza. 2014. "Colliding bodies optimization: a novel meta-heuristic method". Computers and Structures, No. 139: 18-27. https://doi.org/10.1016/j.compstruc.2014.04.005

Kaveh, Ali; and Talatahari, Siamak. 2010. "A novel heuristic optimization method: charged system search". Acta Mechanica, No. 213(3): 267-289. https://doi.org/10.1007/s00707-009-0270-4

Kennedy, Jim; and Eberhart, Russel. 1995. "Particle swarm optimization". In Proceedings of ICNN'95 – International Conference on Neural Networks, Perth, Australia: IEEE Service Center. https://doi.org/10.1109/ICNN.1995.488968

Khalafallah, Ahmed; and El-Rayes, Khaled. 2011. "Automated multi-objective optimization system for airport site layouts". Automation in Construction, No. 20(4): 313-320. https://doi.org/10.1016/j.autcon.2010.11.001

Khan, Ameer Tamoor; Senior, Shuai Li; Stanimirovic, Predrag S.; and Zhang, Yinyan. 2018. "Model-free optimization using eagle perching optimizer". arXiv preprint arXiv:1807.02754. https://doi.org/10.48550/arXiv.1807.02754

Kim, Hyeonseung; Moon, Soyeong; Moon, Hyounseok; and Kang, Leenseok. 2013. "Application of information technology for visualizing and optimizing construction project schedule". In ICEIS 2013 – Proceedings of the 15th International Conference on Enterprise Information Systems, 329-332. France: SciTePress. https://doi.org/10.5220/0004565303290332

Kirkpatrick, Scott; Gelatt, Charles D.; and Vecchi, Mario P. 1983. "Optimization by simulated annealing". Science, No. 220(4598): 671-680. https://doi.org/10.1126/science.220.4598.671

Kumar, Neetesh; Singh, Navjot; and Vidyarthi, Deo Prakash. 2021. "Artificial lizard search optimization (ALSO): a novel nature-inspired meta-heuristic algorithm". Soft Computing, No. 25(8): 6179-6201. https://doi.org/10.1007/s00500-021-05606-7

Kumar, Srinath Shiv; and Cheng, Jack Chin Pang. 2015. “A BIM-based automated site layout planning framework for congested construction sites”. Automation in Construction, No. 59: 24-37. https://doi.org/10.1016/j.autcon.2015.07.008

Land, Ailsa H.; and Doig, Alison G. 1960. “An automatic method of solving discrete programming problems”. In: 50 Years of Integer Programming 1958-2008. Berlin, Heidelberg: Springer. https://doi.org/10.1007/978-3-540-68279-0_5

Li, Jingming; Afsari, Kereshmeh; Li, Nianping; Peng, Jinqing; Wu, Zhibin; and Cui, Haijiao. 2020. “A review for presenting building information modeling education and research in China”. *Journal of Cleaner Production*, No. 259: 120885. https://doi.org/10.1016/j.jclepro.2020.120885

Lindo System Inc. 2021. “LINGO”. Accessed July 13, 2021. https://www.lindo.com/index.php/products/lingo-and-optimization-modeling

Lindo Systems Inc. 2021. “What'sBest”. Accessed July 13, 2021. https://www.lindo.com/index.php/products/what-sbest-and-excel-optimization

Liu, Hexu; Al-Hussein, Mohamed; and Lu, Ming. 2015. “BIM-based integrated approach for detailed construction scheduling under resource constraints”. Automation in Construction, No. 53: 29-43. https://doi.org/10.1016/j.autcon.2015.03.008

Liu, Zhen; Jiang, Lijun; Osmani, Mohamed; and Demian, Peter. 2019. “Building information management (BIM) and blockchain (BC) for sustainable building design information management framework”. *Electronics*, No. 8(7): 724. https://doi.org/10.3390/electronics8070724

Lumivero. 2021. “Evolver”. Accessed July 13, 2021. https://www.palisade.com/evolver

Ma, Guofeng; and Zhang, Lingzhi. 2019. “Exact overlap rate analysis and the combination with 4D BIM of time-cost tradeoff problem in project scheduling”. *Advances in Civil Engineering*, No. 2019: 9120795. https://doi.org/10.1155/2019/9120795

Manderson, Aaron; Jefferies, Marcus; and Brewer, Graham. 2015. “Building information modelling and standardised construction contracts: a content analysis of the GC21 contract”. Construction Economics and Building, No. 15(3): 72-84. https://doi.org/10.5130/AJCEB.v15i3.4608

Marzouk, Mohamed; and Abdelakder, Eslam Mohammed. 2020. "A hybrid fuzzy-optimization method for modeling construction emissions". *Decision Science Letters*, No. 9(1): 1-20. http://dx.doi.org/10.5267/j.dsl.2019.9.002

Marzouk, Mohamed; and Abubakr, Ahmed. 2016. "Decision support for tower crane selection with building information models and genetic algorithms". Automation in Construction, No. 61: 1-15. https://doi.org/10.1016/j.autcon.2015.09.008

MathWorks. 2021. "Matlab". Accessed July 13, 2021. https://www.mathworks.com/products/matlab.html

Mawengkang, Herman; and Murtagh, Bruce A. 1986. "Solving nonlinear integer programs with large-scale optimization software". *Annals of Operations Research*, No. 5(2): 425-437. https://doi.org/10.1007/BF02022084

Maximal Software. "MPL Modeling System". 2021. Accessed July 13, 2021. http://www.maximalsoftware.com/mpl

Mirjalili, Seyedali; and Lewis, Andrew. 2016. "The whale optimization algorithm". *Advances in Engineering Software*, No. 95: 51-67. https://doi.org/10.1016/j.advengsoft.2016.01.008

Mirjalili, Seyedali; Mirjalili, Seyed Mohammad; and Lewis, Andrew. 2014. "Grey wolf optimizer". Advances in Engineering Software, No. 69: 46-61. https://doi.org/10.1016/j.advengsoft.2013.12.007

Moon, Hyounseok; Kim, Hyeonseung; Kang, Leenseok; and Kim, Changhak. 2012. "BIM functions for optimised construction management in civil engineering". In Proceedings of the International Symposium on Automation and Robotics in Construction, edited by van Bronswijk, J. E. M. H.; Maas, Geer J.; and van Gassel, Fans J. M. Eindhoven: IAARC Publications. https://doi.org/10.22260/ISARC2012/0003

Moon, Hyounseok; Kim, Hyeonseung; Kamat, Vineet R.; and Kang, Leenseok. 2015. "BIM-based construction scheduling method using optimization theory for reducing activity overlaps". Journal of Computing in Civil Engineering, No. 29(3): 04014048. https://doi.org/10.1061/(ASCE)CP.1943-5487.0000342

Moon, Hyounseok; Kim, Hyeonseung; Kim, Changhak; and Kang, Leenseok. 2014. "Development of a schedule-workspace interference management system simultaneously considering the overlap level of parallel schedules and workspaces". Automation in Construction, No. 39: 93-105. https://doi.org/10.1016/j.autcon.2013.06.001

Mozaffari, Mohammad Hamed; Abdy, Hamed; and Zahiri, Seyed-Hamid. 2016. "IPO: an inclined planes system optimization algorithm". Computing and Informatics, No. 35(1): 222-240.

Muthiah-Nakarajan, Venkataraman; and Noel, Mathew Mithra. 2016. "Galactic swarm optimization: a new global optimization metaheuristic inspired by galactic motion". Applied Soft Computing, No. 38: 771-787. https://doi.org/10.1016/j.asoc.2015.10.034

Nawari, Nawari O.; and Ravindran, Shiraam. 2019. "Blockchain technologies in BIM workflow environment". In Computing in Civil Engineering 2019: Visualisation, Information Modelling, and Simulation, edited by Cho, Yong K.; Leite, Fernanda; Behzadan, Amir; and Wang, Chao, 343-352. Reston, VA: American Society of Civil Engineers. https://doi.org/10.1061/9780784482421.044

Nemetschek Group. 2018. "Allplan". Accessed July 7, 2021. https://www.allplan.com

NEOS. 2021. "NEOS server: state-of-the-art solvers for numerical optimization". Accessed July 13, 2021. https://neos-server.org/neos

Nusen, Pornpote; Boonyung, Wanarut; Nusen, Sunita; Panuwatwanich, Kriengsak; Champrasert, Paskorn; and Kaewmoracharoen, Manop. 2021. "Construction planning and scheduling of a renovation project using BIM-based multi-objective genetic algorithm". Applied Sciences, No. 11(11): 4716. https://doi.org/10.3390/app11114716

Olatunji, Oluwole Alfred. 2019. "Promoting student commitment to BIM in construction education". Engineering, Construction and Architectural Management. No. 26(7): 1240-1260. https://doi.org/10.1108/ECAM-04-2018-0173

Olowa, Theophilus; Witt, Emlyn; and Lill, Irene. 2020. "Conceptualising building information modelling for construction education". Journal of Civil Engineering and Management, No. 26(6): 551-563. https://doi.org/10.3846/jcem.2020.12918

Olsen, Gregory R.; and Vanderplaats, Garret N. 1989. "Method for nonlinear optimization with discrete design variables". AIAA Journal, No. 27(11): 1584-1589. https://doi.org/10.2514/3.10305

OpenSolver. 2021. "About OpenSolver". Accessed July 13, 2021. https://opensolver.org

Osman, Hesham M.; Georgy, Maged E.; and Ibrahim, Moheeb E. 2003. "A hybrid CAD-based construction site layout planning system using genetic algorithms". *Automation in Construction, No. 12(6): 749-764. https://doi.org/10.1016/S0926-5805(03)00058-X*

Ozturk, Gozde Basak. 2020. "Interoperability in building information modeling for AECO/FM industry". Automation in Construction, No. 113: 103122. https://doi.org/10.1016/j.autcon.2020.103122

Padberg, Manfred W.; and Rinaldi, Giovanni. 1987. "Optimization of a 532-city symmetric traveling salesman problem by branch and cut". *Operations Research Letters*, No. 6(1): 1-7. https://doi.org/10.1016/0167-6377(87)90002-2

Passino, Kevin M. 2002. "Biomimicry of bacterial foraging for distributed optimization and control". IEEE Control Systems Magazine, No. 22(3): 52-67. https://doi.org/10.1109/MCS.2002.1004010

Powell, Michael J. D. 1969. "A method for nonlinear constraints in minimization problems". Optimization, 283-298.

Powell, Michael J. D. 1978. "A fast algorithm for nonlinearly constrained optimization calculations". In Numerical analysis, edited by Watson, G. A., 144-157. Berlin, Heidelberg: Springer. https://doi.org/10.1007/BFb0067703

Qi, Xiangbo Qi; Zhu, Yunlong; and Zhang, Hao. 2017. "A new meta-heuristic butterfly-inspired algorithm". *Journal of Computational Science*, No. 23: 226-239. https://doi.org/10.1016/j.jocs.2017.06.003

Rao, Ravipudi Venkata; Savsani, Vimal J.; and Vakharia, Dipakkumar P. 2011. "Teaching–learning-based optimization: a novel method for constrained mechanical design optimization problems". *Computer-Aided Design*, No. 43(3): 303-315. https://doi.org/10.1016/j.cad.2010.12.015

Rashedi, Esmat; Nezamabadi-pour, Hossein; and Saryazdi, Saeid. 2009. "GSA: a gravitational search algorithm". Information Sciences, No. 179(13): 2232-2248. https://doi.org/10.1016/j.ins.2009.03.004

Ren, Ran; and Zhang, Jiansong. 2021. "A new framework to address BIM interoperability in the AEC domain from technical and process dimensions". *Advances in Civil Engineering*, 2021: 8824613. https://doi.org/10.1155/2021/8824613

Rumelhart, David E.; Hinton, Geoffrey E.; and Williams, Ronald J. 1986. "Learning representations by back-propagating errors". Nature, No. 323(6088): 533-536. https://doi.org/10.1038/323533a0

Ryoo, Hong S.; and Sahinidis, Nikolaos V. 1996. "A branch-and-reduce approach to global optimization". Journal of Global Optimization, No. 8(2): 107-138. https://doi.org/10.1007/BF00138689

Said, Hisham; and El-Rayes, Khaled. 2014. "Automated multi-objective construction logistics optimization system". *Automation in Construction*, No. 43: 110-122. https://doi.org/10.1016/j.autcon.2014.03.017

Sang, Hong-Yan; Pan, Quan-Ke; and Duan, Pei-yon. 2019. "Self-adaptive fruit fly optimizer for global optimization". Natural Computing, No. 18(4): 785-813. https://doi.org/10.1007/s11047-016-9604-z

Construction 4.0: *An innovation platform for the built environment*, edited by Sawhney, Anil; Riley, Michael; and Irizarry, Javier. 2020. London: Routledge.

Schwab, Klaus. 2017. *The fourth industrial revolution.* New York: Currency Books.

Shah-Hosseini, Hamed. 2009. "The intelligent water drops algorithm: a nature-inspired swarm-based optimization algorithm". *International Journal of Bio-inspired Computation*, No. 1(1-2): 71-79. https://doi.org/10.1504/IJBIC.2009.022775

Shah-Hosseini, Hamed. 2011. "Principal components analysis by the galaxy-based search algorithm: a novel metaheuristic for continuous optimization". *International Journal of Computational Science and Engineering*, No. 6(1-2): 132-140. https://doi.org/10.1504/IJCSE.2011.041221

Shayanfar, Human; and Gharehchopogh, Farhad Soleimania. 2018. "Farmland fertility: a new metaheuristic algorithm for solving continuous optimization problems". *Applied Soft Computing*, No. 71: 728-746. https://doi.org/10.1016/j.asoc.2018.07.033

Shehzad, Hafiz Muhammad Faisal; Ibrahim, Roliana Binti; Yusof, Ahmad Fadhi; Khaidzir, Khairul Anwar Mohamed; Iqbal, Muhammad; and Razzaq, Saad. 2021. "The role of interoperability dimensions in building information modelling". *Computers in Industry*, No. 129: 103444. https://doi.org/10.1016/j.compind.2021.103444

Simon, Dan. 2008. "Biogeography-based optimization". IEEE Transactions on Evolutionary Computation, No. 12(6): 702-713. https://doi.org/10.1109/TEVC.2008.919004

Singh, Abhishek Raj; Patil, Yash; and Delhi, Venkata Santosh Kumar. 2019. "Optimizing site layout planning utilizing building information modelling". In Proceedings of the International Symposium on Automation and Robotics in Construction, 376-383. IAARC Publications. https://doi.org/10.22260/ISARC2019%2F0051

Storn, Rainer; and Price, Kenneth. 1997. "Differential evolution – a simple and efficient heuristic for global optimization over continuous spaces". *Journal of Global Optimization*, No. 11(4): 341-359. https://doi.org/10.1023/A:1008202821328

Sušnik, Mija; Tagliabue, Lavinia Chiara; and Cairoli, Maria. 2021. "BIM-based energy and acoustic analysis through CVE tools". Energy Reports, No. 7: 8228-8237. https://doi.org/10.1016/j.egyr.2021.06.013

Tan, Yi; Song, Yonze; Liu, Xin; Wang, Xiangyu; and Cheng, Jack C. P. 2017. "A BIM-based framework for lift planning in topsides disassembly of offshore oil and gas platforms". *Automation in Construction*, No. 79: 19-30. https://doi.org/10.1016/j.autcon.2017.02.008

Tan, Yi; Song, Yonze: Zhu, Junxiang; Long, Qiang; Wang, Xiangyu; and Cheng, Jack C. P. 2018. "Optimizing lift operations and vessel transport schedules for disassembly of multiple offshore platforms using BIM and GIS". Automation in Construction, No. 94: 328-339. https://doi.org/10.1016/j.autcon.2018.07.012

Tao, Xingyu; Das, Moumita; Liu, Yuhan; and Cheng, Jack C. P. 2021. "Distributed common data environment using blockchain and interplanetary file system for secure BIM-based collaborative design". *Automation in Construction*, No. 130: 103851. https://doi.org/10.1016/j.autcon.2021.103851

Tilahun, Surafel Luleseged; and Ong, Hong Choon. 2015. "Prey-predator algorithm: a new metaheuristic algorithm for optimization problems". *International Journal of Information Technology and Decision Making*, No. 14(06): 1331-1352. https://doi.org/10.1142/S021962201450031X

UIMP. 2021. "UIMP: user interface for mathematical programming". Accessed July 13, 2021. https://optirisk-systems.com/whitepapers/uimp-user-interface-for-mathematical-programming

Vilutiene, Tatjana; Kalibatiene, Diana; Hosseini, M. Reza; Pellicer, Eugenio; and Zavadskas, Edmundas Kazimieras. 2019. "Building information modeling (BIM) for structural engineering: a bibliometric analysis of the literature". *Advances in Civil Engineering*, 2019: 5290690. https://doi.org/10.1155/2019/5290690

Viswanathan, Jagadisan; and Grossmann, Ignacio E. 1990. "A combined penalty function and outer-approximation method for MINLP optimization". Computers and Chemical Engineering, No. 14(7): 769-782. https://doi.org/10.1016/0098-1354(90)87085-4

Volk, Rebekka; Luu, Thu Huong; Mueller-Roemer, Johannes Sebastian; Sevilmis, Neyir; and Schultmann, Frank. 2018. "Deconstruction project planning of existing buildings based on automated acquisition and reconstruction of building information". Automation in Construction, No. 91: 226-245. https://doi.org/10.1016/j.autcon.2018.03.017

Wang, Heng-Wei; Lin, Jia-Rui; and Zhang, Jian-Ping. 2020. "Work package-based information modeling for resource-constrained scheduling of construction projects". Automation in Construction, No. 109: 102958. https://doi.org/10.1016/j.autcon.2019.102958

Wang, Haiyan; and Song, XiaoSan. 2015. "Research on BIM construction schedule generating algorithm". International Journal of Simulation: Systems, Science and Technology, No. 16(1B): 10.1-10.7. https://doi.org/10.5013/IJSSST.a.16.1B.10

Wang, Jun; Zhang, Xuedong; Shou, Wenchi; Wang, Xianyu; Xu, Bo; Kim, Mi Jeong; and Wu, Peng. 2015. "A BIM-based approach for automated tower crane layout planning". Automation in Construction, No. 59: 168-178. https://doi.org/10.1016/j.autcon.2015.05.006

Wang, Liyuan; Huang, Meiping; Zhang, Xiaohua; Jin, Ruoyu; and Yang, Tong. 2020. "Review of BIM adoption in the Higher Education of AEC disciplines". Journal of Civil Engineering Education, No. 146(3): 06020001. https://doi.org/10.1061/(ASCE)EI.2643-9115.0000018

Wang, Yaowu; Yuan, Zhenmin; and Sun, Chengshuang. 2018. "Research on assembly sequence planning and optimization of precast concrete buildings". Journal of Civil Engineering and Management, No. 24(2): 106-115. https://doi.org/10.3846/jcem.2018.458

Westerlund, Tapio; and Pettersson, Frank. 1995. "An extended cutting plane method for solving convex MINLP problems". Computers and Chemical Engineering, No. 19(1): 131-136. https://doi.org/10.1016/0098-1354(95)87027-X

Wolfram. 2021. "Mathematica". Accessed July 13, 2021. https://www.wolfram.com/mathematica

Wu, Jin; Sadraddin, Hezha Lutfalla; Ren, Ran; Zhang, Jiansong; and Shao, Xiaoyun. 2021. "Invariant signatures of architecture, engineering, and construction objects to support BIM interoperability between architectural design and structural analysis". Journal of Construction Engineering and Management, No. 147(1): 04020148. https://doi.org/10.1061/(ASCE)CO.1943-7862.0001943

Wu, Keyi; and de Soto, Borja Garcia. 2020. "Spatiotemporal modeling of lifting task scheduling for tower cranes with a tabu search and 4-D simulation". *Frontiers in Built Environment*, No. 6: 79. https://doi.org/10.3389/fbuil.2020.00079

Wu, Ping; Jin, Ruoyu; Xu, Yidong; Lin, Feng; Dong, Yiting; and Pan, Zhihong. 2021. "The analysis of barriers to BIM implementation for industrialized building construction: a China study". *Journal of Civil Engineering and Management,* No. 27(1): 1-13. https://doi.org/10.3846/jcem.2021.14105

Xu, Zhao; Wang, Xiang; and Rao, Zezhi. 2020. "Automated optimization for the production scheduling of prefabricated elements based on the genetic algorithm and IFC object segmentation". Processes, No. 8(12): 1593. https://doi.org/10.3390/pr8121593

Xu, Yongge; and Wei, Ya. 2015. "Study on trade-off of time-cost-quality in construction project based on BIM". In Proceedings of the 2015 International Conference on Economics, Social Science, Arts, Education and Management Engineering, 864-870. Atlantis Press. https://doi.org/10.2991/essaeme-15.2015.184

Xue, Fan; and Lu, Weisheng. 2020. "A semantic differential transaction approach to minimizing information redundancy for BIM and blockchain integration". *Automation in Construction*, No. 118: 103270. https://doi.org/10.1016/j.autcon.2020.103270

Yang, Xin-She. 2009. "Firefly algorithms for multimodal optimization". In International symposium on stochastic algorithms, Stochastic Algorithms: Foundations and Applications, edited by Watanabe, Osamu; and Zaugmann, Thomas, 169-178. Berlin, Heidelberg: Springer. https://doi.org/10.1007/978-3-642-04944-6_14

Yang, Xin-She. 2010. "A new metaheuristic bat-inspired algorithm". In Nature inspired cooperative strategies for optimisation (NICSO 2010), edited by González, Juan R.; Pelta, David Alejandro; Cruz, Carlos; Terrazas, Germán; and Krasnogor, Natalio, 65-74. Berlin, Heidelberg: Springer. https://doi.org/10.1007/978-3-642-12538-6_6

Yang, Xin-She; and Deb, Suash. 2009. "Cuckoo search via Lévy flights". In 2009 World Congress on Nature and Biologically Inspired Computing (NaBIC), 210-214. IEEE. https://doi.org/10.1109/NABIC.2009.5393690

Yang, Xin-She; Karamanoglu, Mehmet; and He, Xingshi. 2014. "Flower pollination algorithm: a novel approach for multiobjective optimization". *Engineering Optimization*, No. 46(9): 1222-1237. https://doi.org/10.1080/0305215X.2013.832237

Yu, Jingyu; Wang, Jingfeng; Hua, Zhengmao; and Wang, Xingxing. 2021. "BIM-based time-cost optimization of a large-span spatial steel structure in an airport terminal building". Journal of Facilities Management, No. 20(3): 469-484. https://doi.org/10.1108/JFM-12-2020-0097

Mario Galić is an associate professor at the Josip Juraj Strossmayer University of Osijek, Faculty of Civil and Architectural Engineering Osijek, Croatia. His teaching and research interests are construction engineering, process modelling, simulation and optimization; construction project planning and scheduling; construction technology; logistics and supply chain management.

Uroš Klanšek is a full professor of construction management at the Faculty of Civil Engineering, Transportation Engineering and Architecture, University of Maribor, Slovenia. His current research interest mainly focuses on optimization methods and their applications in construction engineering and management.

IV

Advanced Construction Project Management: The Meaning and Importance of the New Learning Paradigm

Zoran Pučko and Nataša Šuman

4.1 Learning construction management for tomorrow

Project management as a scientific and professional discipline has radically changed in recent decades due to the rapid development of advanced technologies and the methods of Industry 4.0, which focuses on digitalisation and automation in all industrial sectors. According to a study by the McKinsey Global Institute (Manyika 2015), the construction industry is lagging far behind in this area.

Awareness of the importance of a healthy lifestyle, concern for the environment and society's development orientations align with the guidelines of the New European Bauhaus Initiative (European Union 2022). The trends of green building (Li et al. 2021), sustainable building (Boyle 2005; Sourani and Sohail 2008), a circular economy (Norouzi et al. 2021), and smart cities and buildings (Ghaffarianhoseini et al. 2018) are the main directions for construction projects today. The priorities of smart specialisation strategies in the European Union have been developed (European Commission 2021) and serve as guidelines for all member states. The Slovenian Smart Specialization Strategy S4 [Služba Vlade Republike Slovenije za razvoj in evropsko kohezijsko politiko 2017] has been submitted in Slovenia and contributes to the draft Smart Specialization Strategy 2030–S5 (Republika Slovenija 2021). The strategy has five main objectives: 1. An inclusive, healthy, safe and responsible society; 2. High levels of collaboration, competence and managerial efficiency; 3. A preserved healthy natural environment; 4. A highly productive economy that creates value for all; and 5. Learning for and throughout life.

All this has a direct impact on construction project management. Nowadays, these are the main directions that require a responsible and lifelong approach to construction project planning and execution, and the integration of advanced technologies and methodologies into construction project management is urgently needed (Xavier & Jacob 2018).

With regard to new methods and technologies in the construction industry or for the stakeholders in the construction project processes where the term architecture, engineering, construction, and operations (AECO) industry is often used, trends in development and implementation are recognised in both academic and professional circles (Hasan & Sacks 2021). These trends include building information modelling, construction robotics, construction project management, advanced construction materials, offsite construction, construction worker safety, construction monitoring, green building, 3D printing and connected construction sites (StartUs 2021).

4.1.1 Importance of BIM and Industry 4.0 for construction project management

BIM has grown exponentially in construction practice as it enables the digitalisation of construction projects, often called a digital twin, throughout the entire life cycle of construction projects (Borrmann et al. 2018; Eastman et al. 2018). Compared to the traditional approach, the main advantage of the BIM approach is that all expert treatment information is collected in one place that is automatically updated and accessible to all project stakeholders. Traditional project management uses various tools and methods to measure the success of projects from different points of view, such as time (e.g. with MS Project), cost (e.g. construction project management software) and quality. Ilozor and Kelly (2012) provide insight into the traditional approach to managing construction projects as well as a more detailed and critical review of the implementation of the BIM approach, and an analysis of the benefits of using BIM in commercial construction projects was conducted, commonly known as the Macleamy Curve Effect. The following describes the synergy of the main common points of the two main disciplines for advanced construction project management, i.e. the BIM approach and Project Management. The BIM approach includes four pillars of BIM (Turner 2017; Matthews 2016; Dawood & Vukovic 2015), as shown in Figure 4.1, Policy, People, Technology and Process. The four pillars are also meaningfully included in the educational process.

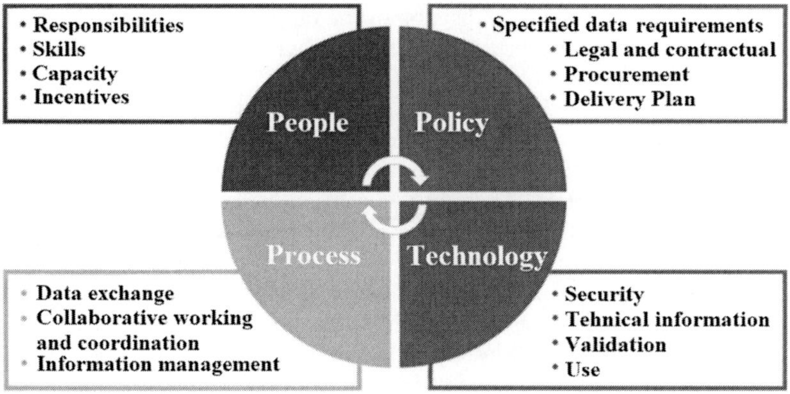

Figure 4.1 *Pillars of BIM (Turner 2017; Matthews 2016; Dawood & Vukovic 2015)*

Following the guidelines of the Project Management Institute (PMI n.d.) and the *Guide to the Project Management Body of Knowledge* (PMBOK® 2017), processes and definitions for project management can be found, as shown in Figure 4.2.

Figure 4.2 *The PMBOK Process Groups*

The specificity of construction projects is that they are unique projects that cannot be compared to mass production. Each construction project must be planned separately. Construction projects are divided into several phases, forming the life cycle of construction projects. Combined with the BIM approach, processes can be considered a BIM process model. The result of the BIM in terms of the digitalisation of the building, which includes both geometric and non-geometric elements of the building, is understood as the BIM object model.

Considering technological progress, increasingly complex and well-planned construction projects require the modernisation of project management, leading to advanced construction project management (Šuman & Pučko 2021). Therefore, construction sector companies must strive to keep up with the numerous novelties related to using advanced technologies and methods in Industry 4.0. The project manager must have the knowledge, skills, and abilities to manage construction projects. All these circumstances put universities in a situation where these challenges must be addressed by updating learning content and methods. They should also encourage students to research and write theses on Industry 4.0 for the construction industry, focusing on digitalisation and automation. Active learning is particularly important, a well-established teaching method in civil engineering study programmes and includes teaching techniques such as activating students through interactive lectures, experiential learning, collaborative learning, and project-based learning (Lassen et al. 2018).

4.1.2 Introducing the BIM concept in the education process

Some frameworks are proposed in the literature for introducing BIM into the educational process. Each of them addresses individual challenges related to education BIM, which can be divided into seven main groups: the skills to be acquired, the teaching approach, the evaluation methods, the technological environment, the industrial partnerships, the implementation approach, and the timing (Boton et al. 2018). MacDonald and Mills (2013) proposed one of the first such frameworks, the "IMAC" framework, which consists of four stages: illustration, manipulation, application, and collaboration. These stages relate to different levels of achievement and consist of two components to help a) educators benchmark their curricula and b) develop their own improvement strategies. Sacks and Pikas (2013) propose a framework for a) eliciting the requirements of BIM education, b) the levels of achievement, and c) the topics that relate to each level of study. A total of 39 topics were identified. Shelbourn et al. (2016) developed a BIM educational framework for the higher education sector that essentially improves the IMAC framework (Macdonald 2012). The framework is discussed with a case study showing how it can be used. Boton et al. (2018) proposed a framework for implementing BIM in engineering education that includes three main elements: a) the skills to be acquired by students, b) the teaching approach to be adopted, and c) the implementation strategy. A study also includes a case study from a Canadian engineering school. Zamora-Polo et al. (2019) proposed a conceptual framework for using BIM in engineering education. It has three dimensions: a) competencies, b) a pedagogical approach, and c) the level of integration, and it allows for planning and analysis of future experiences with teaching BIM in a higher education context.

When introducing BIM into engineering education, higher education institutions face several limiting factors and challenges, so they do not include BIM in degrees. The most important of these are the number of credits required to introduce modern content (Sacks & Barak 2010), the lack of people qualified to teach BIM (Becerik-Gerber et al. 2011), the lack of appropriate tools to make the change and the lack of appropriate classrooms and technical equipment (Witt & Kähkönen 2019).

The book chapter aims to present a framework for introducing the BIM approach to the educational process with a focus on construction engineering and management and a case study of the teaching experience on BIM and Industry 4.0 at the Faculty of Civil Engineering, Transportation Engineering and Architecture (FCETEA), of the University of Maribor, Slovenia. The case study presents current educational activities on advanced technologies in more detail. First, we outline how digitalisation topics are integrated into the learning process, both in the teaching subjects and other forms of student learning. It then shows some examples of how students are involved in projects. In evaluating the proposed framework, an analysis of the acquired competencies of the students under the given framework and in the discussion of challenges and barriers in the implementation of digitalisation in educational processes in construction management is given. By presenting the educational framework and activities carried out for education on BIM and digitalisation at a university in Slovenia, the chapter aims to share educational experiences from a university perspective and to open this topic to a wider international community of experts for discussion and suggestions for improvement.

4.2 Methodology

The proposed framework considers universities' challenges in integrating BIM into engineering education before introducing methods and technologies for advanced construction project management. Like the two previous proposals by Boton et al. (2018) and Zamora-Polo et al. (2019), it includes three main aspects to consider when implementing BIM: a) competencies, b) pedagogical approach and c) level of integration. The framework is limited to construction project management, taught in the departments of construction engineering and management (CEM) and is one of the fields of the AECO industry. CEM represents a project's overall planning, coordination, and control from beginning to completion to meet the client's requirements to produce a functionally and financially viable project (Chegu Badrinath et al. 2016).

The main elements of the framework, focusing on the CEM, are shown in Figure 4.3 and discussed in more detail below.

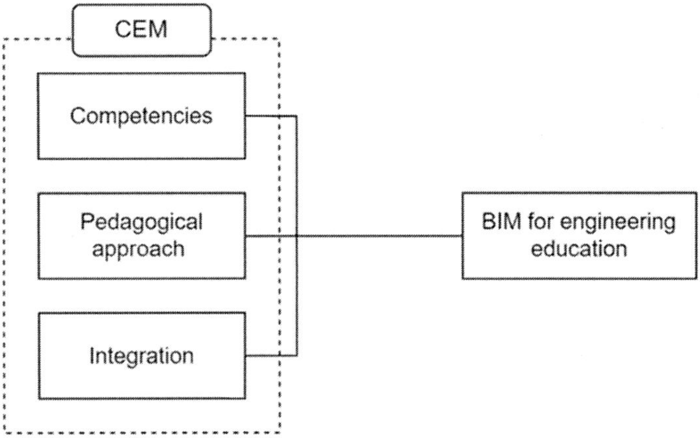

Figure 4.3 *Main elements of the proposed framework*

4.2.1 Competencies to be acquired

The first element of the proposed framework is the competencies and skills students should acquire in the classroom using the BIM methodology. Here, the integration of knowledge, skills, and attitudes (KSA) is understood as competencies (Uhm et al. 2017). Since the BIM approach has been used in the AECO industry, the challenge for the higher education sector is to determine which skills should be acquired by students in order to use them in their professional work.

Several studies have been conducted to analyse the professionals' skills required for work in the BIM sector (Lucas 2017; Sacks & Pikas 2013; Uhm et al. 2017). As indicated in previous studies, capabilities in the proposed framework include core competencies developed in existing engineering competency models and BIM-specific knowledge. The latter are categorised into three main groups: technology-related, process-related, and policy-related competencies (Succar 2009).

Table 4.1 *Knowledge set and skill set for the CEM (summarised by Bozoglu 2016)*

Knowledge Set			
Competencies	Skills	Teaching Methods	Learning Tools
Construction Planning	• Understanding 4D Model Information Exchange • Understanding Mobility and Logistics • Creating and Adjusting the Schedule • 4D Model Creation and Review • Creating 4D Simulation • Data Interpretation • Reporting	• Lecture • Hands-on • In-lab example • Case Video • Case Reading • Self-Learning • Tutorial	• Vico Office Schedule Planner • Revit • Tekla Structure
Cost Estimation	• Understanding 5D Model Information Exchange • Understanding Cost Estimation • Creating Quantity Take-off • Creating Cost Estimation • Cost Comparison • Using Cost Data • Cost Report	• Lecture • Hands-on • In-lab example • Case Video • Case Reading • Self-Learning • Tutorial	• Vico Office Cost Planner • Vico Office Cost Explorer • Revit
Coordination	• Model Coordination • Interdisciplinary Project and Teamwork • Communication between team members • Compare and Select Options	• Lecture • Hands-on • Case Video • Case Reading • Self-Learning • Tutorial	• Vico Office • Trimble Connect • Plan-Radar • Dalux

In this framework, we limit ourselves to the area of CEM, where the skills are acquired in connection with the training of BIM specialists such as BIM managers, BIM analysts and BIM consultants.

Table 4.1 shows the knowledge set and skill set of the CEM. The primary competencies listed are construction planning, cost estimation, and coordination. Skills, teaching methods and learning tools are given for each competency. Competency levels in each area are defined based on Bloom's Taxonomy, which includes: know, remember, understand, apply, analyse, evaluate, and create (Anderson et al. 2001).

In defining skills, it is important to understand the level of education, which Barison and Santos (2019) call the "level of a BIM course." The three levels are distinguished, introductory, intermediary and advanced, and project-based learning is proposed as an appropriate strategy for all three levels. In the proposed framework, we assume that the educational level is related to the academic level. Skills important for CEM are acquired at the intermediate and especially at the advanced level, the second level of study up from the academic level.

4.2.2 Pedagogical approach

The second dimension of the proposed framework is the pedagogical approach, including teaching methods and the technological environment. For the inclusion of BIM in the pedagogical process, it is important to choose an appropriate approach to implementing activities in the teaching process. For the introduction of modern digitalisation content, it is important to use modern collaborative learning methods and the newest active learning methodologies, such as problem-based learning (Kwan 2009). In any case, the paradigm of collaborative learning (teamwork and coordination) is promoted in BIM. This stems from the goals of BIM, which allow all participants to access up-to-date information simultaneously. From the perspective of BIM teaching, it is important to ensure that the teacher has BIM teaching knowledge that spans three areas: BIM software knowledge, BIM knowledge of standards and policies, and pedagogical knowledge (Boton et al. 2018).

The success of a BIM curriculum also depends on the technological environment. It is important to teach students the principles underlying software BIM because technology is rapidly evolving, and graduates must adapt to new technologies during their careers. It is useful to compare different solutions from different vendors and practise mutual interoperability using a real project or various realistic examples. Project management software such as Vico Office, Bexel Manager, iTWO, and costX are suitable for the CEM.

4.2.3 Levels of integration

The third dimension of the proposed framework is dedicated to integrating methodology into the curriculum. There are several strategies for integrating BIM into the curriculum (Ahn et al. 2013; Lucas 2017; Sacks & Pikas 2013; Solnosky & Parfitt 2015). As in previous studies (Ahn et al. 2013; Sacks & Pikas 2013), in the proposed framework, we grouped the strategies developed into three: teaching BIM in an individual course or workshop, a transversal approach, and learning by doing.

The first group (first level) is the most common, in which students develop competence in either a compulsory or elective course. It is usually used in the first initiatives appearing on CAD or design subjects with BIM-related content. For the CEM field, these competencies are acquired primarily in second-level courses that address in-depth content for construction project management needs. Higher-level teaching of BIM represents a transversal approach (second level) where BIM content is integrated into the existing curriculum, i.e. BIM knowledge is introduced into other subjects. In doing so, individual subjects address the inclusion of BIM from their own perspective. The gradual introduction of content ensures that it is included in the curriculum according to the maturity of the students and at the right time. An even higher level of integration can be achieved with the so-called learning by doing, which can be used, for example, to work on multidisciplinary projects involving various courses and degrees. Therefore, the third level means that subjects address common problems in order to increase the efficiency of the teaching and learning process. However, all three levels must be understood as not being selective but complementary to each other, thus representing the natural evolution of the integration of BIM into higher education.

4.3 Case study

In this section, we present the context of current educational activities on implementing advanced technologies such as the BIM approach and Industry 4.0 conducted at the University of Maribor FCETEA. It then shows some examples of how students are involved in projects. The results, according to three main elements of the proposed framework, emphasising CEM, are given in the next chapter.

4.3.1 Learning process in subjects that involve the BIM approach

At FCETEA, during the first and second levels of study, training is provided on digitalisation in construction. The importance of digitalisation is gradually being incorporated into most professional teaching subjects. However, at the second level of study, we have the compulsory subjects BIM, which is about introducing the general concept of the BIM approach, the role of BIM and the technology for BIM. In The Chair of Construction Management, Technology and Economics Department, digitalisation topics are included in construction management, construction economics, project management in construction, and operative planning to meet the needs of construction project management. These subjects are mainly about teaching the use of the basic 3D BIM model and upgrading it to 4D and 5D BIM models. In doing so, the 3D BIM, extended to include the construction schedule, yields the 4D BIM, while the extension to include estimated construction costs yields the 5D BIM model.

At FCETEA, students are taught the fundamentals of digitisation and BIM at the first level of study in courses such as Computer Modelling of Construction Objects and Digital Modelling. At the second level, students are also offered elective courses with in-depth content on the BIM approach, such as the BIM Project for Construction and Infrastructure and the BIM Approach in Operational Construction. These advanced-level subjects focus specifically on BIM and the latest and advanced topics from BIM. These courses are appropriate for students who want in-depth knowledge and advanced skills from BIM and are interested in a BIM-related position. In-depth teaching according to the BIM approach was introduced at FCETEA in the 2015/16 academic year in second-level subjects with the introduction of compulsory and some elective subjects. Some elective subjects were added gradually over the years.

The teaching of advanced technologies focused on using the BIM approach, more specifically for creating 4D, 5D and 6D BIMs, is carried out within the subject of project management in construction. The subject is taught in two study programmes at the second level, i.e. civil engineering and industrial engineering, and in the professional study programme of civil engineering at the first level. In these subjects, students acquire theoretical knowledge about modelling higher BIM dimensional levels and creating 4D, 5D and 6D BIM models. The acquired knowledge is used in the tutorial and computer work, where they create 4D and 5D BIMs for the selected building. Each year they work on various tasks in a real building. For the creation of 4D and 5D BIMs, Trimble Vico Office™ software modules, such as Quantity Take-off, Task Manager, Cost Planner, and 4D Simulation (Trimble 2022) are used, as well as some other tools, such as 4BUILD for cost estimation (Hermes 2022) and MS Project (Microsoft 2022) for scheduling.

Work on tutorials and computer work is done in groups. Each group receives input data in the form of a 3D BIM and technical descriptions for the building considered in each academic year. Each group is assigned a set of elements to be analysed. The groups first analyse the elements (dimensions, materials, technology, quantity, etc.) and obtain cost estimation and scheduling data. Then, a 5D BIM is first created in the Cost Planner module. To determine the unit cost for each element, norms of work items per unit of measure and market prices for materials, equipment and machinery are used. The 5D BIM prepared in the Trimble Vico Office™ software allows cost information to be linked directly and bidirectionally to model elements. This means that if the geometry of the 3D BIM model changes, the costs associated with the element will be automatically updated. After the 5D model is created, the next step is to define the activities and their order of implementation. For this purpose, a 4D BIM is prepared in the Task Manager module. It is a time analysis where the elements in the 3D BIM model are directly linked to the activities in the schedule. The time analysis considers activities, the connections between them and the assigned resources. The quantity and norm of work per unit of measure are important in determining the activity duration. The joint results of all groups give an overall estimate and schedule for the construction under consideration. A simulation of the construction process is also produced. Figure 4.4 shows a process scheme for creating BIMs in the learning process.

Since the 2016/17 academic year, students have created BIMs for a school gym, a single-family house with associated infrastructure, a commercial office building, a two-apartment house, an apartment building and a single-family house. In the 2021/2022 academic year, students created 4D and 5D BIMs for a single-family house in Tepanje, Slovenia cadastral municipality. The conceptual design was previously created by a student using ArchiCAD BIM software. The student has given permission to use this 3D BIM model for study purposes on this course. The 3D BIM model of a single-family house and the location of the plot are shown in Figure 4.5.

An overview of the division of students into five groups, the assigned project tasks and the visualisation of the building elements can be found in Table 4.2.

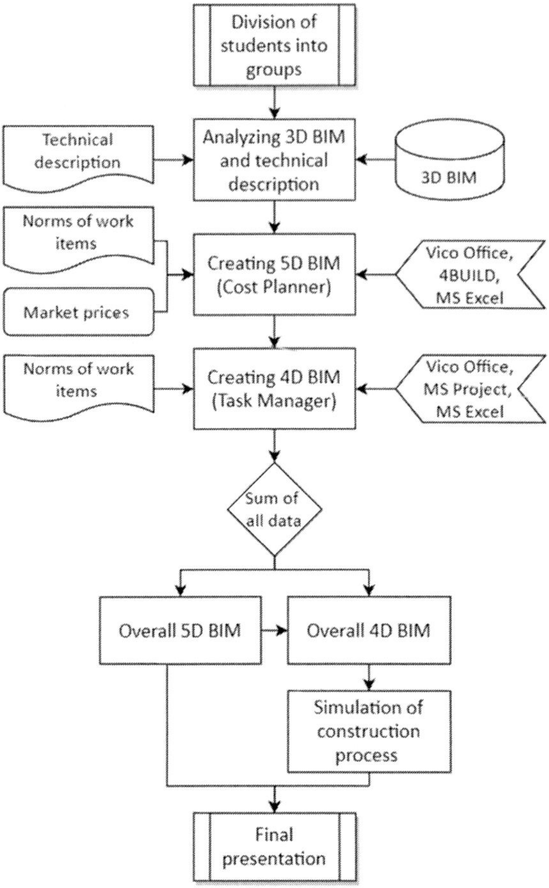

Figure 4.4 *Process scheme for the creation of 4D and 5D BIMs in the learning process*

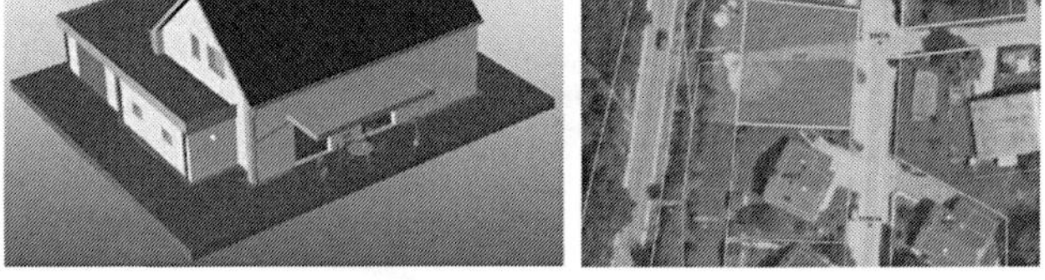

Figure 4.5 *3D BIM model of a single-family house (left) and the location of the plot (right)*

Table 4.2 *Students group number, assigned project tasks and visualisation of building elements*

Group number	The topic of the project task	Visualisation (set in Vico Office)
1	**CODE_building element** 013_foundation slab 011_strip foundations 012_pad foundation 001_façades 015_façades - borders 016_gutters 017_steel construction 018_roofing of the garage and terrace	
2	**CODE_building element** 002a_external walls of the ground floor 002b_external walls of the first floor 003a_inner walls of the ground floor 003b_inner walls of the first floor 006_RC ties 007_RC stairs 008_RC slab above the ground floor	
3	**CODE_building element** 009_terrain 010_filling 026_curbs	
4	**CODE_building element** 014_finishing floors - wood 022_housing equipment 024_doors 025_windows	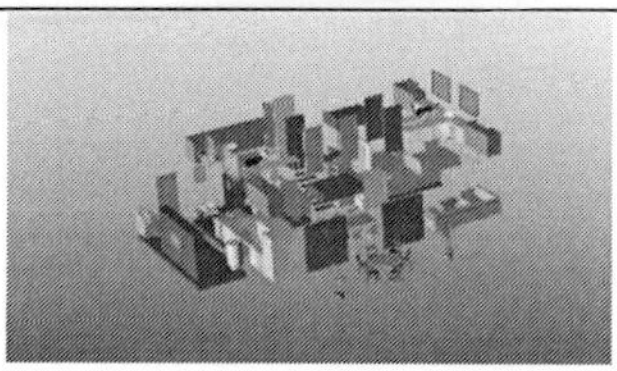

5	**CODE_building element** 004_roofing 005_roof construction 019_wooden wall of the garage 020_chimney 021_glass roof 020a_chimney-coil	

At the end of the study term, as shown in the diagram (see Figure 4.4), a presentation was made in which the groups were first presented with the results of their work (see Figure 4.6). Finally, as a conclusion of the whole work, the combined results of all groups were presented as comprehensive 3D, 4D and 5D BIM models, as shown in Figure 4.7. The final presentation also simulated a construction process (see Figure 4.8). Details of the presentation can be found on the faculty website (https://www.fgpa.um.si/2022/01/vodenje-gradbenih-projektov/).

Figure 4.6 *Presentation of the results of five groups of students*

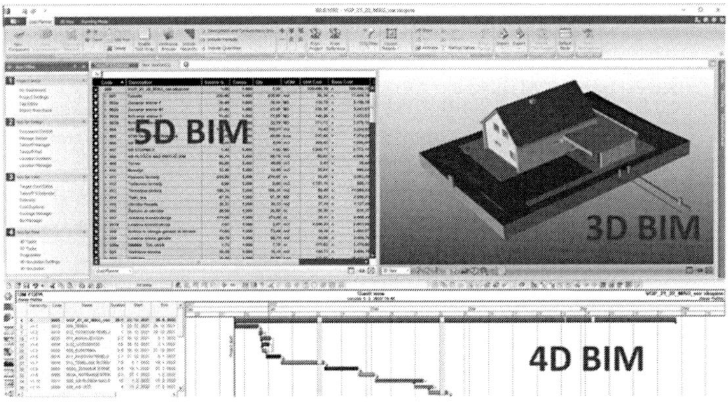

Figure 4.7 *Combined results as a comprehensive 3D, 4D and 5D BIM model of the building*

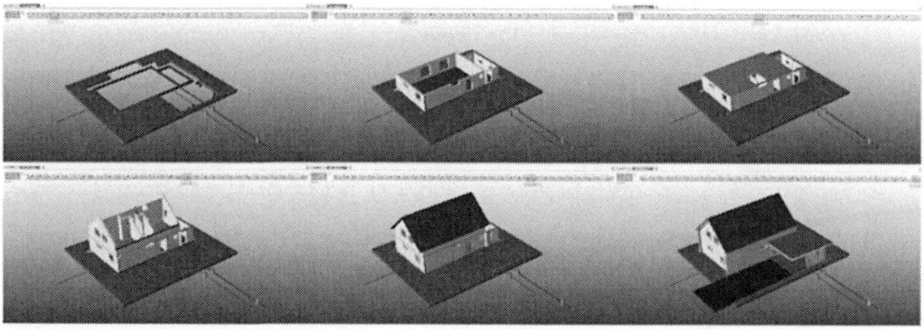

Figure 4.8 *Construction simulation (images from left to right and from top to bottom)*

Descriptions of the learning process of previous generations of students have already been published in publications such as the practical example of the building "Park Villa" (Pučko et al. 2015), the business and commercial building LESDOM (Pučko et al. 2019), the apartment building Ljutomer, the kindergarten Pekre, the semi-detached house and some more (Pučko et al. 2017; Pučko 2017, Pučko 2019).

4.3.2 Learning process implementing Industry 4.0

FCETEA students can also learn about Industry 4.0 and the use of advanced Industry 4.0 methods and technologies in other subjects, such as Safety at Construction Work, Spatial Arrangement and Advanced Planning, and Maintenance and Rehabilitation of Structures. For example, the data capture of the environment with a 3D laser scanner is used for various purposes: to acquire the actual condition of the environment, to determine the progress of work on the construction site and to create a 4D As-built BIM model, to help ensure safety on the construction site, etc. For study purposes, a Leica RTC360 3D Laser Scanner (Leica Geosystems 2022) was used to capture point cloud data at various locations (see Figure 4.9).

Figure 4.9 *Point clouds acquired with Leica RTC360 3D Laser Scanner and bottom right the presence of students during the scan*

During the learning process, advanced augmented reality technologies were also used with the Trimble XR10 with HoloLens 2 device (Trimble n.d.). The advanced technology enables mixed reality, i.e., a combination of a real environment with digital elements, providing the possibility of visualisation in a 1:1 scale-built environment, as shown in Figure 4.10. The technology is quite new in the construction industry, with only a few applications. However, it has a very high potential for use in the construction industry, and more innovations are expected to be developed in the coming years.

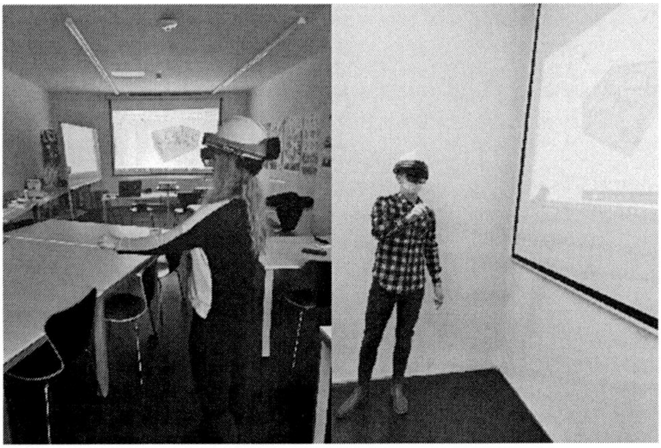

Figure 4.10 *Examples of the use of advanced mixed reality in the learning process*

4.3.3 Other forms of student learning

In the process of student learning, both for formal education within the learning process and for non-formal learning, many important activities help to broaden horizons and provide a more accurate insight into construction practices and the application of modern techniques and methods. These activities include student participation in various professional events, conferences, trade fairs, excursions and site visits.

Figure 4.11 *a) Construction site in Obersalzberg, b) Construction site in Munich and c) BIM WORLD Munich Congress*

In 2018, a two-day working excursion was organised for students that included a visit to the construction site of the Archive of Recent History in Obersalzberg (Figure 4.11-a), a visit to the construction site of the Großlappen Central Wastewater Treatment plant in Munich (Figure 4.11-b), and participation in the BIM WORLD Munich Congress (Figure 4.11-c) (Fakulteta za gradbeništvo prometno inženirstvo in arhitekturo Univerze v Mariboru 2018).

In addition, an excursion was organised for students in 2021 (Figure 4.12); namely, they visited three construction sites on the route of the second track (2TDK d.o.o. 2021), which is currently the largest construction project in Slovenia using modern technology. On all construction sites, the BIM approach is used, and all detailed construction plans are created using the BIM approach (Fakulteta za gradbeništvo prometno inženirstvo in arhitekturo Univerze v Mariboru 2022).

Figure 4.12 *Visit to construction sites in 2021*

As part of the learning process, short visits to construction sites, known as fieldwork, are also conducted and are a regular part of the learning process. Figure 4.13 shows a visit to the construction site in 2021 for the energy and structural renovation of the building of the Secondary School of Hospitality and Tourism in Maribor, where modern technologies such as the BIM approach, communication tools such as Dalux (Dalux 2021), etc. are used. (Fakulteta za gradbeništvo prometno inženirstvo in arhitekturo Univerze v Mariboru 2021)

Figure 4.13 *Short visits to construction sites*

Formal and non-formal forms of teaching are also offered to students through participation in international conferences. One such conference is held every year under the auspices of the siBIM association (Slovensko Združenje Za Informacijsko Modeliranje Gradenj - SIBIM n.d.). In 2016 the "BIMathlon" competition was held in Maribor as part of this conference (SiBIM 2016). The competition aimed to create the most complete BIM model of the selected building within a few hours of the competition day. A BIM TREK team was formed to participate in the competition, consisting of two faculty members, three company representatives, and five students, as shown in Figure 4.14.

Figure 4.14 *The BIM TREK team on the "BIMathlon" competition in 2016*

4.3.3 the Participation of students in projects in the fields of Industry 4.0, digitalisation and automation in construction

Under the auspices of the Public Scholarship, Development, Disability and Maintenance Fund of the Republic of Slovenia, the projects are suitable for the participation of students during their studies under the title "Creative path to knowledge" (Public Scholarship Development Disability and Maintenance Fund of the Republic of Slovenia 2020). Nine students were involved in an "Integration of Industry 4.0 Technologies for Automation of Construction Process Monitoring" project with the acronym APP4ACCPM. The project lasted six months, and the students were divided into four teams: Team A—Builders, Team B—Architects, Team C—Programmers and Team D—Management and Technical Project Support. Educational and professional mentors guided students.

The project's main objective was to develop a prototype for a comprehensive system for automated construction progress monitoring by integrating 4.0 technologies. A 3D scanner was used, which enables the automatic acquisition of actual data in the form of a point cloud, and based on this, the creation of the so-called 4D As-built BIM model. A list of deviations is generated by directly comparing this model with the planned

As-design BIM model. Details of this project are available in the DKUM repository (Pučko et al. 2020) and the FCETEA 2019/2020 yearbook (Fakulteta za gradbeništvo, prometno inženirstvo in arhitekturo 2021).

4.4 Results and discussion

For the case study of learning BIM at the University of Maribor FCETEA, an assessment of the proposed framework is presented by illustrating the inclusion of content for all three main elements. The evaluation is limited to subjects that include the BIM approach. An ex-post perspective was used to evaluate the proposed framework, i.e., proposals are evaluated after implementation. Based on the evaluation and review of other studies on the integration of BIM, this section discusses the challenges and barriers that engineering universities face in adopting BIM.

4.4.1 Skills and competencies

In light of the framework presented, the educational level, the knowledge set, and the BIM-specific knowledge related to the FCETEA teaching experience are discussed. In Slovenia, BIM education is provided within the higher education system at two levels: a university bachelor's degree, where students acquire core engineering competencies and are trained in 3D BIM modelling, and at a master's degree level, where students are trained in the use of a basic 3D BIM model and then upgrade to higher nBIM models to manage BIM projects in connection with other engineering content, such as BIM and structural design. It is about acquiring BIM-specific knowledge.

At FCETEA, the content of upgrading the basic 3D BIM model is taught at the master's degree level through two compulsory courses (BIM and Project Management.4.2 in Construction) and two elective courses (BIM Project for Construction and Infrastructure and BIM Approach in Operational Construction). These are intermediate and advanced levels of a BIM course. Project-based learning is used to a greater or lesser extent in all subjects.

The Project Management in Construction course is particularly important to achieve advanced construction project management. The knowledge set analysis of this course has shown that all the competencies listed in Table 4.1 are acquired through the educational process. In addition, students acquire all the skills except for construction planning, not for creating a 4D simulation, and for cost estimation, not for cost reports. To acquire all three competencies, the following learning methods are used in class: lecture, tutorial, in-lab example, case reading and self-learning.

4.4.2 Pedagogical approach

BIM learning promoted the paradigm of collaborative learning, which involves teamwork and coordination. At FCETEA, the teaching method of project-based learning is used in subjects that include the BIM approach, at least in the tutorial. The analysis of Project Management in Construction at the second level of study has shown that the pedagogical work in the tutorial is organised throughout the entire semester in such a way that students are divided into small teams (three to four students each) and creatively involved in the analysis and modelling of 4D and 5D BIM on a real project example.

At FCETEA, several software packages are used for teaching, including Autodesk Revit, Design Review, Tekla Structure, Autodesk Navisworks, and Vico Office. Teachers with appropriate BIM teaching knowledge teach classes in an IT lab. Project management software is important for CEM. Therefore, Trimble Vico Office™ software and its modules are used in the Project Management in Construction course: Take-off Manager, Task Manager, Cost Planner, Document Control, Schedule Planner and 4D Simulation (Trimble 2022).

4.4.3 Level of integration

In FCETEA, BIM knowledge is integrated at the first and second levels of study. Competencies are developed in a stand-alone compulsory or elective course at the first level. For the needs of the CEM, specific competencies are acquired in the compulsory courses of the second level. As it is in-depth knowledge, it deals with the second level of integration, while the topic deals with the inclusion of BIM from the perspective of the fourth, fifth and even higher dimensions of the BIM model, which are important for advanced construction project management.

4.4.4 Lessons learned

The specifics, professional management, scope and complexity of today's construction projects have exceeded traditional project management skills, leading to the emergence of advanced construction project management. Today, the BIM approach is used as an effective support for advanced project management. The BIM approach to construction practice, introduced by individual countries in different periods and phases (Galić et al. 2017), has clearly shown the need for new professions and changes in learning content.

Many engineering universities are developing a BIM-based curriculum to improve their teaching methods. The development of BIM-based curricula is also active in teaching construction project management. In developing the implementation of BIM into the construction project management curriculum, the introduction of BIM technology with 3D visualisation, 4D scheduling, 5D estimating, and laser scanning technology is particularly important, as is the broader integration of BIM into other courses such as construction surveying, project administration, sustainability in construction, known as 6D BIM, facility management, known as 7D BIM, and even construction safety, known as 9D BIM.

The challenge for higher education institutions is to create the right framework with the right goals and assist educators with integrating BIM into their respective courses. It is always important to understand that introducing BIM into the construction project management department is more complex than simply adding new courses to the curriculum.

In developing the framework, educators must consider the limitations they have and with which they are particularly connected:

- to how BIM is introduced, i.e. either as stand-alone subjects or workshops or as a transversal approach or even learning by doing, with some opting to introduce additional modules;
- to students, meaning that the different needs of students with different computer skills and practical experiences are taken into account;
- to the educational levels, which means finding the appropriate time and scope to include BIM-related education in study programmes;
- to various teaching methods that involve teamwork and collaboration, which means coordinating and motivating students to work together in a multidisciplinary manner; and
- to classrooms and technical equipment, e.g., that classrooms are appropriately designed and equipped for collaboration and that interoperability between different software packages is ensured.

Our further research will focus on upgrading the proposal framework so that it can be used to implement other Industry 4.0 methods and technologies in general and specifically for the needs of construction project management. At FCETEA, Industry 4.0 methods are gradually being incorporated into teaching, as described in subchapter 3.2. In addition, in the paper, we also present various other forms of non-formal education conducted at the faculty, all of which contribute to students acquiring additional knowledge and skills to gain a broader picture of understanding the importance of BIM integration for advanced construction project management.

4.5 Conclusion

The rapid development of new technologies and methods, and the continuous improvement of existing ones that Industry 4.0 brings, require a commitment to mastering them and constantly monitoring development trends. The construction industry lags far behind in digitalisation and automation compared to other industries. However, a radical change has occurred in recent years, and the development and implementation of Industry 4.0 technologies and methods, i.e., digitalisation and automation, has rapidly increased. New paradigms in construction project management require rapid adaptation and active learning of new project management skills, especially for large and complex construction projects. Currently, advanced approaches are being developed in project management, introducing new principles and advanced technologies, and consequently, Industry 4.0 methods are being introduced in the construction industry. All this leads to radical changes in the management of construction projects. Therefore, comprehensive and in-depth knowledge of these modern fields is required, especially at universities. So, engineering universities today face a major dilemma when successfully introducing Industry 4.0 and digitalisation into their curricula. For the needs of construction project management, the introduction of the BIM approach is particularly important. To date, many frameworks have been proposed for introducing BIM into the educational process. However, a comprehensive framework to support the introduction of BIM in engineering colleges focusing on construction project management has not yet been presented. This chapter proposes a framework for introducing BIM into the field of CEM, including the competencies and skills to be acquired, the teaching methods, the technological environment, and the level of integration. The University of Maribor FCETEA case study illustrates the application of the proposed framework for introducing BIM knowledge into the curriculum. Future work will focus on how such a framework can be used to implement other Industry 4.0 methods and technologies in general and specifically for construction project management needs.

Further evaluation and validation of introducing new technologies into the educational process should also be conducted to identify and formalise the best way to introduce these technologies into the engineering universities' curriculum. In parallel, future work should also aim to investigate the required competencies of students in the future, considering the needs of the AECO industry. It follows that the aim of the academic environment must be to constantly monitor and analyse the development trends and thus constantly update the competencies and skills and implement them in the curricula or even establish new modules or study programmes.

References

2TDK d.o.o. 2021. "Za Razvoj Slovenije | Drugi Tir." 2021. http://www.drugitir.si/.

Ahn, Yong Han, Chung Suk Cho, and Namhun Lee. 2013. "Building Information Modeling: Systematic Course Development for Undergraduate Construction Students." Journal of Professional Issues in Engineering Education and Practice 139 (4): 290–300. https://doi.org/10.1061/(ASCE)EI.1943-5541.0000164.

Anderson, Lorin W, David R Krathwohl, Peter W Airasian, Kathleen A Cruikshank, Richard E Mayer, Paul R Pintrich, James Raths, and Merlin C Wittrock. 2001. A Revision of Bloom's Taxonomy of Educational Objetives. https://www.uky.edu/~rsand1/china2018/texts/Anderson-Krathwohl—A taxonomy for learning teaching and assessing.pdf.

Barison, Maria Bernardete, and Eduardo Toledo Santos. 2019. "An Overview of BIM Specialists." *EG-ICE 2010 - 17th International Workshop on Intelligent Computing in Engineering*, January.

Becerik-Gerber, Burcin, David J. Gerber, and Kihong Ku. 2011. "The Pace of Technological Innovation in Architecture, Engineering, and Construction Education: Integrating Recent Trends into the Curricula." Electronic Journal of Information Technology in Construction 16: 411–32.

Borrmann, André, Markus König, Christian Koch, and Jakob Beetz. 2018. Building Information Modeling: Technology Foundations and Industry Practice. Building Information Modeling: Technology Foundations and Industry Practice. Springer International Publishing. https://doi.org/10.1007/978-3-319-92862-3.

Boton, Conrad, Daniel Forgues, and Gilles Halin. 2018. "A Framework for Building Information Modeling Implementation in Engineering Education." *Canadian Journal of Civil Engineering* 45 (10): 866–77. https://doi.org/10.1139/cjce-2018-0047.

Boyle, Carol A. 2005. "Sustainable Buildings." Proceedings of the Institution of Civil Engineers: Engineering Sustainability 158 (1): 41–48. https://doi.org/10.1680/ensu.2005.158.1.41.

Chegu Badrinath, Amarnath, Yun Tsui Chang, and Shang Hsien Hsieh. 2016. "A Review of Tertiary BIM Education for Advanced Engineering Communication with Visualization." *Visualisation in Engineering*. Springer. https://doi.org/10.1186/s40327-016-0038-6.

Dalux. 2021. "Dalux | Digitalizing Construction Industry." 2021. https://www.dalux.com/sl/.

Dawood, Nashwan, and Vladimir Vukovic. 2015. "Whole Lifecycle Information Flow Underpinned by Bim: Technology, Process, Policy and People." second International Conference on Civil and Building Engineering Informatics 7 (May): 1–7.

Eastman, Charles M, Paul; Teicholz, Rafael Sacks, and Kathleen Liston. 2018. BIM Handbook: A Guide to Building Information Modeling for Owners, Managers. Wiley. https://books.google.com.br/books?id=aCi7Ozwkoj0C&printsec=frontcover&dq=BIM+handbook:+a+guide+to+building+information+modeling+for+owners,+managers,+designers,+engineers+and+contractors+(second.+ed.)&hl=fr&sa=X&redir_esc=y#v=onepage&q=BIM handbook%3A a guide.

European Commission. 2021. Study on Prioritisation in Smart Specialisation Strategies in the EU. Luxembourg: Publications Office of the European Union. https://op.europa.eu/it/publication-detail/-/publication/fd1c28cd-fb18-11eb-b520-01aa75ed71a1.

European Union. 2022. "About the Initiative New European Bauhaus." 2022. https://europa.eu/new-european-bauhaus/about/about-initiative_en.

Fakulteta za gradbeništvo prometno inženirstvo in arhitekturo Univerze v Mariboru. 2018. "Poročilo: Strokovna Ekskurzija v Obersalzberg in München | Fakulteta Za Gradbeništvo, Prometno Inženirstvo in Arhitekturo Univerza v Mariboru." 2018. https://www.fgpa.um.si/2018/12/porocilo-strokovna-ekskurzija-v-obersalzberg-in-munchen/.

Fakulteta za Gradbeništvo, Prometno Inženirstvo in Arhitekturo Univerza v Mariboru. 2021. "Terenske Vaje (Ogled Gradbišča) Pri Predmetih Planiranje in Vodenje Gradbenih Projektov in Varstvo Pri Gradbenem Delu | Fakulteta Za Gradbeništvo, Prometno Inženirstvo in Arhitekturo Univerza v Mariboru." 2021. https://www.fgpa.um.si/2021/12/terenske-vaje-ogled-gradbisca-pri-predmetih-planiranje-in-vodenje-gradbenih-projektov-in-varstvo-pri-gradbenem-delu/.

Fakulteta za Gradbeništvo, Prometno Inženirstvo in Arhitekturo Univerza v Mariboru. 2022. "Strokovna Ekskurzija | Fakulteta Za Gradbeništvo,

Prometno Inženirstvo in Arhitekturo Univerza v Mariboru." 2022. https://www.fgpa.um.si/2021/11/strokovna-ekskurzija-3/.

Galić, Mario, Vaclav Venkrbec, Franziska Chmelik, Immo Feine, Zoran Pučko, and Uroš Klanšek. 2017. "Survey of Accomplishments in Bim Implementation in Croatia, the Czech Republic, Germany, and Slovenia." Elektronički Časopis Građevinskog Fakulteta Osijek 8 (15): 23–35. https://doi.org/10.13167/2017.15.3.

Ghaffarianhoseini, Amirhosein, Husam AlWaer, Ali Ghaffarianhoseini, Derek Clements-Croome, Umberto Berardi, Kaamran Raahemifar, and John Tookey. 2018. "Intelligent or Smart Cities and Buildings: A Critical Exposition and a Way Forward." *Intelligent Buildings International* 10 (2): 122–29. https://doi.org/10.1080/17508975.2017.1394810.

Hasan, Saed, and Rafael Sacks. 2021. "Building Information Modeling (BIM) and Construction Tech Integration for Construction Operations: State of the Art." Proceedings of the 2021 European Conference on Computing in Construction 2 (3): 358–65. https://doi.org/10.35490/ec3.2021.179.

Hermes. 2022. "Hermes 4Build." 2022. https://www.hbs.si/sl_SI/hermes-4-bulid.

Ilozor, Benedict D., and David J. Kelly. 2012. "Building Information Modeling and Integrated Project Delivery in the Commercial Construction Industry: A Conceptual Study." *Journal of Engineering, Project, and Production Management* 2 (1): 23–36. https://doi.org/10.32738/jeppm.201201.0004.

Kwan, Anna. 2009. "Problem-Based Learning." In *The Routledge International Handbook of Higher Education*, 91–107. https://doi.org/10.4324/9780203882221-8.

Lassen, Ann Karina, Eilif Hjelseth, and Tor Tollnes. 2018. "Enhancing Learning Outcomes by Introducing Bim in Civil Engineering Studies – Experiences from a University College in Norway." *International Journal of Sustainable Development and Planning* 13 (1): 62–72. https://doi.org/10.2495/SDP-V13-N1-62-72.

Leica Geosystems. 2022. "Leica RTC360 3D Laser Scanner | Leica Geosystems." 2022. https://leica-geosystems.com/en-us/products/laser-scanners/scanners/leica-rtc360.

Li, Ying, Yanyu Rong, Umme Marium Ahmad, Xiaotong Wang, Jian Zuo, and Guozhu Mao. 2021. "A Comprehensive Review on Green Buildings Research: Bibliometric Analysis during 1998–2018." *Environmental Science and Pollution Research* 28 (34): 46196–214.

https://doi.org/10.1007/s11356-021-12739-7.

Lucas, Jason D. 2017. "Identifying Learning Objectives by Seeking a Balance between Student and Industry Expectations for Technology Exposure in Construction Education." *Journal of Professional Issues in Engineering Education and Practice* 143 (3). https://doi.org/10.1061/(ASCE)EI.1943-5541.0000318.

Macdonald, Jennifer A. 2012. "A Framework for Collaborative BIM Education Across the Aec Disciplines." *37th Annual Conference of the Australasian Universities Building Educators Association (AUBEA).*

MacDonald, Jennifer, and Julie Mills. 2013. "An IPD Approach to Construction Education." *Australasian Journal of Construction Economics and Building* 13 (2): 93–103. https://doi.org/10.5130/ajceb.v13i2.3324.

Manyika, James. 2015. "Digital America: A Tale of Haves and Have-Mores." San Francisco: McKinsey Global Institute, no. December. https://www.mckinsey.com/~/media/McKinsey/Industries/Technology Media and Telecommunications/High Tech/Our Insights/Digital America A tale of the haves and have mores/Digital America Full Report December 2015.pdf.

Matthews, Adam. 2016. "Working towards a Unified Approach to BIM in Europe." 2016. https://www.thenbs.com/knowledge/working-towards-a-unified-approach-to-bim-in-europe.

Microsoft. 2022. "Project Management Software | Microsoft Project | Learn More." 2022. https://www.microsoft.com/en-us/microsoft-365/project/project-management-software%0A.

Norouzi, Masoud, Marta Chàfer, Luisa F. Cabeza, Laureano Jiménez, and Dieter Boer. 2021. "Circular Economy in the Building and Construction Sector: A Scientific Evolution Analysis." *Journal of Building Engineering* 44 (December): 102704. https://doi.org/10.1016/j.jobe.2021.102704.

PMBOK® Guide-5th Edition. 2017. Sixth edit. Newtown Square, Pennsylvania: Project Management Institute. https://app.knovel.com/web/toc.v/cid:kpGPMBKPM1/viewerType:toc/root_slug:guide-project-management/url_slug:guide-project-management?b-q=pmi&sort_on=default&b-subscription=TRUE&b-group-by=true&b-search-type=tech-reference&b-sort-on=default&scrollto=pmi.

PMI. n.d. "Project Management Institute." Accessed 1 February 2022. https://www.pmi.org/.

Public Scholarship Development Disability and Maintenance Fund of the Republic of Slovenia. 2020. "Creative Path to Knowledge." 2020. https://www.srips-rs.si/en/human-resource-development/creative-path-knowledge.

Pučko, Zoran. 2017. "4D in 5D BIM Modeliranje s Primeri." https://plus.si.cobiss.net/opac7/bib/20994326.

Pučko, Zoran. 2019. "BIM v -Izobraževalni- Praksi." https://plus.si.cobiss.net/opac7/bib/22075670.

Pučko, Zoran, Danijel Rebolj, Karl Gotlih, Timi Karner, and Rok Cajzek. 2020. "Integracija Tehnologij Industrije 4.0 Za Avtomatizacijo Spremljanja Procesa Gradnje : Končno in Vsebinsko Poročilo Za Projekt 'Po Kreativni Poti Do Praktičnega Znanja.'" Fakulteta za gradbeništvo, prometno inženirstvo in arhitekturo. https://dk.um.si/IzpisGradiva.php?id=78062.

Pučko, Zoran, Andrej Štrukelj, and Nataša Šuman. 2015. "Project Management Software Based on BIM to Evaluate Construction Time and Cost." In *12th International Conference Organization, Technology and Management in Construction*, 309–23.

Pučko, Zoran, Nataša Šuman, and Uroš Klanšek. 2019. "Teaching and Lifelong Education on Bim at Fcetea in Maribor, Slovenia." In *14th International Conference Organization, Technology and Management in Construction*, edited by Ding Ronggui Ivica Završki, Anita Cerić, Mladen Vukomanović, Martina Huemann, 465–73. Zagreb: Croatian Association for Construction Management and the University of Zagreb, Faculty of Civil Engineering. http://www.otmc-conference.com/wp-content/uploads/2019/09/OTMC2019_Conference-Proceedings-01092019-v_9-resize.pdf.

Pučko, Zoran, Nataša Šuman, Uroš Klanšek, and Andrej Štrukelj. 2017. "Recent Works and Activities on BIM Conducted at FCETEA in Maribor Slovenia." In *13th International Conference on Organization, Technology and Management in Construction.*

Republika Slovenija. 2021. "Strategija Pametne Specializacije 2030 (Draft)." https://www.eu-skladi.si/sl/dokumenti/kljucni-dokumenti/2021-12-20-osnutek-strategije-pametne-specializacije.docx.

Sacks, R., and R. Barak. 2010. "Teaching Building Information Modeling as an Integral Part of Freshman Year Civil Engineering Education." *Journal of Professional Issues in Engineering Education and Practice* 136 (1): 30–38. https://doi.org/10.1061/(ASCE)EI.1943-5541.0000003.

Sacks, R., and E. Pikas. 2013. "Building Information Modeling Education for Construction Engineering and Management. I: Industry Requirements,

State of the Art, and Gap Analysis." Journal of Construction Engineering and Management 139 (11): 1–12. https://doi.org/10.1061/(asce)co.1943-7862.0000759.

Shelbourn, M.A, J. Macdonald, and J. Mills. 2016. "Developing an International Framework for BIM Education in the HE Sector." *Proceedings of the 10th BIM Academic Symposium*, no. April: 43–51.

SiBIM. 2016. "Dogodki - SiBIM 2016 - BIMathlon (Poročilo) - SIBIM." 2016. https://www.sibim.si/dogodki/siBIM2016_BIMathlon_porocilo/.

Slovensko Združenje Za Informacijsko Modeliranje Gradenj - SIBIM. n.d. Accessed February 6, 2022. https://www.sibim.si/.

Služba Vlade Republike Slovenije za razvoj in evropsko kohezijsko politiko. 2017. "Slovenska Strategija Pametne Specializacije S4," no. December. https://www.gov.si/assets/vladne-sluzbe/SVRK/S4-Slovenska-strategija-pametne-specializacije/Slovenska-strategija-pametne-specializacije.pdf.

Solnosky, Ryan L., and M. Kevin Parfitt. 2015. "A Curriculum Approach to Deploying BIM in Architectural Engineering." AEI 2015: Birth and Life of the Integrated Building - Proceedings of the AEI Conference 2015, no. Nibs 2007: 651–62. https://doi.org/10.1061/9780784479070.057.

Sourani, Amr, and M Sohail. 2008. "A Review of Sustainability in Construction and Its Dimensions." *Journal of Sustainability*, 536–47.

StartUs. 2021. "Discover the Top 10 Industry 4.0 Trends & Innovations in 2021." 2021. https://www.startus-insights.com/innovators-guide/top-10-industry-4-0-trends-innovations-in-2021/.

Succar, Bilal. 2009. "Building Information Modelling Framework: A Research and Delivery Foundation for Industry Stakeholders." *Automation in Construction* 18 (3): 357–75. https://doi.org/10.1016/j.autcon.2008.10.003.

Šuman, Nataša, and Zoran Pučko. 2021. "Integration of Industry 4.0 for Advanced Construction Project Management." In *Research Anthology on Cross-Industry Challenges of Industry* 4.0, 1277–1311. IGI Global. https://doi.org/10.4018/978-1-7998-8548-1.ch065.

Trimble. n.d. "HoloLens for Construction | Trimble XR10 with HoloLens 2." Accessed 7 February 2022. https://fieldtech.trimble.com/en/products/mixed-reality/trimble-xr10-with-hololens-2.

Trimble. 2022. "Vico Office." 2022. https://vicooffice.dk/en/.

Turner, Jeff. 2017. "The Four Pillars of NLP." 2017.

https://lifemanagement.co.uk/index.php/2018/05/23/the-four-pillars-of-nlp/.
Uhm, Miyoung, Ghang Lee, and Boyoung Jeon. 2017. "An Analysis of BIM Jobs and Competencies Based on the Use of Terms in the Industry." *Automation in Construction* 81 (October 2016): 67–98. https://doi.org/10.1016/j.autcon.2017.06.002.
Witt, Emlyn, and Kalle Kähkönen. 2019. "BIM-Enabled Education: A Systematic Literature Review." In Emerald Reach Proceedings Series, 2:261–69. Emerald Group Holdings Ltd. https://doi.org/10.1108/S2516-285320190000002042.
Xavier, David Kaufmann, and Ruaux Michael Jacob. 2018. "Digitalisation of the Construction Industry: The Revolution Is Underway." Oliver Wyman 3 (10 January): 1–14. https://www.oliverwyman.com/our-expertise/insights/2018/sep/digitalization-of-the-construction-industry.html.
Zamora-Polo, Francisco, Amalia Luque-Sendra, Francisco Aguayo-González, and Jesús Sánchez-Martín. 2019. "Conceptual Framework for the Use of Building Information Modeling in Engineering Education." International Journal of Engineering Education. Vol. 35.

Zoran Pučko is an assistant professor at the Faculty of Civil Engineering, Transportation Engineering and Architecture at the University of Maribor. He has published more than 70 works, including articles (8), books (1), chapters (3), conference papers (17) etc. His research interests include topics such as (BIM), digitalisation and automation in construction, point clouds, data acquisition (photogrammetry, laser scanning and depth images), Scan-vs-BIM and Scan-to-BIM, positioning, tracking and mapping, extended reality (VR/AR/MR) as well as other highly advanced technologies 4.0 and 5.0 for the AEC industry. He is a member of the Slovenian Association for Building Information Modelling (SiBIM), buildingSMART Chapter Slovenija and the Technical Committee SIST/TC BIM at the Slovenian Institute of Standardization (SIST). He is also a member of DIH UM, a leading partner of the Consortium DIGI-SI with the Status of EDIH—European Digital Innovation Hub.

Nataša Šuman is an associate professor at the Faculty of Civil Engineering, Transportation Engineering and Architecture at the University of Maribor. She is chair of the Construction Management, Technology and Economics course. She has published more than 100 works, including articles (16 scientific and two professional), chapters in a monograph (3), conference papers (26), university textbooks (3), interviews (4) etc.

Her research fields are construction economics; construction cost analysis; advanced construction project management; 5D BIM, economic evaluation of building renovation, models for the assessment of sustainable construction and renovation of buildings. She heads the second degree industrial engineering study program at FCETEA and is a member of the Association of Economic Engineers of Slovenia and the GING Council.

V

Project Complexity Framework of International Development Projects

Iztok Palčič and Slađana Rajinac

5.1 International Development Projects are complex

The area of Project Management is still gaining importance. Many project management elements are evolving continuously, two of which are project success and complexity. This is the case in all types of projects, especially in International Development Projects (IDP), which is confirmed by a study pointing out that as many as 64% of externally funded IDPs fail to meet the intended effect for end users (Hekala 2012).

Managing IDP requires new management approaches, due to all the specificities that characterise them compared to commercial projects. These projects are most often implemented in the public sector, characterised by cultural complexity, a unique context and institutional challenges. IDPs are specific because of the immeasurable uniqueness of the general goals. The broad objectives of IDP are realised uniquely with the application of various management tools and the involvement of numerous interest groups.

Contemporary challenges, such as a dynamic and uncertain environment and a large number of interest groups on projects, affect the success of IDP, and are related closely to the specific complexities of this type of project (Brady & Davies 2014; Cicmil et al. 2009; Geraldi et al. 2011; Vidal & Marle 2008; Saynisch 2010). In the scientific community it is emphasised that the degree of complexity has been increasing constantly (Vidal & Marle 2008; Baccarini 1996; Gidado 1996; Williams 1999). Scientific papers in the most prominent journals in the field of Project Management emphasise the existence of a link between project performance and complexity, but how complexity is connected to the practice of ID project management with all the specificities that characterise them is still researched insufficiently. In addition, in the scientific literature, a generally accepted model of project complexity in the field of IDP has still not been adopted (Kiridena & Sense 2016; Willaimson & Winter 1993; Winter et al. 2006; He et al. 2015).

Therefore, the main goal of the research in this chapter is to examine the complexity factors that affect the performance of IDP. The individual research questions answered by the research are:

- What complexity factors are significant in the field of ID Project Management according to the literature?
- What complexity factors are significant in the field of ID Project Management according to the experts?

The framework in this research includes some of the elements of the TOE (technology-organization-environment) framework, proposed by Bosch-Rekveldt et al. (2011), as well as the complexity model proposed by Vidal and Marle (2008). This research investigates the complexity factors that contribute to the overall complexity of IDP from the perspective of the experts. To conduct our research the Delphi survey method was used as the research methodology. The Delphi method is particularly useful in areas of limited research, since survey instruments and ideas are generated from a knowledgeable participant pool (Hasson et al. 2000), and it is suited to explore areas where controversy, debate, or a lack of clarity exists. In the case of this research, the Delphi method has been used to verify the significance of existing complexity factors proposed in the literature, and to update the list of complexity factors further in the context of IDP. It is believed that there is no clear consensus among the researchers on the complexity measures.

This chapter is organised as follows. Section 2 presents a short theoretical background on IDP and the complexity related to IDP. The next Section outlines the research methodology. Firstly, it presents the used Delphi method briefly in general, and secondly describes the research process, including data collection. Section 4 presents the results from the Delphi process in terms of practitioners' and experts' input, and proposes a refined measuring framework for complexity in IDP. The final section presents the conclusions, limitations, and potential implications of the proposed framework with an outlook for future research.

5.2 Theoretical background

5.2.1 International Development Projects

IDP projects need to be considered in the context of globalisation and the increasing economic interdependence of countries. In this sense, regional development is cited as a prerequisite that affects the creation of economically advanced and competitive regions that are capable of integration into global economic flows. Several types of donor organisations implement their activities fully through IDP. Some of them are the European Union, the OECD, the World Bank, and others. They highlight the importance of the region for economic development at the national and international levels.

IDP are the projects that deal mainly with poverty reduction, and cover sectors of agriculture, transportation, water, energy, health, population, education, reform and governance, etc. (Williams 1999).

Ika and Hodgson (2014) pointed out that, due to the specificity of IDP, these projects are on the right end of the spectrum when looking at the continuum that starts with projects from the private sector, towards projects of public institutions, and up to IDP. Figure 5.1 illustrates the scaling of project complexity depending on the group to which the projects belong. Namely, private sector projects are considered to be much less complex than IDP, which are considered more complex than projects implemented in the public sector and IDP.

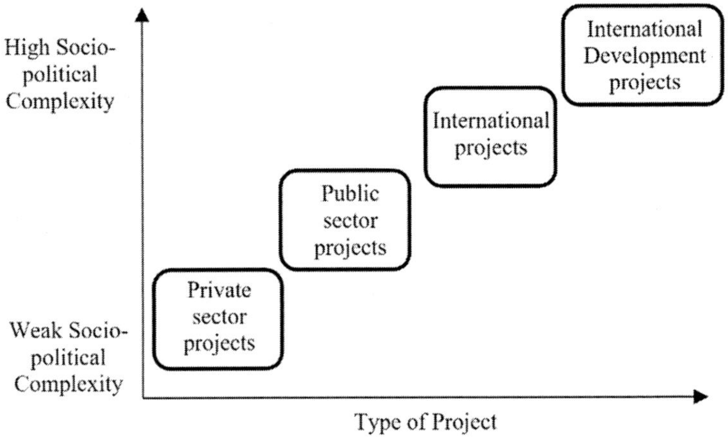

Figure 5.1 *Socio-political complexity in different types of projects*

5.2.1 Project Complexity and IDP

Baccarini (1996) was one of the first authors to review project complexity, and concluded that project complexity consists of a large number of interconnected parts that can be operationalised in the context of differentiation or mutual dependence. Complexity as a project characteristic is, in his opinion, different from other project characteristics, such as size or uncertainty.

Organisational and technological complexity was elaborated further by Williams (1999). He pointed out that, in the organisational context, differentiation implies the number of hierarchical levels, the number of formal organisational units, the mismatch of tasks, the number of specialisations, etc., while interdependence refers to the degree of interdependence between the organisational elements.

When it comes to technological complexity, differentiation refers to the number and diversity of inputs, outputs and activities; interdependence refers to the interdependence between activities, teams, technologies, or inputs.

Although the aforementioned authors focused on "structural complexity" and "uncertainty", it is assumed that "soft aspects" and environmental influences also affect project complexity (Bosch-Rekveldt et al. 2011; Jaafari 2003; Geraldi & Adlbrecht 2007).

In the literature, complexity is most often placed explicitly with uncertainty (Soomer & Loh 2004; Pich et al. 2002). Uncertainty undeniably appears as a factor affecting modern project management. During the duration of the project cycle, uncertainty decreases, but a certain level of uncertainty is present in every phase of project management.

Risk can be seen as a type of uncertainty, and is important for project implementation. Risk consists of the cause of the risk, the event itself and its consequences, as well as the probability of occurrence of the given impact. Complexity is caused by both uncertainty and risk.

In the subject research, the opinion of the author Bosch-Reckvelt (2011) was respected, who interpreted uncertainty as a characteristic of projects: a project can be characterised according to its "imprint" of complexity.

Mitchell and other authors introduced a model of identification and visibility of interest groups, which distinguishes the attributes of power, legitimacy and urgency (Mitchell et al. 1997). According to them, these three attributes should be viewed as dynamic and sociologically constructed. Although this typology can be useful for identifying and classifying interest groups on a project, it is mostly oriented towards interest groups that are outside the project (external interest groups). Achterkamp and Voss defined interest groups based on their role in the project. They developed a model that acts as a useful starting point in differentiating interest groups within a project (Achterkamp & Vos 2008). Their model distinguished four potential stakeholder roles: client, decision maker, project planner and passively involved parties. Here, we can recognise Freeman's basic definition of an interest group (Freeman 1999): "An interest group in an organisation is any group or individual who can influence or be influenced by the satisfaction of the organisation's goals...".

Interest groups who can influence the project are represented by active roles, and interest groups who are influenced are represented by their fourth, passive role. Certain roles in projects are often distinguished in the project management literature. Apart from the identification of interest groups (roles) in project management, their engagement is also important. Hilson and Simon recommended assessing three dimensions for each interest group: their attitude (supportive or resistant), their power, and their level of interest (Hillson & Simon 2007). Depending on these three results, it should be decided how to include or manage them in the project.

Table 5.1 *Complexity measuring in the literature*

Factor / Sub-factor	**Elements: sub-elements**	**Source**
Structural complexity / technological complexity	Goals: • Number of goals • Goal alignment • Clarity of goals Scope: • Scope largeness • Quality requirements Tasks: • Number of tasks • Variety of tasks • Dependencies between tasks • Interrelations between technical processes • Conflicting norms and Standards Experience: • Newness of technology • Experience with Risk: Technical risks	Lu et al. (2015); Brady and Davies (2014); Senescu, Aranda-Mena, & Haymaker (2013); Geraldi et al. (2011); Whitty and Maylor (2009); Vidal & Marle (2008); Geraldi & Adlbrecht (2007); Remington & Pollack (2007); Ives (2005); Williams (2003); Xia and Lee (2004); Williams (1999); Baccarini (1996); Shenhar and Dvir (1996); Maylor et al. (2008)
	Size: Project duration	

Structural complexity / organisational complexity	Resources: • Compatibility of different project management methods and tools • Size in budget • Size in Engineering hours • Size of a project team • Number of locations included Resources: • Resources and skills availability • Experience with parties involved • Interfaces between different disciplines • Number of financial resources • Contract types Team: • Number of different nationalities • Number of different languages • Cooperation JV partner • Overlapping office hours Trust: • Trust in a project team • Trust in the contractor Risk: Organisational risks	
Structural complexity / environmental complexity	Stakeholders: • Number of stakeholders • Variety of stakeholders' perspectives • Dependencies on other stakeholders • Political influence • Company (implementing body) internal support Location: • Interference with existing site - N/A • Weather conditions – N/A • Remoteness of location • Experience in the country Market conditions: N/A Risk: Risks from environment	

Dynamical complexity / -	Changes in all the elements that consist in the structural complexity	Kiridena &Sense (2016)
Socio-political complexity / -		Beach (2016); Geraldi et al. (2011); Maylor et al. (2008); Bresnen et al. (2005); Cicmil and Marshall (2005); Ives (2005); Shenhar and Dvir (1996); Jones and Deckro (1993); Maylor et al. (2008)
Uncertainty / structural	Uncertainties in scope	(Shenhar, 2001; Tatikonda and Rosenthal, 2000, Mykytyn and Green, 1992; Geraldi and Adlbrecht, 2007; Hobday, 1998;
Uncertainty / dynamical	Change in elements: • Change in scope • changes • deviations External uncertainty: • External contexts • Unclear organisational context • External elements • External political influence	Geraldi and Adlbrecht, 2007; Collyer and Warren, 2009; Petit, 2012; Atkinson et al., 2006; Bosch-Rekveldt et al., 2011; Maylor et al., 2008
Pace / -		Geraldi et al. 2011; Dvir, et al., 2006; Shenhar and Dvir, 2007; Williams, 2003
Project success / short-term	Time, Cost, Objectives	Ika, L. A., Diallo, A., & Thuillier, D. (2012)
Project success / long-term	Impact, Sustainability, Relevance	Ika, L. A., Diallo, A., & Thuillier, D. (2012)

In this research, interest groups related to the project influence it in two ways. First, all the interest groups (all types), internal as well as external, can influence the complexity of the project, and therefore should be and will be included in the research on the complexity of the project. Second, different interest groups involved in the project may have different interpretations of the project. In this context, the relevant interest groups included in the research are the Project Manager, the project owner (client/sponsor), and the team members.

Previous complexity studies have focused predominantly on the technical aspect of complexity. Contemporary literature focuses mainly on aspects of technical complexity, although, at the same time, it recognises the importance of "softer" aspects of complexity. Based on a detailed analysis of the literature (Bosch-Rekveld et al. 2011; Jaafari 2003; De Bruijn & Herder 2009) the division of complexity into technical, organisational and environmental complexity was adopted in this research. Furthermore, it is assumed that project complexity is dynamic, i.e. to change the project cycle. Therefore, a model that should characterise project complexity should take into account its dynamic nature. Contrary to certain literature sources that consider complexity and uncertainty as project characteristics (Sommer & Loch 2004; Pich et al. 2002), in the subject research, uncertainty is interpreted as one of the sources of project complexity (Williams 2003).

5.3 Methodology

5.3.1 Delphi method

The Delphi method is a systematic and qualitative method of forecasting by collecting opinions from a group of experts through several rounds of questions. The Delphi method relies on experts who are knowledgeable about a certain topic, so they can forecast the outcome of future scenarios, predict the likelihood of an event, or reach a consensus about a particular topic.

There are several variations of the Delphi method, developed according to the different types of problems that researchers face, i.e. according to the objectives of the implementation of the Delphi method itself. One of the variations that are accepted by the scientific community and spread widely in scientific practice is called the ranking-type Delphi method. It is used to develop a group consensus regarding the relative importance of a problem. Schmidt (1997) provided detailed information on how to perform this type of Delphi method. In addition, it includes guidelines for data collection, data analysis (based on non-parametric statistical techniques), and the reporting of study results. The selection of appropriate experts is the most important and neglected aspect in scientific works that apply the Delphi method.

Research that involves the application of the Delphi method usually consists of three steps. Namely, the factors that can answer the first two research questions are identified first. This step is characterised by a significant degree of subjectivity, as it depends on the process of identifying plausible factors. The second step refers to the inclusion of quantitative testing of the identified factors using a quasi-experimental design, to confirm the relevance of the factors themselves. This step contributes to the objectivity of the whole process. Finally, the third step offers practical recommendations for solving the problem of the research question.

The Delphi method is a research technique that increases the effectiveness of the group dynamics process. The implementation of this technique takes place through a process that must satisfy the criteria of anonymity and written form, and it must also contain a multi-stage survey procedure, after which a record of feedback concerning the group's attitude is kept after each round. In most cases, studies of this type focus further on reaching a consensus among the experts. If there are certain differences in the definitions of the method itself between different researchers, or slightly different implementation procedures, the following four characteristics overcome all the differences between them, and represent the basis of the Delphi technique itself (Rowe & Wright 2001):

1. Anonymity;
2. Repeating iterations;
3. Controlled feedback;
4. Statistical "group response".

When it comes to anonymity, it is guaranteed in Delphi studies, since the study participants usually do not know each other, and the communication process itself is coordinated by a moderator. Questionnaires are completed by each participant independently and returned to the research facilitator, who then analyses the group response. This procedure has certain advantages compared to other types of group communication. First of all, anonymity reduces the effect of the dominance of certain individuals in communication. On the other hand, it is important to point out the absence of socio-psychological pressure on the panelists from the rest of the group. Then, anonymity encourages panelists to change their previously expressed opinion without hesitation, without thinking about the possible condemnation of the group (Strauss & Zeigler 1975). Finally, anonymity in the conduct of the study most often leads to an increase in the degree of cooperation of the participants - a higher degree of response to the sent inquiries. The assumption is that the participants feel more comfortable, and, for this reason, decide more easily to give their assessments about complex problems in an anonymous form. Strauss and Ziegler particularly pointed out anonymity as an important factor in the success of Delphi studies (Strauss & Zeigler 1975). Namely, these authors came to an insight that shows that the largest number of participants emphasised anonymity as a key factor in the success of the given research.

The multilevel survey procedure is another important feature of the Delphi study. After each completed stage of the survey the answers of the respondents are summarised by the researcher, and, thus, they represent the basic feedback for the next round of the survey. This process is repeated until a certain degree of stability is achieved in the responses. Repeating the rounds, along with the orderly collection of answers from respondents, contributes to a significant reduction of potential misunderstandings during communication between participants (Strauss & Zeigler 1975). Also, this entire process enables the modification of previously reached conclusions, as well as the cumulative increase in knowledge about the topic being investigated.

During the development of the Delphi method, various criteria were used to determine the moment at which the multi-stage survey procedure should be terminated. Subjective analysis, descriptive statistics and inferential statistics were used to that end. In classic Delphi studies, the measurement of consensus among experts is based on descriptive statistics. Group response feedback, as well as potential corrections to the questions by the researcher, usually leads to a decrease in statistical variance in subsequent rounds.

A third important feature of Delphi studies is controlled feedback. This characteristic is called "controlled" because the researcher decides the type of feedback and its delivery. After each conducted round, the data are analysed again statistically and reported again in aggregate form.

Group response statistics, as the fourth important feature of Delphi studies, can be presented numerically or graphically, and most often contain measures of central tendency (median and arithmetic mean), dispersion (interquartile range and Standard Deviation), and frequency distribution (Dunn 2015).

5.3.1 Research process

In this research the Delphi method was implemented by ranking in two rounds (two-round ranking-type Delphi), to reach a group consensus on the relative importance of the proposed complexity factors within IDP (Figure 5.2).

Within Delphi research it is not necessary to select a representative sample of any population. Participants in Delphi research are qualified experts who have a better understanding of the selected research items, which makes the selection of participants a very important prerequisite for quality research implementation (Okoli & Pawlowski 2004). Within the subject research the experts were divided into two panels: scientists and practitioners. Heterogeneous groups of participants allow different perspectives on the chosen topic, as well as a comparison of the perspectives of different groups of stakeholders. Panels generally consist of 15 to 30 participants within the same discipline, or five to ten participants from different professional groups (Okoli & Pawlowski 2004). Following the guidelines from the relevant literature on Delphi research, 11 participants were selected in the first round of research, of whom seven participants also contributed to the second round of research.

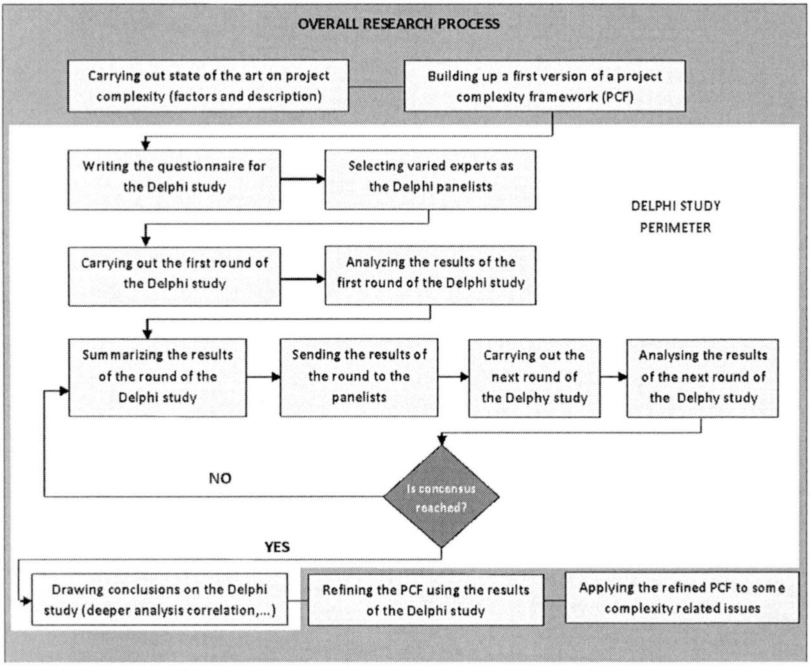

Figure 5.2 *Delphi algorithm in IDP research*

The following steps were involved in the selection of experts for the Delphi survey:

- Step 1 – preparation of the knowledge resources – determination of relevant disciplines or skills: scientists and practitioners; determination of relevant literature;
- Step 2 – compiling a list of contacts of knowledge resources;
- Step 3 – nomination of additional experts by existing contacts;
- Step 4 – inviting experts for each of the panels until the target panel size is reached.

5.4 Results and Discussion

Questionnaires for the Delphi survey were sent by email over the Internet. Within this phase the panelists were asked to rank the proposed complexity factors on a five-point Likert scale. They were classified into the three most important groups: technological, organisational, and environmental factors (TOE factors).

Table 5.2 *TOE complexity factors*

Complexity type	Element name
Organisational complexity	Duration, Compatibility of different project management methods and tools, Size in CAPEX, Size of the project team, Number of locations, Resources and skills, Experience with parties involved, Interfaces between different disciplines in IDP, Number of different nationalities in IDP, Number of different languages, Cooperation of JV partners, Trust in the project team (JV partner), Organisational risks
Technological complexity	Number of goals, Goal alignment, Clarity of goals, Scope largeness, Uncertainties in scope, Quality requirements, Number of tasks, Variety of tasks, Dependencies between tasks, Uncertainty in technical methods, Conflicting norms and Standards, Newness of technology, Experience with technology
Environmental complexity	Number of stakeholders (internal and external), Variety of stakeholders' perspectives, Dependencies on other stakeholders, Political influence, Organisational internal support, required local content, Experience in the country of implementation, Stability of project environment, Risks from the environment

In addition, participants were asked to list additional relevant complexity factors affecting IDP projects, with a brief explanation of each suggested factor. As part of the analysis, duplicates were removed, new complexity factors (Table 5.2) were classified and the terminology was unified for the proposed factors. After that, a consolidated list of factors was sent to the participantts.In the next phase the panelists were given a list of consolidated factors collected in the first round of questionnaires, grouped into categories, with a brief description of each factor based on information from the first round. In addition, participants were sent a copy of their responses from the first phase. The panelists were asked to verify that the answers were interpreted correctly and to place them in the appropriate categories.

In the first round, the following new elements were proposed by the experts:

- Overlapping project phases;
- Interdependence between different interest groups;
- Different expectations of interest groups;
- Lack of clarity or consensus regarding project benefits among interest groups;
- Variation – the first type of uncertainty;
- Anticipated uncertainty – another type of uncertainty;
- Unforeseen uncertainty - the third type of uncertainty;
- Chaos – the fourth type of uncertainty.

The panelists rated the TOE factors on a five-point Likert scale. Consensus measurement plays a key role in Delphi research, and can be defined as clustering around mean values with minimal divergence (Murry & Hammonds 1995). In this research two criteria were chosen for measuring consensus: Mean value >3 and Interquartile range < 1 (IQR).

Five elements had a mean value of less than three, which is why they were not included in the next round of Delphi research:

- Quality requirements;
- Duration of the IDP;
- Compatibility of different methods and tools for project management;
- The size of the capital investment;
- Cooperation with JV partners.

Consensus between the two groups of panelists was not reached on certain factors (IQR>1), so they were re-ranked in the next stage:

- Number of objectives;
- Alignment of goals;
- Clarity of goals;
- Number of activities;
- Interdependence between activities;
- Conflicting norms and Standards;
- New technology;
- Experience with technology;
- Availability of resources and skills;
- Overlapping of different disciplines;
- Trust in the project team (JV partner);
- Experience in the country of implementation.

In the second stage the original list of factors was narrowed down. Four participants did not continue their participation in the study; seven panelists continued to participate in the second round of research (four scientists and three practitioners). The main objective of this round was to understand the ranking of factors based on different perspectives of the interest groups.

All the new factors proposed by the participants had a mean value of less than 3, which makes them significant for the complexity of an IDP, according to the panelists.

A consensus was not reached for the following factors (IQR > 1):

- The number of different nationalities on an IDP affects their complexity;
- The political influence of an IDP affects the complexity of projects;
- The stability of the project environment (changes in the exchange rate, changes in material prices, etc.) in an IDP affects the complexity of the project;
- Interdependence between interest groups affects the complexity of projects.
- Chaos (the fourth type of uncertainty) affects the complexity of projects.

The t-test measures the differences in arithmetic means between the two groups. Two t-tests for independent samples were conducted, one for each round. In the first round, there were statistically significant differences, while, in the second round, no statistically significant differences were identified in the opinions of scientists and practitioners. In the first round respondents showed differences in opinion on seven questions, and in the second round, there were no differences in the answers.

Project coordinators believe that the number of objectives, the compatibility of different project management methods and tools, the size of the capital investment, and the required local environment in IDP have a more significant effect on project complexity than scientists think. A t-test measures the difference in opinion between two groups of panelists. In the first round, the respondents showed differences of opinion on seven questions, and in the second round, there were no differences in the answers.

The Wilcoxon test measures changes in consensus between the first and second rounds of the Delphi survey. The purpose of the Wilcoxon test is to measure the stability of the data, and help researchers determine if there was a difference in the data between the two Delphi rounds.

All concepts reached stability (a significance level set at 0.05), which is why it was decided to terminate the Delphi after the second round. For 11 questions that were repeated in both rounds, there was no significant statistical difference (Table 5.3).

Table 5.3 *Wilcox test*

Factor	**Z**	**Asymp. Sig. (2-tailed)**
Num. of goals	-1.300[b]	.194
Goal alignment	-1.13[b]	.257
Clarity of goals	-1.134[c]	.257
Number of tasks	-1.633[c]	.102
Dependencies between tasks	-1.000[c]	.317
Conflicting norms and standards	-.816[b]	.414
Newness of technology (world-wide)	-.333[c]	.739
Experience with technology	-1.000[c]	.317
Resource and skills availability	-.577[c]	.564
Interfaces between different disciplines	-1.604[c]	.109
Number of different nationalities	-.736[c]	.461

[a] *Wilcoxon Signed Ranks Test*
[b] *Based on positive ranks*
[c] *Based on negative ranks*

When it comes to the importance of factors according to the mean value indices, the following factors were selected as the most important according to the opinion of the panelists:

1. Clarity of goals (4.57);
2. Variations in the perspectives of interest groups (4.45);
3. Interdependence between activities (4.43);
4. Overlapping of different disciplines (4.29);
5. Interdependence with other interest groups (4.27);
6. Risks from the environment (4.27);
7. Lack of clarity or consensus regarding project benefits among the interest groups (4.14);
8. Unforeseen uncertainty (4.14);
9. Political influence (4.14);
10. The number of interest groups - internal and external (4.09).

Most of the factors with a mean value greater than three belonged to the Environment Complexity group. It can be concluded that project coordinators and scientists agree that the complexity of the environment is the most important in IDP, which can be considered the biggest contribution of this research phase. Similar research conducted on different types of projects generally concluded that organisational complexity has the greatest impact on projects. In addition, it was concluded that uncertainty has a significant impact on the project complexity of IDP, which is supported by the group of uncertainty factors proposed by experts in the Delphi research. The complexity framework shown in Figure 5.3 was proposed after the qualitative research phase.

5.5 Conclusions

By reviewing the relevant scientific literature it was determined that most authors classified project complexity into three most important units: 1) Organisational complexity (project duration, compatibility of different methods and tools for project management, size of the project team, number of locations, resources and skills, existing experience with the involved parties, overlapping of different areas in IDP, number of different nationalities, number of different languages, cooperation with project partners, trust in the project team, organisational risks), 2) Technological complexity (number of goals, alignment of goals, clarity of goals, size of the project scope, uncertainties in the project scope, quality requirements, number of tasks in the project, variations in tasks, dependencies between different tasks, uncertainties in technical methods, conflicting norms and Standards, novelty in technology, experience with technology) and 3) Complexity of the environment (number of stakeholders, variations in interested foreign perspectives, political influence, organisational internal support, required local context, experience in the country where the project is carried out, stability of the project environment, risks from the environment). A literature review provided a list of factors relevant to IDP, thus providing an answer to the first research question.

The Delphi method of qualitative research was applied to answer the second research question. The main idea of this part of the research was to establish a consensus among experts – scientists and practitioners who deal with IDP, about which complexity factors are the most relevant when it comes to this type of project.

Within the Delphi research, completely new factors of the complexity of IDP were proposed: overlapping of project phases, interdependence between different stakeholders, different expectations of stakeholders, lack of clarity or consensus about the utility of the project between stakeholders, variation, predictable uncertainty, unpredictable uncertainty and chaos. Both scientists and practitioners reached a consensus that these factors are important for the complexity of IDP.

According to the practitioners, the number of objectives, the compatibility of different methods and tools in project management, as well as the size of the capital investment and the local context had a significantly greater impact on project complexity than according to the scientists. This can be interpreted by the specific implementation experience that practitioners have compared to scientists, which makes it difficult for them to manage IDP on a day-to-day basis.

According to scientists, variations in interest group perspectives, interdependence between interest groups and political influence have a much greater effect on the complexity of IDP than practitioners realise. It could be concluded that, according to the practitioners, technological complexity has much greater importance on IDP, while, according to the scientists, the most important influence is the complexity of the environment.

In conclusion, the panelists reached a consensus, and concluded that among the selected factors, the most important factors of the complexity of IDP are: clarity of goals, diversity of perspectives between interest groups, interdependence between project activities, overlapping of different disciplines, the interdependence of interest groups, risks from the environment, lack of consensus regarding the usefulness of the project between interest groups, unpredictable uncertainty, political influence, as well as the number of interest groups – internal and external.

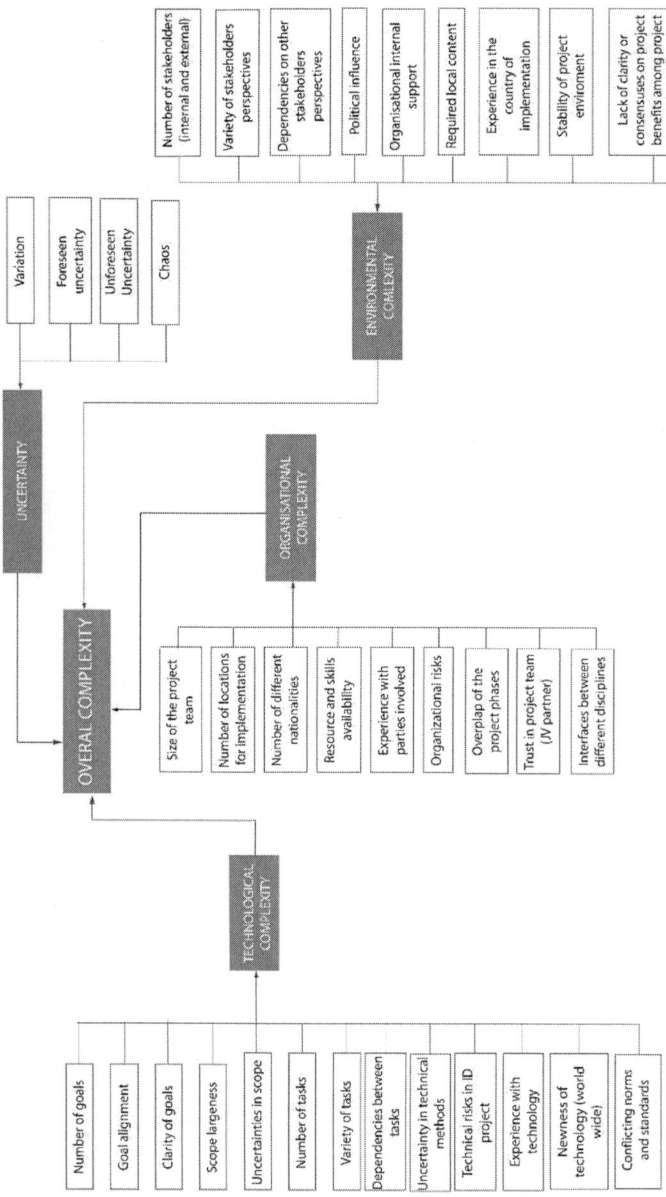

Figure 5.3 *Modified TOE framework*

After summarising the results from this qualitative research, the important conclusion is that factors from the group of environmental complexity have the greatest influence on the overall complexity of IDP, which is a completely original scientific contribution.

In previous research, TOE complexity factors have never been considered in the context of IDP. Studies that examined mainly complexity in large infrastructure, IT, or construction projects concluded that complexity factors from the group of organisational complexity are more influential than the other two groups. It can be concluded that each type of project is characterised by the specificity of the industry in which it is carried out, and thus by the types of factors and sources of complexity that make it up. In addition, it is necessary to work on the assessment of complexity in all phases of the project, to take adequate actions and achieve satisfactory project performance. This provides a comprehensive answer to the second research question.

The insights of the study can be used by both academics and practitioners. The framework could be used to assess the complexity of the IDP. The existing framework has an objective to contribute to a better understanding of project complexity in the context of international development, and identification of complexity areas in specific projects, that could lead to better management of potential risks, as well as improvements in the process of project planning and implementation.

This research has several limitations. The implemented Delphi study is a qualitative research approach, which means that certain subjectivity cannot be avoided. This is especially the case when the sample of respondents is rather low, which was even more evident in the second Delphi round in this research. The major limitations of the study will be removed by investigating the framework by employing a quantitative approach. Therefore, the research will be upgraded by sending questionnaires to Erasmus and Tempus project coordinators and structural equation modelling as an advanced statistical method.

References

Achterkamp, Marjolein. C., and Vos, Janita. F.J. "Investigating the use of the stakeholder notion in project management literature, a meta-analysis." International Journal of Project Management, No. 26, Vol. 7. (2008): 749–757.

Atkinson, Roger, Crawford, Lynn, and Ward, Stephen. "Fundamental uncertainties in projects and the scope of project management."

International Journal of Project Management, Vol. 24, No. 8. (2006): 687-698.

Baccarini, David. "The concept of project complexity—a review." International Journal of Project Management, Vol. 14, No. 4. (1996): 201–204.

Beach, Yvonne. "The Socio-political dynamics and complexity of organisational change projects: A research agenda, in Project Managemement Development-Practice and Perspectives, 20–30.

Bosch-Rekveldt, Marian, Jongkind, Yuri, Mooi, Herman, Bakker, Hans, and Verbraeck, Alexander. "Grasping project complexity in large engineering projects: The TOE (Technical, Organisational and Environmental) framework." International Journal of Project Management, Vol. 29, No. 6. (2011): 728–739.

Brady, Tim, and Davies, Andy. "Managing structural and dynamic complexity: A tale of two projects." Project Management Journal, Vol. 45, No. 4. (2014): 21–38.

Bresnen, Mike, Edelman, Linda, Newell, Sue, Scarbrough, Harry, and Swan, Jacky. "Exploring social capital in the construction firm." Building Research and Information, Vol. 33, No. 3. (2005): 235-244.

Cicmil, Svetlana, Cooke-Davies, Terry, Crawford, Lynn, and Richardson, Kurt Anthony. 2009. Exploring the complexity of projects: Implications of complexity theory for project management practice, PMI.

Cicmil, Svetlana, and Marshall, David. "Insights into collaboration at the project level: Complexity, social interaction and procurement mechanisms." Building Research & Information, Vol. 33, No. 6. (2005): 523-535.

Collyer, Simon, and Warren, Clive M. J. "Project management approaches for dynamic environments." International Journal of Project Management, Vol. 27, No. 4. (2009): 355-364.

De Bruijn, Hans, and Herder, Paulien. M. "System and actor perspectives on socsiotechnical systems." IEEE Transactions on Systems, Man and Cybernetics – Part A Systems and Humans, Vol. 39, No. 5. (2009): 981–992.

Dunn, William. N. 2015. Public policy analysis, Routledge.

Freeman, Edward, R. "Divergent stakeholder theory." Academy of Management Review, Vol. 24, No. 2. (1999); 233–236.

Geraldi, Joana. G., and Adlbrecht, Gerald. "On faith, fact, and interaction in projects." Project Management Journal, Vol. 38, No. 1, (2007): 32–43.

Geraldi, Joana, Maylor, Harvey, and Williams, Terry. "Now, let's make it really complex (complicated): A systematic review of the complexities of projects." International Journal of Operations & Production Management, Vol. 31, No. 9. (2011): 966–990.

Gidado, K. I. "Project complexity: The focal point of construction production planning." Construction Management Economics, Vol. 14, No. 3. (1996): 213–225.

Hasson, Felicity, Keeney Sinead, and McKenna Hugh. "Research guidelines for the Delphi survey technique." Journal of Advanced Nursing, Vol. 32. (2000): 1008–1015.

He, Qinghua, Luo, Lan, Hu, Yi, and Chan, Albert P. C. "Measuring the complexity of mega construction projects in China – A fuzzy analytic network process analysis." International Journal of Project Management, Vol. 33, No. 3. (2015): 549–563.

Hekala, Walter. "Why donors should care more about project management." Accessed October 21, 2022. https://www.devex.com/news/why-donors-should-care-more-about-project-management-77595

Hillson, David, and Simon, Peter. 2007. Practical Project Risk Management: The ATOM Methodology, Berrett-Koehler Publishers.

Hobday, Mike. "Product complexity, innovation and industrial organisation." Research Policy, Vol 26. (1998): 689-710.

Ika, Lavagnon, Diallo, Amadou, and Thuillier, Denis. Critical success factors for World Bank projects: an empirical investigation." International Journal of Project Management, Vol. 30, No. 1. (2012): 105–116.

Ika, Lavagnon, and Hodgson, David. "Learning from international development projects: Blending Critical Project Studies and Critical Development Studies." International Journal of Project Management, Vol. 32, No. 7. (2014): 1182–1196.

Ives, Mark. "Identifying the Contextual Elements of Project Management within Organizations and their Impact on Project Success." Project Management Journal, Vol. 36, No. 1. (2005): 37-50.

Jaafari, Ali. "Project management in the age of complexity and change." Project Management Journal, Vol. 34, No. 4. (2003): 47–57.

Jones, Robert E., and Deckro, Richard F. "The social psychology of Project management conflict." European Journal of Operational Research, Vol. 64. (1993): 216-228.

Kiridena, S., Sense, A. (1999). Profiling Project Complexity: Insights from Complexity Science and Project Management Literature. Project Management Journal, 47(6), 56–74.

Lu, Y., Luo, L, Wang, H., Le, Y., Shi, Q. (2015). Measurement model of project complexity for large-scale projects from task and organisation perspective. International Journal of Project Management, 33(3), pp. 610–622.

Maylor, Harvey, Vidgen, Richard, and Carver, Stephen. "Managerial complexity in project-based operations: A grounded model and its implications for practice." Project Management Journal, Vol. 39, No. 1. (2008): 15-26.

Mitchell, Ronald. K., Agle, Bradley. R., and Wood, Donna. J. "Toward a theory of stakeholder identification and salience: Defining the principle of who and what really counts." Academy of Management Review, Vol. 22, No. 4. (1997): 853–886.

Murry Jr, John. W., and Hammons, James O. "Delphi: A versatile methodology for conducting qualitative research." The Review of Higher Education, Vol. 18, No. 4. (1995): 423–436.

Mykytyn Jr., Peter P., and Green, Gary. I. "Effects of computer experience and task complexity on attitudes of managers." Information Management, Vol. 23, No. 5. (1992): 263-278.

Okoli, Chitu, and Pawlowski, Susanne. "The Delphi method as a research tool: an example, design considerations and applications." Information Management, Vol. 42, No. 1. (2004): 15–29.

Petit, Yvan. "Project portfolios in dynamic environments: organising for uncertainty." International Journal of Project Management, Vol. 30, No. 5. (2012): 539-553.

Pich, Michael T., Loch, Christoph. H., and de Meyer, Arnoud. "On uncertainty, ambiguity, and complexity in project management." Management Science, Vol. 48, No. 8. (2002): 1008–1023.

Remington, Kaye, and Pollack, Julien. 2007. Tools for Complex Projects, Aldershot, UK: Gower Publishing.

Rowe, G., Wright, George. "Expert opinions in forecasting: the role of the Delphi technique". In Principles of forecasting, 125–144. (Springer, 2001).

Saynisch, Manfred. "Beyond frontiers of traditional project management: An approach to evolutionary, self-organisational principles and the complexity theory—results of the research program." Project Management Journal, Vol. 41, No. 2. (2010): 21–37.

Schmidt, Roy C. "Managing Delphi surveys using nonparametric statistical techniques." Decision Science, Vol. 28, No. 3. (1997): 763–774.

Senescu, Reid, Aranda-Mena, Guillermo, and Haymaker, John. "Relationships between Project Complexity." Journal of Management Engineering, Vol. 29, No. 2. (2013): 183-197.

Shenhar, Aaron. J., and Dvir, Dov. "Toward a Typological Theory of Project Management." Research Policy,Vol. 25. (1996): 607–32.

Sommer, Svenja. C., and Loch, Christoph. H. "Selectionism and learning in projects with complexity and unforeseeable uncertainty." Management Science, Vol. 50, No. 10. (2004): 1334–1347.

Strauss, Harlan. J., and Zeigler, Harmon L. "The Delphi technique and its uses in social science research." Journal of Creative Behaviour, Vol. 9, No. 4. (1975): 253–259.

Tatikonda, Mohan. V., and Rosenthal, S. R. "Technology novelty, project complexity, and product development project execution success: a deeper look at task uncertainty in product innovation." IEEE Transactions on Engineering Management, Vol. 47. (2000): 74-87.

Vidal, Ludovic-Alexandre, and Marle, Franck. "Understanding project complexity: implications on project management." Kybernetes, Vol. 37, No. 8. (2008): 1094–1110.

Whitty, Jonathan, and Maylor, Harvey. "And then came complex project management (revised)." International Journal of Project Management, Vol. 27, No. 3. (2009): 304–310.

Williams, Terry. "The need for new paradigms for complex projects." International Journal of Project Management, Vol. 17, No. 5. (1999): 269–273.

Williams, Terry. 2003. Modelling Complex Projects. UK: John Wiley & Sons, Ltd.

Williamson, Oliver E., Winter, Sidney G. 1993. The nature of the firm: origins, evolution, and development. UK: Oxford University Press.

Winter, Mark, Smith, Charles, Morris, Peter, and Cicmil, Svetlana. "Directions for future research in project management: The main findings of a UK government-funded research network." International Journal of Project Management, Vol. 24, No. 8. (2006): 638–649.

Xia, Weidong, and Lee, Gwanhoo. "Grasping the complexity of IS development projects." Communications of the ACM, Vol. 47, No. 5. (2004): 68-74.

Iztok Palčič is employed at the University of Maribor, Faculty of Mechanical Engineering, Laboratory for Production and Operations Management as full professor. His areas of expertise are Production Management, Project Management, Innovation, and Technology Management. He is the author of over 40 scientific papers and six scientific monographs. Prof. Palčič is a visiting researcher and Professor at Graz University of Technology in Austria and the Faculty of Technical Sciences Novi Sad in Serbia. He has been a visiting researcher at the Vienna University of Technology and Leeds University Business School. He has experiences in different national and international R&D

projects as a Project Manager or team member: 6. FP, Leonardo, PHARE, Tempus, Erasmus, Slovenian Research Agency projects, CEEPUS, etc. He is a member of EurOMA.

Slađana Rajinac finished her PhD at the Faculty of Technical Sciences, University of Novi Sad. She has been engaged in several business and academic projects for several years, and has published more than 20 scientific and professional papers.

VI

DATA ANALYSIS, REPORTING AND DATA REPRESENTATION IN PROJECT MANAGEMENT

JOSIP MESARIĆ AND DARIO ŠEBALJ

6.1 Digital Transformation in Project Management

Any project needs to collect and analyse numerous external and internal organisational data. When starting a project, or its initialisation and further processes and activities, the data will multiply exponentially and become complex due to different types, formats and relationships. They will be concretised in each phase and process (process groups) in structured and unstructured data, metadata and formal or informal documents and knowledge bases for each process group. Extending the project's complexity (or portfolio), a formal or informal project information system will be developed as an indispensable support mechanism for more efficient decision-making and control.

The contextual framework of the organisational system in which the project is performed determines the data sets that need to be collected and processed from functionally organised information systems such as ERP, SCM, CRM, e-commerce and related external systems. These data, together with the data preceding the project and the data generated in the project, will be interconnected, thus forming multidimensional data structures. Project management tools can use these data directly or indirectly through the various business intelligence system creating new data that are used in the management of project activities and stored in common multidimensional data repositories, which can be used in further project life cycle phases.

The amount, types, dynamics, formats and methods of data collection, processing, representation, distribution and storage depend on the general and specific characteristics of the project to which they are related, such as:

- nature of the project and project organisation,
- size (scope) of the project,
- number of stakeholders,
- duration,
- dynamics and number of changes recorded in the project,
- size of the project team,
- type and number of resources,
- number and contents of documents that must be created,
- intensity and dynamics of communication and cooperation,
- the intensity of the relationship between the project organisation and the environment,
- applied tools, and
- the organisational structure of the project organisation.

With the project's progression, the amount of data and metadata increases linearly at the beginning and exponentially in the execution process group. In the pre-project and initial phase, the data are usually unstructured (in text documents, web pages, images, and videos), with a small share of data that are part of structured databases. The data are mostly external. The project initiators will systematise or classify such data by areas of interest and form a set of metadata. The analysis of these data aims to define the project's purpose and objectives clearly. In these phases, software solutions in office operations and traditional project management packages are usually sufficient for collecting and manipulating project data. When the amount of data begins to multiply and the speed of their creation, heterogeneity of sources, formats and the number of connections and relationships between data increase, the need for more complex analytical procedures arises, and more complex processes for data manipulation are required. Unstructured data will be supplemented with metadata that, together with already structured data, can be analysed to identify patterns of behaviour, trends and other more complex forms of relationships.

The research problem of this chapter is how to integrate an enormous amount of data related to various aspects of projects and thus represent different project instances. Most of these data are digitalised and could serve for analytics, representation, execution, decision-making, communication, collaboration and tracking project activities and results. The question is whether modern project management software solutions lead to integrations and transformation of the project into its "digital twin", ensuring reuse, making each new project more effective, easier to learn, execute and add new instances for different purposes and different users including post-project maintenance and upgrading results through the entire project life cycle.

This chapter aims to present the current methods of digital transformation of projects in the collection, analysis and representation of data in modern PM tools, as well as find out trends in the creation of a digital twin—integrated software solutions that will be used in the entire life cycle of the project. Research is based on desktop research and consists of analysing theoretical and practical research on project management, including analysing several project management tools orientated to agile project management.

6.2 Desk Research Results

6.2.1 Project data sources, transformation and destination

Project data, data origin, transformations and destinations, analysis and representation, monitoring and updating are the subjects of all detailed manuals on project management. In the following, an overview of data sources and categories of data relevant to the execution and management of projects will be given.

Professional project management associations place project management problems in the context of:

- business organisations—strategies, organisations, structures;
- project environment—stakeholders of different categories;
- project cycle—typical project phases and associated processes and activities;
- key areas of management (PMI 2017): requirements management of stakeholders, scope management, creating an action plan and allocating resources and time, costs, quality, communication, risks, procurement and project integration).

Figure 6.1 lists project management data sources.

Project data that must be collected depends on the project stakeholders' requests and applications. Figure 6.2 provides an overview of key data requested by project stakeholders.

Most of the data in the project is collected and used in creating and updating the project plan as a key document that serves as the basis for project management. Figure 6.3 illustrates project planning as an area of knowledge with data sources and outputs (documents).

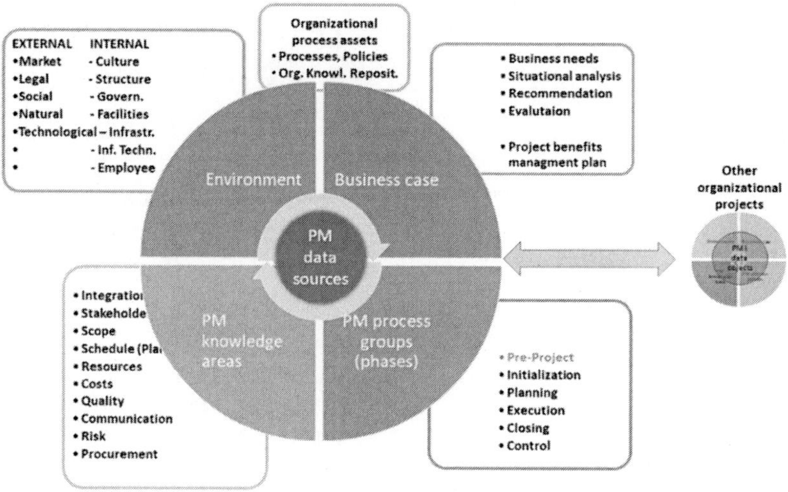

Figure 6.1 *Sources of project management data*

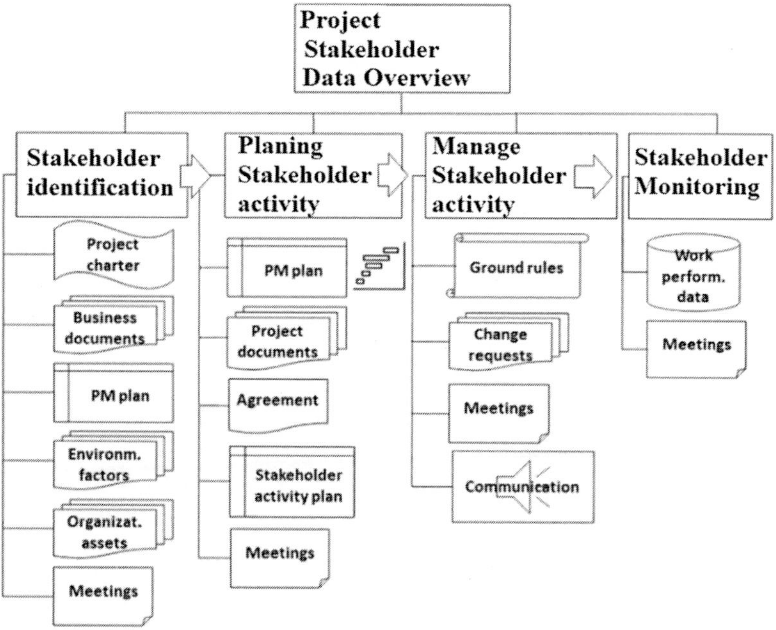

Figure 6.2 *Project stakeholder data overview*

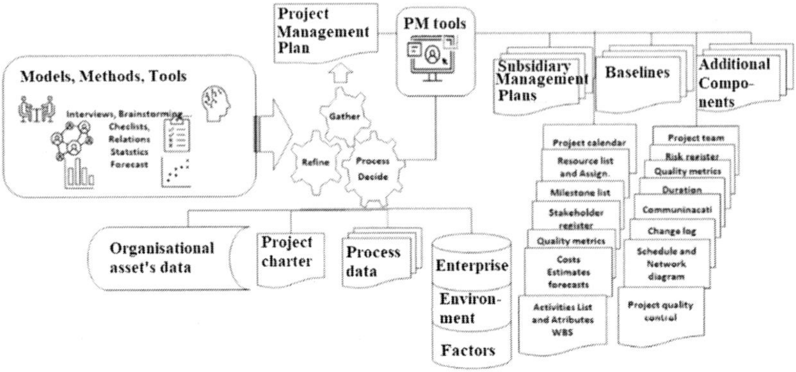

Figure 6.3 *Project planning data, techniques and information content*

6.2.2 Project data and data analysis

The scale of importance of data analysis and manipulation can be seen when all relevant things (features) of the project are identified and when their attributes and relationships are determined, which multiply when the spatial and temporal dimensions of the project are included.

According to PM2 (European Commission 2016), typical project analyses include, but are not limited to:

- The PESTEL Analysis is used "to understand how the environment might impact a project or an objective. PESTEL stands for Political, Economic, Social, Technological, Environmental and Legal factors."
- The Make or Buy analysis "helps the organisation make an informed decision about what to outsource and what not to outsource."
- The Stakeholder Interest/Influence Matrix (SIIM) is used "to facilitate and document the analysis of the interest and influence of each stakeholder in the project."
- The Risk Likelihood/Impact Matrix is used "in the qualitative assessment of risks after the project risks have been identified."
- The Work Breakdown Structure (WBS) is "a hierarchical division of the project into smaller work components that can be used to assign work or to estimate effort and cost."
- The Deliverables Breakdown Structure (DBS) can be used "to identify and document the deliverables of a project (both project deliverables and project management deliverables) and their interdependencies."

- The Effort and Cost Estimates technique derives from the WBS and estimates working tasks by effort and cost.
- The Three-Point Estimate is part of the PERT and calculates the expected duration/cost. The standard deviation of a project's duration or cost is calculated based on three data points: an optimistic estimate of duration or cost, a most likely estimate and a pessimistic estimate.
- Project Scheduling, which "aims to identify dependencies between tasks, to assign resources for each task, to identify task start and end dates, and to work out the overall project duration."
- Resource Levelling is a technique used to analyse the unbalanced use of project resources and resolve resource allocation conflicts.
- The Gantt Chart is a technique used to "represent a project's schedule, phases, and activities in a single visual (generally a type of horizontal bar chart). It focuses on project sequence, duration, dependencies and status."
- The Critical Path Method (CPM) is a modelling technique that uses a mathematically based algorithm to calculate the total duration of a project.
- Different financial analysis methods like NPV, IRR, Earned Value Management (EVM) and other analysis technique are used to monitor and control the performance of projects.
- Capturing Lessons Learned is a "way of identifying development/ improvement areas within a project for the purpose of helping similar projects avoid certain pitfalls in the future."

Advances in IT solutions (processing power, new possibilities of relational databases) from the beginning of this century have led to the possibility of creating multidimensional analytical databases from transaction databases within the data warehousing model and, more recently, graph databases. "Analytics marries large data sets, statistical techniques and predictive modelling. It could be thought of as the practice of mining institutional data to produce 'actionable intelligence.'" (Campbell et al. 2007).

Modern project management tools include a large amount of data about project entities and their relationships (participants, resources, products, services, goals, milestones, including their financial values, communications, controls, activities and time frame). As a result, they are increasingly faced with conducting various analytics, either past and present data or predictions of the future. The key issues of data analytics in projects and project portfolios are the availability of data (quantitative and qualitative, machine and artificial), the speed with which they can be processed, especially in distributed project resources and the simplicity and information value of analyses. The latter request addresses various forms of visualisation and visual communication in which real-time feedback on a request, inquiry or problem occurs, representing various dashboards.

Simple analysis and complex data analytics are performed "because it leads to data-driven decision-making that yields superior project outcomes, and because it requires projects to operate outside the narrow confines of traditional project management practice with its focus on the triple constraints, enabling them to be an integral part of the business." (Frame et al. 2019, 21).

Data analytics in the project holder (or executive) organisation begins before deciding to participate. This decision should be based on good data and knowledge and skills to use them. Before project authorisation and initial project activities, the business case must be analysed and validated to ensure the project is feasible. According to PMBOK (2017), the business case is a "documented economic feasibility study used to establish the validity of the benefits of a selected component lacking sufficient definition, and that is used as a basis for the authorisation of further project management activities." Analytical procedures are focused on targeted benefits (tangible and/or value-based), compliance with strategy and short-term goals, time frame for implementation, selection of metrics for realised benefits and assumptions for successful implementation.

Defining purpose and goals, either strategic, tactical or operational, should provide an answer to the question of why the project is launched. The analysis of preliminary benefits begins for the organisation and other stakeholders, as well as the limitations and parameters of the business organisation and the limitations and parameters imposed by the environment (Spalek 2019, 51).

Data for these analyses are collected from past events, current situations and estimates of project outcomes on the anticipated future of stakeholders affected by the project. This could require a relatively broad set of data and metadata in a particular business case, especially if a goal is to be explained in more detail. This opens the need to filter or remove erroneous data or data that have no value for analysis and add some metadata. Speaking of data analytics, we approach the interpretations of the preliminary analysis, and in terms of project management, we concretise the recommendations for the initialisation of the project.

Data sources for these analyses are data from the organisational environment and data on organisational skills. Dominant methods and tools are focused on estimates and forecasts. From these data, including the business environment analysis, the project charter, the primary document for project authorisation, will be formed (Figure 6.4).

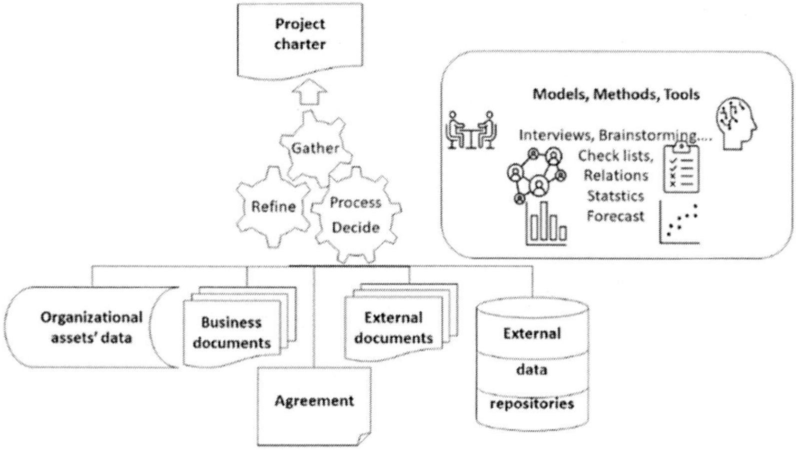

Figure 6.4 *Project analyses and data for project charter design*

Environmental Factors Analysis

The greater the number of the organisation's relationships with the environment, the more likely the project will have more variables affecting its outcomes. The response to these variables, which may positively or negatively impact the project, will depend primarily on the set of different capabilities that, in PM terms, are called organisational process assets. When the project takes place in an organisation that runs an occasional project within its core business or if it is a multi-project organisation, it is useful to consider the key factors coming from the internal organisational environment. This may include organisational culture, structure and management, geographical distribution, infrastructure, information technology, resource availability and employee capabilities.

Data sources for these analyses are formalised and non-formalised organisational documents such as strategy, vision, leadership styles, hierarchical structures, shared values and norms, ICT infrastructure including hardware, software solutions and data, their use and availability, availability of shared resources and suppliers, formal actual competencies and skills of employees. Most of these data can be found in enterprise ERP systems.

Typical external data include market data, social and cultural influences, legal frameworks and assumptions, commercial databases, research status, national and industry standards, financial market data, physical conditions and other external data.

Data sources for this analysis include competition, competitive and alternative products, brands, political climate and ethical norms, legislation and legal certainty, labour market, procurement conditions, business databases, audit reports and structure of key operating costs and risks. Furthermore, it includes data on regulatory bodies and standards, environmental constraints, labour force and characteristics. Also of particular importance are data on exchange rates, interest rates, inflation, customs duties, taxes and non-tax payments, and data on working conditions and the legal protection of employees.

Organisational Project Assets

Organisational process assets used to perform project work are described by data on standard processes and procedures in formalised information systems and subsystems. They contain data on human resources, confidential data on production processes and recipes as well as their software solutions, data from quality control systems, contracts with suppliers and customers, software solutions for management and support of the entire project cycle, control and audit procedures, numerous formalised forms with detailed data contents for input data and reporting data from the process. In the execution of software solutions, a large amount of data on the project plan's structure, implementation methods and approval of changes, time reports and review of activities are predefined. The list of data is not finished, and in different specific conditions, it can include many other data.

Part of the organisational project assets are documents, software and hardware components in the knowledge repositories of past activities and experiences. These repositories contain baseline, procedures and other digitised project documents and logs. They also contain all the financial data on the unit cost of resources, the resources expended, the budget and the time commitment of people and material resources. Furthermore, the repositories contain information on project performance, approved changes, descriptions of all achievements (milestones), data on performed controls, risk registers and methods of risk management, metrics and method of measuring data on processes and products, closing data, stakeholder data and many other data. These data in organisational repositories on similar projects can significantly shorten the preparation time and initialisation processes, provide less uncertainty and errors in execution, and increase the productivity of all participants in the project.

Special circumstances that contribute to creating such repositories arise from multiple data content in organisational systems that project programmes or have portfolios of differentiated projects.

6.2.3 Project documenting and data visualisation

Projects are preceded by and create many different documents. According to PM2, the purposes of documenting the project are to:

- help people think something through: documentation sharpens thinking through the process of having to put vague thoughts and plans into words,
- crystallise planning,
- define the project scope for approval: ensure agreement by all project stakeholders and project team members (so that everybody shares the same expectations on what is to be delivered, what to do, when to do it, etc.),
- provide all stakeholders with a clear picture of the project requirements,
- facilitate communication with internal and external groups,
- provide a baseline for the monitoring and control of a project's progress,
- document important decisions made,
- provide the information required by official audits, and
- support organisational memory and act as a historical reference which can be used to increase the chances of success of future projects (European Commission 2016).

6.2.4. Project data visualisation

Data visualisation generally is a graphical representation of data to facilitate business decision-making. Manole and Grabara (2016) define visualisation as "the process of encoding information in the form of a variety of images that stimulates [the] imagination and creative thinking to find the best solutions to existing problems." The visualisation should be clear, unambiguous, concise and user-orientated. Therefore, it is first necessary to consider the context in which the data are visualised. According to Nussbaumer Knaflic (2015), three main questions need to be answered before visualising data or creating content: Who, what, and how or "To whom are you communicating?", "What do you want your audience to know or do?" and "How can you use data to make your point?" The first step in presenting project deliverables and results is to accurately define the audience to make the communication as successful as possible and achieve the goal of the visualisation. If the visualisation is aimed at different audiences, creating a separate visualisation for each is necessary. It is not the same as presenting the project results to your team members, the management or the client (project sponsor). Each of them needs different information and different levels of detail.

After defining the target audience, it is necessary to determine what they should know or what information should be presented to them. The client will be interested in the realisation of the budget, the progress of the activities and the percentage of completion of certain tasks, project phases and the project itself. On the other hand, the project team members will be interested in information about the utilisation and commitment of resources, the activities to be performed, the project, the baseline and the like.

Only in the third step do the data come into play, i.e., it must be determined what data are needed and whether they are available to achieve the goal of the visualisation. The data should be cleaned and prepared for analysis in this step.

According to MindManager (2020) and Gerdisch (2021), the benefits of visual project management are as follows:

- Effective planning of each project phase in advance
- Improving team speed and saving time by providing managers with insights at a glance
- Making data-driven decisions from a bird's eye view of the project
- Providing a clear perspective on project goals and the steps needed to achieve them
- Help project managers gain clarity on progress and identify potential obstacles that may arise
- Make communication easier and clearer at all levels (stakeholders and team members)
- Help project managers to understand the impact of project changes in real time.

The third category of tools is visual project collaboration tools, which may include modern project management tools such as Asana, Jira, Trello, Microsoft Project, etc. The main focus of this chapter is on the second group of visual project management tools, especially on creating dashboards, which have become increasingly popular recently due to their many benefits. However, to create a high-quality dashboard that provides users (stakeholders, project sponsors...) with insight into key project information, it is necessary to master certain rules of successful data visualisation.

Tools for Visual Project Management

According to Williams (2015), there are three basic categories of information visualisation tools in project management:

- Visual thinking tools that support project management,
- Visual project reporting tools,
- Visual project collaboration tools.

Visual thinking tools that support project management are used before the formal project planning phase, i.e., during the project idea and concept development. These are, for example (Williams 2015):

- mind maps,
- process maps (Flowcharts, EPC, BPMN diagrams…),
- storyboards,
- mockups, wireframes, and prototypes,
- charts.

According to Williams (2015), visual project reporting tools are used when communicating with key stakeholders in a project. The project manager is responsible for summarising data, analysing them and reporting on key indicators of project success. Project sponsors and key stakeholders rely on high-quality project reporting to assess progress and performance, make informed decisions and ensure that scope and deliverables align with business strategy. Most project reporting is still done traditionally through written reports. However, due to increasing demands on time and the complexity of information, project reporting is increasingly shifting to visual techniques. These include:

- dashboards,
- road maps,
- Kanban boards,
- SCRUM boards,
- burn down charts,
- infographics.

The most common way to present project results and other project-related data is through a dashboard. A dashboard is "a visual display of the most important information needed to achieve one or more objectives, consolidated and arranged on a single screen so the information can be monitored at a glance" (Few 2013, 26).

Few (2013) lists six features to be considered when creating a dashboard:

- Update frequency—specifies how often the information on the dashboard should be updated. For example, this can be daily or hourly and in real-time.
- User expertise—the level of user expertise determines how complex the dashboard will be, i.e., how detailed the visualisations on the dashboard will be. Someone who is an expert in their field (e.g., project team members) may be presented with a more complex dashboard with a lot of detail and information. However, for a project sponsor who often lacks project management expertise, a simpler and more readable dashboard needs to be created that does not include unnecessary details and complex visualisations.
- Size of audience—the more customisable a dashboard can be, the more effective it will be. If a dashboard is designed for an individual (such as a project sponsor), it can be designed and customised entirely for that user. On the other hand, if the dashboard is to be presented to a larger group of people, those people may be interested in the same information and have the same purpose (project team members), but they are different and different information is important to each of them.
- Technology platform—three platforms can be distinguished on which the dashboard is located: desktop/laptop, web server/browser or mobile device. Nowadays, dashboards that can be accessed through a web server or browser and mobile devices such as tablets are preferred.
- Screen type—the screen size on which a dashboard is displayed can significantly affect how dashboards are designed and formatted. A smaller screen requires a less complex dashboard that displays only a few key pieces of information. The dashboard can be more complex on larger screens and include more details. However, it can often be a mistake to put too much information on the dashboard (since there is not enough space) that the human eye cannot examine simultaneously.
- Data type—data are mainly divided into quantitative and qualitative data. Dashboards mainly display quantitative data as they show various metrics, movement of some value over time, frequencies, etc. Dashboards that provide insight into information about a project are often a combination of quantitative (budget realisation, number of resources used and their utilisation, percentage of completed tasks/phases/ project, costs of individual phases, material inventory, etc.) and qualitative data (list and schedule of tasks to be executed, top

five resources used the most, list of tasks not executed on time, list of upcoming deadlines, etc.).

As mentioned earlier, data are mainly divided into quantitative and qualitative data. Qualitative data can be further divided into categorical and ordinal data. Categorical (nominal) data are textual data that represent specific names, categories or groups. For example, these can be project team members, project activity names, city names, etc. Ordinal data has a meaningful order (rank), such as the project completion level, the project phases, the level of satisfaction, the level of human resources education, etc.

Quantitative (numerical) data are expressed in numbers, and mathematical operations can be performed on these data. These are, for example, the budget, the cost of each phase of the project, the number of resources working on a task in the project, and the like.

A very important point in creating a dashboard, but also visualisations in general, is how to attract the audience's attention or design visualisations so that the audience focuses on some of the important parts of visualisation. Our brain has three basic types of memory: iconic memory, short-term memory (working memory), and long-term memory. According to Nussbaumer Knaflic (2015) and Few (2013), iconic memory is super fast, and information stays there for a fraction of a second before being passed on to short-term memory. Iconic memory is very important in data visualisation and is related to preattentive attributes, which will be discussed later.

Short-term or working memory lasts longer (a few seconds to a few hours), but people can store about four pieces of visual information in the short term (Few, 2013). If a line chart is created with ten different coloured lines and the legend is on the side, the user will have difficulty remembering what all ten lines mean at once but must constantly look at the lines and the legend.

Long-term memory is a memory that develops over time and is important for pattern recognition. For example, by using an image in visualisation, we want to encourage the audience to associate that image with something else.

As mentioned earlier, iconic memory is closely related to 'preattentive attributes.' With their help, we direct the audience's attention to a certain part of the visualisation. Some preattentive attributes are (Wexler et al. 2017): colour, size, orientation, length, width, enclosure and shape. Figure 6.6 shows the 12 most common preattentive attributes used in data visualisations.

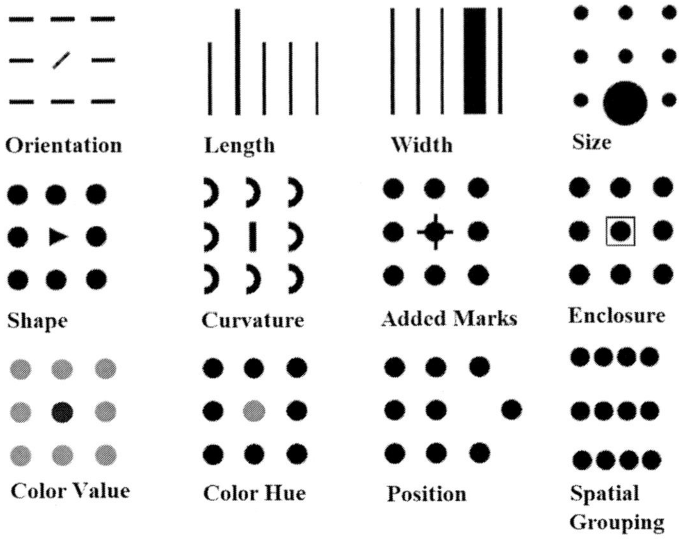

Figure 6.6 *The most commonly used preattentive attributes*
Source: Wexler et al. 2017

Colour can easily highlight detail in the visualisation that the users perceive in a split second (using their iconic memory). For example, in a bar chart showing resource engagement on a project, a different colour can indicate the column with the greatest engagement. The audience will automatically be drawn to that part of the chart.

Size is also a very good attribute to increase attention. A larger font can indicate the part of the text that is more important than the rest. For example, budget realisation is important information in project management. Therefore, the realisation percentage can be displayed at the top of the dashboard in a larger font to draw attention to it.

Preattentive attributes do not necessarily have to be used only in charts. They can also be used in the text.

Choosing the appropriate charts to represent a particular data type is crucial when designing a dashboard. There are also some rules and recommendations here. For example, using a line chart to show the movement of a numerical value over time is common. Table 6.1 provides an overview of the most appropriate charts used in dashboard design and their purpose and adds an example.

In addition to the charts in Table 6.1, various tables are often used in project management. They are not intended to display concise and visual information but to present complete data. Some rules should be followed when designing tables.

Table 6.1 Different *charts used in dashboard design*

Chart type	Example Chart	Purpose of use	Example
Bar chart	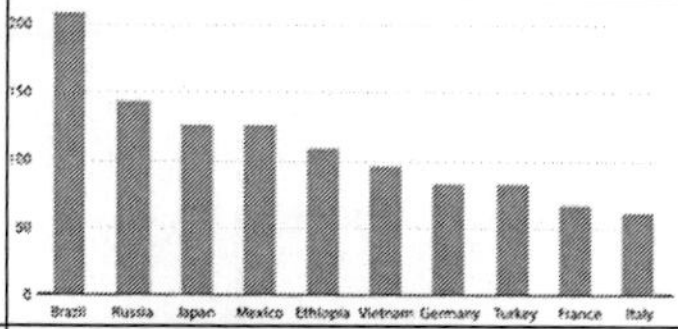	Presentation of quantitative data by specific categories/ groups	To show costs by project phases
Heatmap	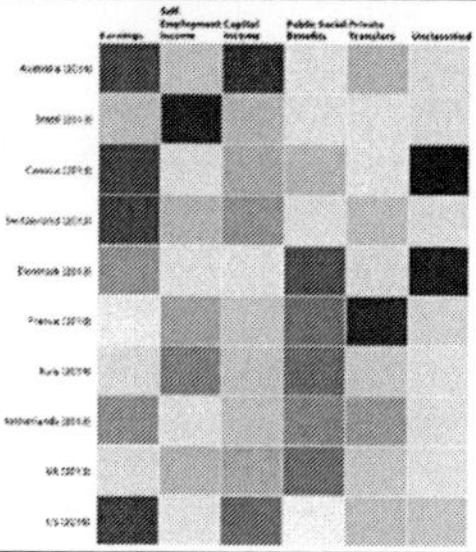	Presentation of quantitative data in the form of a table, the value of which is shown in different shades of colour	To show costs (in shades of colour) by project phases for each month of the year
Bullet chart	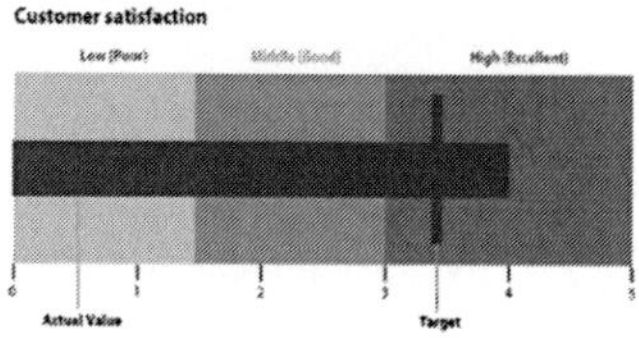	Presentation of the quantitative data value, divided into certain ranges and with the indicated target value	Budget utilisation rate
Line chart	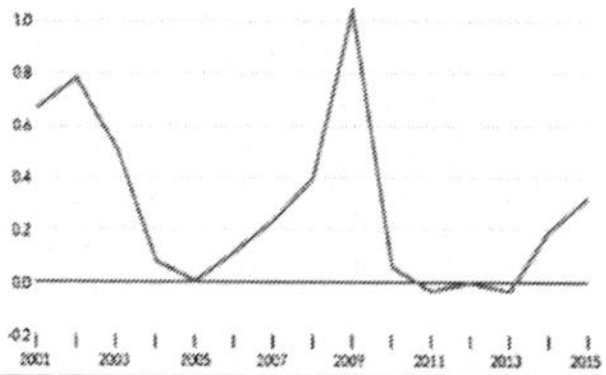	Presentation of quantitative value movement over a period of time	Number of resources engaged during the project duration
Sparkline		Presentation of quantitative value movement over a period of time, without unnecessary details and is	Number of working hours of project team members during a

		usually located at the end of the table	certain period
Gantt chart		Presentation of project tasks schedule	Project tasks schedule
Histogram	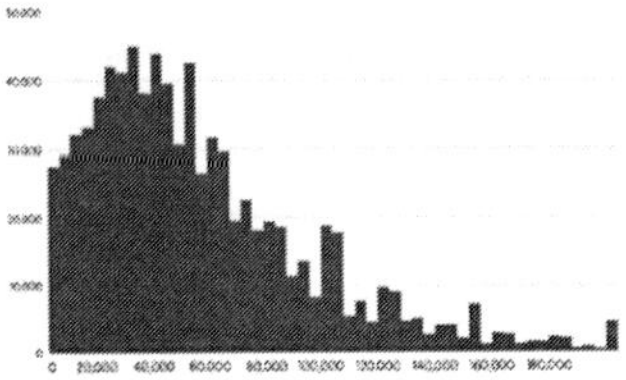	Distribution of frequencies by bins	Distribution of human resources salaries by selected bins (e.g., 0-999)
Scatter-plot	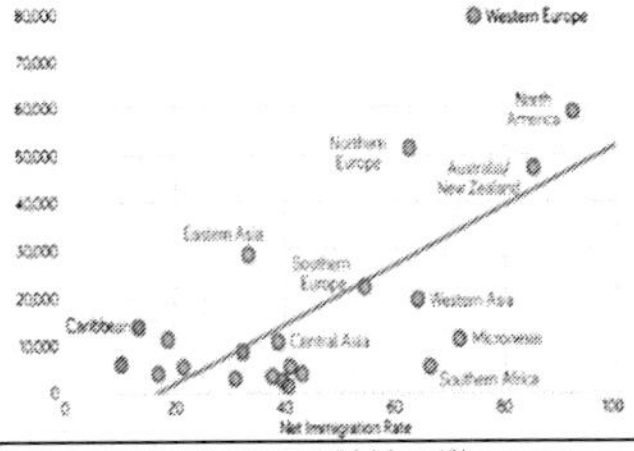	Presentation of correlation between two quantitative variables	Relationship between employee salaries and hours worked on a project
Pie chart	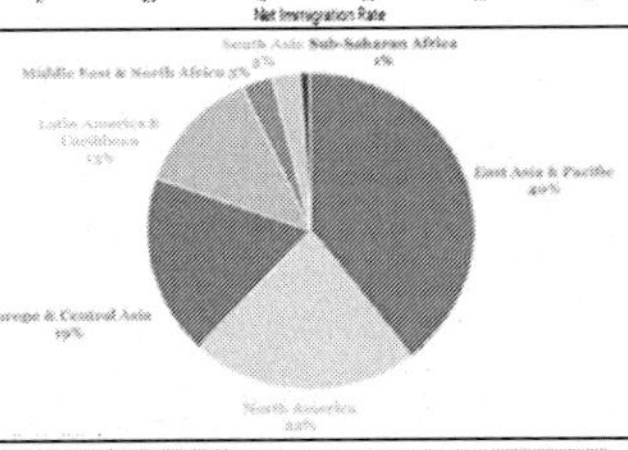	Share of individual quantitative values in the total	To present the share of costs by project phases
Treemap		The proportion of individual quantitative values in the whole, in the form of rectangles	To present costs by individual project phase

Source: Own, according to Schwabish (2021), Nussbaumer Knaflic (2015) and Few (2013)

Schwabish (2020) listed ten of the most important guidelines for well-designed tables:

1. Offset the heads from the body—it is necessary to highlight the column names from the rest (body) of the table. This can be done by using boldface or separating it from the data.
2. Use subtle dividers rather than heavy gridlines—use light borders within the body of the table or remove them altogether. If a row in the table shows the total, the entire row can be shaded, bolded or separated from the rest of the table by a bold line.
3. Right-align numbers and heads—the numbers in the table must be right-aligned. The name of the column containing the numbers is also right-aligned. This makes the numbers easier to read and the right-aligned values easier to compare. In tables, it is necessary to pay attention to the font because, in some fonts, the numbers are not the same size and therefore do not align correctly.
4. Left-align text and heads—text values must be left-aligned, as well as the headings of such columns.
5. Select the appropriate level of precision—the number of decimal places is something to pay attention to. Too many decimal places (e.g. 4 or 5) are often unnecessary, and it is difficult to compare such numbers. Often it is enough to display numbers with one or two decimal places.
6. Guide your reader with space between rows and columns—if the spacing between columns in the table is too large, readers will most likely read the table from top to bottom. If the spacing between rows is too large, readers will read the data horizontally, from left to right. Therefore, the spacing between the columns and rows must be strategically determined based on how you want the reader to read the data in the table.
7. Remove unit repetition—it is unnecessary to write the symbols that define some values (e.g., %, $, €) after/before each number in the table. Specifying it in the column name (e.g., budget (in €)) is enough.
8. Highlight outliers—if a table contains a large amount of data, outliers should be highlighted in some way to make them easier for the reader to notice. This can be done by making the text boldface, shading it with colour or even shading the entire cell.
9. Group similar data and increase white space—if there are repeating values in a column, they should be grouped to avoid data redundancy.
10. Add visualisations when appropriate—tables can become much nicer and clearer if small visualisations are added. These can be sparkline charts, heatmaps, icons, etc.

Visualisation tools used to create visualisations and dashboards are becoming increasingly popular. Tableau is one of the best-known software for this purpose (Figure 6.8). According to the 2022 Gartner Magic Quadrant for Analytics and Business Intelligence Platforms (Gartner 2022), Tableau is one of the market leaders in this segment, along with Microsoft and its PowerBI tool.

Tableau works on the principle of pivot tables and is characterised by ease of use and extensive visualisation capabilities. It also allows you to connect to numerous files (e.g. Excel, CSV, various databases, cloud services, etc.) and also includes the Tableau Prep plugin for cleaning and editing data before starting visualisation. The created dashboards can be integrated into existing applications and websites and run through the Tableau Online service.

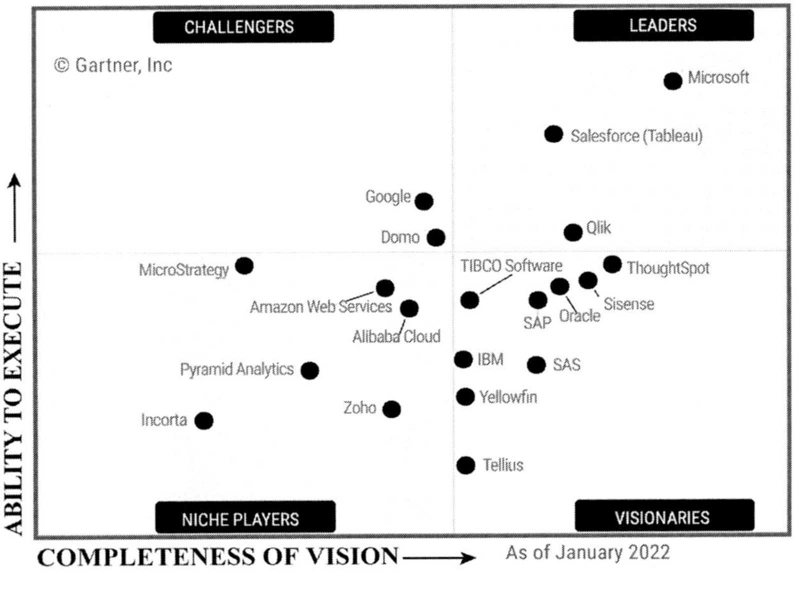

Figure 6.8 *Magic Quadrant for Analytics and Business Intelligence Platforms*
Source: Gartner 2022

6.2.5 Data Visualisation in Project Management information systems

Nowadays, there are many project management software programs. Some are suitable for smaller projects and beginners (e.g. Trello), others for large projects (e.g. MS Project), and still others focus on simplicity (e.g. Wrike). However, they all offer very good solutions for reporting and collaboration.

Here are a few of the best software packages on the market (Dean 2021; Duffy 2022; DeMuro et al. 2022; TechnologyAdvice 2022; Aston n.d.):

- Asana (asana.com)—in addition to the standard features, such as the Gantt chart, Asana stands out for its excellent visualisation capabilities, such as dashboards with real-time project data, various reports in the form of charts, Kanban boards, calendars, timeline. The interface is also visually nice and enables collaboration between project team members.
- Basecamp (basecamp.com)—this tool focuses on collaboration. It offers email integration and the ability to share tasks and messages with people outside the organisation.
- Celoxis (celoxis.com)—offers great reporting capabilities and customisable and dynamic dashboards, and also includes a tool for What-If Analysis tool—an interactive report where users can see how a particular action affects their people, budgets and other resources.
- Jira (atlassian.com/software/jira)—Jira's main features are Kanban and SCRUM boards. However, reporting is still more traditional and not as visually advanced and customisable as Asana or Celoxis.
- LiquidPlanner (liquidplanner.com)—one of the tools suitable for large companies, used by companies such as Bayer, Cisco or Daimler. It is complex and includes a predictive (automatic) scheduling feature that allows LiquidPlanner to determine when tasks should be done and when a project will be completed based on several factors. LiquidPlanner also supports the Kanban board and has extensive reports and dashboards.
- Microsoft Project (microsoft.com/en-us/microsoft-365/project/project-management-software) is one of the oldest and best PM tools on the market and somewhat more traditional tools. Large companies mostly use it, and it features excellent budgeting, resource and task-planning capabilities. Reporting is also very powerful, with pre-built and customisable reports.
- Trello (trello.com)—is based on the Kanban board, has a simple interface and is easy to use. It includes a dashboard but is not as powerful as other tools.
- Wrike (wrike.com) is a user-friendly tool with interactive Gantt charts, simple dashboards and Kanban boards.

The project management software listed above includes pre-built dashboards and reports.

6.3 Integration of Data and Programmes—project Knowledge Bases, Projects and Their Digital Twins

Project management is a set of abilities, knowledge and skills translated into the activities of different participants orientated to the achievements and goals of the project. These skills include integrative knowledge for identifying and recognising problems or opportunities, clearly defining goals and shaping them into documents for initialising and planning necessary, feasible and measurable project activities. They provide intermediate results, using already acquired knowledge and experience, to determine criteria and methods of implementation of control and closure of individual project phases. In addition, project management includes skills for project scope, allocation of activities and resources, cost management (including planning, budgeting and control), quality management and outcomes, and resource management (human, material and financial), including their planning, collection and allocation and control. In addition to the above, project management includes abilities, knowledge and skills for communication management, including its planning, implementation and control, identification and risk management and ways of responding to risks and their implementation and supervision. A special area of project management includes skills to cover and manage the engagement of different project participants and in cases where the project needs complex procurement, implementation, supervision and control of procurement.

The term “knowledge base” in the context of this chapter is used as an organised set of different contents that include documents or files of previous knowledge (versions of PM plans from PM tools, register of lessons learned, WBS and RBS, deliverables, source selection criteria, stakeholder register…) software for creating new knowledge, software for analytics, inference mechanisms supported by artificial intelligence methods, options for collaboration and communication through different channels and ways to share knowledge. An example of a tool that allows the creation of a “knowledge base” and the integration of all other listed functionalities and cooperation with many other applications is Freshworks. In traditional project management, these data are usually in text form, and their analysis is more demanding and time-consuming. In addition, reporting on project results often involves many different reports and tables, and stakeholders want quick, concise and timely information on project progress and results. Various techniques and tools for visualising project information help plan and manage projects. Using data visualisation tools in projects is often called visual project management.

Digitised project data are created in different heterogeneous systems, where the backbone for integration is some of the project management programmes, either conventional ones focused on large projects or those from the agile management domain focused on relatively small projects from different domains (increasingly from the IT domain projects). Do such programmes represent reality in a way that they can be categorised as digital twins?

The digital twin consortium (2020) defines a digital twin as "a virtual representation of real-world entities and processes, synchronised at a specified frequency and fidelity." Virtual representation is a set of correlated digital models and supporting data (e.g. metadata, master data, reference data, etc.), which provide cohesive information about their subject matter.

Subsystems in integrated digital twin systems include (Olcott & Mullen 2021):

- Digital models (e.g., legacy business systems, engineering models, purpose-built knowledge graphs, other databases, IoT data feeds and data historians, satellite imagery, point clouds, video, etc.).
- One or more observational and interventional synchronisation mechanisms (that keep the digital models in sync with the real world).
- A digital thread implementation which weaves digital models together along different dimensions to achieve a holistic view.
- Subsystems for visualisation, analysis, automation, data integration, security and other functionality.

The described programmes that support project management in an agile approach and complex programmes for project management have all the properties of project twins up to a certain level. At the same time, the development of synchronisation mechanisms and the frequency of refreshing digital data and their precision is expected in the future. Functional integration will be carried out on new scalable software solutions and platforms that will provide interfaces for different types of requests in terms of processes and data in the formats of previously used applications and their use in such a way as to connect with current software solutions (interoperability) that describe the existing project. These data will necessarily be distributed, and it is to be expected that access to them will be provided through Internet protocols. The construction of such systems will be challenging to meet all foreseeable user requirements and will likely be focused on integrating project solutions and data from specific project domains.

6.4 Conclusions

Project management encompasses a wide range of activities, the result of which is a large amount of data collected or created through various project process groups, even before the actual authorisation and launch of the project. These are, for example, the data required for the economic feasibility carried out before the decision on the project implementation. They also include data about the project's potential costs and benefits for different stakeholders.

Visualisation tools are very useful for easier reporting in the phase of initialisation, implementation and closing of the project and post-project activities. Besides the Gant and related charts about resources and activities, including their simulation, a dashboard is the most common way to present the project, project results, and other data types. The advantage of this way of presenting information is, in addition to the visual impression, the speed of noticing important information, the possibility of adapting the dashboard to the appropriate type of user, and the dynamism and interactivity of such displays. This type of presentation of project data and information is still relatively new and not so accepted by project managers, but surely, with the increase of data and the complexity of their analysis, the need for such good visualisation will grow.

An enormous amount of data that appears in the project and is relevant for the project's entire life cycle are digitised today. PM tools ensure the use and manipulation of a large amount of data and often provide the basis for setting a project plan for similar projects. However, each project is associated with a large amount of data collected and processed in other applications, creating different data formats that are not mutually exchangeable. All these data provide insight into different project instances. The project in execution and exploitation must also ensure the collection and recording of new data, whether intermittent or continuous (e.g., IoT technology).

Although in modern digital transformation, the concept of digital twins is mentioned primarily in the context of products or processes life cycle development, both are an integral part of project management that is well formulated in complex applications, regardless of whether they use the so-called "classic" programming tools for complex projects with a broad systemic approach or tools with a focus on effective achievement with an agile approach.

Modern software tools of project management in the current stage of development tend to integrate a large amount of data for different purposes. All of the above leads to an objective requirement for integrations at different levels and creating digital twins for the project. Digital twins are software solutions that should ensure this integrative role in collecting and exploiting almost all project data. Mayr (2021) states, "Most of today's digital twin solutions are siloed applications with a minimal scope regarding the life cycle or value chain. We are just beginning a robust growing technology ecosystem that will transform businesses worldwide by rapidly increasing their process efficiency and automation".

Although increasingly complex, transformational technologies that will strongly connect the virtual representation and reality of physical entities and processes of different kinds are becoming increasingly available. According to Civil+Structural Engineer Media (2021),

> the cost of creating digital twins has been dropping, and they are expected to become a more commonly used project planning and management tool. The benefits of digital twins, including faster approval cycles, lower and more predictable construction costs, and greater client satisfaction, can greatly improve project economics. We see Digital Twins moving forwards as a fusion of real-time, people-focused data sets and traditional building and process-based BIM systems.

References

European Commission. 2016. The PM² Project Management Methodology Guide—Open Edition. Luxembourg: Publications Office of the European Union.

Gerdisch, Evan. 2021. "The Ultimate Guide to Visual Project Management". Accessed December 4, 2022. https://clickup.com/blog/visual-project-management/.

Nussbaumer Knaflic, Cole. 2015. *Storytelling with data: A data visualisation guide for business professionals*. New Jersey: Wiley.

Few, Stephen. 2013. *Information Dashboard Design: Displaying data for at-a-glance monitoring*. El Dorado Hills: Analytics Press.

Wexler, Steve, Shaffer, Jeffrey and Cotgreave, Andy. 2017. *The Big Book of Dashboards: Visualising Your Data Using Real-World Business Scenarios*. New Jersey: Wiley.

Schwabish, Jonathan. 2020. "Ten Guidelines for Better Tables". *Journal of Benefit-Cost Analysis*, No. 2: 151-178.

Schwabish, Jonathan. 2021. Better Data Visualisations: A Guide for Scholars, Researchers, and Wonks. New York: Columbia University Press.

TechnologyAdvice. 2022. "TechnologyAdvice Project Management Software Buyer's Guide: Top Project Management Software Recommendations". Accessed November 27, 2022. https://technologyadvice.com/project-management/#compare-the-best-project-management-software-2021.

DeMuro, Jonas P., Turner, Brian and Ballard, Barclay. 2022. "Best project management software of 2022". Accessed November 27, 2022. https://www.techradar.com/best/best-project-management-software.

Duffy, Jill. 2022. "The Best Project Management Software for 2022". Accessed November 27, 2022. https://www.pcmag.com/picks/the-best-project-management-software.

Aston, Ben. n.d. "Compare The 15 Best Project Management Software Of 2022". Accessed November 27, 2022. https://thedigitalprojectmanager.com/tools/best-project-management-software/.

Campbell, John, DeBlois, Peter and Oblinger, Diana. 2007. "Academic Analytics: A New Tool for a New Era". Accessed February 2, 2023. https://er.educause.edu/articles/2007/7/academic-analytics-a-new-tool-for-a-new-era

Gartner. 2022. Magic Quadrant for Analytics and Business Intelligence Platforms.

Mayr, Maximilian. 2021. "An Introduction to the Next Generation of Digital Twins". Accessed January 27, 2023. https://www.digitaltwinconsortium.org/2021/11/an-introduction-to-the-next-generation-of-digital-twins.

Digital twin consortium. 2020. "Digital Twin Consortium Defines Digital Twin". Accessed January 27, 2023. https://www.digitaltwinconsortium.org/2020/12/digital-twin-consortium-defines-digital-twin.

Olcott, Sean and Mullen, Casey. 2021. "Transforming Businesses using Digital Twin", Accessed January 27, 2023. https://www.digitaltwinconsortium.org/2021/01/transforming-businesses-using-digital-twin-

Civil+structural Engineer media. 2021. "Digital Twins for Project Planning and Management: Key Considerations". Accessed January 27, 2023. https://csengineermag.com/digital-twins-for-project-planning-and-management-key-considerations/.

PMI. 2017. *A Guide to the Project Management Body of Knowledge (PMBOK).* Pennsylvania: Project Management Institute.

Frame, Davidson J. and Chen, Yanping. 2019. "Why Data Analytics in Project Management". In *Data Analytics in Project Management*, edited by Spalek, Seweryn, 7-22. London: CRC Press.
Spalek, Seweryn. 2019. "Analytical Challenges of a Modern PMO". In *Data Analytics in Project Management*, edited by Spalek, Seweryn, 43-62. London: CRC Press.
Williams, Paul R. 2015. Visual project management. Paper presented at PMI Global Congress 2015, EMEA, London, England. Newtown Square: Project Management Institute.
MindManager. 2020. The Ultimate Guide to Visual Project Planning. Corel Corporation.
Manole, Alexandru Lucian and Grabara, Iwona. 2016. "Methodologies and visualisation tools of effective project management". *Polish Journal of Management Studies*, No. 2: 137-149.

Josip Mesarić worked as a full professor at the University of Osijek, Faculty of Economics in Osijek, where he taught, among others, project management, business process management, information system design and information resource management. As a vice dean for science he initialised and participated in creating new study programmes and participated in different types of projects. He is (co)author of five books on information technology, information systems and supply chain. He published over 80 scientific and professional papers.

Dario Šebalj defended his doctoral dissertation entitled: "Simulation model of the natural gas supply chain in the Republic of Croatia in the function of cost optimisation". Since July 2022, he has worked as an assistant professor at the Department of Quantitative Methods and Informatics at the Faculty of Economics in Osijek (Croatia). From 2020 to now, he has been involved in the publishing activities of the faculty as an executive editor of the journal Ekonomski vjesnik. He has published 11 papers in scientific journals and 15 papers in proceedings of international scientific conferences. He was involved as a researcher in a scientific project of the Croatian Science Foundation and in two Erasmus+ projects. He is a member of the Project Management Institute and the International Institute of Business Analysis.

VII

OPEN INNOVATION DEVELOPMENT PROJECTS: MEDICINE VENTILATOR SHORTAGES

ARMAND FAGANEL AND BOJAN MEVLJA

7.1 SARS-CoV-2 and Medical Ventilator Emergencies

When coronavirus from SARS-CoV-2 was reported in China in 2019, people could not imagine its consequences and impact on the global economy and health. A growing number of countries introduced the quarantine regime following this global pandemic, and many declared states of emergency while the cases constantly increased. Governments implemented quarantines and social distancing measures. Many companies had to cease or close down operations (Vermicelli et al. 2021, 183).

The COVID-19 pandemic (the pandemic) represents the worst social, health and industrial crisis in humanity since 1945. Juxtaposed to another pandemic—Spanish flu—the most endangered group was different, as about two-thirds of the deaths were young adults between 18 and 50. Whereas with the new pandemic, older people were most at risk (Jallow et al. 2020).

The pandemic has caused a public health and economic crisis of unseen proportions. Scientists and innovators made a fundamental contribution to solving this crisis with their efforts to help the acute situation in many ways (Vermicelli et al. 2021, 183).

The pandemic severely tested public health systems around the world. It will be challenging to recover from COVID-19. Innovation should play a crucial role in regaining economic stability too. This article discusses innovation and project management during recovery through case studies and lessons learned, as they strongly influenced innovation management (Chesbrough 2020, 410). The pandemic generated large and diverse changes in the development of technologies throughout the sectors, converting the functioning of the economy and society (Liu et al. 2022, 1).

Technology and societal pressures propel innovating potential, and distinct circumstances cause ultimate economic and societal forces. As both factors were present during the pandemic, several innovations were developed worldwide, some of which have the potential to influence society long-term (Zimmerling & Chen 2021).

On the other hand, the pandemic can have a ripple effect on other sectors like infrastructure and policymakers, so it is necessary to understand how it affected them (Jallow et al. 2020). The pandemic has stimulated an increase in open innovation initiatives to provide policy decision-makers with knowledge and tools (Elia et al. 2022, 419).

Because the pandemic is a major challenge of global proportions, joint stakeholders' efforts are needed to allow scientific progress and technology development to be able to accomplish similar open innovation outlooks; different creative approaches were seen to leverage common knowledge origins which surpass sources usually accessible to one company (Bertello et al. 2022, 178).

Numerous initiatives have been seen to promote networking occasions, to increase interaction among various actors (those taking part within the health services, manufacturing, decision making, universities, individuals), advancing radical resolutions and shared frameworks (rapid development and production of individual safeguarding appliances and medical equipment, as well as tests, therapies and innovative technology) to assist medically (Vermicelli et al. 2021, Liu et al. 2022).

Such progressive ventures occur outside corporate limits through cooperation and open innovation (Liu et al. 2022, 1). These innovative activities and collaborations are carried out as project activities, which take place as one-time processes, have a defined beginning and end, and precisely defined goals, objectives and budget.

7.2 Open Innovation Projects

In the 1980s, the raise of competitiveness emphasised the capability of manufacturing companies to upgrade the level of quality, decrease costs, shorten market introduction time for new products and oversee the growing products' intricacies (Beaume et al. 2009, 167).

Platform approaches and projectification were the two most important transformation shifts for manufacturing companies in the 1990s and early 2000s. Maylor et al. (2006, 663) determined organisational projectification "as a change in organisational and governance structure to increase the primacy of the processes of projects within a central organisation and its supply networks". For these companies, innovation management is no longer about introducing radical and completely new products but applying innovative features within a range of new platforms and products. The interaction between advancing products' innovative characteristics and the consistent flow of evolutionary projects stemming from current competencies implies that this interplay should be managed (Beaume et al. 2009, 166).

Mass-manufactured products resulted from the predominant industrial concept until the 21st century, whereas contemporary businesses prefer a conversion to project production. It is true not only for businesses producing specialised equipment for new investments—but this change might also be observed in organisations that traditionally relied on mass production, so today, businesses must employ project-based and continuous processes simultaneously (Kušar et al. 2008, 588). The automotive industry is traditionally a typical shop floor production process. But projects are the most widely used tool for innovation, development of new products, producing and delivery of services. Such evolution, earlier defined as projectification, also leads to meaningful organisational transformation. As Wagner (2021, 127) explains: "Organisational structures, processes and above all mindset and culture adapt to the requirements of project work."

The project management introduction in an organisation is challenging because it demands adjustments in incorporating and aligning the company's operational units to the organisation's goals. Project-friendly conditions must be built inside an organisation by prioritising project-based goals over operational ones (Kušar et al. 2008, 605).

The project-based perspective is certainly a quite widely used approach to foster innovation. Risk analysis and risk management inside projects dealing with innovations are very challenging for project management, as innovative projects involve an elevated level of uncertainty. The risk management variables in innovation projects are conditional on the innovation's life cycle stage, which requires adopting different methods. Kozlov et al. (2021) argue that the parameters of innovative projects might be classified into target and controlled parameters. The most important risks in an innovative project's development and enactment stage embrace the possibility that the project idea might not be realisable along with timeliness, budget shortages and the non-achievement of the objectives of the innovation (Batkovskiy et al. 2015, 243).

The pandemic's repercussions on individuals could be seen from different angles in social development, public health and commercial sustainability sectors. Various challenges of the pandemic might be responded to with multiple mechanisms, and innovation is crucial. Innovations and innovation culture are key factors in the success of companies. Many ways to innovate are described in the literature. The ones that relate to process or product innovations are called technological innovations. Innovation might also tackle novel organisational methods, improved business models, different markets or advanced processes. Social innovation is gaining huge importance, which could be described as processing dynamic response patterns to profound social requirements. Existing norms, institutionalised values and power structures must be broken to succeed. An open-sharing approach and consolidating strengths are indispensable in the struggle to beat the pandemic (Vermicelli et al. 2021, 183).

Social evaluation impact might also be found in businesses. Management is applying strategic learning to examine social environment changes in their organisations, improve strategies and simulate results to understand how they might affect their competition, buyers, and organisation (Becker 2001, 312).

Oeij et al. (2019) argue that social innovation develops through an action that moves away from the usual stream and entails a comprehensible, imaginative and significant conversion. Plans for social change are in the background because processes are in the foreground. Barriers to its acceptance are primarily unwillingness to adapt to new circumstances, resistance to change, prioritising production optimisation and worries about the operational models' efficiency. Alterations are taking place, however, because these obstacles are beginning to collapse. A small group often recognises the urgency to change and successfully forces a paradigm shift (Almeida 2020b, 64-65).

The whole development and carrying out resolution cycle to introduce a novel product in the company must be understood as project management. To introduce an innovative product, the project's implementation must consist of all or most phases of the project lifecycle (Papelniuk 2017).

7.3 Open Innovation Projects

At the heart of an open innovation project and model is an important process of creating a range of new, promising ideas to puzzle out a research question or utilise an occasion. The other important process is selecting the idea which has been recognised as the one that is well worth developing further and fund. Both processes are growing in complexity daily, overtaking the mechanisms depicting the current knowledge situation. The Open Innovation paradigm brought together some operations to respond to the pandemic. The other important process is selecting the idea that has been recognised as well worth developing further and funding. Both processes are growing in complexity daily, overtaking the mechanisms depicting the current knowledge situation. The magnitude, nature and intricacy of the collaborations and partnerships have solely lessened the effects of the health emergency during the pandemic (Robbins et al. 2021, 2).

Innovating activities never stop and require a willingness to adapt when an opportunity for change is recognised as a way to operate more efficiently in the capital and product markets. Chances to differentiate a company's products from those offered by their competition, to alter their goods to particular buyers' needs, and to reach the competition 'red line' with a favourable level of costs are being given to every organisation, no matter how big it is (Gawlik & Kiełbus 2010, 176).

Innovating in industries is evolving and changing to be more open, which requires adaptations in companies' innovation management. Knowledge sources from outside companies are gaining importance, and access to the market through external channels is also more promising. These changes intensify the judgement of the technology project's first phases; they are frequently associated with compelling market and technology uncertainties. The open innovation model takes for granted that companies can and have the will to employ as many external as internal ideas and all the available routes to advance their technology. Open innovation further presumes that ideas from inside could be brought to market along independent channels, aside from the company's usual business units, to create added value (Chesbrough 2004, 23).

According to Gassmann and Enkel (2004), three distinct open innovation processes exist. The outside-in process bolsters the company's knowledge base by integrating outside resources such as universities, industries, buyers and suppliers. The inside-out process allocates several of the company's assets outside its walls and takes its ideas to the external environment. Such an example would be other companies using the company's intellectual property rights. Several companies possess numerous intellectual property rights held for no profit. Licencing unused intellectual property rights to other companies might be a beneficial inside-out open innovation. The coupled process is the last open innovation model; it focuses on harmoniously integrating outside-in and inside-out processes with collaborators from joint ventures, cooperations and alliances.

When using open innovation to solve strategic innovation problems, firms opt for different modes to solve challenging projects: open innovation partnerships, contests and communities. To explain: open innovation partnerships describe bilateral open innovation relationships, while open innovation contests and open innovation communities require firms to interact with multiple external actors. Open innovation partnerships are successfully used for complex projects related to well-known technological solution areas (i.e., two partners jointly developed a new rendering technology for a complex business problem with high market uncertainty and technological unpredictability) (Brunswicker et al. 2018, 3).

Several ways exist for research and development projects to gain from such partnerships based on innovation. Open innovation collaboration might escalate the chances of project survival during product development and lead to the product launching on the market, thereby reducing the likelihood of failed project if access to assets has been given to the R&D partners. If R&D projects are implemented through open innovation partnerships, they might yield a superior profit if directed appropriately. If we have badly managed projects, partnerships based on the market lead to inferior performance, while process management of formal projects allows beneficial correlation to the project. In contrast, partnerships based on science demonstrate better project returns only on projects managed more liberally (Du et al. 2014, 828–830).

Bagherzadeh et al. (2019, 301) surveyed 201 American innovation projects. They revealed that two crucial attributes of innovation projects (uncertainty and complexity) are bound to five elements, which could lead to thriving open innovation management: 1) degree of openness, 2) choice of an external partner, 3) choice of open innovation model, 4) formalisation of the cooperation process, and 5) internal company practices.

In their recent open innovation research, Brunswicker et al. (2016, 2) discovered that open innovation brings strategic value to bigger companies. These companies strongly fund open innovation projects, allowing them to leverage the company's productivity. There are different modes of open innovation, such as intellectual property licencing contracts, bilateral partnerships, communities, innovation contests, etc.

Strategic open innovation projects vary in complexity, the firm's depth of solution know-how, or the hiddenness of knowledge. Complex problems imply technological and market uncertainty and unpredictable outcomes. The depth of solution know-how describes a firm's ability to locate potential solution know-how. If the knowledge is hidden, then the firms lack this ability. Projects with high complexity or 'hiddenness' cause management challenges even though they could benefit the most from open innovation approaches (Brunswicker et al. 2018, 2).

The data from Liu et al.'s research (2002, 11-12) propose the importance of technology adaptation and crowdsourcing, especially when companies face crises if they are juxtaposed with alternative open innovation models. Crowdsourcing, complemented by social engagement, is an unconventional way of achieving solutions that might make the most of the innovation. The exaptation of technology allows rapid innovation in emergencies when innovators do not have time to design the development of new products traditionally. Furthermore, crisis innovation shows cooperation characteristics that surpass the usual dynamic and supply chain changes, which is compatible with the business ecosystems' common evolution view.

The pandemic's influence on lives was significant because of the severe situation in the health sector, sudden changes in people's lives, and the stopping of economic activity. In order to relieve this impact, the private sector, governments and all organisations and institutions that help people are jointly performing and seeking new ways and innovations. A survey from Almeida (2021a) has identified 212 projects in EU countries. The public health sector stands out in most of these projects, but other areas of life were also addressed, like detecting and controlling infection, virtualising school activities, retail and restaurants etc. The projects were considered because they demonstrate an original novelty element in the response to fight the virus and its consequences. About three-quarters of these projects have been underpinned by the activities and legislature of local governments, which have been very supportive, even though the motor leading this resourcefulness is often the civil and business actors. Austria and Portugal had the highest number of projects, accounting for one-third of the EU projects. Most of these projects involve exchanging practices and information, with public service delivery in second place and third, the analysis of collected real-time data.

In this crisis, there was a huge demand for ventilators. In order to procure sufficient quantities as quickly as possible, it was necessary to engage many stakeholders, i.e., businesses, non-governmental organisations, research institutions and persons prone to the invention. Faced with a modest offer of ventilators vital to some patients' critical care, ventilator producers partnered with car manufacturers, aerospace companies and other stakeholders to increase production simultaneously. The Massachusetts Institute of Technology and other universities tried to help alleviate the hospital shortages through competition calls for the design of open-source ventilators (Chesbrough 2020, 411). Also, in Slovenia, we found several cases, especially in the field of medical ventilator shortages.

7.4 Methodology and Results

In the empirical part, the content analysis method has been adopted. Content analysis is a broad array of techniques. We used it to analyse the content of texts and documents, using "predetermined categories and in a systematic and replicable manner" (Bryman & Bell 2011, 288). Based on an internet search of relevant keywords in Slovenian, five significant sources have been identified and analysed.

At the height of the COVID-19 pandemic, there was a shortage of respirators in Italy, which were essential for patients who need intensive coronavirus treatment. In order to prevent a similar scenario from occurring in Slovenia, the “Slovenian Respirator” initiative was launched in mid-March 2020 on several parallel paths. Extremely short development times, a limited supply of components and the introduction of emergencies were severe obstacles, but some development groups were not intimidated. Teams in different organisations and inter-organisational teams joined their forces, skills, knowledge and finances and started to develop prototypes based on open innovation projects. In this chapter, a content analysis of available articles from newspapers and electronic media has been used to present their efforts. Following the announcement from the Chamber of Commerce and Industry of Slovenia (2020), 176 companies expressed their willingness to join the initiative with their capacities. This shows the high awareness of how important this project is for Slovenia and its population.

The associations CENELEC (the European Committee for Electrotechnical Standardization) and CEN (the European Committee for Standardization), together with all their members, agreed to provide temporary free access to the European Standards for medical devices and personal protective equipment (European Commission 2020). Such intervention helped companies start producing the right products simultaneously while ensuring the desired safety. These standards were published on the 21st of March 2020 on the government of Slovenia’s (2020) web pages. This was an important push for cooperation from different companies to join forces in an open innovation project, which would benefit Slovenia.

Two meaningful knowledge flows drive open innovation; one is determined as inside-out and the other outside-in. The first is about businesses allowing their unused knowledge to be used by other companies. Chesbrough (2017) suggests that this flow needs more researchers’ attention to understand its potential. The other one, outside-in, is being researched by many more academics and practitioners and is often erroneously seen as the main open innovation field.

Four development teams have succeeded in prototyping respirators. Two groups created a prototype of a respiratory-assisted respirator designed for conscious and self-breathing patients. Two groups, however, created a prototype respirator for critical patients who no longer breathe independently or are unconscious. The prototypes differed, but they had to obtain the appropriate certificates before they could be used to treat people.

One of the spontaneous initiatives was born at the University of Ljubljana, Faculty of Electrical Engineering, on the initiative of Prof. Dr Marko Topič, who returned early from touring in the USA on the 16th of March. Just an hour and a half after his landing, the Department of Electronics colleagues decided to undertake a feasibility study and develop the simplest fan possible. On the 22nd of March, the government published requirements for professional ventilators, which were the basis for the Slovenian respirator, calling on institutions and companies with the appropriate knowledge and competencies to develop a medical ventilator in cooperation with the University Medical Center Ljubljana. Medical ventilators were almost impossible to obtain at the outbreak of the pandemic, and delivery times were too long. The faculty responded to the call. With great zeal, together with industry partners, they began work and developed a medical ventilator, which they named the FEspirator (Faculty of Electrical Engineering 2020).

Lotrič Metrology joined forces in the project Diham [I breath] with Domel, EKWB, Tehnološki Park Ljubljana, Zavod 404 and BPMC in cooperation with the team UKC Ljubljana, consisting of Dr Tomislav Mirković, Andriy Grynyuk, PhD and Janko Rakef, who provided the teams with user requests (Špende 2020). The partners in the project designed a turbine pressure respirator with its motor and blower without inflatable bellows, which operates both in a hospital environment and in mobile hospitals or even independently. It does not need compressed air to operate, as it has its source of pressure and airflow, but only electricity and a source of oxygen—a cylinder or wiring. The respirator works in three ways and adapts to the patient when breathing alone or with the help of apparatus. According to the development team, if necessary, the so-called zero series could be produced in a month, with only materials and labour input costs (around €4,900). Until regular production, if they opted for it, they would have some more development work to do, and above all, they needed to check whether they had infringed any patent or intellectual property rights during the rush. The appliance should also have a certification process, which can take a year or more (Špende 2020).

In the FEspirator project, in addition to the seven employees of the Laboratory for Photovoltaics and Optoelectronics UL FE (LPVO), six electrical engineering students also participated in the development, helping with the initial hardware testing and programming. Professor Damijan Miljavec from the Laboratory for Electrical Machines at the University of Ljubljana, Faculty of Electrical Engineering and the Laboratory for Measurements in Process Mechanical Engineering from the University of Ljubljana, Faculty of Mechanical Engineering, helped calibrate the flow sensor. The necessary materials and production of the mechanical parts of the fan were also contributed by partners from various Slovenian and foreign companies led by ZAXCSS, where Igor Stražišnik and Aljaž Žavrlan took over the entire implementation of the mechanical part of the device. More than 30 people participated in developing the FEspirator and spent more than 1000 hours developing the prototype together. The first testing of prototypes on a simulation dummy took place on Friday, the 10th of April, at the University College Ljubljana.

In addition to the group from the University of Ljubljana, Faculty of Electrical Engineering, the ventilator was also developed by Janez Pirc's group with colleagues from the Fotona company and the Lotrič Metrology group under the auspices of the Ljubljana Technology Park. All three groups presented working prototypes with extraordinary innovation, which were evaluated by the expert commission of the Ljubljana Clinical Center through four phases of testing, setting a date for the final testing of prototypes after 14 days. Even though the groups presented different solutions, they cooperated in the development (Faculty of Electrical Engineering 2020).

It can be seen that an enormous input in terms of time, energy, money, knowledge and human resources has been invested in the development of this project. All this would not be possible (at least not on short notice) if people from different backgrounds would not join forces and the standards for respirator building would not be freely available. The motivation was high; people worked long nights, without any reimbursement, just from their resolution to get involved and help the nation.

The anesthesiologist Bojan Kontestabile, for example, who worked intensively with the developers all the time, said (Slovenian Press Agency 2020):

> I read about the faculty's initiative in the online news. Of course, this is my field and I immediately asked my colleagues who is involved in these projects. The younger colleagues have already helped other teams, so I immediately decided and got in touch with Professor Topič and the cooperation started immediately. With great mutual respect, we embarked on a project in which we were already two weeks behind at the beginning.

As Kontestabile explained, he prepared an introductory lecture for the team, explaining the theory and, above all, emphasised the awareness that they are not just making an inflating machine but that the goal of the device is to treat people.

On the 24th of April 2020, the second round of testing took place at the University of Ljubljana. The Faculty of Electrical Engineering, House of

Experiments, the project Diham (Lotrič Metrology, Domel, EKWB, Technology Park Ljubljana, Institute 404, BPMC) and the group led by Janez Pirc, which connects a group of individuals from different companies, presented their prototypes to the public.

Individual interests were put aside, and care for society and the common good became primary, a rarity for an increasingly individualised and consumer-orientated Western society. As Latemore (2021, 257) defines it, "The common good is regarded as the communion of a person in good living. Addressing the relationship between the economy and society, it is proposed that the marketplace subsists within society." He highlighted the significance of mutuality, generosity and relationships as public common good features. Public discourse disclosed two narratives during COVID-19, one based on selfishness and fear and the other characterised by generosity and hope. Generosity was highly recognised in this case because, as Morabia (2020) observes, the "pandemic shines a spotlight on how injustices intersect and channel the brunt of the burden to low-wage earners, those discriminated against, the poor and the marginalised".

Innovative solutions and advanced algorithms distinguish the prototype of the FEspirator for many functionalities typical of professional medical ventilators. Among other things, it has fast and accurate pressure regulation, automatic breath detection and multi-stage alarms. This brings the device beyond the breathing device level and closer to professional medical ventilators. The device was ready to save lives in a pandemic emergency (Slovenian Press Agency 2020).

Lotrič wanted to learn something from the collaboration on the project Diham, and they planned to set up the production of medical devices on their production premises within two months. The experience with breathing respirators is a good start for a new development cycle. There is also a product in this medical story that they are already making, i.e. a control system to capture the temperature, humidity, carbon dioxide and other functions primarily for cold chain tracking, such as refrigeration control in healthcare. They want to establish a laboratory that will be certified according to the system of achieving good manufacturing practices for medical devices, which is a great opportunity for them, as they have open paths to partners (Špende 2020).

The findings by Du, Leten and Vanhaverbeke (2014) demonstrate that R&D projects, including open innovation partnerships, perform better financially, provided they are conducted appropriately. A positive correlation to the project's success is detected by market-based partnerships when the partners use formal project management. Nevertheless, these partnerships result in lower performance for loosely managed projects. This case shows that in an emergency, an open innovation project can help society and increase the company's market competitiveness in the long run.

7.5 Discussion

(Un)fortunately, the ventilators' development projects did not go into production; after an initial standoff, the government procured enough tested ventilators from imports to meet urgent hospital needs. Nevertheless, the open innovation approach demonstrated that innovative product development could be successfully channelled by combining knowledge and the innovative potential of companies, creative individuals, universities and other institutions. It would be wise to continue promoting and financing national know-how and thus position Slovenia even more decisively on the map of the most influential societies and economies.

It is well known that the market conditions demand an ever shorter development time and reduced costs if the businesses want to compete in the market with more sustainable advantages. Shorter process and product development schedules combined with lower costs to achieve the expected quality can only be realised if project management methods are integrated with contemporaneous elements (Kušar et al. 2008, 588).

The pandemic has shown the world new challenges in the last few years. These challenges, personal and for businesses, were related to the changes that were forced on us. Companies and people began to cooperate openly, putting added value and open innovation first, not just opportunities for competitive advantage. All this made it possible for us to come out stronger together and to see many undiscovered opportunities that probably would not have been possible under normal conditions.

However, the volume of open innovation projects during the pandemic evokes the enormous potential that it brings—no matter if the crisis is present at that moment. In this way, the window for creating value remains wide open, as it offers a plethora of opportunities for value creation, whether new partners have been involved that possess skills which complement skills already inside the company or the existing partnerships unlock undetected potential (Dahlander & Wallin 2020).

Due to the strong pressures that were exercised on the health sector, the economy and people's lives, open innovation projects mitigated these effects. Governments, NGOs and businesses have delivered innovative proposals through joint ventures. At the beginning of the pandemic, there was a shortage of respirators in Europe, essential for patients needing intensive coronavirus treatment. To prevent a similar scenario in Slovenia, the "Slovenian Respirator" initiative was launched in mid-March 2020 on several parallel paths.

7.6 Conclusion

This chapter deals with innovative initiatives that responded to Slovenia's shortage of respirators. They have been identified and analysed through content analysis. The analysis shows spontaneous initiatives and stories about the FEspirator and the project Diham. The remarkable cooperation between researchers, the health sector, the business sector and the government has also been highlighted. All this demonstrates how open innovation partnerships help to leverage the achievements of open innovation projects and lead their product to the market, thereby reducing the likelihood of project failure and supporting project take-up.

Findings prove that there is no clear division between outbound and inbound open innovation but that collaboration with partners involving digital platforms, co-creation and informal partnerships remain critical to resilience and flexibility during the pandemic. Innovation hard factors, i.e. products, patents, and existing technologies, are very important. However, there are other meaningful elements, called soft factors, which might represent a crucial push to fasten innovation; strategic alliances, personal relationships, and cross-sector consortia (Liu et al. 2002, 11–12).

As Robbins et al. (2021, 1) suggest, the open innovation mission and contribution to addressing the consequences of the pandemic demonstrated massive and crucial support. Innovation management's complex and unpredictable nature has been exposed and highlighted unprecedentedly.

The pandemic has rapidly changed business models and organisational systems, generating significant upheavals. This contribution highlights some open innovation strategies and innovation ecosystems implemented in the healthcare sector in response to emergencies. In the end, we suggest the presence of some identified future trends and a roadmap to follow. First, it has been noticed how through crowdsourcing, organisations can effectively solve concrete problems, thanks to digital technologies. These can accelerate innovation, harnessing the power of the online community. Second, in product design and development, it has emerged as organisations, starting from re-design and production flexibility, can leverage technology exaptation as a potential pool of resources. Finally, we showed how collaborations between universities, industries and government entities might be strategically important for developing innovation and revitalising the country. In conclusion, it appears essential for the health sector to understand the innovation systems and know how to modify the supply network adapted to the swapped organisational ecosystems. Only in this way will organisations be able to react effectively to unpredictable shocks and gain resilience that can endure long-term.

References

Almeida, Fernando. "Innovative response initiatives in the European Union to mitigate the effects of COVID-19." *Journal of Enabling Technologies*, No. 15(1) (2021a): 40-52. https://doi.org/10.1108/JET-09-2020-0039.

Almeida, Fernando. "The role of tech startups in the fight against COVID-19." *World Journal of Science, Technology and Sustainable Development*, No. 18(1) (2021b): 64-75. https://doi.org/10.1108/WJSTSD-04-2020-0030.

Batkovskiy, Aleksandr M., Konovalova, Alina V., Semenova, Elena G., Trofimets, Valerij Y. and Fomina, Alena V. "Risks of development and implementation of innovative projects." *Mediterranean Journal of Social Sciences*, No. 6(4) (2015): 243-243. https://doi.org/10.5901/mjss.2015.v6n4s4p243.

Beaume, Romain, Maniak, Rémi and Midler, Cristophe. "Crossing innovation and product projects management: A comparative analysis in the automotive industry." *International Journal of Project Management*, No. 27(2) (2009): 166-174. https://doi.org/10.1016/j.ijproman.2008.09.004.

Becker, Henk A. "Social impact assessment." *European Journal of Operational Research*, No. 128(2) (2001): 311-321. https://doi.org/10.1016/S0377-2217(00)00074-6.

Bertello, Alberto, Bogers, Marcel L.A.M. and De Bernardi, Paola. "Open innovation in the face of the COVID-19 grand challenge: insights from the Pan-European hackathon 'EUvsVirus'." *R&D Management*, No. 52(2) (2022): 178-192. https://doi.org/10.1111/radm.12456.

Bhaskar, Sonu, Tan, Jeremy, Bogers, Marcel L.A.M., Minssen, Timo, Badaruddin, Hishamuddin, Israeli-Korn, Simon and Chesbrough, Henry. "At the epicentre of COVID-19–the tragic failure of the global supply chain for medical supplies." *Frontiers in Public Health*, No. (2020): 821. https://doi.org/10.3389/fpubh.2020.562882.

Brem, Alexander, Viardot, Eric and Nylund, Petra A. "Implications of the coronavirus (COVID-19) outbreak for innovation: Which technologies will improve our lives?" *Technological Forecasting and Social Change*, No. 163, (2021): 120451. https://doi.org/10.1016/j.techfore.2020.120451.

Brunswicker, Sabine, Bagherzadeh, Mehdi, Lamb, Allison, Narsalay, Raghav and Jing, Yu. Managing open innovation projects with impact. SSRN whitepaper series, No. July (2016): 1-67. http://dx.doi.org/10.2139/ssrn.2821203.

Bryman, Alan and Emma Bell. 2011. Business research methods. Cambridge: Oxford University Press.

Chamber of Commerce and Industry of Slovenia. 2020. Seznam zainteresiranih ponudnikov kapacitet [List of interested capacity providers]. Accessed November 10, 2022 https://www.gzs.si/zbornica_elektronske_in_elektroindustrije/vsebina/RESPIRATOR/Seznam-zainteresiranih-ponudnikov-kapacitet.

Chesbrough, Henry. "Managing open innovation." *Research-Technology Management*, No. 47(1) (2004): 23-26. https://doi.org/10.1080/08956308.2004.11671604.

Chesbrough, Henry. "The future of open innovation: The future of open innovation is more extensive, more collaborative, and more engaged with a wider variety of participants." *Research-Technology Management*, No. 60(1) (2017): 35-38. https://doi.org/10.1080/08956308.2017.1255054.

Chesbrough, Henry. "To recover faster from COVID-19, open up: Managerial implications from an open innovation perspective." *Industrial Marketing Management*, No. 88 (2020): 410-413. https://doi.org/10.1016/j.indmarman.2020.04.010.

Dahlander, Linus and Wallin, Martin. "Why now is the time for "Open Innovation". *Harvard Business Review*, No. 6 (2020): 5. Accessed the 12th of December, 2022. https://hbr.org/2020/06/why-now-is-the-time-for-open-innovation.

Du, Jingshu, Leten, Bart and Vanhaverbeke, Wim. "Managing open innovation projects with science-based and market-based partners." Research Policy, No. 43(5) (2014): 828-840. https://doi.org/10.1016/j.respol.2013.12.008.

Elia, Gianluca, Margherita, Alessandro, Massaro, Alessandro and Vacca, Angelo. "Adoption of open innovation in the COVID-19 emergency: developing a process-based information coordination system." *Business Process Management Journal*, No. 28(2) (2022): 419-441. https://doi.org/10.1108/BPMJ-11-2020-0507.

European Commission. 2020. Coronavirus: European standards for medical supplies made freely available to facilitate increase in production. Accessed the 2nd of December, 2022. https://ec.europa.eu/commission/presscorner/detail/en/ip_20_502.

Faculty of Electrical Engineering. 2020. FEspirator—Elektrotehniški prototip medicinskega respiratorja [FEspirator—Electrotechnical prototype of medical respirator]. Accessed the 12th of December, 2022. https://fe.uni-lj.si/aktualno/novice/2020042413101721/.

Gawlik, J., & Kiełbus, A. (2010). Chosen aspects of innovative project management. Archives of foundry engineering, 10(3), 175.

Government of Slovenia. 2020. Standardi za izdelavo respiratorjev [Standards for the manufacture of respirators]. Accessed the 22nd of November, 2022. https://www.gov.si/novice/2020-03-21-standardi-za-izdelavo-respiratorjev/.

Jallow, Haddy, Renukappa, Suresh and Suresh, Subashini. "The impact of COVID-19 outbreak on United Kingdom infrastructure sector." *Smart and Sustainable Built Environment*, No. 10(4) (2020): 581-593. https://doi.org/10.1108/SASBE-05-2020-0068.

Keogh, Colin. "Open innovation in response to COVID-19: a case study of the open source ventilator Ireland project." Qeios, No. The 10th of February (2021): 1-18. Accessed the 22nd of November, 2022. https://www.qeios.com/read/VF6WTE/pdf

Kozlov, Alexandr, Pavlova, Elizaveta and Królas, Pawel. "Classification of parameters of innovative projects in the framework of digital transformation programs for sustainable development of industrial enterprises." E3S Web of Conferences, No. 258(02021) (2021): 1-9. https://doi.org/10.1051/e3sconf/202125802021.

Latemore, Greg. "COVID and the Common Good." *Philosophy of Management*, No. 20 (2021): 257–269. https://doi.org/10.1007/s40926-020-00154-w.

Lee, Sang M., Hwang, Taewon and Choi, Donghyun. "Open innovation in the public sector of leading countries." Management decision, No. 50(1) (2012): 147-162. https://doi.org/10.1108/00251741211194921.

Liu, Zheng, Shi, Yongjiang and Yang, Bo. "Open Innovation in Times of Crisis: An Overview of the Healthcare Sector in Response to the COVID-19 Pandemic." *Journal of Open Innovation: Technology, Market, and Complexity*, No. 8(1) (2022): 21. https://doi.org/10.3390/joitmc8010021.

Maylor, Harvey, Brady, Tim, Cooke-Davies, Terry and Hodgson, Damian. "From projectification to programmification." *International Journal of Project Management*, No. 4(8) (2006): 663-674. https://doi.org/10.1016/j.ijproman.2006.09.014

Morabia, Alfredo. "COVID-19: Health as a Common Good." American Journal of Public Health, No. 110(8) (2020): 1111-1112.

https://doi.org/10.2105/AJPH.2020.305802.

Papelniuk, Oksana. 2017. Development of methods of innovative project management in developer organisations. In MATEC Web of Conferences, No. 106(08044). EDP Sciences. https://doi.org/10.1051/matecconf/201710608044.

Pearce, Joshua M. "A review of open source ventilators for COVID-19 and future pandemics." F1000Research, No. 9 (2020): 218. https://doi.org/10.12688/f1000research.22942.2.

Robbins, Peter, O'Gorman, Colm, Huff, Anne and Moeslein, Kathrin. "Multidexterity—A New Metaphor for Open Innovation." *Journal of Open Innovation: Technology, Market, and Complexity*, No. 7(1) (2021): 99. https://doi.org/10.3390/joitmc7010099.

Sandmeier, Patricia, Jamali, Nadia, Kobe, Carmen, Enkel, Ellen, Gassmann, Oliver and Meier, Markus. 2004. Towards a structured and integrative front-end of product innovation. R&D Management Conference (RADMA) 2004.—Lisbon. Accessed the 22nd of November, 2022. https://www.alexandria.unisg.ch/publications/275.

Slovenian Press Agency. 2020. "FEspirator": Kako se je razvoja slovenskega prototipa medicinskega ventilatorja lotila Fakulteta za elektrotehniko UL? ["FEspirator": How did the Faculty of Electrical Engineering of the University of Ljubljana approach the development of the Slovenian prototype of a medical ventilator?]. Accessed November 22, 2022. https://o-sta.si/26946/-fespirator-kako-se-je-razvoja-slovenskega-prototipa-medicinskega-ventilatorja-lotila-fakulteta-za-elektrotehniko-ul.

Špende, Romana. 2020. Respirator diham Lotrič Meroslovju zagon za nov razvojni cikel [respirator breathe gives Lotrič Metrology impetus for a new development cycle]. Dnevnik, the 11th of May. Accessed 22nd of November, 2022. https://www.dnevnik.si/1042929010.

Vanclay, Frank, Esteves, Ana Maria, Aucamp, Ilse and Franks, Daniel M. 2015. Social Impact Assessment: Guidance for assessing and managing the social impacts of projects. Fargo ND: International Association for Impact Assessment. Accessed the 20th of December, 2022. https://www.iaia.org/uploads/pdf/SIA_Guidance_Document_IAIA.pdf.

Vermicelli, Silvia, Cricelli, Livio and Grimaldi, Michele. "How can crowdsourcing help tackle the COVID-19 pandemic? An explorative overview of innovative collaborative practices." *R&D Management*, No. 51(2) (2021): 183-194. https://doi.org/10.1111/radm.12443.

Zimmerling, Amanda and Chen, Xiongbiao. "Innovation and possible long-term impact driven by COVID-19: Manufacturing, personal protective equipment and digital technologies." *Technology in Society*, 65(101541) (2021). https://doi.org/10.1016/j.techsoc.2021.101541.

Wagner, Reinhard. 2021. The Role of Projects in the Process of Transforming Automotive Industry. In: Cuevas, R., Bodea, CN., Torres-Lima, P. (eds) Research on Project, Programme and Portfolio Management, pp 127–136. Lecture Notes in Management and Industrial Engineering. Springer, Cham. https://doi.org/10.1007/978-3-030-60139-3_9.

Armand Faganel earned the title of Doctor of Science at the University of Primorska, Faculty of Management in Koper, where he is acting as head of the marketing department and vice-dean. Before his employment at the university, he gained work experience in the field of commerce; he was head of marketing, head of sales and business unit manager at different international companies. For eight years, he taught three courses at the XAMK University in Finland and performed various professional seminars in sales and marketing in Slovenia and abroad. He participated in and led a dozen research projects. Among his research interests are scientific fields of perception of service quality, branding, consumer behaviour and higher education issues. He is also an international expert in quality assurance for several European agencies. He has already published 30 scientific articles, 25 chapters and five monographs.

Bojan Mevlja is a habilitated assistant professor in management at the University of Primorska Faculty of Management. He has skill and experience in management, strategic management and non-profit organisations. He led the development of advisory projects for the public administration, non-governmental sectors and the economy. He was also a member of the Council of the Republic of Slovenia for Sustainable Development. His research interests include management, strategic management and non-profit organisations. He has published five scientific articles and authored two scientific monographs.

VIII

Artificial Intelligence and Machine Learning in Project Management

Ali Bidhendi and Mohammad Mahoud

8.1 Smart Systems

Learning is acquiring new or modifying and reinforcing existing knowledge, behaviours, skills, values or preferences. Humans, animals and some machines possess the ability to learn.

Machine learning creates a program that automatically enhances performance based on experience. (Zhang 1999) Machine learning is one of the most important parts of artificial intelligence (AI). A system in a changing environment must learn to be clever. In such a case, designers only need to anticipate some possible situations.

Machine learning (ML) has progressed significantly in the last decade and has developed three technological trends. First, more data have been collected with the dramatic growth of measurement technologies and the Internet of Things (IoT). As data storage becomes insufficient, more data are stored. As a result, vast amounts of data are available in universities and industries. Second, machine-learning chips such as GPU (GPU) and TPU (Tensor Processing Unit) have been designed and manufactured to give people access to powerful, cost-effective computing resources. Third, advanced ML algorithms have been developed and validated. Big data, high-performance computing and advanced ML algorithms are integral to advancing and applying machine learning in various fields. (Hong et al. 2020)

Over the past few decades, significant advances in modelling techniques and concepts for predicting ML, statistics, and computer science have been valuable to researchers and those involved in organisations (Putka et al. 2017).

ML is a sub-field of AI that activates computational systems to learn from specific task data. ML tasks can be classified as follows: (i) classification (or supervised learning); (ii) clustering (or unsupervised learning); (iii) association; and (iv) numeric prediction (Witten et al. 2005).

Due to its numerous applications in various fields and disciplines, ML has been recognised as an effective predictor tool (Kavakiotis et al. 2017). To this end, ML has often been surpassed in predictive work, by many human professionals. It has also been shown that ML can predict nonlinear and complex phenomena (e.g., building accidents) and helps management make better decisions (Zhou et al. 2015).

Although several studies have used modern project management techniques (e.g., Chulani et al. 1999; Paliwal & Kumar 2009; Wang & Gibson 2010; Shmueli & Koppius 2011), there is also a need to understand more about the potential use of these methods in project management. Therefore, a new approach uses a perspective that primarily relates to project performance forecasting using forecasting analysis methods (Sabahi & Parast 2020).

ML can improve the management processes like decision-making in long-term planning and daily operations. ML can be used in project management areas such as time (Kim et al. 2008), cost (Williams & Gong 2014), quality (Zheng et al. 2010), safety (Miang & Faddilah 2015), and operational performance (Xiao & Fan 2014).

ML often performed better than the existing methods when a combination of factors caused the domain problem. For example, Hammad et al. (2014) reported that estimating the time it takes to make steel using ML is better than the existing estimation method. In another study, Yu & Skibniewski (2010) proposed an ML cost estimation model, which is stronger and more precise than the conventional cost estimators using unit cost-level items, which are prone to fluctuations.

The challenges that have led to the neglect of ML in project management include the following: 1. lack of large-scale data for model training and validation. 2. Lack of model transferability limits a trained model with one data-rich project to be used in another with limited data. 3. Refraining from justifying the costs and benefits of deploying ML in projects. 4. Performance may need to be more reliable and stronger for the stated purposes, as this method may work for some projects but cannot be generalised to others. The difference between machine learning and deep learning is explained in Figure 8.1.

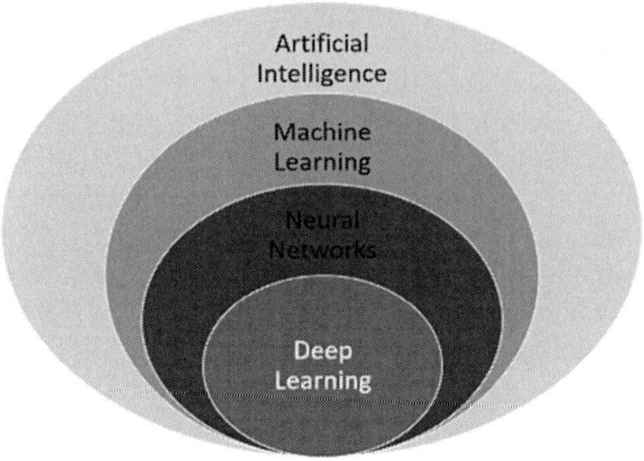

Figure 8.1 *Background – Artificial Intelligence*

AI is a sub-field of computer science concerned with developing computers capable of doing tasks ordinarily performed by humans, specifically those associated with intelligent human behaviour. Understanding how these new technologies function is critical in the workplace. Black boxes that provide us with answers without explanations or technologies that fail to interact with us cannot be trusted partners. We need to comprehend the fundamentals of how these systems reason, and the systems must be able to explain how they arrive at their conclusions.

Intelligence or cognition may be divided into three major areas: sensing, reasoning and acting. Because this research does not include robotics, our focus on "acting" is on speech generation.

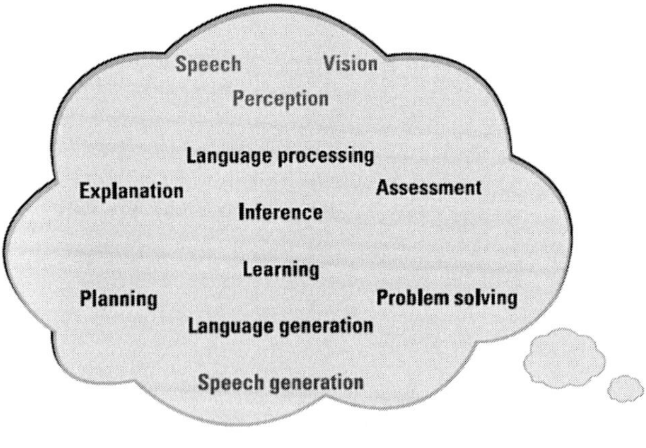

Figure 8.2 *Various capabilities within the three components of AI*

As seen in Figure 8.2, we may identify fine-grained differences within these macro areas relating to voice and picture recognition, different flavours of reasoning (logic vs evidence-based) and creating speech (and other more physical acts) to assist communication.

There are blue areas among these activities, especially regarding the function of reasoning. However, considering intelligence as described by sensing, reasoning and acting is important for defining behaviours:

- Sensing: gathering sensor data about the world, such as:
  - Image processing: recognising important objects, paths, faces, cars or kittens.
  - Speech recognition: filtering out the noise and recognising specific words.
  - Other sensors: mostly for robotics, sonar, accelerometers, balance detection, etc.
- Reasoning: consider how objects connect to what is known, for example:
  - Language processing is the process of converting words into concepts and their relationships.
  - Situation assessment: determining what is happening in the world on a larger scale than just thoughts.
  - Inference based on logic: deciding that something is true because it must be true logically.
  - Evidence-based inference: deciding whether something is true based on the weight of the evidence available.
  - Planning/problem solving: determining what to do to reach a goal.
  - Learning is the process of acquiring new information via the use of examples or the analysis of facts. Natural language generation is creating the words required to achieve a communication objective.
- Acting: creating and directing acts such as:
  - Speech generation by creating audio that expresses a piece of text.
  - Robotic control is the movement and management of the many effectors that move you. (Narrative Science 2015).

8.2 Artificial Intelligence in Project Management

The implementation of AI has increased rapidly in recent years. Nevertheless, many businesses must realise the projected benefits or abandon projects before completion (Westenberger et al. 2022).

Moreover, AI is no longer limited to cutting-edge IT and technology applications. AI has already begun to make inroads into more traditional contexts to augment or replace functions typically performed by humans, including project managers.

AI and ML have several business applications. The most significant AI skills are rapidly processing enormous volumes of data, recognising patterns in data, learning from it and generating predictions. AI is and will continue to be an emerging trend in project management due to its unique capacity to analyse particular trends and foresee project situations and results. AI has revolutionised and will continue to change project management.

The following are some instances of the influence of AI on various aspects of project management:

- Productivity and Business Insights:
  - Because AI is created to follow precise, rule-based procedures, bottlenecks may be solved rapidly. AI helps project management deliver additional insights into potential outcomes, resulting in better decision-making quality.
  - By automating various monotonous operations, AI can increase corporate efficiency.
- Allocation of Resources and Planning—AI may increase project planning accuracy and assist the project manager in tracking the project's progress. This is extremely useful while working on large and complex projects. AI-enhanced project management solutions can assist you in making the optimum resource allocation choice for your project:
  - ML algorithms may estimate project activity time, resource and budget needs based on historical data from past projects.
  - Project planning may be strengthened by enabling auto-scheduling via programmed logic and rules. Furthermore, progress and task status may be automatically tracked, informing the project manager.
  - Historical data may be used to create custom workflows and forecast workload, assess work and time-off calendars, identify training needs for a specific resource, and even advise new employees based on applications in the employment portal that match the capabilities necessary for the project.
- Overview of the Integrated Project:
  - Through data visualisation, AI can deliver real-time data and project progress updates. This helps the team and management to discuss the status of a project and make educated decisions about its length, cost and strategy.
  - Prioritising tasks is difficult, especially when working in groups. AI can assist the team in better understanding essential operations, true priorities or focusing on a specific job. (https://www.pmi.org/)

8.3 Machine Learning

Before 2000, AI approaches such as expert systems, neural networks and case-based reasoning (CBR) were used. In addition, the cost forecasting model has been studied since the 2000s. (Kim et al. 2013)

ML is one of the most important innovative inventions and competitive advantages in the workplace. Although ML has existed for over 60 years, it has recently shown significant potential for transforming economies and societies. Many industries, such as healthcare, banking, manufacturing and transportation, have been affected by ML. According to Accenture (2018), ML can reduce costs by 20% to 25% in banking, IT operations, infrastructure and maintenance and generate new revenue in products and services. By transforming human processes into intelligent and automated processes, organisations can focus their resources on more valuable activities, such as providing better customer products and services and improving customer acquisition and retention.

Due to the increasing growth of ML technologies and most organisations' adaptation, managers at all levels must learn ML techniques to create the most value for their companies by using the portfolio of ML projects (Lee & Shin 2020).

8.4 Methodology

This section describes the method of obtaining relevant literature from publicly available databases. Each step of the process leading to the classification of the selected literature into different categories is explained.

Figure 8.3 shows the process of literature retrieval used in this article. In step 1, the keywords describing the topic are determined. A pilot keyword search showed that citation databases, such as Web of Science and Google Scholar, performed poorly, with inconsistent and scattered results compared to Scopus and Elsevier. Therefore, this article selected Scopus and Elsevier as the citation databases.

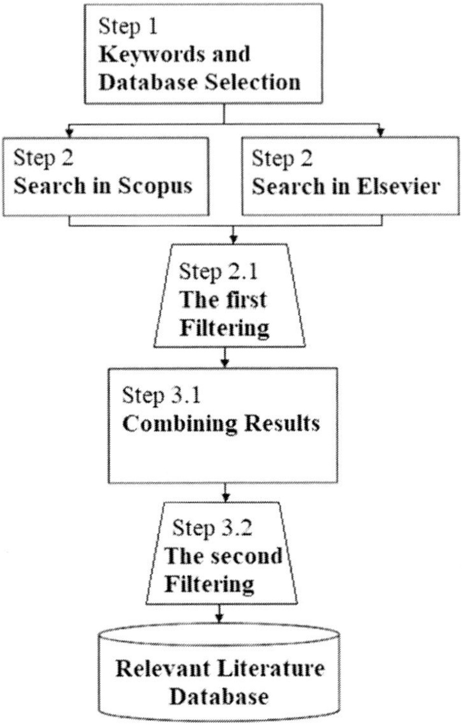

Figure 8.3 *Literature retrieval process*

In addition to the keywords in Table 8.1, the corresponding filters in Scopus and Elsevier were chosen to avoid duplicate entries and limit the scope of the project management.

Table 8.1 *List of search keywords used in Scopus and Elsevier*

No.	Selected search keywords
1	Machine Learning AND Engineering AND Project Management
2	Artificial Intelligence AND Engineering AND Project Management
3	Data Mining AND Engineering AND Project Management
4	Big Data AND Engineering AND Project Management
5	Data Fusion AND Engineering AND Project Management

In step 2, a keyword search was performed in Scopus and Elsevier. In step 2.1, a filtering process was applied to limit the range of search results by evaluating the search results based on four selection criteria. These four criteria are explained in Table 8.2.

Table 8.2 *Criteria used in the step 2.1 literature filtering process*

Criterion	Description
C1	The article should be written in English.
C2	Studies indexed in databases other than Scopus or Elsevier are out of scope.
C3	Only journal articles are considered. Conference papers are out of scope.
C4	Only articles using AI/ML algorithms for project management are selected.

Although conference papers may suggest more interesting methods, their inclusion in this review would result in a collection of papers. Filtering and reviewing these articles require much more time and resources. Therefore, criterion C3 was presented to limit the scope of the study to a review article published in journals. Step 3.1 combines the database obtained from the first filtering process, and duplicates are removed from the combined Scopus and Elsevier datasets. A second filtering process was performed in step 3.2 to limit the search results. The two criteria in the second filtering process are C5 and C6, as described in Table 8.3. The filtered dataset from step 3.2 resulted in a sample space of articles focusing on risk assessment using ML algorithms.

Table 8.3 *Criteria used in the step 3.2 literature filtering process*

Criterion	Description
C5	Focuses on project management, time and cost management. Focuses on project-based control/system feedback.
C6	Focuses on ML or deep learning methods. AI-based methods, such as expert systems, genetic algorithms, search problems and Bayesian belief networks are out of scope.

8.5 Results

Bellow, the results of the literature review process are presented.

8.5.1 Machine Learning in Industry and Safety

One of the problems of many industries, including the construction industry, is decision-making with uncertainty. Wrong decisions can have dire consequences, endangering lives. An experienced worker or safety manager needs to gain more personal experience with such hazards, as they may misdiagnose or not recognise the potential hazards of a project situation. Therefore, individuals' lack of risk recognition is one of the most important causes of hazards and serious injuries in the construction industry. People working in the upstream construction phase, such as designers, are at greater risk of not recognising hazards and misjudging. The situation always causes serious mistakes. Humans cannot draw logical conclusions from many observations over time, and this is because short-term memory can only perceive up to seven features simultaneously.

On the other hand, ML can infer general rules from large volumes of data in multidimensional spaces. Therefore, it is considered a solution for safety decisions under uncertainty in empirical knowledge and leads to improved decision-making and saves lives (Tixier et al. 2016).

The use of ML techniques to build models from data and information is constantly growing. Building such models requires properly understanding ML tools' data, knowledge and characteristics. A systematic approach ensures that all important modelling aspects are considered, which can lead to good-quality models. ML models are made for different applications, including models to improve data comprehension and forecasting models. Regardless of their role, evaluating models is one of the most important steps in building them. Evaluating these models determines whether the modelling activity's stated goal has been achieved and allows us to compare different modelling approaches and guide future research. However, despite its importance, evaluation has received less attention than other modelling steps (Reich & Barai 1999).

8.5.2 Machine Learning in Conflict Management

Some studies show that conflict management is better used as a process of continuous improvement in projects from a knowledge management perspective rather than just focusing on one project. Love and Smith (2016) found that project people should view each error as a learning opportunity instead of having zero tolerance for errors. They concluded that creating a learning culture in organisations or projects could prevent mistakes in the future. Therefore, learning from past experiences is an effective way to improve conflict management. In addition, the knowledge gained from past project experiences has been widely used to assist in appropriate decision-making in other projects in current research. In this regard, Williams and Gong (2014) investigated the possibility of predicting project cost increases through numerical data from previous projects. Gerassis et al. (2016) and Leu and Chang (2013) also used different machine-learning methods. They predicted the safety risk of different types of projects using incident data from previous projects. Wang and Light (2013) confirmed that historical data could be used to discover knowledge to improve the conflict management process.

The ML classification process consists of several steps: problem identification, data collection, data preparation and processing, algorithm selection, model training, and evaluation (Yuqing & Daniel 2019).

8.5.3 Machine Learning in Design

Using ML in design evaluation also helps designers in decision-making processes. Design goals focus on using space, safety, energy efficiency and people's well-being, which can be accelerated by using ML (Bidhendi & Azizi 2021).

Studies have shown that the energy consumption of buildings once built and in operation is much higher than the energy consumption predictions made during the design, leading to the term "performance gap." A traditional prediction method, based on building physics, is a real-world data-based approach in which behaviour is learned through observation. Screen energy certifications are the source of building "behaviour" observed in the UK, and ML, a subset of AI, can predict global behaviour in complex systems such as buildings. Accordingly, artificial neural networks, an ML technique, have been collected and trained to predict the annual use of thermal (gaseous) and electrical energy in building designs based on various design parameters; for example, the research focused on school design in the UK. The mean absolute percentage errors were 22.9% and 22.5% for annual thermal and electrical energy use forecasts. This compares with the current performance gap sources, 9.1% for forecasting annual thermal energy use and 24.5% for forecasting annual energy use (Pasichnyi et al. 2019).

8.5.4 Machine Learning in Cost Management

OCost management is one of the most important applications of ML techniques in construction. Predicting construction costs can help project managers identify potential problems, adopt accountability strategies and better control project costs. However, it is difficult to accurately predict construction costs in the planning or early stages when project information is limited (Ahiaga-Dagbui & Smith 2012). With advances in computing power, recent cost estimation approaches tend to use more sophisticated methods and larger volumes of data. ML methods have been used in recent years, which allow the study of multivariate and nonlinear relationships between final costs and design variables (Günaydin & Doğan 2004).

Using forecasting models or algorithms, automatic cost estimation aims to identify the correlation between the influencing factors and the project cost. Elfaki et al. (2014) distinguished four different advanced methods based on AI, namely ML, knowledge-based systems (KBS), evolutionary systems (ES), and hybrid systems (HS) (Elfaki et al.2014). Kim et al. (2004) analysed three cost estimation models, namely artificial neural networks (ANN), multiple regression analysis (MRA), and a CBR system. They concluded that ANNs were more accurate than the model. MRA and CBR estimate work (Marzouk & Ahmed 2011). In addition, according to Cheng et al. (2010), ANN has the best approach to estimating the duration and cost of construction projects in the initial design stage (Cheng et al. 2010).

8.5.5 Machine Learning in Reporting

Progress reporting is an important managerial function for successfully implementing construction projects. Because images are more eloquent than text, digital photos of a construction site gradually replace their traditional counterparts, paper reports and records of the construction process. Computer vision techniques can also store, process, and analyse images taken from a construction site more automatically and efficiently (Bender & Friedman 2018).

8.5.6 Machine Learning in Quality Control

ML, especially image processing techniques, can diagnose construction defects and monitor buildings' structural health. Akinci et al. (2006) proposed a method of quality control of construction through the automatic detection of construction defects and their management (Akinci et al. 2006). The approach used a convolution neural network (CNN) to analyse the laser scanner data and then compared the fabrications with predetermined programs to detect aberrations and defects. Zhu and Brilakis (2009) used computer vision techniques to automatically detect concrete surface defects such as air bubbles and discolouration. This method can identify the location and number of air pockets and discolouration areas on concrete surfaces.

Some studies have focused specifically on the structural health of bridges (Zhenhua & Ioannis 2009).

8.5.7 Machine Learning in Building Information Modelling

Building Information Modelling (BIM) has attracted the attention of more universities and industries. BIM is an emerging technology to digitise the construction industry and has created a new model for storing and exchanging building data. Made from an AutoCAD model, it usually cannot fully capture a built-in facility's details (Bidhendi et al. 2022).

Laser scanners can capture dense 3D measurements of a facility's as-built condition, and the resulting point cloud can be manually processed to create an as-built BIM.

However, this process is time-consuming, subjective and error prone. To solve this problem, ML can automatically convert cloud 3D points of raw data collected from a laser scanner to BIM. Tang et al. (2010) examined techniques for automating the BIM creation process, such as constructing laser scanner data, which can be divided into three main operations: geometric modelling, object recognition and object relation modelling. Methods and algorithms for providing knowledge about form, identity, and relationships are also described and summarised (Hong et al. 2020).

8.6 Discussion

AI changes how companies work, and project management is an important area positively affected. The applications of AI in project management are comprehensive. These systems provide advanced solutions, precision, strategy and support for the project manager. It also improves project managers' emotional intelligence and creativity and eliminates individual decision-making biases.

We have reached a stage where AI has reduced the need for excessive human intervention. For the first time, it can do more in less time. AI tools such as data warehousing have more storage capacity than ever.

Even with the rise of technology, the need for human interaction, input and discussion in the project management industry will always remain. There is no doubt that technology promotes projects. However, as the agile project management process has shown, face-to-face conversation is the only effective way to convy information.

8.7 Conclusions

Various ML techniques, such as safety, cost, risk, conflict and more, are currently used to manage projects. Historical and real-time data for developing ML models can provide input to traditional project management techniques. This paradigm shift occurs in various industrial sectors, including automobiles, aviation, construction and railways.

About half of the proposed ML model implementation methods use a case study method. About a quarter of the proposed methods are implemented in a real environment. Risk identification and cost management are some of the most popular things the proposed ML models help in the literature. This study's results show that due to the increasing trend in annual publications, ML techniques in project management are an emerging field for study. By gathering more data on various technical and social systems, adopting ML methods may help traditional project management by providing data-driven inputs. In the future, the industry's need for project management may lead to ML methods. Different authorities should validate ML use in project management.

References

Ahiaga-Dagbui, Dominic and Smith, Simon. 2012. "Neural networks for modelling the final target cost of water projects", Association of Researchers in Construction Management, ARCOM 2012, Proceedings of the 28th Annual Conference, 1(September), pp. 307–316.

Akinci, Burcu and Boukamp, Frank and Gordon, Chris and Huber, Daniel and Lyons, Catherine and Park, Kuhn. 2006. "A formalism for utilisation of sensor systems and integrated project models for active construction quality control" *Automation in Construction*, 15(2), pp. 124–138. doi 10.1016/J.AUTCON.2005.01.008.

Bidhendi, Ali and Arbabi, Hani and Mahoud, Mohammad. 2022. "Perceived effect of using BIM for improving construction safety," *Asian Journal of Civil Engineering*. doi 10.1007/s42107-022-00449-5.

Bidhendi, Ali and Azizi, Mojtaba. 2021 "Application of machine learning in project management". Available at: https://www.researchgate.net/publication/360757417 (Accessed: 1 June 2022).

Cheng, Min-Yuan and Tsai, Hsing-Chih and Sudjono, Erick. 2010. "Conceptual cost estimates using evolutionary fuzzy hybrid neural network for projects in the construction industry," Expert Systems with Applications, 37(6), 4224–4231. doi:10.1016/J.ESWA.2009.11.080.

Chulani, Sunita and Boehm, Barry and Steece, Bert. 1999. "Bayesian analysis of empirical software engineering cost models", *IEEE Transactions on Software Engineering*, 25(4), 573–583. doi:10.1109/32.799958.

Elfaki, Osman and Alatawi, Saleh. 2014. "Using Intelligent Techniques in Construction Project Cost Estimation: 10-Year Survey," *Advances in Civil Engineering*. Edited by S. Madanat, 2014, p. 107926. doi:10.1155/2014/107926.

Emily, Bender and Batya, Friedman. 2018. "Data Statements for Natural Language Processing: Toward Mitigating System Bias and Enabling Better Science," Transactions of the Association for Computational Linguistics, 6, 587–604. doi: 10.1162/tacl_a_00041.

Günaydin, Hasaim and Doğan, Salima. 2004. "A neural network approach for early cost estimation of structural systems of buildings," *International Journal of Project Management*, 22(7), 595–602. doi: 10.1016/J.IJPROMAN.2004.04.002.

Hammad, Ahmed and AbouRizk, Simaan and Mohamed, Yasser. 2014. "Application of KDD Techniques to Extract Useful Knowledge from Labor Resources Data in Industrial Construction Projects," *Journal of Management in Engineering*, 30(6), p. 5014011. doi:10.1061/(ASCE)ME.1943-5479.0000280.

Hong, Tianzhen and Wang, Zhe and Luo, Xuan and Zhang, Wanni. 2020. "State-of-the-art on research and applications of machine learning in the building life cycle," *Energy and Buildings*, 212, 109831. doi:10.1016/J.ENBUILD.2020.109831.

Hu, Yuqing and Castro-Lacouture, Daniel. 2019. "Clash Relevance Prediction Based on Machine Learning," *Journal of Computing in Civil Engineering,* 33(2), 4018060. doi: 10.1061/(ASCE)CP.1943-5487.0000810.

Hyunjoo, Kim and Soibelman, Lucio and Grobler, Francois. 2008. "Factor selection for delay analysis using Knowledge Discovery in Databases," *Automation in Construction*, 17(5), 550–560. doi:10.1016/J.AUTCON.2007.10.001. In, Lee and Yong Jae, Shin. 2020. "Machine learning for enterprises: Applications, algorithm selection, and challenges," *Business Horizons*, 63(2), 157–170. doi: 10.1016/J.BUSHOR.2019.10.005.

Kavakiotis, Ioannis and Tsave, Olga and Salifoglou, Athanasios. 2017. "Machine Learning and Data Mining Methods in Diabetes Research," *Computational and Structural Biotechnology Journal*, 15, 104–116. doi: 10.1016/J.CSBJ.2016.12.005.

Kim, Gwang-Hee and Kim, Sangyong and Shin, Yoonseok. 2013. "Comparison of School Building Construction Costs Estimation Methods Using Regression Analysis, Neural Network, and Support Vector Machine," *Journal of Building Construction and Planning Research*, 01(01), 1–7. doi: 10.4236/jbcpr.2013.11001.

Liu, Zheng and Sadiq, Rehan and Rajani, Bogarapu. 2010. "Exploring the Relationship between Soil Properties and Deterioration of Metallic Pipes Using Predictive Data Mining Methods," *Journal of Computing in Civil Engineering,* 24(3), pp. 289–301. doi:10.1061/(ASCE)CP.1943-5487.0000032.

Marzouk, Mohamed and Ahmed, Rasha. 2011. "A case-based reasoning approach for estimating the costs of pump station projects," *Journal of Advanced Research*, 2(4), 289–295. doi:10.1016/J.JARE.2011.01.007.

Miang, Yang and Nur, Faddilah. 2015. "Cognitive Factors Influencing Safety Behaviour at Height: A Multimethod Exploratory Study," *Journal of Construction Engineering and Management*, 141(6), 4015003. doi: 10.1061/(ASCE)CO.1943-7862.0000972.

Mohammad, Muamer and Sulaiman, Norrozila and Muhsin, Osama. 2011. "A novel intrusion detection system by using intelligent data mining Artificial Intelligence and Machine Learning in Project Management in WEKA environment," *Procedia Computer Science*, 3, 1237–1242. doi: 10.1016/J.PROCS.2010.12.198.

Narrative Science (2015) "Practical Artificial Intelligence For Dummies" Available at: https://www.businesswire.com/news/home/20150728005453/en/Narrative-Science-Publishes-Practical-Artificial-Intelligence-For-Dummies-Book (Accessed: 1 June 2022).

Paliwal, Mukta and Kumar, UshaA. 2009. "Neural networks and statistical techniques: A review of applications," *Expert Systems with Applications*, 36(1), 2–17. doi: 10.1016/J.ESWA.2007.10.005.

Pasichnyi, Oleksii and Wallin, Jörgen and Levihn, Fabian. 2019. "Energy performance certificates—New opportunities for data-enabled urban energy policy instruments?" *Energy Policy*, 127, 486–499. doi:10.1016/J.ENPOL.2018.11.051.

Project Management Institute (PMI), https://www.pmi.org/.

Putka, Dan and Beatty, Adam and Reeder, Matthew. 2017. "Modern Prediction Methods: New Perspectives on a Common Problem," Organizational Research Methods, 21(3), pp. 689–732. doi:10.1177/1094428117697041.

Reich, Yoram and Barai, Sliva. 1999. "Evaluating machine learning models for engineering problems," Artificial Intelligence in Engineering, 13(3), pp. 257–272.
doi: 10.1016/S0954-1810(98)00021-1.

Sabahi, Sima and Parast, Mahour. 2020. "The impact of entrepreneurship orientation on project performance: A machine learning approach," *International Journal of Production Economics*, 226, 107621.
doi:10.1016/J.IJPE.2020.107621.

Shmueli, Galit and Koppius, Otto. 2011. "Predictive Analytics in Information Systems Research," MIS Quarterly, 35(3), pp. 553–572.
doi: 10.2307/23042796.

Tixier, Antoine and Hallowell, Matthew and Rajagopalan, Balaji and Bowman, Dean. 2016. "Application of machine learning to construction injury prediction," Automation in Construction, 69, 102–114. doi: 10.1016/J.AUTCON.2016.05.016.

Wang, Yu-Ren and Gibson, Edward. 2010. "A study of pre-project planning and project success using ANNs and regression models," *Automation in Construction*, 19(3), 341–346.
doi:10.1016/J.AUTCON.2009.12.007.

Westenberger, Jens and Schuler, Kajetan and Schlegel, Dennis. 2022. "Failure of AI projects: understanding the critical factors," *Procedia Computer Science*, 196, 69–76. doi:10.1016/J.PROCS.2021.11.074.

Williams, Trefor and Gong, Jie. 2014. "Predicting construction cost overruns using text mining, numerical data and ensemble classifiers," *Automation in Construction*, 43, 23–29.
doi:10.1016/J.AUTCON.2014.02.014.

Witten, Iovn and Hall, Minoa and Frank, Edvardo. 2005. *Practical Machine Learning Third Edition*.

Xiao, Fu and Fan, Cheng. 2014. "Data mining in building automation system for improving building operational performance," *Energy and Buildings*, 75, 109–118. doi: 10.1016/J.ENBUILD.2014.02.005.

Yu, Wender and Skibniewski, Mirosław. 2010. "Integrating Neurofuzzy System with Conceptual Cost Estimation to Discover Cost-Related Knowledge from Residential Construction Projects," *Journal of Computing in Civil Engineering*, 24(1), 35–44.
doi:10.1061/(ASCE)0887-3801(2010)24:1(35).

Zhang, Yi. 1999. "Smart PCA". IJCAI 2009, Proceedings of the 21st International Joint Conference on Artificial Intelligence.

Zhenhua, Zhu and Ioannis, Brilakis. 2009. "Comparison of Optical Sensor-Based Spatial Data Collection Techniques for Civil Infrastructure

Modelling," *Journal of Computing in Civil Engineering*, 23(3), 170–177. doi: 10.1061/(ASCE)0887-3801(2009)23:3(170).
Zhou, Zhipeng and Goh, Y. M. Yang and Li, Qiming. 2015. "Overview and analysis of safety management studies in the construction industry," *Safety Science*, 72, 337–350. doi:10.1016/J.SSCI.2014.10.006.

Ali Bidhendi is an M.Sc. in construction and project management at Tarbiat Modares University (TMU) and achieved PMP in 2022. His professional field is in the construction and information technology industry, and duc to his effort in R&D, he earned the required points of Iran"s National Elites Foundation. He also achieved the award for best local organiser (LO) in this global competition in 2021 and won first place in the project management championship (PMC) in Iran 2020. He is also the YC Stars in International Project Management Association (IPMA) project manager.

Mohammad Mahoud is a visiting lecturer for post-graduate business/project management students at the State University of Management. Due to his scientific and research background, he is an international peer reviewer of the Infrastructure Asset Management & Municipal Engineer & Urban Design and Planning Journals—Proceedings of the Institution of Civil Engineers (UK), the Asian Journal of Civil Engineering (Building and Housing) from the proceedings of Springer Nature, the Journal of Civil, Construction and Environmental Engineering from Science Publishing Group (US), the International Journal of Construction Supply Chain Management from Massey University (New Zealand), and an editorial board member of the Project Leadership and Society Journal from the proceedings of Elsevier. He has more than ten years of managing and development experience outside academia. He is the Founder and CEO of the 3M-CEPM R&D Institute. In his professional career, he has been educated as a trainer (TOT) in entrepreneurship, leadership and business management based on the learning model LENA by the Austrian Chamber of Commerce (WIFI). Moreover, he has been selected as the judge at the accredited Global Individual Achievement Awards of the International Project Management Association (IPMA). Lastly, he has already been selected as the judge at the world's largest and most prestigious awards for PMOs and PMO Leaders by PMO Global Awards (PMOGA).

IX

DEVELOPMENT OF AN EDUCATION MODEL FOR PRODUCERS AND PROJECT MANAGERS IN MULTIMEDIA PRODUCTION

SREČKO ZAKRAJŠEK, NEJC ZAKRAJŠEK AND MIHA ZAKRAJŠEK

9.1 Project management in multimedia production

The preparation and development of a higher education programme in multimedia production, which is rapidly evolving and changing, is very demanding and requires the consideration of various requirements and the participation of different and numerous stakeholders.

In preparation and implementation of programmes, relatively rigid and demanding rules for higher education programmes must be adhered to, and graduates also go into a working environment where they must learn about different technologies, equipment and procedures and consider relevant standards and certificates. The work environment generally requires more knowledge, skills and competencies than graduates usually have when they enter it. These differences can partly be mitigated by the fact that students have already been involved in the organisation's work during their studies by preparing various seminar assignments, projects, compulsory practical training and preparation of diploma projects.

Part of the knowledge, skills and competencies in the certificates are to be included in the educational programme by the education institution. Those specific to individual professional fields can be included in elective courses.

In this paper, we will focus on including elements of certificates established in project and production work and the standards of digital competencies.

Students tend to obtain certificates after graduation when they decide to work in a certain field, as they must have a certain number of years of work on projects to obtain a certificate, especially at higher levels, and they must also present relevant performed work. In schools, students prepare several projects, usually sufficient to obtain certificates of lower to medium difficulty; the highest certificates require many years of successful work in practice.

We decided to manage the design and implementation of the study programme as a portfolio of projects, as the educational process is characterised by years and subjects that have specific goals, responsible persons (the dean, lecturers, and mentors), a target public (students, organisations which employ graduates, etc.), time and financial frameworks and requirements for quality, risk and uncertainty, etc., which are all characteristics of the project. At the same time, all projects also have post-project activities, as each project's results (knowledge, skills) (subject or other activities) are transferred through academic years and into practice after graduation.

9.1.1 The Definition of a research problem

This chapter presents the course of research and the bases at the IAM (Institute and Academy of Multimedia) used to prepare and upgrade the higher education programme Multimedia Production. In the first phase, we developed an IAM higher education programme from the idea we prepared in 1995 to its actual beginnings in 2000. The independent higher education programme prepares graduates for quality performance work in a specific elective field (animation, audio, photography, graphic design, web, video etc.) of multimedia production in practice in two years. Students also gain competencies for planning and implementing simpler projects.

We monitored and developed the short-cycle higher education programme and upgraded it to the higher education programme we developed at IAM, where the first students enrolled in 2010. In preparation for this programme, we set the acquisition of knowledge, skills and competencies for production and project work among the initial goals. We defined these competencies in detail in the subject-specific competencies of the study programme.

After 2017 (when the European Digital Competence Framework DigComp was established), we began to systematically include the acquisition of digital competencies in the study programme and, by this, upgrade the existing system of acquiring and optimising multimedia competencies.

Whilst preparing the new study programme, we encountered many unknown issues because there were no similar educational programmes before the year 2000, as the field of multimedia production had only just started to develop.

In an article from 2003, Picard (2003) pointed out that the development of global physical distribution systems for audio, video and software products and digital distribution based on the Internet and cable and satellite systems has created the possibility of new global markets for multimedia products and services. He also noted that only a few companies effectively use these opportunities, as multimedia production still has much ambiguity and uncertainties.

Uncertainties and ambiguities in practice created issues for preparing the study programme. However, they posed a great challenge simultaneously, as we had the opportunity to create an innovative, interesting and useful study programme for students and the environment.

In preparing study programmes, an important requirement is that the programme must be prepared according to certain criteria and established rules based on extensive theoretical knowledge and only to a lesser extent on the acquisition of competencies, usually in practical work in organisations. The implementation should be planned as lectures and exercises, and research work should also be important.

Preparing a programme where the necessary core and special knowledge, skills and competencies can be provided in multimedia production is extremely demanding because multimedia production is extensive and diverse. Therefore, selectivity and specialisation are also essential.

A special challenge in planning and implementing the programme was that it was only after 2000 that modern technologies and portals that realistically provide proper organisation and management of the study process started to be systematically introduced to education (Baule 2019).

E-learning began to emerge in the late 1990s and was introduced in some institutions with the LMS—learning management system when the implementation models of online education were considered from a technological point of view (Siemens & Tittenberger 2009). This was the start of using LMS, such as Blackboard, Moodle, combinations of digital tools, such as blogs, wikis, Skype, discussion forums, online lectures (synchronous) with virtual classes supported by LMS or a combination of digital tools, podcasts, video lectures and OER either with LMS or a combination of digital tools.

Using cloud computing, smartphones and other personal devices (BYOD) have recently become predominant. Open educational resources (OER), big data and learning analysts became common.

However, the rapid development of modern technologies and distance education has been accelerated by the COVID-19 crisis. Mishra et al. (2021) describe innovative and effective ways to use multimedia for education during the pandemic. The authors believe this is the most effective and influential teaching and learning methodology.

Difficult challenges also arose in introducing certain certificate requirements in the educational programme since, e.g., certificates for project work take three years minimum to obtain a certificate at the first D level. In production work, programmes are implemented mainly for film producers, whilst programmes are rare or included as an optional part of study programmes in other fields. In digital competencies, criteria for professional fields of multimedia production have not yet been developed, but some certificates can be used in preparing the programme and evaluating results.

All this has enabled us to conduct continuous research since 1995 by preparing an appropriate work programme for each period.

Before beginning the research, we defined the purpose and goals of the research and set the research questions.

9.1.2 Purpose and goals of the research

We prepared the research to thoroughly explore all the areas required to prepare, develop and implement a quality higher education programme and the relations between them. This should enable achieving goals: developing, realising, implementing and evaluating a quality higher education programme in multimedia production.

9.1.3 Research questions

Based on introductory research and experience from practical work, we set three research questions which covered areas that are crucial for the preparation of a modern study programme:

1. How should the higher education professional study programme be conceived and structured for graduates to acquire relevant knowledge, skills and competencies in project and production work in multimedia production?

2. What are the possible and meaningful links between education and obtaining certain certificates?
3. What are the optimal approaches to acquiring digital competencies of students in the study process of multimedia production?

9.2 Basic information on fields that are important for the preparation of the study programme

For reviewing the segments that are crucial for the preparation of a higher education programme, we focused on five fields, namely:

- the requirements for the preparation of the programme as defined in the Higher Education Act (2016) and the requirements of the SQAA (Slovenian Quality Assurance Agency for Higher Education) (SQAA Criteria 2019);
- the issue of programme planning and review of similar programmes around the globe;
- the analysis of multimedia production to obtain data for the preparation of goals and competencies of the programme;
- obtaining digital competencies that are required for work in multimedia production, and
- certificates that exist in design and production work.

Based on reviewing the situation and selecting relevant sources, we conducted research in individual areas per the methodology and methods described in Chapter Three. The results of partial research were integrated into the educational programme, which is composed to enable constant innovation and updating per the development of the profession and the requirements of science, the profession and the labour market.

9.2.1 Requirements for the preparation of the study programme

The basic requirements set out in the Higher Education Act must be considered when preparing a study programme. Given that higher education in the EU is standardised, the same rules apply to all institutions in the EU.

Compulsory components of study programmes for further education are defined in Article 35 of the Higher Education Act (2016):

- general information about the programme (name, type, duration);
- definition of basic goals of the programme or general and subject-specific competencies acquired in the programme;

- syllabus with credit valuation of study obligations in accordance with ECTS and definition of the share of electives in the programme;
- enrolment requirements and criteria for selection in the event of enrolment limits;
- provisions on acknowledging knowledge and skills acquired before enrolment in the programme;
- assessment methods;
- criteria for advancing the programme;
- the manner of conducting the study;
- criteria for completion of the study.

Basic requirements also include the components of study programmes determined by the year's credit evaluation, semester, and syllabus (Credit Evaluation Criteria 2019).

Study programmes must be composed so that each year has 60 credit points, and a semester should have 30.

The syllabus must present the number of credit points required to complete each programme unit (i.e. subject, module, practical training etc.) and learning outcomes or competencies of the entire study programme and individual units. The programme must include at least 10% of elective subjects. The diploma thesis must also be credit-evaluated for completing the study. Students must be able to transfer at least ten credits from the compulsory or elective units of the programme from one study programme to another.

Self et al. (2019) present the results of a study proving that interdisciplinary study aimed at practical project implementation is very effective. Projects were prepared in design, and it was found that it is possible to perform the synthesis and integration of knowledge successfully in this way. For this type of work, students must have appropriate prior knowledge and skills, be motivated and be properly guided.

Based on general starting points, it is necessary to prepare the study programme's structure and content, which differs depending on the chosen field of study. The structure and content of the programme are reviewed by an external institution (SQAA) which focuses on achieving certain standards (Accreditation Criteria 2021).

In doing so, the first standard is that, according to its composition and content, the study programme offers students comprehensive knowledge and enables them to achieve the set goals and planned competencies or learning outcomes. The syllabus must be prepared so that the subjects have appropriate credit-valuation and are distributed by years and semesters, consequently being consistent and substantively related, and that the programme integrates the necessary scientific, professional, research or artistic content.

To achieve the second standard, the study programme must be appropriately placed in the planned field and disciplines in terms of name, purpose and content and how the contents of the study programme are related, what their relation is to useful or basic knowledge in the field and discipline and the conceptual selection of contents that are clearly defined and meaningfully related to the current situation and development trends.

For the third standard, the study programme must be connected to the environment in which the higher education institution operates to the extent that the higher education institution's scientific, professional, research or artistic cooperation is established in the field from which the study programme originates.

Analyses or research of the needs of the employment environment, labour market and employability of graduates or the need for knowledge and society's goals must be performed. It is also very important that the environment is favourable for students' practical education and that mentors' involvement and education are ensured. An appropriate financial strategy must be provided to prepare and implement the programme.

In any case, the preparation of the study programme requires the participation of motivated experts from the educational institution, from the profession and professional associations, as well as chambers and government organisations.

9.2.2 Overview of some institutions and study programmes

In the preparation phase of the higher education study programme before 2010, we reviewed and analysed some higher education institutions and study programmes, and it should be noted that most of the programmes at that time were mainly focused on film and TV production. In 2022, we also assessed the changes implemented since 2010.

Within the programmes, we analysed their structure, purpose and goals, distribution and content of subjects, competencies, content that provides acquisition of project and production knowledge and skills, and competencies for work in practice.

Middlesex University, United Kingdom

In 2010, Middlesex University (http://www.mdx.ac.uk) implemented two programmes: a BA (Hons) in Television Production. In 2022, they also offered a creative media and writing programme.

The television production course is technically designed but includes some "soft" content. The programme focused on the technically specific requirements of television production whilst leaving enough space for students to become familiar with the content requirements of television production, which allows quality cooperation with all those involved and highly technical knowledge. The programme included extensive practical work in the studio and other locations, giving the student a sense of working in real media.

Students learned how to produce documentaries and programmes, how a news programme on television works, and how to prepare an entertainment programme.

In addition to the content work, students also learned how to research an interesting story, prepare it for production and write, direct, produce and publish it in the media.

The course required effective study and personal and professional development. It motivated students to communicate with each other and engage in teamwork, and they also required sufficient knowledge of information technology. In short, everything was lacking in former television technicians' courses.

Loyalist College, Ontario, Canada

BA Television and New Media Production programme conducted by Loyalist College of Ontario (https://www.loyalistcollege.com/) since 2010 offers students a course tailored to the needs of television, video and online production.

Students acquire extensive knowledge, deepening in selected fields of study. In the first year, they learn the technical basics of television and new media. During the first year of study, students get to know all the jobs in production during their practical work. In the second academic year, students start to decide on their specialisation. They upgrade their practical work in a real production provided by a local cable TV station in cooperation with the school. They begin to prepare various contributions and train in teamwork simultaneously in collaboration with journalism students. In the third year, they specialise in the field that they then develop in their dissertation.

In 2013, the Digital Media Centre (http://www.loyalistcollege.com/our-campus/campus-facilities/digital-media-centre/) was opened, in which television, film, digital content creation, animation, gaming, journalism, communications and photojournalism are taught.

Students write, report, share photos, host programmes and create online social media, video and audio content. They use all modern technologies and media, ensuring constant updating of the study programme. They also gain basic knowledge about production and project work.

The college also offers one-year work programmes: project manager, project control analyst, project schedule analyst, project control officer, project coordinator, project planner and project team leader.

University of Canberra, Australia

The BA (Hons) Communication in Media/Multimedia Production course, provided since 2010 at the University of Canberra (https://www.canberra.edu.au/) in Australia, is a balanced programme of advanced practical technical knowledge and integrated analytical studies. The acquired knowledge and skills enable students to upgrade their professional work with new, creative solutions and successfully transfer them to the world of the constantly changing media industry. The study emphasises technique and creativity in dynamic media production and industry processes.

In the first year of study, students become acquainted with digital photography, cinematography, and the Internet and in the second year, they deepen their knowledge of animation in the technology field and communication and media studies in social sciences. In the third and final year, the interlinked technical and social science knowledge is used for a graduate project in media production. In 2022, the communication and media course Art in Design focused on creative artwork in production.

An example of multimedia teaching was presented in an article by Jennifer Goode (2021). The pilot programme conducted in the autumn of 2017 was presented with an attempt to link the teaching of multimedia project management skills in higher education and a master's course. The same lecturer managed the programme. At the higher education institution, they developed mainly technical skills and implementation management (the multimedia programme) and project management (the Management of Multimedia programme) in the master's. Both groups came together on the same projects and thus achieved good results. This paper proposes concrete multimedia projects, and one of the possibilities is a cooperation between high school students mainly focused on production and management skills and the master's degree, for which students obtain advanced project knowledge and skills. This way, postgraduate students plan and lead projects whilst lower-year students technically implement them.

9.2.3 Presentation of multimedia production

The scope of the field of multimedia production is best seen by listing the areas in which it is crucial: audio production, AV products and film, MM equipment and various applications for vehicles, blogs, digital library, 2D animation, DJ, digital illustration, e-learning, film industry, photography, graphic design, gambling, gaming, web and mobile applications, multimedia installations, multimedia equipment, advertising products and campaigns, podcasts, materials for electronic boards and educational platforms, billboards, promotional projects, simulations, scenarios (films, commercials, risks, etc.), web production, technical organisation of events, teleconferences, printing, video production, 3D modelling and animation, VJ, virtual reality, vlogs, etc.

Jin et al. (2021) explain the importance of multimedia materials and presentations in the media, as the organisations that use them gain a market advantage. The design, quality and options for interactive use are very important because we promote information and social motivation for entertainment with these products.

Youn et al. (2021) show multimedia materials' development, importance and effectiveness in education. The development of creative multimedia products is based on quality educational content, from which multimedia materials, films, animations, documentaries, cartoons etc., are created, which are constantly checked in practice on various media (especially online and mobile devices) and also improve with the help of teachers and user feedback (students).

We encounter certain peculiarities in multimedia production, often similar to those in the IT sector and which are probably also present in other areas to a lesser extent.

It is extremely important that an innovative and highly specialised individual can prepare certain products or services for the global market from home and with affordable equipment.

Multimedia technologies are also associated with negative impacts as computer systems and connections consume a huge amount of electricity; the environment is negatively affected by the acquisition of materials for devices, the use of certain products increases light pollution, and large amounts of electronic waste are generated. It is also worth mentioning the negative effects, such as various forms of addiction.

Multimedia production is characterised by:

- including at least two types of media;
- being based on digital technologies and mobile and online services;

- globalisation, connectivity, interactivity, and the constant development of "smart" products that can quickly establish themselves in the international market;
- operation in a global market economy-great opportunities, fierce competition, constant scrutiny, etc.;
- strict copyright law;
- being present and mandatory in all areas that have the largest market (entertainment, advertising, education, etc.) and a local and global market;
- based on creativity, innovation, and interactivity;
- constantly needs new content, events, approaches, solutions, etc.;
- enabling continuous, practical instant monitoring, display and assessment of the quality and (business) performance of products;
- most multimedia production is performed in the form of projects and is led by project managers or producers.

Multimedia production is characterised by creativity and innovation, as well as constantly new and innovative products and services and production requirements, and that is why we encounter uncertainties and risks in most projects. As multimedia production is based on stories and other authorial products, it employs many creative and artistically talented staff, which makes knowledge of the organisation and teamwork especially important.

Figure 9.1 shows the phases and course of multimedia production according to the IAM methodology. The methodology was developed at the IAM, Ljubljana.

In multimedia production, the following division is often used:

- pre-production, which represents the strategic part of the project and product selection;
- production when product production takes place;
- post-production when the final version of the product is prepared;
- product distribution when marketing and sales activities take place.

Most multimedia production is performed on a project basis, with many projects followed up with post-project (post-production) activities in which the product is put into practice and marketed for many years through copyright and related rights (e.g. films, TV series, books, music catalogues) or where product maintenance and upgrades must be provided.

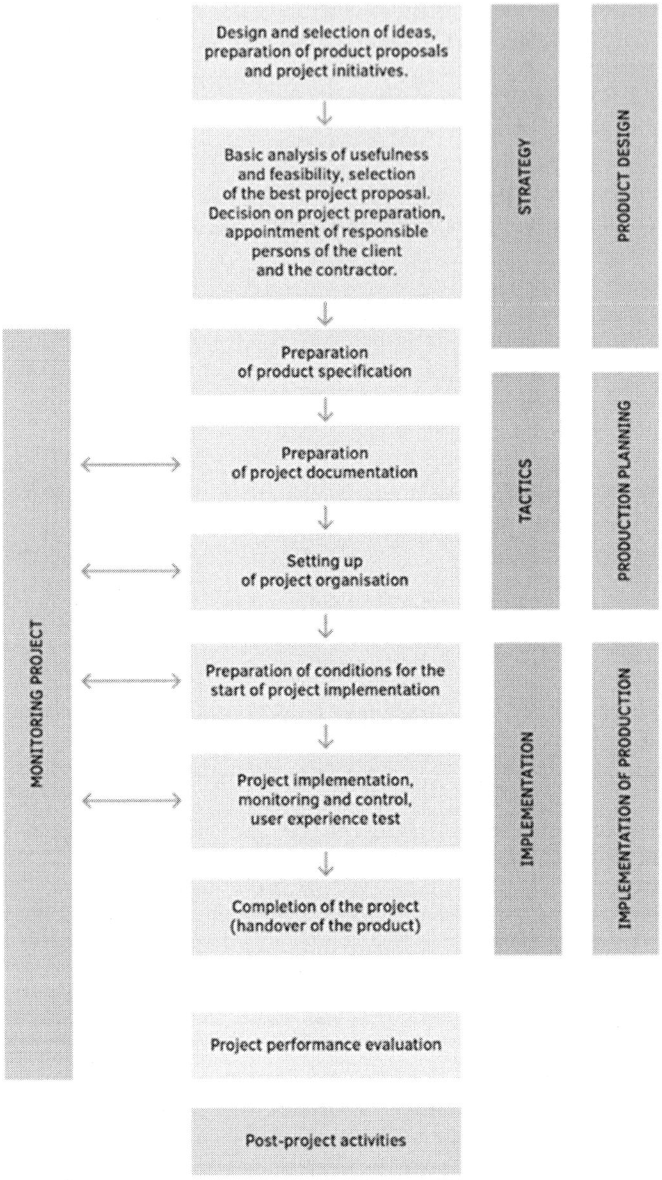

Figure 9.1 *Assemblies, phases and activities of the project in accordance with IAM methodology*

As shown in Figure 9.1, the basic skeleton is the same for all multimedia production, allowing the design of a core educational programme. However, the differences are in individual segments, which can be arranged by selecting part of the programme involving specialists and cooperating with organisations.

In order to prepare a study programme, it is necessary to be familiar with and consider the generic and subject-specific competencies required for work in this field, which must be included in the higher level of education.

Attempts to define skills or competencies for work in multimedia were made in 2001 (Richey et al. 2001), and competencies were determined for visualisation, interaction and simulation processes in 2005 (Earle et al. 2005) when requirements were set for knowledge of copyright tools for creating effective hypermedia/multimedia learning materials.

In 2012 (Sugar 2012), the results were published of an extensive survey which analysed the required competencies needed in different professional fields. It was found that creating products for use in real media is the most important for acquiring digital and professional competencies, and it is necessary to achieve an appropriate balance between study and the production process. It was stressed that students must learn about effective online work, have oral and written communication competencies, and be trained for participation. The research results also showed that students involved in the preparation of real projects are more competent than students who are only involved in the study process at educational institutions.

9.2.4 Digital competencies

Digital competencies that define the use of knowledge and skills in the digital environment are among the key competencies of an expert in multimedia production. These competencies are relatively new and were mainly considered as part of various other competencies, such as computer and media literacy, before 2010.

In 2006, the European Parliament and Commission noted (Punie and Cabrera 2006) that digital literacy includes the safe and critical use of information society technologies (IST) in communications and leisure time at work. Basic ICT skills support it using computers to search, evaluate, store, produce, present and exchange information and to communicate and participate in collaborative networks over the Internet. Certain recommendations were also included (Recommendations 2006).

In 2013, the EU was ready to prepare an Open Education Action Plan of the Committee to increase innovation and digital competencies in schools and universities (Action Plan 2013).

DigComp digital competencies framework

In 2016, the Joint Research Centre (JRC) released DigComp 2.0 (DigComp 2016), which introduced a conceptual model of the digital competencies framework, which was then upgraded to DigComp 2.1, released in 2017 (DigComp 2017).

The Digital Competence Framework developed in Europe aimed to identify and describe the key components of digital competence in terms of knowledge, skills and attitudes. Competence areas represent the basic framework:

- information,
- communication,
- content creation,
- protection,
- problem-solving.

The main goals of DigComp are:

- DigCompOrg seeks to promote self-reflection and self-assessment in educational organisations that are intended to introduce digital learning in accordance with their capabilities;
- DigCompOrg is designed to focus primarily on teaching, learning, assessment and related learning support activities carried out by a particular educational organisation. However, it is not focused on organisational forms of implementation, which is left to the capabilities of different countries and institutions.

Learning outcomes are the basis for each level, and Bloom's Taxonomy and the European Qualifications Framework are considered. The aim is to prepare tests for different areas that could realistically measure digital competencies and apply them universally to all societal areas and levels. As there are 21 types of digital competencies and eight levels of competencies, 168 descriptors need to be prepared for each specific field or process, in accordance with which the digital competencies of individuals can be determined.

Table 9.1 lists the levels of competencies and basic requirements for the public (DigComp 2.1 2017, 13).

IPMA presented a paper in 2018 (Wagner 2018), "Competencies-an update for the digital era," describing digital competencies' importance and their great influence on project work and proposing the necessary changes. The author pointed out that the most important task is developing competencies related to digitisation, using digital tools and applications, and understanding potentials and threats. This includes finding collaborators for projects through social media. It puts data analytics in second place because the most important data must be selected, analysed and evaluated quickly. This is about accurate customer and stakeholder data allowing quick action, adaptation, forecasting trends and planning development. Also included was the necessity of agile project work forms in these processes. Project managers must be able to reflect on the completed work critically and have a self-organisation and participatory leadership style based on dynamic learning processes, collaboration with others and the exchange of experience and knowledge. The competence for stakeholder participation and involvement is becoming the central competence of every project manager.

As a follow-up to the 2018 Action Plan (Communication from the Commission 2018), in September 2020, the EU published the Digital Education Action Plan 2021-2027 (2020), which sets out a vision for high-quality, inclusive and accessible digital education in Europe. The plan has two strategic priorities:

- promoting the development of a highly efficient digital education ecosystem,
- improving digital skills and competencies for digital transformation.

The priority included infrastructure, connectivity, digital equipment, effective digital capacity planning, teacher education and training, high-quality content and the development of user-friendly tools and secure platforms that respect privacy and ethical standards.

Specifically, a European content framework for digital education, building on European cultural and creative diversity, should be developed in the short term, and a feasibility study on a possible European platform for sharing certified online resources and linking to existing educational platforms should be prepared. Digital transformation plans at all levels of education and training through Erasmus cooperation projects should also be supported.

The platforms support digital pedagogy and expertise in using digital tools for teachers through the Erasmus Teacher Academy and the online tool for teacher self-assessment-SELFIE (self-reflection on effective learning by promoting innovative educational technologies). They will also develop ethical guidelines on artificial intelligence and support Horizon Europe's research and innovation.

The second priority is improving digital competencies for digital transformation, which will develop common guidelines for teachers and educational staff to promote digital literacy and address misinformation and problems in this field. Special emphasis will be placed on integrating artificial intelligence and data-related skills. Activities to increase women's participation in areas involving ICT (science, technology, engineering and mathematics) are also important. This will help increase EU citizens' digital competencies at all levels.

Table 9.1 *Levels of digital competence for EU citizens and keywords for each level*

Levels of digital. competencies in DigComp 2.1	Difficulty of tasks	Independence	Predominant cognitive level
1 Helplessness	Simple tasks	With the support of others	Remembering
2 Helplessness	Simple tasks	Independently and with the support of others when needed	Remembering
3 Survival	Normal tasks and simple problems	Independently	Understanding
4 Survival	Tasks and well-defined and unusual problems	Independently and in accordance with their own needs	Understanding
5 Overcoming obstacles	A variety of tasks and problems	Providing support to others	Use
6 Overcoming obstacles	Demanding tasks	Adapting to others in demanding tasks	Evaluation
7 Mastery	Solving complex	Involvement and contribution	Production

	problems with a limited number of solutions	to professional solutions, leading others	
8 Mastery	Solving complex problems with many interdependent factors	Proposing new ideas and processes for the professional field	Production

ECDL Certificates

ECDL certificates (ECDL 2021), which are already well established, cover most digital competencies. Their advantage is that they are already operationally implemented in practice and are constantly being updated and upgraded, depending on changes in the professions.

There are three different ECDL certificates: base, standard and advanced ECDL profiles, each representing a different level of knowledge, skills and competencies. The base certificate is obtained by completing four modules (computer essentials, online essentials, word processing and spreadsheets). The standard certificate is an upgrade of the Base option, which means that, in addition to the four basic exams, three more exams must be passed from the standard modules group (presentation, using databases, IT security, online collaboration, image editing, web editing, 2D design and project planning). One of the advanced modules (advanced databases, advanced spreadsheets, advanced word processing and advanced presentation) must be completed for the advanced certificate.

9.2.5 Certificates for project work

When preparing courses that must include certain goals and competencies, it is sensible to consider certificates for individual fields and include them in the competencies and contents of individual subjects. This way, the connection, coordination and updating of curricula in accordance with the requirements and needs of practice are ensured in the most meaningful and rational way, and there is a certain feedback effect simultaneously.

As part of this research, we focused on certificates related to design and production work.

The IPMA (International Project Management Association) organisation has the most detailed competency system for project work. The IPMA is an international organisation working in project management, and the Slovenian Project Management Association (ZPM) is one of the members of this organisation. There is an international certification of experts within the framework of IPMA in project management, which is carried out in Slovenia by ZPM alongside the "IPMA SloCert" programme. A certificate is a document to demonstrate the qualifications and competence of its holder regarding the ability to use the necessary knowledge and/or skills and the suitability of personality traits for successful and efficient project management (IPMA SloCert 2002).

To obtain the international IPMA certificate for a project manager, candidates had to demonstrate competencies in various fields before 2010 (ICB IPMA 2006), when we were preparing our higher education study programme Multimedia Production. A total of the 46 most important competencies had to be mastered, namely:

- environmental competencies (11)-including organisational competencies and ability to work in a project-orientated organisation (project orientation, programme orientation, portfolio orientation, project, programme and portfolio implementation, permanent organisation, business, systems, products and technology, human management, health, protection, security, environment, finance, legislation);
- technical competencies (20)-mastering the contents of project management (success of project management, stakeholders, project requirements and objectives, risks and opportunities, quality, project organisation, teamwork, problem-solving, project structures, scope and achievements, time and phases of the project, resources, costs and finances, supply and contracts, changes, controls and reports, information and documentation, communications, project launch, project completion);
- behavioural competencies (15)-personal qualities (leadership, belonging and motivation, self-control, perseverance, relaxation, openness, creativity, result orientation, efficiency, consultation, negotiation, conflicts and crises, reliability, values, ethics).

The programme and competencies have been supplemented over the years (ICB 4.0 2015). Various certificates are possible within IPMA 4LC certification, which is related to the characteristics of the project, programme or portfolio of projects and is divided into four levels accordingly, meaning that the certificate can also be obtained only to demonstrate knowledge in project management (IPMA CCT).

It is possible to obtain the following D certificates for projects: (project task manager), C (project manager), B (senior project manager) and A (project director). Certificates B and A can be obtained for programmes and portfolios.

In order to obtain certificates, it is necessary to acquire further theoretical knowledge and relevant skills and experience with work and in practice with workshops organised by IPMA.

As our higher professional education course, Multimedia Production takes three years, we have focused on obtaining D and C certificates.

The basic level is the D level: Certified Project Management Associate-IPMA level D-(certified project manager)-an expert who masters project management knowledge. The certificate is intended for: members of project teams, project managers and anyone who wants confirmation of their knowledge in project management. Conditions for obtaining the certificate are that the candidate must know all areas of ICB competencies. However, no work experience is required.

Level C is higher (Certified Project Manager-IPMA level C)-a certified project manager who independently manages less complex projects or participates in managing complex projects. The certificate is intended for: managers of all non-complex projects (commercial, strategic, development, etc.). The candidate planning to obtain this title must meet the following conditions: at least three years of work experience in managing less complex projects as a project manager (or as a subproject manager in complex projects) and a qualification in managing less complex projects for which the candidate uses appropriate management methods, techniques and tools.

We provide basic data with an explanation from extensive material to understand the system of competencies in accordance with the current certification system (ICB 4.0 2015).

Individual competence is using knowledge, skills and abilities to achieve the desired results. There are also team (linking individual competencies) and organisational competencies that address strategic competencies.

Areas of competence are divided into:

Human competencies that are personal or interpersonal and enable participation in projects or their management (they have ten elements). They originate from the ability to self-reflect and must enable the successful implementation of projects. Communication and building relationships with customers and teammates are important, as well as the ability to lead in crises:

- Self-reflection and management of one's own activities,
- Personal integrity and reliability,

- Personal communication,
- Relationships and commitment,
- Leadership,
- Teamwork,
- Conflicts and crises,
- Ingenuity and ability to create a creative environment,
- Negotiation,
- Focus on results, ability to lead teams to goals.

Practical (implementation) competencies refer to the specific methods, tools and techniques required to work on projects from planning to implementation (they have 14 elements). Therefore, they are in the same order as the work on the project:

- Project, programme or portfolio design when structure and connections are formed.
- Purpose, goals and requirements. A precise definition of objectives and requirements.
- Scope. Defining the scope of the project.
- Time. Project timeline and milestones.
- Organisation and information. Preparation of an organisational chart and communication plan.
- Quality. Preparation of quality criteria and control methods.
- Finances. Definition of financial resources.
- Resources. Preparation of project resources (personnel, space, equipment, materials, logistics, etc.).
- Procurement and partnerships.
- Plan and control. Project progress monitoring and control plan.
- Risks and opportunities. Identification of risks and opportunities.
- Stakeholders. Stakeholder cooperation programme.
- Change and transformation. Identification of possible changes and actions if changes are needed.

Perspective competencies include methods, tools and techniques by which individuals interact with the environment (they have five elements):

- Strategy (to set clear goals and guidelines).
- Management, structures, and processes (to prepare an appropriate, optimal organisation).
- Compliance, standards, and regulations (to ensure organised operation in accordance with regulations).

- Strengths and interests (that the participants have the interest and ability to prepare the project).
- Culture and evaluation (knowledge and provision of an appropriate culture of cooperation).

Each competency has a description, purpose, definition, knowledge, skills and connections to other areas. The main competency indicators have a description and criteria.

9.3 Methodology

To find answers to research questions, we prepared a research plan and determined which elements and variables we would monitor and in what manner. We used approaches and methods from qualitative (observation, interview and conversation, brainstorming, focus groups, action research) and quantitative research (surveys). In doing so, we observed the situation in educational systems and organisations globally, Slovenia and associations dealing with certification. We have systematically analysed certain elements in over a hundred production organisations in audio, video, TV and radio production, graphics, the web and event organisation. Our students and graduates do internships or work in these organisations. That is why we also have regular contact with human resources departments, mentors and experts who know our work and, at the same time, influence it with proposals for changes and comments on the work.

For project competencies, we adopted the criteria of IPMA certificates; for digital competencies, the Dig.Comp methodology and the requirements of SQAA for the structure of study programmes and subjects. In the requirements for producers, we mainly adopted the opinions of successful producers.

9.3.1 Design Science Research methodology

We used the research approach, design and development method of DSRM (design science research methodology) products (Hevner et al. 2004; Peffers 2007). This strategy aims to create new products or solutions (artefacts), enable the restructuring of organisations or prepare new ones, etc. The strategy is based on seven guidelines that must be followed if the research is to be completed (Figure 9.2).

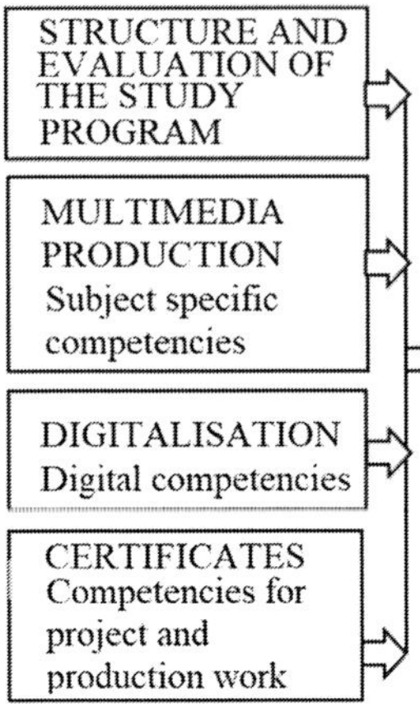

Figure 9.2 *Conceptual research model*

Figure 9.3 shows the planned course of research in accordance with the DSRM. The methodology is based on seven guidelines.

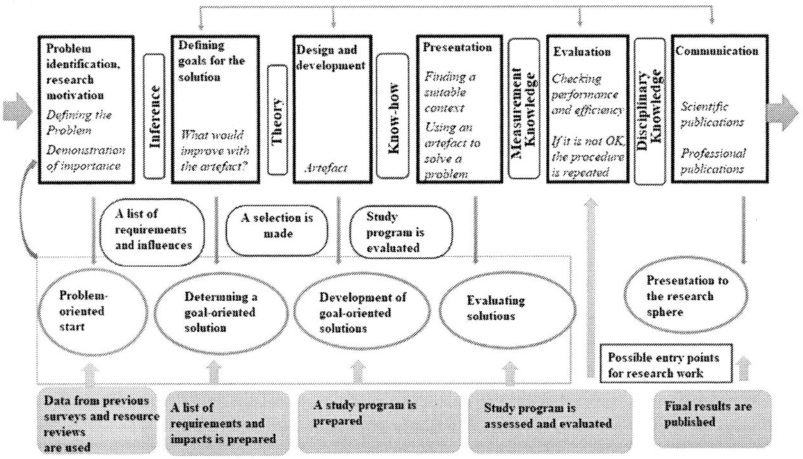

Figure 9.3 *Expected course of research in accordance with the DSRM*

In accordance with the first guideline, we planned the preparation of an artefact which should ensure the optimisation of the acquisition of competencies required for project management and production of our graduates in accordance with the second guideline. We had to study several possible scenarios, courses, multimedia production, digital competencies and certification systems and determine the factors present, how these factors are involved in acquiring design and production competencies, and how all the elements can be included in the preparation of the courses.

The DSR product planning and development strategy needs to evaluate the artefact's quality, usability and efficiency; thus, we also evaluated the study programme and its usability at our university per the third guideline.

Following the fourth guideline of the DSR product planning and development strategy, we provided key contributions to the research-the artefact (the study programme) and, thus, the basis for further research.

Following the fifth guideline of the DSR product design and development strategy, we used appropriate work methods in all research phases described in detail in this chapter.

In our work, we ensured constant communication and interactivity with all stakeholders, constantly checked and evaluated research achievements, and optimised the course of research and the artefact.

We did this through annual self-evaluation procedures and with the participation of external representatives of multimedia production in commissions when we assessed the knowledge and skills of students and graduates in project presentations, surveys among mentors on practical work and employers of our students. The operation of the school and the programme were verified three times by the SQAA (School Quality Assessment and Assurance).

Following the sixth guideline, the research strategy for designing and developing DSR products must be considered as a process of finding an optimal and effective solution. This was implemented by regular monitoring, analysis and updating of the programme. In doing so, we considered the profession's and market's development and requirements.

Following the seventh guideline of the DSR product design and development strategy, we successfully communicated with many stakeholders throughout the research, both in the design phase and in the validation and verification phase of the model in practice, resulting in a very positive response from the students, users (multimedia production) and the SQAA at all stages of the research.

The method of reviewing and studying sources was very important in almost all phases of the research. In secondary sources, we reviewed and studied 34 scientific articles and monographs in multidisciplinary bibliographic databases:

- Science Citation Index-SCI (WoS),
- EBSCO (eBook Collection (EBSCOhost)),

- EBSCOhost, Academic Search Complete (ERIC),
- ProQuest (Interdisciplinary-Doctoral dissertations only), and
- other sources of scientific articles and monographs.

The following keywords and phrases were used in the literature search: project work, multimedia production, educational programmes, project manager, producer, project work competencies, digital competencies and certificates.

We did not set the language, accessibility, publication date, location or other restrictions when searching bibliographic databases.

A systematic review of the literature showed that the databases have a higher number of hits related to research keywords, whilst the selected combination of keywords in the narrower research area showed only five hits that did not address our research subject. We used this to conclude that the proposed topic is topical and the proposed area is poorly researched.

We also reviewed 45 documents prepared by the EU, JRC, OECD, SQAA, IPMA, SloCert and other organisations and tertiary sources such as, e.g. project and blog websites, summaries, reviews, etc. The most relevant ones are also listed in the references of this document.

In addition to reviewing sources and literature, we mainly used the method of conversation and interviews with individuals and in groups, and surveys.

An interview is a qualitative form of data collection primarily aimed at individuals and small groups, as it allows in-depth data acquisition and discussion of different views, beliefs and dilemmas. In addition to an individual interview, we also used group interviews, in which questions are answered by a suitably selected group (Vogrinc 2008; Taylor et al. 2015).

The most common is a direct conversation or interview between the researcher and the respondent, in which the former asks questions and the latter provides answers. The researcher and the respondent can discuss certain answers or topics thoroughly, so this interview is also referred to as an in-depth interview. It is unstructured (ethnographic or friendly), as the researcher only has the set goals, adjusts the questions to the course of the conversation, and can also introduce new elements and questions that arise during the interview.

In a semi-structured or partially structured interview, the researcher prepares framework topics and questions, whilst the selection and number of questions and the method of questioning depend on the respondent. A partially structured interview enables the systematic organisation and communicative validation of the obtained data.

In the case of structured questions (focused interview), the questions are specific and the same for everyone; everything is done in a precise order, which makes it easier to edit and compare data and results. It is suitable for studying subjective positions and interpretations.

Surveys belong to the quantitative research methods (Groves et al. 2009; Rek 2011) and are used to collect data from respondents. Surveys can be conducted through a variety of media.

An important part of the survey is the processing and interpreting the results, so surveys should be prepared to elicit the desired responses with as few questions as possible. We use different types of questions in the survey. Open-ended questions allowed free answers when we did not have enough information and wanted to obtain certain data from the respondents, which we then used in compiling more specific closed-ended questions. Closed-ended questions already offer answers and only require the respondents to choose between them or evaluate certain options. With these questions, we need to obtain data that are as accurate as possible for our research.

Likert scales are characteristic of ordinal (descriptive) variables characterised by a uniform distance between answers, allowing the respondent to classify or rank their grade. Sorting can be achieved using numbers (e.g. 1-worst and 5-best) or words (e.g. I disagree, strongly agree, bad, excellent, etc.).

9.4 Results

We prepared Multimedia Production based on the requirements for preparing study programmes in accordance with the legislation and the requirements of the SQAA and after comparing similar programmes offered by foreign educational institutions.

A comparison of the IAM VŠMM (School of Multimedia Production) course with similar higher education institutions is shown in Table 9.2.

With selected foreign courses, the course is related and comparable in concept and goals and formal and substantive composition by offering various choices based on a single basic concept or structure of the course and individual subject. Our course partly differs from a more competently designed study programme.

By analysing production procedures, tasks and staff structure in certain areas and sets of multimedia production, we determined the characteristics of project work in multimedia production. We found that they are also led by different producers, either by themselves or with the participation of project managers and experts from different areas. For smaller projects, this is often the same person. Larger projects require the distribution of responsibilities and cooperation.

The responsible project manager and the owner's representative are the executive producers, and the creative and financial producers work together. The creative producer must find and choose the appropriate theme and story, work with publishers and agents of creatives and actors, and acquire and motivate the best staff, screenwriter, director and production team. The financial producer is responsible for obtaining financial resources from various sources and their economic management.

The target audience and sales in multimedia production are very important as it is easier to make products with tremendous technological advances in a field of fierce competition than it is to determine how they can ensure commercial success. Therefore, the keys are the initial pre-production activities until the project's approval and the last phase of distribution, marketing and sales activities. In the first and last phases, talented, motivated and capable creative, promotional and sales staff are needed, and the production part requires the teamwork of specialists and, as a rule, creators and clients are also involved throughout the production.

Table 9.2 *Comparison of some key parameters in study programmes of higher education institutions*

Name of the institution	**IAM Higher Education Programme, Ljubljana**	**Middlesex University**	**University of Lincoln**	**University of Canberra**	**Loyalist College, Ontario**
Programme name	Multimedia Production	BA Honours Television Production in Programm e BA Honours Television production – Technical Arts	BA (Hons) Media Production	BA Hons Communi-cation in Media / Multimedia Production	BA Hons Television and New Media Production
Number of ECTS	180	180	180	180	180
Duration of studies	Three years	Three years	Three years	Three years	Three years

Student responsibilities	Compulsory subjects, partial selectivity in 1st and 2nd year, strong selectivity in 3rd year	Compulsory subjects, specialisation in 2nd year, two elective courses in 3rd year	Compulsory subjects, specialisation in 2nd year, two elective courses in 3rd year	Compulsory subjects, specialisation in 2nd year, two elective courses in 3rd year	Compulsory subjects, specialisation in 2nd year, two elective courses in 3rd year
Completion of studies	Project diploma thesis	Project diploma thesis	Project diploma thesis	Project diploma thesis	Project diploma thesis

Project managers are already involved in the pre-production phase but usually take over the implementation of production and post-production and then usually finalise their work. Creative producers participate in all stages and certify the product. The financial producer, known as a financial analyst in other types of projects, monitors the financial part of the project.

Successful product preparation usually completes the project for the project manager, and producers continue with distribution, marketing and sales, which can take several decades (e.g. showing films, music, books, etc.).

Based on analysing the requirements of knowledge, skills and competencies in multimedia production, we have prepared a selection that can be implemented in a three-year higher professional programme. Certain knowledge, especially in advertising, financial analysis and marketing, must be provided in postgraduate studies and through many years of practical work.

We defined the goals of the programme earlier. The three-year higher professional course Multimedia Production must be modern, the graduates of which are capable of planning and managing demanding multimedia projects, as well as being professionally trained producers in individual fields of multimedia production. The course is designed to encourage and require the students to develop and implement demanding real-world production projects during their studies—for themselves, the companies or institutions from which they come, or other clients.

Reviewing the course, the SQAA found that it complies with the set goals and learning outcomes. The vertical and horizontal connectivity is appropriate. Industry representatives confirmed that the contents of the course are up to date. The high employability of graduates confirms its relevance. However, their opinion was that it is too focused on acquiring engineering skills and that there should be an even greater emphasis on production skills at the higher education level (Evaluation Process Report 2019). In addition to this report, it should be noted that the commission members were mainly drawn from university study courses that are more theoretical and research-orientated. At the same time, the vocational college is based on competencies that are as directly applicable in practice as possible.

The Multimedia Projects for Students page describes the benefits of project work for the study process. Process and product evaluation is carried out, learning objectives, objectives and audiences are defined, various options must be explored, and appropriate proposals and prototypes prepared. It is necessary to determine all production parameters, such as stories, content, activities, time and financial frameworks and the implementation strategy. Students are motivated for project work, effective integration into professional media production is enabled, the school's operation and with the students' products and services, as well as control over the operation of the educational institution.

9.4.1 Definition of key general and subject-specific competencies

At the beginning of the programme, we also defined general and subject-specific competencies, including the results of the analysis of similar programmes, the requirements of IPMA certificates, and trends in introducing digital competencies in education. Some competencies were later supplemented mainly with competencies for producers and digital competencies. The general competencies of the programme are:

- knowing and understanding social processes;
- knowing and understanding the functioning of media and multimedia;
- ability to successfully lead, participate in a team and solve specific problems in the professional environment;
- mastering techniques, methods, procedures, programmes and equipment relevant to successful professional work;
- development of critical and self-critical judgement, personal integrity and reliability;
- ability to flexibly apply knowledge in practice;
- knowing the concept of quality and the persistent pursuit of the quality of professional work through autonomy, (self) criticism, (self) reflexivity and (self) evaluation in professional work;
- development of communication skills in the domestic and international environments;
- ethical reflection and commitment to professional ethics in the social environment with conscientious respect for the principles of

truthfulness, freedom, responsibility, openness, tolerance, pluralism, creativity, originality, balance, justice, and fairness;
- ability to work in a team, ability to establish and maintain cooperative relationships for working in a group and with users;
- ability to identify and take advantage of opportunities offered in the work and social environment (which manifest as an entrepreneurial spirit and active citizenship).

Subject-specific competencies of the programme (special competencies acquired in individual highly specialised contents are given for each subject separately):

- knowledge of basic concepts, devices, equipment and technologies in media or multimedia technologies and informatics;
- knowledge of production, project and production work in media and multimedia production;
- ability to choose devices and programmes in media and multimedia production and use them; knowledge of connecting to systems;
- ability to purchase and maintain devices in media and multimedia production;
- knowledge of basic and current principles of operation of information systems in various segments of society and especially of companies and institutions from the media and multimedia production sectors;
- ability to select appropriate databases;
- knowledge of professions, roles, tasks and responsibilities in the media production team and in media and multimedia production in general;
- professionally based knowledge and understanding of the social role of the media;
- deeper understanding and appropriate practical mastery of media creation technologies;
- ability to use information and communication technology and systems in media, media production, and multimedia production;
- knowledge and mastery of processes and techniques of creative creation of media content;
- ability to solve specific problems in media and media production or multimedia productions using appropriate methods, techniques and procedures;
- ability to integrate coherent basic knowledge acquired in compulsory subjects and its application in practice;
- ability to obtain, select, evaluate and place new information in media and the ability to interpret it;

- understanding the methods of critical analysis and development and their use in solving specific problems at work in contemporary media;
- development of skills and abilities in the application of knowledge in media and multimedia production by solving theoretical, empirical or practical problems;
- education and development of the need for independent creation based on acquired relevant professional knowledge and practical skills;
- organisational and managerial skills required for planning, leading, directing, promoting, supervising, evaluating and rewarding independent, conscientious and professional work and/or the creation of individuals and groups;
- constructive communication with various stakeholders in media and multimedia production;
- digital competencies in multimedia production for the 7th level-mastery for EU citizens (DigComp 2.1, in information, communication, content creation, protection and problem-solving).

The 3rd year subject preparation and implementation of a demanding project includes specific subject competencies, including most of the competencies required by the IPMA certificate.

The learning unit contributes to the development of the following subject-specific competencies:

- the ability to integrate coherently mastered basic and specialised multimedia expertise and practical application;
- the development of project and production skills for the preparation and implementation of projects in multimedia production on a specific demanding project;
- the ability to determine strategy, complex analysis of starting points or project plan, preparation of proposals and selection of optimal solutions in the preparation of the project for the media or MM product or service;
- the ability to work in a project team, knowing and ensuring an appropriate culture of cooperation;
- ability to perform the task from idea to product, taking into account business, legal, ethical and other requirements;
- developing a critical attitude towards media messages and products and the ability to judge demanding products or services from basic aspects of ethics and aesthetics;
- integrating elements of creativity and innovation into individual phases of the project;

- mastering the technique of preparing projects for the production of media products;
- mastering the technique of preparing and managing projects for the production of a multimedia product or service;
- knowledge of documentation and programmes for the preparation, management and monitoring of projects in multimedia production;
- knowledge of preparation of final documentation and knowledge of evaluation of results;
- knowledge of professions, roles, tasks and responsibilities in the media production team; organisational and managerial skills for directing and coordinating work in preparation and management of projects in media production, flexibility and adaptability, i.e. the ability to work professionally in different environments;
- the ability to analyse finances and understand all phases of project work and to obtain funds for projects;
- knowledge of marketing and sales activities.

Special additional requirements for digital competencies and production work related to financial and marketing have been included in the last two indents of specific competencies.

9.4.2 Description of the new programme

We present individual subjects by year and include solutions obtained through research.

The first year

The first year includes subjects in which students gain basic knowledge, skills and competencies in multimedia production, as all subjects are designed so that students prepare seminar papers or small projects in areas of special interest or work on them in practice because most students study whilst working. This way, we also ensure that students continue to work in a certain field or become involved in it, as in this way, the motivation for study and success at work is greatly increased.

First-year subjects: introduction to multimedia, Slovenian language in media production, multimedia Practicum, computer graphics, photography, the economic and legal basis of multimedia production, the basics of informatics and multimedia technologies, the basics of media communications, multimedia Practicum 2 and an elective course 1.

The subjects are designed to allow constant updating (equipment, technology, programmes, concepts, knowledge, skills), innovation and inclusion of new fields.

The second year

The second year includes subjects in which students acquire or upgrade knowledge of the basics of organisation and management of multimedia production and expand or upgrade basic knowledge in audio and video production, animation and multimedia programmes. The second-year subjcets are also prepared in a way that allows for constant updating.

Second-year subjects: organisation and management of multimedia production, the basics of audio-video production and animation, multimedia programmes, multimedia production and practical training.

In the second year, most students are already involved in real projects in multimedia production in which practical education is also important, and they prepare two projects at the school. They prepare the first project in cooperation with one of the external organisations, for which students are divided into groups of five and prepare complex promotional AV materials and promotional campaigns. They work under the mentorship of practising experts and acquire an understanding of project and production work in practice. A presentation and selection of the best projects are performed at the end, and the organisation usually buys several of them from students for practical use. Table 9.3 shows the results of a survey conducted among students after completing a project in 2018 in collaboration with an external organisation.

In the second year, each student also prepares a small project in their elective field. The areas to choose from are animation, audio, photography, graphics, Internet, video and event organisation.

The third year

In the third year, students are made familiar with all areas of multimedia production, and they are also trained to prepare products and services in the electives. Therefore, the third year emphasises the analysis of products and services, creativity and the planning, preparation and implementation of a demanding product. The study programme includes the acquisition and use of demanding project and production knowledge, with the final product being documentation and a plan for implementing a demanding project which is also partially carried out in the context of practical training. Each student also prepares a complex multimedia project: a family tree for which they also perform a research task that helps them to obtain relevant information about their family.

Third-year subjects: creativity techniques, analysis of multimedia products and services, multimedia production planning, preparation and implementation of a demanding project, and practical training.

In preparing the courses and individual topics from the project work, we focused on the requirements of levels D and C (IPMA SloCert 2002), as students can formally obtain a D certificate at the end of their studies, and they can complete the requirements for taking certificate C in the year after graduation, as they have the appropriate competencies, have implemented projects and have a formal period of three years of participation in projects.

Students prepare projects with mentors—experts-producers. During their studies, they meet 12 experts at lectures and talks from various fields of multimedia production and six experts—producers and four experts for individual segments of project work (law, finance, ethics and marketing and quality). The expert prepares students for the presentation of projects before a commission which includes external experts.

Table 9.3 *Level of students' agreement with statements on the project implementation (Zakrajšek 2021)*

Statement	Strongly disagree	Disagree	Uncertain [% of responses]	Agree	Strongly agree
1. Tenders for student projects are more suited than students applying to projects which are available to professionals as well.	0	5	12	29	54
2. It is important that appropriate awards are given at the end of the project.	0	3	14	15	68
3. Cooperation with experts is also considered an award.	0	1	7	23	69
4. It is important that company projects are made for specific subjects and suggest tasks with useful effects.	0	1	3	20	76
5. When creating the project, we also learn of real problems which we haven't previously considered.	0	9	10	22	59
6. Companies could obtain many useful products or services or solve a certain problem with award projects for students.	0	3	12	32	53

The multimedia production programme is designed to enable students and requires the continuous acquisition of digital competencies in all five competency areas: information, communication, content creation, protection and problem-solving. In the implementation part of the programme, we took from Table 9.1 levels of digital competence as criterion 7—Mastery—to be achieved by our graduates.

Table 9.4 presents students' grades for individual subjects in the 3rd year of 2020/2021.

Table 9.4 *Total grades for subjects—third-year multimedia production for two academic years (Self-Evaluation Report 2021)*

Indicators	2019/2020	2020/2021
Creativity techniques	4.8	4.6
Multimedia product and service analysis	4.7	4.7
Planning multimedia production	4.3	4.1
Preparation and implementation of a demanding project	4.5	4.3

As we applied more demanding theoretical content and higher requirements required by project and production work, the grades are around 4.5 (very good), with additional issues posed by COVID-19. Top production knowledge and competencies can only be acquired through years of practical experience. As there were several younger students with elective or very little practical experience in the elective courses, they assessed that the programme and assignments were very demanding. However, after a successful external product inspection and diploma preparation, they found that our high demands were justified.

The study of multimedia production requires constant work with computers, networks, media, applications, databases and various clients, performers and users, so students must achieve at least Level 7—Mastery at which the ability to create and solve various problems is an important requirement, and this is also a requirement for good project managers and producers.

9.5 Discussion

The contribution presents the development of an educational model for producers and project managers in multimedia production. We started the research and development in 1998, and we established the IAM at the beginning of the millennium when a two-year multimedia college started operating in 2000, focusing on staff education and training for work in audio and video production, animation and photography and graphics.

According to the concept and legal requirements for short-cycle higher education programmes, students complete about 40% of the programme in practice, and the school must prepare them for this by teaching them the theoretical basics. At the same time, they must also become familiar with the equipment, procedures and basic skills in practice, allowing them quick and successful integration into the work environment. We found that people in organisations want students to become involved in work as quickly as possible and to help them with mentoring, but they do not have the time to teach them the basics. Due to this, we have established close relationships with organisations by ensuring constant updating and integration of the latest technologies and equipment in the study programme, as well as the participation of experts in the study process—lecturers, instructors, mentors, external evaluators, etc. At the same time, we introduced knowledge of project work and the acquisition of soft skills to the programme that students need when working on projects and working groups that are being used in practical work.

The development of the profession, especially the desire of young people for higher education and the interest of organisations, have encouraged us to prepare a professional higher education programme in multimedia production. Based on our experience with implementing the short-cycle higher education programme, we have set ourselves the goal that the higher education programme must also be development-orientated, competent and prepared and implemented in close cooperation with the professional environment. We paid special attention to the acquisition of digital competencies and competencies for project and production work for which we wanted to take into account the requirements of established certificates, as this allows the study programme to comply with the requirements in practice, as well as the possibility of active influence on certification systems.

We designed the development of the programme as a special research and development project and initially asked ourselves three research questions. The answers are presented below:

- How should the higher education professional study programme be conceived and structured for graduates to acquire the relevant knowledge, skills and competencies in project and production work in multimedia production?
  In finding the answer to the first research question, we examined the legal requirements for study programmes and criteria and analysed study

programmes available in this field. We considered the research results in integrating the competence concept of teaching into study processes. We found that it is possible to prepare a quality higher education programme of multimedia production within the existing legal requirements by setting goals, competencies and content that is sufficiently general and can be regularly upgraded and updated and to which new topical content and resources could be added.

The programme formed in this manner allows the latest specific goals and competencies, including requirements and requests from the environment and students, to be included each year before lectures.

In the event of major deviations from the initially applied programme, the programme must be sent for evaluation and confirmation to the SQAA if the higher education institution is operating in Slovenia.

Graduates acquire the relevant knowledge, skills and competencies in project and production work in multimedia production with the participation of external experts who conduct over 50 hours of lectures, with the participation of visiting organisations, practical training in organisations and preparation of projects.

- What are the possible and meaningful links between education and obtaining certain certificates?

  We have mentioned the possibilities for meaningfully including and upgrading knowledge, skills and competencies from various fields in the study programme in answer to the first research question. This way, we ensure that the programme's planning and subject contents, knowledge, skills and competencies include the most important, as anticipated and needed by the profession at this time.

  In incorporating the competencies from project work, we cooperated with the organisation SloCert, which deals with the certification of Slovenian experts in project work. Whilst preparing the programme in 2010, we considered the criteria from 2006 and 2015 (ICB 4.0 2015).

  During their studies, our graduates acquire the knowledge required for the D certificate, and at the same time, they participate in and manage several projects; this requires the C certificate, which they can formally acquire within a year after graduation.

- What are the optimal approaches to acquiring digital competencies of students in the study process of multimedia production?

  We introduced those digital competencies into our programme from the seventh level (master) of digital competencies for EU citizens, which we have assessed as most suitable for our students, as the list of digital competencies for this field is not yet ready. We are monitoring and, as far as possible, taking into account the solutions that will be created within the EU project Digital Education Action Plan (2021–2027), which plans infrastructure development, preparation of quality content, integration of artificial intelligence, development of friendly tools and training through the Erasmus project, which will also develop common guidelines for teachers and produce a European Digital Skills Certificate (EDSC).

As digital competencies represent the ability to successfully use knowledge and skills in the digital environment, we have included the acquisition and development of these competencies in all practical exercises in individual subjects, in project and production work and in practical education.

We considered the findings of researchers and practitioners (Harpreet 2021), which show problems and solutions when introducing the acquisition of digital competencies in education, in which the process includes creativity, critical thinking, communication and cooperation as core competencies. Acquiring skills for using devices and technologies is only one part of the programme for acquiring digital competencies. They also reflect on the problems and dangers posed by modern technologies and suggest various innovative teaching methods.

9.6 Conclusion

Finally, we can say that we have managed to prepare a quality programme as we have been receiving approval from students, the environment and the SQAA. We managed to prepare a flexible and efficient, development-orientated study programme, giving students a good basis for quality preparation and management of demanding multimedia projects and production work. Successful work on demanding projects requires years of practice with quality mentoring in both professions.

In the future, we will continue with research and development work to constantly update the programme and develop a quality postgraduate study in which project managers and producers can gain special knowledge and competencies.

References

Commission launches "Opening up Education" to boost innovation and digital skills in schools and universities (2013). European Commission. https://ec.europa.eu/commission/presscorner/detail/sl/IP_13_859.

Baule, Steve. (9. 4. 2019). From LMS to NGDLE: the Acronyms of the Future of Online Learning. eCampus News.

https://www.ecampusnews.com/2019/04/09/lms-ngdle-future-online-learning/.

DigComp 2.0 – The Digital Competence Framework for EU Citizens (2016). https://www.digitalsme.eu/digcomp-2-0-digital-competence-framework-eu-citizens/.

DigComp 2.1: The Digital Competence Framework for Citizens with eight proficiency levels and examples of use. (2017). Luxembourg: Publications Office of the European Union. https://publications.jrc.ec.europa.eu/repository/handle/JRC106281.

Digital Education Action Plan (2021–2027). (2020). Resetting education and training for the digital age. European Commission. https://ec.europa.eu/education/education-in-the-eu/digital-education-action-plan_en.

Earle, Rodney. S. and Persichitte, Kay. A. (Eds.). (2005). *Standards for the accreditation of school media specialist and educational technology specialist programmes* (4th ed.). Bloomington, IN: Association for Educational Communications and Technology.

Goode, Jennifer. (2021). "A Collaborative Multimedia Project Model for Online Graduate Students Supported by On-Campus Undergraduate Students." *Journal of Technical Writing & Communication*, 51(1), 53–69.

Harpreet, Kaur. D. (2021). Handbook of Research on Barriers to Teaching 21st-Century Competencies and the Impact of Digitalization. IGI Global.

Hevner, Alan and R., March T. Salvatore and Park, Jinsoo and Ram, Sudha. (2004). "Design Science in Information System Research." *MIS Quarterly*, 28(1), 75–105.

Hong Jin, Yunting Miao, Xinping Chen, Joung-Hae Seo and Eun-Mi Park. (2021). "Motivation research on the participation of multimedia Web page users in 'share' behaviour: a case study of Alipay." Multimedia Tools and Applications, 80, 34571–34589.

Individual Competence Baseline for Project Management, IPMA global standard, version 4.0. (2015). IPMA.

IPMA. (n.d.). ICB IPMA Competence Baseline Version 3.0. (2006). IPMA.

International Project Management Association (IPMA). (2022). IPMA CCT Certification product update. https://www.ipma.world/news/ipma-cct-certification-products-update/

Jeong-Jin, Youn and Su-Jeong, Jeong and Kang-Hoon, Lee and Byung-Man, Kim. (2021). "Development and application of a digital curation system to promote total creative personality based on multimedia." *Multimedia Tools and Applications,* 80, 34369-34387.

Annual report with a quality report for the 2020/2021 study year, IAM, Ljubljana.

Mishra, Deepanjali and Chuang, Yuangshan. (2021). Learning How to Learn Using Multimedia. Springer Nature.

Multimedia Projects for Students | Multimedia Project Topic. (academiccollegeprojects.com).

SQAA. (2019). Criteria for valuation of study programmes with ECTS. https://view.officeapps.live.com/op/view.aspx?src=https%3A%2F%2Fwww.nakvis.si%2Fwp-content%2Fuploads%2F2019%2F11%2FMerila-za-kreditno-vrednotenje-%25C5%25A1tudijskih-programmeov-po-ECTS.docx&wdOrigin=BROWSELINK.

Peffers, Ken. And Tuunanen, Tuure and Rothenberger, Z.,Marcus and Chatterjee, Samir. (2007). A Design Science Research Methodology for Information Systems Research. *Journal of Management Information Systems*, 24(3), 45–78.

Report on the evaluation process of the higher education programme Multimedia Production at IAM Ljubljana. (2019). Ljubljana, SQAA.

Legal Information System of the Republic of Slovenia (PIS). (2021). Criteria for accreditation and external evaluation of higher education institutions and study programmes. http://www.pisrs.si/Pis.web/pregledPredpisa?id=DRUG4397

Punie, Yves and Cabrera, Marcelino. (editor). (2006). The Future of ICT and Learning in the Knowledge Society. Luxembourg: European Commission.

Recommendation 2006/962/EC of the European Parliament and of the Council of 18 December 2006 on key competencies for lifelong learning. (2006). *Official Journal L* 394.

Peffers, Ken & Tuunanen, Tuure & Rothenberger, Marcus & Chatterjee, S "Research Methodology for Information Systems Research." *Journal of Management Information Systems*, 24(3), 45–78.

Richey, Rita and Fields, Dennis. C.,and Foxon, Marguerite. (2001). Instructional design competencies: The standards (3rd ed.). Syracuse, NY: ERIC Clearinghouse on Information & Technology.

Self, James & Evans, Mark & Jun, Thomas & Southee, Darren. (2019). "Interdisciplinary: challenges and opportunities for design education." *International Journal of Technology and Design Education*, 29, 843–876.

Siemens, George and Tittenberger, Peter. (2009). *Handbook of Emerging Technologies for Learning*. University of Manitoba.

https://www.bucks.edu/media/bcccmedialibrary/documents/academics/facultywebresources/Handbook_Emerging-Technologies.pdf.

Sugar, William and Hoard, Brent and Lee Daniels. (2012). Identifying Multimedia Production Competencies and Skills of Instructional Design and Technology Professionals: An Analysis of Recent Job Postings. *J. Educational, Technology Systems*, 40(3), 227–249.

Taylor, Steven, and Bogdan, Robert, And DeVault, Marjorie. (2015). Introduction to Qualitative Research Methods: A Guidebook and Resource. New Jersey: John Wiley & Sons.

Vogrinc, Janez. (2008). Qualitative research in pedagogy. University of Ljubljana, Faculty of Education. 99–118. http://pefprints.pef.uni-lj.si/179/1/Vogrinc1.pdf.

Higher Education Act (ZViS-NPB23). Article 35a (Components of study programmes for advanced training). https://zakonodaja.com/zakon/zvis/35a-clen-sestavine-studijskih-programmeov-za-izpopolnjevanje.

Zakrajšek, Miha. (2021). Cooperation with the economy as a key factor for quality study. Master's thesis. Faculty of Media, Ljubljana.

Wagner, Reinhard. (5. 2. 2018). Competencies—an update for the digital era. IPMA International Project Management Association. https://www.ipma.world/competencies-update-digital-era/.

Srečko Zakrajšek is a doctor of chemical sciences and educational management, dean of the IAM College for Multimedia, and docent for the courses Management and Organization of Multimedia Production and Planning of Multimedia Production, the IPMA Senior project manager certificate holder and research associate at IAM College of Multimedia.

Nejc Zakrajšek is a doctor of chemical sciences. He holds a Master's in media production, and is director of the Institute and Academy for Multimedia. Senior lecturer in the field of Multimedia production. He is a research associate at IAM College of Multimedia.

Miha Zakrajšek is a director of the IAM College for Multimedia, a lecturer in the field of multimedia production, and a research associate at IAM College of Multimedia.

X

The Hybridisation of Project Management Methodologies

Sergiy Bushuyev, Victoria Bushuieva, Denis Bushuiev and Natalia Bushuyeva

10.1 Hybridisation challenges

Today, many organisations often face the problem of selecting the necessary rational methodologies for effective programmes, portfolios and project management. With the specific conditions for the programmes and project implementation, it is difficult for organisation methodologists to choose a methodology suitable for the coverage goals from the methodologies presented on the global market (PMI 2021). If applying a systematic approach to creating a methodology, then it is obvious the 'boxed' product in such a situation cannot be suitable since this product was developed for a certain application that does not coincide with the specifics of the organisation. This problem sets the task for project management methodologists to either adapt the 'box' methodology or develop their own, for the specifics of the projects of this organisation, under the conditions in which it operates. Considering management methodology as the language of effective stakeholder interaction, using classical methodologies is a priority. A sound project management methodology will guide the project manager through the controlled, manageable and visible activities to achieve project output (International Project Management Association (IPMA), 2015; IPMA 2013).

Developing a new performed methodology is a costly undertaking that requires highly qualified methodological resources, versatile managers' experience, time, etc. In professional cases, managers-methodologists adapt existing project management methodologies when solving this problem. The adaptation of project management (PM) methodologies can happen with the use of convergence or hybridisation.

The convergence of PM methodologies means a systematically verified merger, a combination or penetration of methodologies, subject to the conditions for the consistency of the elements of the hybridised methodologies.

10.2 Conceptual model of hybridisation of PM methodology

The goal of applying the mechanisms of convergence of methodologies is the synergy of the elements of hybrid methodologies in developing PM methodology for specific conditions (IPMA 2013; PM^2 2018).

Let us look at the basic definition of the hybridisation of PM methodology.

Definition 1. "Convergence"—the convergence by reducing or smoothing gaps between levels. Integration processes and globalisation in the world have mainly led to convergence. However, when there is a state of stagnation or backwardness, an inability to adapt to modern conditions, the situation worsens, and as a result, the gap between such developed institutions increases significantly, i.e. there is divergence.

Definition 2. "Divergence"—movement along divergent lines: increasing the gap between levels of development, increasing differences between models, their structures of competencies and mechanisms; this term is also used to denote deviations from the average for certain indicators or general vision.

The hybridisation of methodologies means the combination of elements of different methodologies into one. This PM methodology will be called hybrid.

Ontologically, the divergence and convergence of PM methodologies arise under the influence of internal and external conditions in fairly complex multifunctional projects or programmes (Obradović et al. 2018). When carrying out multifunctional programmes, the organisation's management is logically forced to follow Ashby's law: to effectively manage the various projects included in the programme. It is necessary to have a set of methodologies covering various projects. The same factors explain this diversity. The feasibility of saving (not spraying) resources: a functionally specific project, in terms of feasibility, quality, time and other project implementation parameters, dictates the choice of a specific methodology optimal for this type of project. Suppose an enterprise methodologist applies a systematic approach and different specialised methodologies to specific projects of an enterprise, starting from the scale of the life cycle of a portfolio of projects within the life cycle of an enterprise, under internal and external influences, then some common characteristics appear (ISO 21502, ISO 21503, ISO 21504, ISO 21505). The methodologies have signs of convergence, a single 'new' methodology applied to the enterprise. This is the result of the methodologies' convergence.

The convergence of PM methodologies is an objective consequence of the impact on the conditions of project implementation. This is possible precisely under a high level of management processes maturity conditions—not lower than the third class according to the IPMA-Delta certification system (IPMA 2013). In the conditions of a high maturity of PM, convergence inevitably proceeds without the decisive active role of methodologists but under the influence of the corporate culture and management processes (IPMA 2013).

In an organisation with a low level of maturity of PM, convergent manifestations in the development of methodologies are insignificant and may occur with a small influence or not at all.

Divergence (from the Latin. *divergentia*—disagreement) in the management of projects determines the field of competence clusters, which characterises the density of their sources.

Divergence considers the competence characteristics of the organisation and which application of the hybrid methodology is manifested in the divergence of competencies in the development of organisations, which is introduced to explain the emergence of various specialities or specialisations in a particular field of study, considering market requirements.

The divergent methodology of organisational development programmes is a system of principles, mechanisms, models, methods and means of organising activities, which is produced or deepens the field of competencies of the moving context based on assessing the gaps in competency clusters (Todorović et al. 2015).

Studies on the problems of automated management of free economic development strategies in conditions of uncertainty and poor formalisation of organisational and technological processes of the environment have shown the following:

- complexity in the effectiveness of the methodology, which is based on the consideration of free economic zones as a complex, probabilistic system;
- the application of convergent methodology requires a complex informational task to form a portfolio of projects in the strategic development of the organisation, similar to the functionality in the information space; and

- the application of divergent technology only partially implements the project approach to the implementation of production, educational, scientific and innovative profitable strategies, as their implementation solves only the problem of effective operational management in an uncertain market environment, i.e. does not solve the problem of project formation and monitoring implementation.

The convergent approach, in which one can create the desired image of a future new convergent world with the so-called concept of the 'bifurcation century': new biology and new systems sciences—seeks and find features of unity in the world's diversity.

The conceptual model of PM methodologies hybridisation (Figure 10.1) involves the consistent application of the mechanisms of convergence, integration and updating, followed by the divergence of the hybrid model into clusters of competence to form teams of projects and programmes based on the role description.

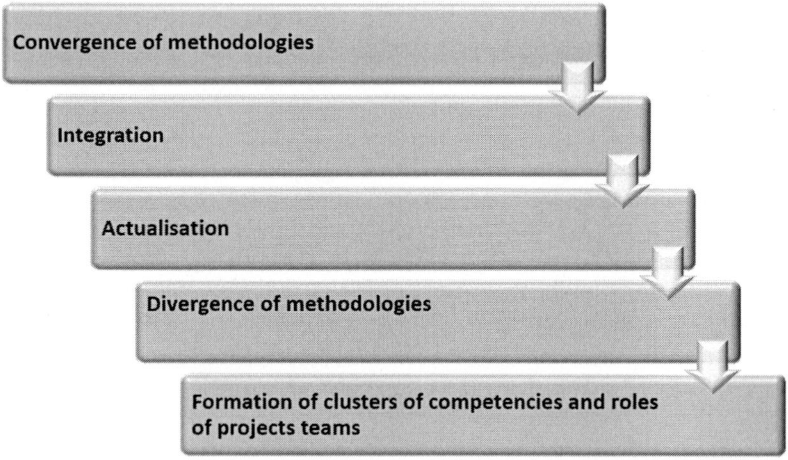

Figure 10.1 *The conceptual model of project management methodologies hybridisation*

In conditions of low maturity of PM, if professional methodologists are in the organisation, the hybridisation of PM principles and tools can be effective. PM methodologists can select some methodologies that are not directly suitable for the implementation of portfolio projects, create a hybrid version of a single methodology, and select from each of the initial original methodologies those components that are useful for the specifics of a project portfolio of a given organisation.

In this case, a high level of maturity of PM, both convergence and hybridisation of methodologies, can be used. In a combined process, convergence can proceed as a synergistic action of methodological transformation with the insignificant ('passive') influence of methodologists, and hybridisation is realised with the influence of a methodologist acting like a sculptor, cutting off everything superfluous from a blank stone.

From the point of view of time parameters and changes in management structures in PM methodologies, convergence technologies can be conditionally classified as evolutionary and hybridisation technologies as revolutionary.

Convergent technologies for creating PM methodologies are relatively well developed; here, we touch on them only partially and will dwell on some aspects of hybridisation technologies for PM methodologies.

10.2.1 The hybridisation of PM methods in the context of digitalisation and artificial intelligence environments

The most fruitful application of hybridising PM methodologies according to digital society's technology lifecycle is automatic systems, particularly cyber management systems.

Practically all existing project management methodologies are developed for the real PM environment and the ordinary level of human intelligence. In this case, artificial intelligence is still significantly different from human intelligence. The main differences between artificial intelligence and natural intelligence are empathy and abilities, complex sensations, the analysis of non-verbal information flows, and the use of the collective unconscious and hereditary (genetically transmitted) information space (PM^2 2018). In some PM methods, an important role is assigned, for example, to such management decision-making tools as intuition (Sternberg & Kaufman 2011) and altered states of consciousness. Naturally, we do not have the right to transfer traditional PM methodologies to the cyber management environment to install them one-on-one into artificial intelligence.

Digital society needs to develop new PM methodologies, and hybridisation can be the most effective at the current stage of these developments after selecting a set of PM methodologies for the digital environment using hybridisation methods. It makes sense to apply the convergence technique as well.

There is a need to develop intelligent PM methodologies that create control tools in natural, artificial intelligence and combined environments.

The difference in the hybridisation of the creation of PM methodologies is that both objects, subjects and process management are fundamentally different in these methodologies.

If existing project managers do not consider some aspects, including the management process and behavioural competence, this can decrease decision-making efficiency. If the hybrid methodologies have artificial intelligence modules, these aspects require a specific development process. Hybrid methodologies of natural intelligence need to take into account the elements that are the functional structure of artificial intelligence.

The hybridisation process gives a special impetus to creating decision support systems (DSS). The application of modern DSS shows their insufficient effectiveness. This effectiveness is determined by the limited number of analysed 'entity attributes' and relationships and the limitation of considering the influence of external and internal conditions on PM. This does not make it possible to give the decision-making based on artificial intelligence (Sternberg & Kaufman 2011). Problems with using DSS arise in legal and social aspects. Socially, the problem of utilisation of released human resources is sharply exacerbated. Legally, conflicts arise associated with the so-called 'guillotine' problem. For the cyber manager, the negative consequences are the responsibility of decisions made by the intelligence system (Intelligence Models 1999).

In practice, project managers use an integrated model with five domains of intelligence:

1. Emotional intelligence (EI). This domain includes the competencies: result orientation, initiative, flexibility and self-confidence.
2. Social intelligence (SI) includes competencies like empathy, influence, networking and distributed team leadership. It also shows significant cognitive competencies like systems thinking and pattern recognition.
3. Cognitive intelligence (CI). This domain of competencies includes effectiveness in acquiring knowledge, creativity and innovation, artificial intelligence and modelling in an organisation (Sternberg & Kaufman 2011). The integrated intelligence model for implementing the project, programme and portfolio management methodology is shown in Figure 10.2.
4. Business intelligence (BI). This domain of competencies includes strategy, culture and values, planning and control, opportunity and risk management (Baker 1975; Bondar 2020).

5. Technical intelligence (TI) competencies include having a vision of the product and result, technical, technological and organisational solutions in the implementation of the project, working in conditions of uncertainty and innovation, clearly defining boundaries and working within context (Bushuyev 2018).

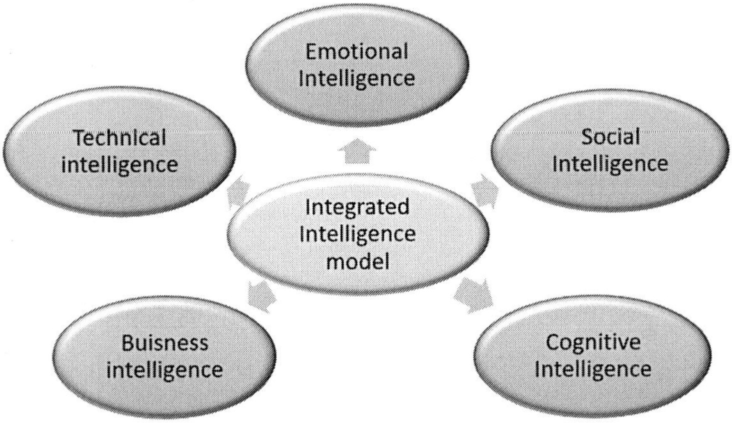

Figure 10.2 *The Integrated intelligence models for implementing project, programme and portfolio management methodology*

10.3 Application principle of hybrid project management methodology

Figure 10.3 lists five application principles of hybrid project, programme and portfolio management methodologies.

A. *The principle of a centralisation project, programme and portfolio management* is the concentration on the strategy and most important decisions.

The advantages of a centralised decision-making process include the good representation of the organisation's managers, who occupy high positions and have extensive knowledge and experience; elimination of duplication of work and the associated reduction in overall management costs; ensuring a unified scientific and technical, production, marketing, personnel policy, etc.

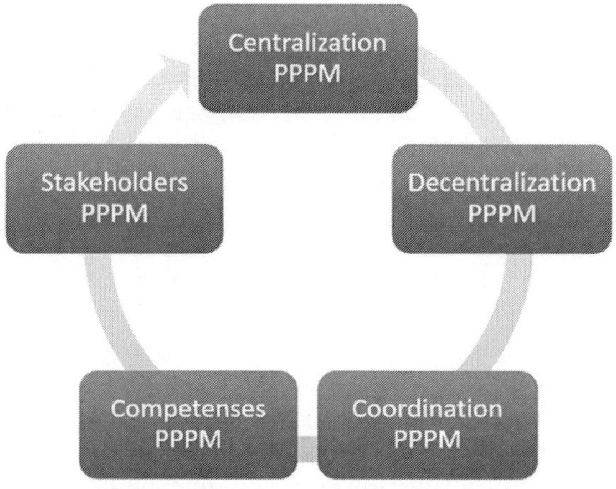

Figure 10.3 *Application principle of the hybrid project, programme and portfolio management methodology*

The disadvantages of centralisation decision-making arise from a manager with poor knowledge of specific circumstances. Much time is spent on information transmission. The lower-level managers are practically eliminated from the decisions subject to execution.

B. *The principle of decentralisation project, programme and portfolio management* is delegating authority to a lower management body (structural unit, official) to make decisions or give orders on behalf of the entire company or unit within certain limits. The need for this is due to the growth in the scale of production and its complexity when not only one person but a whole group of people cannot make and control all decisions, and even more so to carry them out. Decentralisation has many advantages, including the possibility of quick decision-making due to the involvement of middle and lower-level managers, the absence of the need to develop detailed plans and the weakening of bureaucracy. At the same time, with decentralisation, there is a lack of information, which inevitably affects the quality of decisions made; the scale of thinking is changed, and the circle of interests of managers narrows—feelings can take precedence over reason; the unification of rules and decision-making procedures becomes more difficult, which increases the time for coordination and "shaking". The higher the degree of decentralisation, the greater the independence of grassroots units, which can lead to disintegration and separatism. That is why decentralisation can be allowed only within certain limits. A large company should be more decentralised because the number of decisions made in the centre and their approval grows exponentially and eventually exceeds the management system's technical capabilities. The need for decentralisation increases in geographically dispersed organisations and in an unstable and rapidly changing environment since there is often not enough time to coordinate actions that must be carried out immediately. Finally, the degree of decentralisation depends on the experience and qualifications of the managers and employees of the respective departments. The more experienced and qualified people are on the ground, the more rights they can be given, the greater responsibility placed on them, and they can be instructed to make difficult decisions independently.

C. *The principle of coordination project, programme and portfolio management* of the activities of structural divisions and employees of the company. Depending on the circumstances, coordination is either entrusted to the units, jointly developing the necessary measures or may be entrusted to the head of one of them. However, coordination is often entrusted to a specially appointed leader with a staff of employees and consultants.

D. *The principle of using the human project, programme and portfolio management* competence is as follows:

- the bulk of decisions are made not by the entrepreneur or the chief manager unilaterally but by employees at those levels of management where decisions must be implemented;
- performers are focused primarily not on direct instructions from above but on clearly limited areas of action, powers and responsibilities; and
- higher authorities solve only those issues and problems that lower ones cannot (or do not have the right) solve.

E. *The principle of effective use of project, programme and portfolio management* stakeholders. A business' sphere of influence includes a whole range of related activities. The specialists who perform them are called satellites (companions, assistants) of the business. They contribute to the company's relations with the outside world: contractors and the state represented by its numerous bodies and institutions.

10.4 Convergence, integration and actualisation processes in the hybridisation of project management methodologies

At the present stage, the basis of PM can be considered a new philosophy—the philosophy of instability, which radically changes the concept of the world structure, rethinking the role of chaos in the world, considering it as a source of order and organisation, and which legitimises the principles of pluralism, relativism, indeterminacy. The philosophy of instability postulates the idea of abandoning monism, logocentrism and linearity, but the starting point of its worldview and methodological strategies is the idea of openness, plurality, multivariate and nonlinear worldviews, chaos and chance as creative principles. This is because society now has a variety of worldviews and philosophical principles of interpretation and management practices, defined as the organisational activities of people.

The methodological basis of the convergent approach to PM is also formed by general scientific approaches and methods (systemic, functional, institutional, historical, comparative, etc.), which will contribute to a comprehensive analysis of the phenomenon of management. New opportunities for improving and developing innovative approaches to project decision-making to ensure the project's success will create and use their subject area.

There are two directions of hybridisation of methodologies.

The first direction is *vertical hybridisation* within the development of methodologies from PM to programme and project portfolio management. This development is observed in the latest PM^2, P2M (PMAJ 2017), and PMBoK (Project Management Book of Knowledge) versions. An example of vertical hybridisation P2M standard is shown as the new P2M tower as a model of programme integration and PM (Figure 10.4).

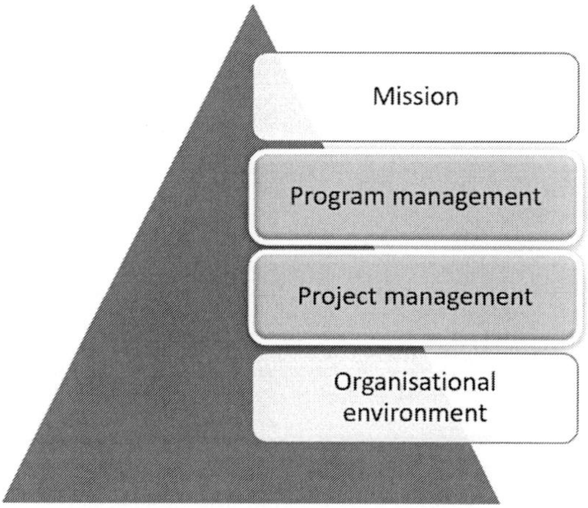

Figure 10.4 *Integration of programme and PM methodology*

The second direction is *horizontal hybridisation* between different P2M and agile methodologies.

Within the framework of the P PM², methodology, an attempt was made to integrate the waterfall process model horizontally with the agile model. The PM² methodology provides:

- a governance structure for the project;
- guidelines for the management process;
- templates for artefacts;
- artefact guidelines;
- effective mindsets.

The PM² agile extension applying for IT projects (Figure 10.5):

- agile roles and responsibilitics;
- integration with the PM² project lifecycle;
- the set of proposed Agile PM² artefacts.

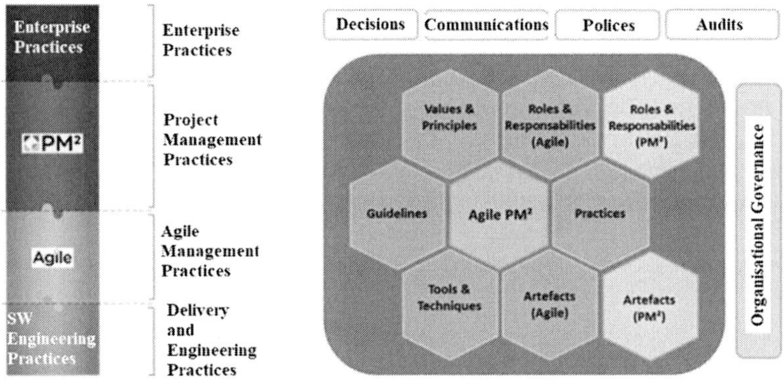

Figure 10.5 The positioning of Agile
Source: PM² within an organisation

The artefacts support the use of Agile PM² methodology. Artefacts capture and document information according to the management approach, implementation, activities, milestones, risks and progress reporting. Artefacts are grouped into three categories (Figure 10.6):

- agile-specific artefacts,
- coordination & reporting artefacts, and
- project governance artefacts.

Let us look at project and programme management integration in PM^2 methodology. Programme management is managing interrelated projects to achieve the programme's objectives. The programme is initiated from the portfolio management layer within the organisation.

Thus, the effectiveness of a convergent approach to PM depends largely on the personal determinant: only a creative, diverse, result-orientated person who does not shirk responsibility for decisions can succeed in project activities. In addition to professional knowledge and skills, a modern manager must have personal competencies especially relevant during economic instability: resilience, responsibility, discipline, ambition, determination and a propensity to innovate.

The question is not whether traditional PM and new, agile (flexible) methodologies can be combined. The problem that appears is rather in terminology and the replacement of entities. Today it is widely believed that there are old and new PM methodologies. If the project manager considers the essence of the applied 'old' methodologies, then it consists of using well-planned, developed packages and documents for the project's life cycle. Documents, starting from the concept, technical specifications, tasks, and project charter up to an integrated project management plan with all regulations and systematically design management processes following PMBoK, ICB4, Agile or PM^2. We will consider the development of competence in the context of the implementation of innovative projects and programmes. At the same time, information and communication technologies will be the key driver. The study's main hypothesis is that the key factor in successfully implementing innovative projects and programmes is actively developing a system of competencies in management processes. Creating and migrating values based on modern project management methodologies such as PMBoK, PM^2, and P2M contain certain solutions for hybridising the waterfall model and agile methodology. Today, these decisions do not have the necessary scientific foundation and are formed based on intuition and good practice.

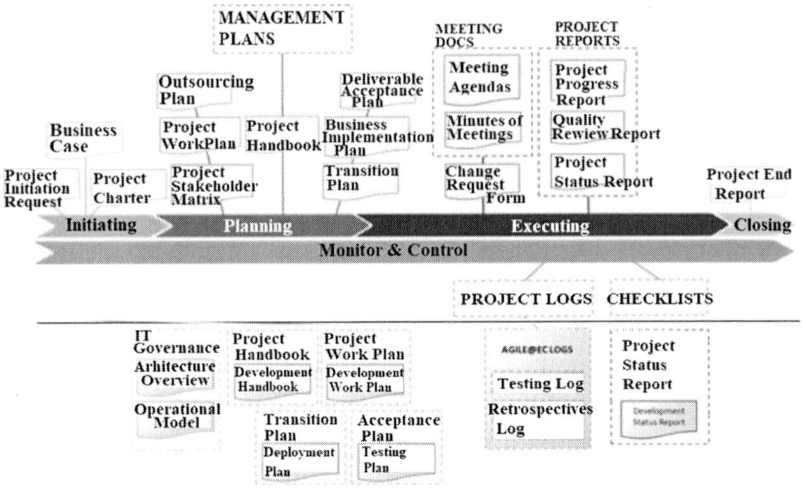

Figure 6. *Agile PM² Artefacts Landscape*
Source: PM² within an organisation

The success of projects and programmes can only be managed by focusing on the vectors of value creation for various stakeholders, using modern trends to accelerate the development process, the convergence of knowledge, a timely change in management paradigms, and understanding the life cycle (IPMA 2013). Each element is a component of the success of programmes, and the formula for project success is determined through the synergy of interaction (Obradović 2018). Projects substantiate the expediency of using genomic representations of the organisation's portfolio management methodologies, programmes and projects. The updating mechanism is preparing a hybrid implementation methodology. Each of these mechanisms has a complex structure and entry and exit functions. Such mechanisms will be defined in detail in future publications by the authors. For example, relationships at the first level between principles and approaches are systematised by an adjacency matrix. At the same time, the matrix elements determine the system compatibility of individual principles and approaches. A value of zero determines the inconsistency of the elements or the absence of their mutual influence, and a value of one indicates full consistency and maximum mutual influence.

Similarly, matrices are formed at other levels of the model. The task of the systematisation mechanism is to determine the system compatibility of the selected elements of the methodologies. In this case, the term the "genetic code of a project (programme)" will mean its system model, which includes the initial idea of the vision of the product of the project or programme, an integrated process for the development of a certain functional activity, built for the entire life cycle of the project, and tools for its interaction with the external environment. At the same time, the genomes of PM methodologies and project and programme portfolio management have the same helical structure for different content.

The convergent development methodology in managing innovative digitalisation projects has been formed on this basis. The methodology determines what a necessary attribute of convergence (interpenetration) is; these are structural or functional changes in PM systems. It should be noted that an immanent feature of a convergent management system establishes a long-term balance of competence of the team and other participants in the innovative digitalisation project relative to each other. The main advantage of the convergent model of competency development in management lies in the possibility of the simultaneous use of the potential of various competency-based management methodologies for the effective interaction of participants in an innovative project. Following the indicated mechanisms and methods, we single out three main concepts for studying and determining the convergence of management systems for innovative digitalisation projects (PM^2 2018):

- Acquisition by the system, the characteristics of other systems are studied under the influence of innovations and external factors over time (evolution).
- Approximation of the characteristics of innovative systems and competencies for their development because of mutual movement towards each other.
- Determination of the degree and measure of similarity of systems in the 'as is' state to assess the necessary competencies.

The first and second concepts consider the system parameters in the dynamic, and the third—is in a static state.

The first concept is displayed as the evolution of competencies, resulting in convergent similarity. This means the similarity of PM competencies, based not on their industry-specific but on a set of features that have formed independently in the different digitalisation processes. The reason for convergent evolution is the same as the nature of the influence of external factors on this competency set (Agile Practice Guide 2017).

The interpenetration occurs as a result of ensuring the digitalisation processes innovation in some fields of science, technology, education, etc. It is an interweaving and interaction of competency elements for managing projects. In this case, organisational pathologies are created regarding the interaction of competencies (Bushuyev et al. 2020).

The second concept is related to the formation of new systems of competencies due to the convergence of the characteristics of systems. This happens in digitalisation projects due to the mutual movement of competencies towards each other. In this case, the key issue is the sustainability of development and the flexibility of the system of competencies (Bushuyev et al. 2020).

It is necessary to implement the second concept:

- to determine the key components of the convergence process of management competencies in the process of new methodologies formation;
- to propose criteria for comparing the system characteristics of objects in their convergence concerning competencies (Bushuyev & Verenych 2018); and
- to highlight the main methods of comparison and analysis of the field of competencies that can be used in creating new competencies of PM methodologies.

10.5 A genetic approach to hybridisation of project management methodologies

Basic definitions of applying the genetic approach in PM are given.

Definition 3. The genetic model of the project is a system model that describes the project with all the hereditary traits, which includes the initial idea of the 'vision' of the project product, the integrated development process in a particular subject area built for the project life cycle, and the tools for its interaction with the environment. If the constructed genetic model is correct, then the possibilities for the head of the programme of development of the organisation expand.

Definition 4. The phenotype is a set of external quantitative features of the project, which are observed taking into account the degree of adaptation (adaptability) to the external environment, which forms a general idea of the project.

Definition 5. A gene is an element of project information reflected in a phenotype that moves from project to project and is a specific information structure that significantly impacts the environment of projects and programmes. Genes are units of heredity. The length of the project genes can be the same or different.

Definition 6. A chromosome is a set of genes that determine project properties (project characteristics, project characteristics, project class, project types, time parameters of the project, project complexity levels, project complexity levels, project scale, project life cycle structures, external project impact factors, project flexibility levels, levels project manageability, etc.). The chromosome has a fixed length. The location of a particular gene on a chromosome is called a locus, and alternative forms of the same gene located at the same locus on a chromosome are called alleles.

Definition 7. Project genetic code (genotype)—represents a set of interconnected structures containing all hereditary information from 'ancestors' with the possibility of transmission to 'descendants.' The genetic code of the project is formed at the time of its birth, but most often, the process of code formation occurs spontaneously, based on intuition and the practice of PM in this class. During the implementation of the project, the genetic code can be modified under the influence of changes and accumulated knowledge about the project outcome, PM processes and interaction with the environment.

An example of the structure of the project's genetic code and its formation process is a carrier methodology for goal setting, management of values and expectations of stakeholders based on the carrier of genome methodologies:

The formation of a new (transferred) methodology takes place on three levels:

- Level 1—the level of innovation (creative thinking);
- Level 2—the level of convergence of system parameters; and
- Level 3—the level of integration and harmonisation of the transferred methodology.

At the first level, there is a process of innovation (creative thinking), which arises from the need to create new approaches to solving unique problems that arise under the influence of turbulent environments.

The driving force (*D*) for developing new methodologies is the creative force of innovation, as the interaction of project context and personality. Such a force disturbs the static balance of the cyclical course of life of the system and raises it to a whole new level. At the same time, managerial innovation is mostly a creative action, and the manager is a bold leader who seeks to break through a wide range of stereotypes. This, in turn, takes the manager beyond routine management.

Such processes reveal the ability to think in a new way, act quickly and confidently and understand intuitively. Creativity realised through innovative behaviour includes not only experimenting with new technologies, and management methods but also the ability to separate from the set of possible methods best suited for the effective solution to tasks.

As we know, the basics of project managers' innovation are creative, innovative behaviour, the main characteristics of which are—intuition (*I*—intuition), fantasy *(F*—fantasy), imagination (*V*—vision), novelty (*N*—novelty), originality (*O*—originality), a game of concepts and reasons (*R*—reason), admiration (*E*—enthusiasm), surprise (*S*-surprise), the harmony of quality (*Q*—quality), and belief in the incredible (*B*—belief). All these elements are components of the driving force *D* of social, emotional and CI (Figure 10.2).

So:

$$D=\langle I,F,V,N,O,R,E,S,Q,B\rangle. \quad (1)$$

The action of *P* leads to a shift of the elements of the systems C_1 and C_2 (*S*—structures, *F*—functions, *A*—goals) in the direction of convergence or divergence.

With:

$$C_1=\left\langle S^{C_1},F^{C_1},A^{C_1}\right\rangle; \quad (2)$$

$$C_2=\left\langle S^{C_2},F^{C_2},A^{C_2}\right\rangle, \quad (3)$$

where:

$$S=\left\langle s_i \middle| s_i\in S, \quad i=\overline{1,n}\right\rangle,$$

$$F=\left\langle f_j \middle| f_j\in F, \quad j=\overline{1,m}\right\rangle, \quad A=\left\langle a_k \middle| a_k\in A, \quad k=\overline{1,l}\right\rangle,$$

for C_1:

$$S^{C_1}=\left\langle s_1^{C_1},s_2^{C_1},s_3^{C_1},\dots,s_n^{C_1}\right\rangle; \quad (4)$$

$$F^{C_1}=\left\langle f_1^{C_1},f_2^{C_1},f_3^{C_1},\dots,f_j^{C_1}\right\rangle; \quad (5)$$

$$A^{C_1}=\left\langle a_1^{C_1},a_2^{C_1},a_3^{C_1},\dots,a_k^{C_1}\right\rangle. \quad (6)$$

for C_2:

$$S^{C_2} = \langle s_1^{C_2}, s_2^{C_2}, s_3^{C_2}, ..., s_n^{C_2} \rangle; \tag{7}$$

$$F^{C_2} = \langle f_1^{C_2}, f_2^{C_2}, f_3^{C_2}, ..., f_m^{C_2} \rangle; \tag{8}$$

$$A^{C_2} = \langle a_1^{C_2}, a_2^{C_2}, a_3^{C_2}, ..., a_l^{C_2} \rangle.$$

At the next stage, these parameters' convergence levels are determined, which shows the degree of convergence of individual elements of systems (*R*). The closer the elements are located, the more realistic and reliable the use of convergence methods when creating new systems (methodologies). It should be noted that several parameters will not converge at all (because the comparison involves mostly completely different systems), so they can be taken beyond certain limits.

In the figure, these limits are marked as BMD—the lower limit of system tolerance, and TDC—the upper limit of system tolerance. These boundaries form a space of tolerance in which, through stratification, new sets are formed according to three main characteristics:

$$(\exists s_i \in (S^{C_1} \vee S^{C_2})) \in S'; \tag{9}$$

$$(\exists f_j \in (F^{C_1} \vee F^{C_2})) \in F'; \tag{10}$$

$$(\exists a_k \in (A^{C_1} \vee A^{C_2})) \in A', \tag{11}$$

where:

$$i = \overline{1,n}, \quad j = \overline{1,m}, \quad k = \overline{1,l}$$

S', *F'*, *A'*—sets formed from elements that detect convergence and form a new system at the next level.

The elements of these sets at the next level are integrated and harmonised to create a new system to which the analogy method can be applied to form new methodologies.

$$\overline{C} = \langle S', F', A' \rangle. \tag{12}$$

Systematic and morphological analysis methods, with the help of expert assessments or statistical analysis, can determine these limits. Information approaches to comparing systems can be considered as a separate area.

To achieve real success in solving such problems, there are new requirements for the project manager, taking into account their ability for holistic and innovative thinking and ability to use methods of convergence of systems in developing new tools for unique project products.

Thus, the task is to determine a convergent approach to forming new methods and models of PM based on the development of innovative thinking of the project manager.

At the present stage, PM is carried out in a certain environment, which is a complex of various (economic, technological, social, cultural, etc.) factors. According to modern domestic experts in the philosophy of management, "in a broad philosophical sense, management is a fundamental general functional property of the objective world, organic and inorganic nature, conscious and natural forces, which are characterised by the qualities of regularity, expediency, purposefulness and purposefulness." Thus, the convergence of ideas is set objectively because the diversity of such complex processes as the evolution of the universe, society, culture, government, etc., is studied on a single conceptual basis.

PM activities are related to solving various problems, encouraging researchers to review traditional management strategies and seek new methodological orientations to converge economic, technical and humanitarian methods of cognition and the development of reality.

After all, even mathematicians today deny the absolute probability and self-evidence of all mathematical postulates and basic definitions (evidence of this is the emergence of non-Euclidean geometry, Boolean algebra, etc.).

Thus, complex, unique management tasks that constantly arise in PM require the researcher to have at least some knowledge in the humanities, social, natural, economic and technical disciplines, which, incidentally, are contained in higher education curricula.

Consider the gradual formation of PM methodology with a built-in immune mechanism. The application of interaction mechanisms depends on the organisational competence (technological maturity) level of the PM system in the organisation. At low levels of technological maturity, the methodology is not required in full and may not be represented by all elements. At high levels of technological maturity, organisations implementing large-scale, comprehensive programmes and projects require a methodology with all the elements and the necessary immune mechanisms. For the most complex and hypothetically diverse portfolio of projects and programmes, the methodology is close to a "hypothetically comprehensive system."

10.6 Intelligence mechanisms of hybridisation of project, programme and portfolio methodologies

An analysis of the development of PM methodologies allows us to identify the following mechanisms of convergence:

- development of knowledge,
- transfer of knowledge and technology,
- benchmarking,
- self-organisation and evolution of systems,
- change (development) of the personality of researchers.

The main prerequisites for the use of convergence mechanisms are (Bushuyev et al. 2015):

- an absence in the modern methodological field of objective generally accepted systematisation of methodologies, which leads to systemic chaos in which it is very difficult for both managers and scientists to understand;
- the development of specialisation in certain areas of PM leads to the disintegration of the discipline of PM as such;
- regulations of enterprise PM are developed with an understanding of the fundamental difference between project and production activities, but the management mechanisms are used in general, which leads to methodological divergence;
- PM is replaced by content management, which leads to the fact that, for example, the quality of the PM process and the quality of competence of project participants is identified with the quality of the project product;
- lack of effective knowledge base at enterprises, which includes the accumulation of high-level collective competencies and opportunities for effective exchange of knowledge, experience and skills, which significantly delays the process of transition of the enterprise to a higher level of maturity;
- underestimation of the possibilities of the processes of planning, development and implementation of organisational capacity development systems due to the lack of systematic proposals on this issue in the existing methodologies; and

- low quality of education in PM, lack of professional quality systems for assessing learning outcomes, and imperfect feedback on teaching and learning due to the low basic training of students.

On this basis, it is possible to form a methodology for the convergent development of PM systems, which will determine that the necessary attributes of convergence are structural and functional changes in PM systems, which in turn are related to changes in the relationship and role of the most important component. Also, it should be noted that an inherent feature of the convergent management system establishes a long-term balance between the team and other project participants concerning each other. The main advantage of the convergent model of management systems development is the possibility of the simultaneous use of the potential of different management methodologies based on the effective interaction of project participants.

According to the presented mechanisms and methods, we can identify three main research and development concepts of PM systems convergence. The first and second concepts consider the project parameters dynamic, and the third—is static.

The first concept is reflected in the evolution of systems. The result of this is convergent similarity. That means the PM systems' similarity is based not on their industry characteristics but on a close set of features formed independently in different systems.

Within the framework of this concept, we will consider the formation of a new methodology in the form of a model of convergence of components of different systems under the influence of internal and external factors. In this case, convergence in PM can be used to create common, aggregate and specialised methodologies that meet the specific needs of businesses of different orientations, different scales and different levels of maturity of management systems.

The model distinguishes three types of systems (the classification may be different and broader, but this will complicate the perception of the model): mechanical, organic and organisational and technical systems to which the project belongs. The known components of the systems are given: *S*—structure, *A*—goals, C—relationships, *P*—elements, and an additional element, *M*—system management methodology. The described systems are considered dynamic, so in their movement and transformation, researchers can identify similar parameters of these systems, which indicates their approximation, i.e. convergence.

Procedural convergence of system elements can occur in several planes (layers), which differ in the scale of the development process. Technical means (information technology) may converge at the basic level to ensure design decisions. A layer of convergence of professionalism follows this, as new methods require additional competencies and convergent formats of management tasks, which create conditions for interaction and interpenetration at the level of PM system components.

Such systems can be built with the researcher's basic knowledge of systems theory, systems analysis and other branches of science. We can say that a project manager has the most invariant knowledge in management, as they can develop and implement projects in completely different directions. This presupposes the rapid development of PM methodologies using a convergent integration approach. The established methodology also becomes a factor of influence for the further development of systems, which is important for ensuring development processes. Therefore, such research needs to be continued, deepening knowledge and ensuring the continuous development of methods and models in various fields of government.

Today, agile is actively used in extreme conditions. From a systemic point of view, creating an extreme situation is a consequence of an insufficiently mature management process.

Despite its methodological fragmentation, but also the fact that agile methodologies are inherent in additional material, human, and sometimes financial costs arise due to 'throwing from side to side' when reacting to internal and external changes (reactions to situations). These methodologies are also partially applied in highly mature management enterprises, usually as a hybrid addition to the main methodologies (Bushuyev et al. 2015). Hybrid methodologies based on traditional ones using artificial intelligence and elements of agile methodologies will reduce the risks of resource dispersion and increase productivity and quality of PM decision-making.

10.7 Conclusion

To create or adapt a PM methodology, convergence and hybridisation technologies are determined by the characteristics of the project, its scale, complexity, basic requirements, success criteria and the organisational structure in which it is implemented. The effective application of convergence and hybridisation technologies largely depends on the project managers' competence, team competence and, generally, the project organisation's maturity level.

From the point of view of the formation and development of individual and especially collective knowledge bases and competencies in PM, hybrid methodologies can significantly increase the system coverage of world experience and increase the speed of knowledge accumulation, productivity and quality of decision-making.

And the approach looks completely strange when, due to the current situation at an enterprise, PM is adjusted to the methodology adopted at it: in mature business organisations, the opposite approach is used—for the effective implementation of projects, specific methodologies are selected, adapted or developed for them. In the latter case, both convergence and hybridisation of methodologies are productively applied.

References

PMAJ. *A Guidebook of Programme & Project Management for Enterprise Innovation*, Third Edition, 2017: 427.

PMI. Project Management Book of Knowledge. Seventh Edition, 2021: 370.

IPMA. Individual Competence Baseline for Project, Programme & Portfolio Management, Version 4, 2015: 415.

IPMA. Organisational Competence Baseline (IPMA OCB). 2013: 67.

PM². Project Management Methodology Guide 3.0, 2018: 113, https://ec.europa.eu/eusurvey/runner/openpm2-contact.

ISO 21502. Guidance on project management. Project Committee ISO / PC 236, 2020: 52.

ISO 21503, project, programme and portfolio management—Guidance on programme management. ISO/PC 236, 2018: 52.

ISO 21504, project, programme and portfolio management—Guidance on portfolio management ISO/PC 236, 2015: 24.

ISO 21505, project, programme and portfolio management —Guidance on governance ISO/PC 236, 2017: 11.

The Cambridge Handbook of Intelligence, Cambridge University Press, 2011: 58–82 DOI: https://doi.org/10.1017/CBO9780511977244.005.

Intelligence Models and Best Practices. IALEIA,1999: 58.

Obradović, Vladimir, Todorović, Marija and Bushuyev Sergiy. 2018, "Sustainability and Agility in Project Management: Contradictory or Complementary?" IEEE 13th International Scientific and Technical Conference on Computer Sciences and Information Technologies, CSIT 2018, 165-169. DOI: 10.1109/STC-CSIT.2018.8526666.

Todorović, Marija, Petrović, Dian, Mihić, Miko, Obradović., Vladimir and Bushuyev, Sergey. 2015. "Project success analysis framework: A knowledge-based approach in project management." *International Journal of Project Management* (2015): 772-783.

Baker, Norman, Freeland James, 1975. "Recent advances in R&D benefit measurement and project selection methods." *Management Science*, Vol. 21, No6., (1975):1164-1175.

Bondar, Alla Bushuyeva, Natalia, Bushuyev, Sergiy, Onyshchenko, Svitlana 2020. "Modelling of Creation Organisational Energy Sergey - Entropy" IEEE 15th International Conference on Computer Sciences and Information Technologies (CSIT), Zbarazh, Ukraine, (2020):141–145, https://doi.org/10.1109/CSIT49958.2020.9321997.

Bushuyev, Sergiy, Verenych, Olena. 2018. "The Blended Mental Space: Mobility and Flexibility as Characteristics of Project/Programme Success." IEEE 13th International Scientific and Technical Conference on Computer Sciences and Information Technologies, (2018): 148-152.

Agile Practice Guide: USA, Project Management Institute, 2017. 210.

Bushuyev Sergiy, Kozyr Boris, Rusan Nadija. 2020. "Modelling of Empathy, Emotional Intelligence and Transformational Leadership to the Project Success." In *Mathematical Modelling and Simulation of Systems. Advances in Intelligent Systems and Computing*. Springer AG. vol. 972, (2020): 209–222.

Bushuyev Sergiy, Babayev Jahid, Bushuiev Denis, Kozyr Boris. 2020. "Emotional Infection of Management Innovation SMART Government Projects." IEEE European Technology & Engineering Management Summit. (2020): 53-58.

Bushuyev, Sergiy, Bushuiev, Denis, Rogozina, Victoria, Mikhieieva, Olga. 2015. "Convergence of knowledge in project management." Proceedings of the 2015 IEEE 8th International Conference on Intelligent Data Acquisition and Advanced Computing Systems: Technology and Applications, IDAACS (2015): 496–500.

Sergey Bushuyev, Dr.Sc. (Habilitation), is a professor at Kyiv National University of Construction and Architecture (KNUCA); since 1986, he has been the head of the Project Management Department, Ukraine, an honorary scientist of Ukraine, a Laureate of the National Scientific Award, and is an honorary member of the International Project Management Association (IPMA). Since 1975, Bushuyev has prepared 40 candidates for science PhDs and 15 Doctors of Science. He has published more than 50 books and 250 scientific papers.

Nataliia Bushuyeva, Dr.Sc. (Habilitation), is a professor at Kyiv National University of Construction and Architecture (KNUCA), Ukraine, a Laureate of the National Scientific Award, and an International Project Management Association (IPMA) member. Since 2004 Bushuyeva has prepared 12 candidates for science PhDs and published more than 80 scientific articles and books.

Denis Bushuiev Dr.Sc. (Habilitation), is a professor at Kyiv National University of Construction and Architecture (KNUCA), Ukraine. In February 2015, he defended his PhD thesis. In 2019 he defended his Doctor of Science. (Habilitation). He is a Laureate of the National Scientific Award and an International Project Management Association (IPMA) member. Professor Bushuiev has published more than 60 scientific articles and books.

Viktoria Bushuieva is an associate professor at Kyiv National University of Construction and Architecture (KNUCA), Ukraine. In March 2015, she defended her PhD thesis. She is a member of the International Project Management Association (IPMA). Viktoria Bushuieva has published more than 40 scientific articles and books.

XI

Hybrid Model of Infusing Agile Project Management Principle in Waterfall Model for the Successful Execution of Capital Project

M. Ramakrishnan, R. Gajanan
and M. Naveenkumar

11.1 Overview of Capital Project

The world is gradually reviving to normality from the pandemic after two years. The nations have begun to loosen their restrictions on development through investment projects, even though the pandemic has not yet been contained. Due to the public interest and national development, investments have begun to increase dramatically. Investors are eager to recoup their investment while minimising risk. The cascading effect of failing to deal with unexpected changes could cause the pipeline of large-scale projects that is currently in place to lose more than USD 1.5 trillion over the course of the next five years (Oracle Corporation, n.d.). In order to manage risk during each stage of the project, various strategies are developed. The practise of remote lean scheduling, which collaborates daily activity by involving the entire team and keeps the task on track, is used in the building of structures that place an emphasis on enhancing productivity with the best available resources. Regulations pertaining to health, safety, and the environment (HSE) are put into effect by organising tasks that would allow for physical separation and prevent trade stacking (Gagen 2020). In addition to the planning task, the organisation must foresee the trend so that the choice will be profitable for the company. It is essential to choose the appropriate data that is extracted by machine learning and then subjected to predictive analytics in order to derive wise decisions (Cheeseman 2021). There is a constellation of connected solutions among various phases of the project through modern technology, which are AI, digital twin, modularization, optimization in construction, and supply chain (Blanco et al. 2018). Because of the ease of executing the project, advanced work packaging techniques by grouping the scope into work areas are in practise (Monteiro & Jagnanan 2016).

Different organisations, including investors, execution agencies, and software developers, are making numerous efforts to complete the project on time and within budget. The pandemic has accelerated development in a new dimension while the resource optimization and digitization of the workplace were already underway. It is essential to look for solutions holistically rather than in a piecemeal or narrowly focused manner in order to complete the project on time and within budget. Retrospective data will serve as a guide, and different technologies will serve as a platform to facilitate business, but the project's execution strategy will be crucial in achieving the goal. There are many factors that affect a project's success, including (i) organisations like stakeholders and shareholders, (ii) environmental elements like legislation, political objectives, and geographic location, (iii) intrinsic characteristics like work culture, and (iv) tools and techniques like project management methodologies, advanced programming tools, or digital platforms. Across different projects, the magnitude of each variable sounds different. The implementation of the Project Management (PM) methodology plays a crucial role in the project's execution because it combines the resource through human analytics with pre-programmed tools. The key members of the organisation must be knowledgeable and experienced to lead the project, be conscious of the workplace culture, foster team cohesion, and be energetic about the project (Gomarn & Pongpeng 2018; Almeida 2017).

The capital projects are intricate, with a detailed schedule and a sizable budget. The waterfall methodology, which has been used for decades and is primarily used for capital projects, is used to carry out capital projects. Second, to lower the risk for the investor, the projects are awarded on a turnkey basis. Thirdly, for the majority of capital projects, the scope will be partially developed when the project is launched. A mature scope, clear resources, and upfront analysis are required for the waterfall methodology (Roecker 2018; Donado n.d.). The scope of the majority of projects has a few ambiguous areas that will be clarified during execution. In these situations, adopting a new project management methodology is challenging. Instead, the traditional approach of sequential workflow in a linear approach, known as the waterfall methodology, needs to be transformed by incorporating the agile principle by handling the scope of each phase in bits of independent iteration and dispensing the result into the main body of the project. In this paper, the present scenario of the capital project with literature has been discussed, followed by proposing the hybrid model of infusing agile into the waterfall method that needs to be pragmatic, and the critical success factor of the hybrid methodology in capital projects.

11.2 Review of the present scenario of the capital project with literature review

With reference to the literature review, this section discusses the current state of capital projects like oil and gas, petrochemical, transmission and distribution (T&D), factories, and buildings. Project life cycle, organisational factor, project manager competency, scheduling approach, digitization, and project management methodology make up this section.

11.2.1 Project development life cycle

Nowadays, the majority of contracts are given out on a lump sum basis in order to significantly lower the risk for the investor or owner. As a collaborative arrangement, a turnkey contract appoints a prospective agency to design, obtain the necessary materials, install, and run the plant (Owusu & Ofusu 2013; Vassileva & Nikolov 2016). The project development life cycle begins with the conception stage, where the project's goals are determined. From there, a feasibility study is conducted until a proposal is prepared (Long 2021). The investor may choose to hire a consulting firm that may be designated as an "Owners Engineer" or EPCM contractor, or they may choose to hire the performing organisation, which would be a turnkey contractor.

After the conceptual design or feasibility study is finished, front-end engineering design (FEED) will be started through the project proposal. Process and design basis descriptions, input and output production and consumption rates, optimised heat and mass balances, process flow diagrams (PFD), partially developed piping and instrumentation diagrams (P&ID), equipment process datasheets and specifications, instrument data sheets, utility flow distribution drawings, equipment lists, line lists, preliminary layouts, environmental design requirements, and other fundamentals are all included in FEED. The detailed engineering phase of an immature FEED may result in a significant change order. The partially developed FEED may occasionally be floated by the owner for competitive bidding, which would result in deviation after the contract is awarded. Few change orders would typically be made in a well-developed FEED because they are unavoidable. It forms the source of delay at the inception of the project (Long 2021).

The owner may use different agencies both before and after the contract is awarded, which would lead to ambiguity in assumptions, particularly in design because information on the interface between systems is missing, estimates are not finalised, and the scope is not developed to its full potential. This will increase the project's risk. There are industry-specific and general factors in every project. Sector-specific factors are only focused on a particular industry vertical, whereas general factors apply to the entire vertical or sector (Pall et al. 2019). The risk must be calculated in accordance with the assumption of the project, which must be defined precisely in the project proposal during the conception stage. During detail engineering, a failure to define assumptions regarding sector-specific and general factors may have serious repercussions. The potential agency will be given the contract at the conclusion of the conception phase. The owner must hire Contract Administration/Construction Claim experts to review the contract procedures that are appropriate for the type of contract, which would be lump sum or cost reimbursable, in order to lessen the contract's ambiguity. It should happen before the award of the contract (Long 2021).

The project development life cycle's second stage is known as "Definition" or "Planning." This phase would start following the awarding of the contract. By developing (i) the project definition, which will convert the proposal into manageable tasks and schedule it in a project roadmap, and (ii) the system definition, measurable short-term goals are created from high-level project goals during this phase. The project management methodology will be approved at the start of this phase, and project execution strategies will be created. The scope of work is broken down into work packages, each of which is completed by a team member under the supervision of the leadership team or project management team (PMT). Following the development of the project's initial requirements, each work package's budget, manpower mobilisation, risk register, and preliminary planning to create a critical path are finished (Herbst 2016). The schedule was developed assuming that risk would be reviewed and changed throughout each period as project planning continued through completion of the handover. For some projects, the scope is carried out using the Engineering, Procurement, and Construction work packages. When dividing the scope into the work package, constructability of the work is taken into consideration. It acts as the project's execution phase's framework (Monteiro & Jagnanan 2016). Cutting the scope requires capable leadership that can anticipate future risks and communication irregularities throughout the project.

The FastTrack principle is used to carry out capital projects, and each project phase overlaps the previous one. There are more design changes in projects with aggressive schedules (Alhomadi et al. 2011). Most change orders would arise from conflicts with FEED and misunderstandings with the vendor during the finalisation of the system's specification, rather than from voluntary or imposed changes (Zadeh et al. 2014). More technical issues which would be unaddressed on time, the ignorance of interfaces, failure to identify risk, poor stakeholder management due to a higher number of Joint Venture (JV), unavailability of design documents for brownfield projects, changes in sub-surface data in Oil & Gas (O&G) are notable concern that has a consequence on the project during the design stage (Suppramaniam et al. 2018; Pall et al. 2019; Wadie 2020; Hatmoko & Khasani 2019).

When a system is finalised or the specification for a system is derived, numerous agencies are involved, including the owner's engineer, principal contractor, turnkey contractor, Engineering, Procurement and Construction Management (EPCM), Original Equipment Manufacturer (OEM), and sub-design agency. To develop the specification, communication is crucial. Poor communication between project parties during the package release or specification finalisation process has a significant impact on the project's execution (Pall et al. 2019). A portion of the capital project's scope is initially undeveloped. The front-end loaded schedule may be prepared by the turnkey contractor or his vendor without validating the available drawings, whether on purpose or accidentally. The project would incur higher costs during the execution stage as a result (Wadie 2020). Lack of in-depth system thinking and poor interface management across the system for design may result in unrealistic duration fixing (Emam et al. 2014), which will have unexpected project outcomes.

"Execution" is the third phase of the project development life cycle. This stage of a project is when the most labor-intensive work is completed. Each phase of the Fastrack project crosses over with the next. This phase starts as the Planning phase is gradually completed. This phase involves the system's detailed engineering, component manufacturing on the premises of the principal contractor and the OEM, fabrication, site installation, testing, and pre-commissioning. It also involves making sure the system is ready for operation.

During the detail engineering,

1. Lack of qualified and experienced personnel,
2. Poor interaction with the vendor during detail design,
3. Late approval from the owner or the consultant,

4. Unclear owner specifications,
5. Erroneous contractor design,
6. Late identification of voids in FEED during detail design,
7. Less knowledge of equipment sizing by the contractor,
8. Lack of value engineering concepts to control scope creep is the source of delay (Suppramaniam et al. 2018; Pall et al. 2019; Wadie 2020; Hatmoko & Khasani 2019).

Other significant causes of delay in detail design include project-specific issues like route change in T&D projects and delay in the design of the topside deck and hull in O&G projects (Pall et al. 2019; Long 2021). Despite the presence of experienced professionals, a protracted approval process for drawings and documents by the owner or his representative could cause the project to be delayed indefinitely (Pall et al. 2019). To lessen the pivot point of the liability gap between the agencies by owner, the majority of capital projects are delivered under a Design-Build contract with liability to a single entity. A single goal drives the engagement of numerous agencies by the prime/turnkey contractor, including design, OEM, and installation groups (Design-Build Institute of America 2014). A turnkey contractor handling such contracts must manage communications effectively. The project could be severely delayed if the project manager is unable to guide and resolve disputes and communication issues (Manavalan 2021). The core of a capital project is detail design, so it's critical to manage vendor and contractor communication. The preparation of realistic and accurate project costs that are comparable to the elaboration of the scope is required alongside detail design (Alhajri & Alshibani 2018).

The procurement process is yet another crucial component of the Execution phase. The delay begins with the vendor being chosen solely based on bid value, regardless of their affiliation with the competition and their qualifications, who may need to firmly stand by their commitment (Alhajri & Alshibani 2018). Delays by a vendor or OEM can affect a system or package that is in the interface or activities that must be carried out in a specific order, which can have a cascading effect on the project. When it comes to sector-specific delays, engineering, the establishment of the procurement system, and long lead times for items are to blame (Gomarn & Pongpeng 2018; Hatmoko & Khasani 2019). On the other hand, general factors include poor communication with vendors, late payments to suppliers, a rigid process for selecting vendors, the provision of inefficient equipment, the late intent on heavy machinery for lifting, subpar finished goods, a lack of material management, and resistance to adopting the new system (Gomarn & Pongpeng 2018; Pall et al. 2019; Wadie 2020; Jobet al.

2018; Daniel et al. 2018). Engineering delays at the project's beginning have a huge impact on procurement activities. Poor material management may lead to waiting and retrieving materials for an average of 80 minutes each day (Lambert 2020).

In the Execution phase, the Installation comes after the procurement. The installed, operationally tested, and commissioning components—both those that were provided and those that were made locally—meet the contractual requirements. Most studies are being conducted to slow down elimination and improve construction. Across the industry, the installation discipline has unique characteristics like lifting tools, technical know-how, and legal requirements. Beginning with the hiring of an incompetent party, poor planning from the start, and a breakdown in communication between the principal contractor and the subcontractor all contribute to delays (Suppramaniam et al. 2018). Sector-specific issues include the long construction cycle and numerous risks in the oil and gas industry, the obstruction of a highway, buildings, or creek as a result of a change in a project's route, the inability of a contractor to afford to abide by the terms of a contract, such as the use of modern equipment and specialists, and the failure to time fabrication with the availability of marine spread. General factors include a lack of a qualified leader to lead the site, an overly ambitious schedule by the contractor, sudden flooding in the transmission line project, unexpected change orders during installation, local community issues, concurrent installation with operation, an ambiguous contract clause, cultural impacts, and an installation error caused by an unskilled workforce (Suppramaniam et al. 2018; Pall et al. 2019; Wadie 2020; Hatmoko & Khasani 2019; Long 2021; Emam et al. 2014). In addition to technical factors, other factors that affect construction activities include government regulations, financial restrictions on the part of the owner or contractor, political issues, and international diplomacy, delays in the approval process for technical queries, and a strict permit process (Suppramaniam et al. 2018; Pall et al. 2019; Hatmoko & Khasani 2019). Additionally, the turnkey contractor's lack of understanding of the relationship between the sub-contractor and vendors has a significant impact on the progress. The projects are tested for operability module by module and then holistically to ensure they meet the contractual requirements. At this stage, there will be a lot of risk because the turnkey contractor needs to work with a variety of equipment vendors and manage their agreed-upon costs through a technical interface to meet plant performance requirements. This phase will be impacted by delays from the project's beginning because of cascading effects, and it won't be possible to shorten its duration; instead, it may lengthen depending on how well each piece of equipment performs. As a result, the phase in the schedule that is created using planning software needs to have enough float.

"Operation" is the fourth stage of the project development life cycle. The project moves from this stage into the operational stage. While the operational phase is taken into account in built-operate-own-transfer projects, the first three phases of the project development cycle make up the project life cycle that is taken into account in design-build projects (Prakash 2015). In order to address the operational improvement that is elaborated in the suggested method, this paper has been restricted to the project life cycle given the design-build project.

11.2.2 Organizational factor

According to ICB version 4.0 clause 4.3.1, each organisation defines its own strategies for achieving benefits for the organization's long-term goal by carrying out the project through specific management domains like programmes or portfolios. Understanding the environment in which the organisation operates, coming up with a plan to achieve the desired outcome, and choosing the best project or programme within the portfolio are all examples of strategic competence. Each organisation would identify the critical success factor (CSF), which would be crucial in defining the mission, as the root of its success. A key performance indicator (KPI) is used by the performance indicator to measure and track the accomplishment of the objectives (Mihăiloaie 2013; Giffhorn et al. 2009). At the start of the project, the management defines these two factors. The organization's strategy, capacity, and experience must be taken into account when choosing a project (Wadie, 2020). According to clause 4.3.1.2 of the ICB 4.0, the executive board developed a top-down strategy at the project's outset that would allow for the realisation of environmental changes, new opportunities, and risk during execution that would deviate from the pre-set strategic goals. In order to achieve the predetermined target, the influences must be managed by an interactive control system using a bottom-up strategy. Additionally, the board and top management must be persuaded to accept the change. The turnkey contractor or sub-agency in a project also has their organisational policies and strategy to carry out the project, even though the aforementioned factor may sound favourable to investors. The alignment of each stakeholder's strategy with the appropriate organisational policy is essential to the capital project's success.

Along with the definition of organisational policies and strategy to complete the project, the workforce is a valuable asset. The success of the project depends on the organisation choosing a capable project manager, and then, with the project manager's assistance, the organisation choosing experienced and technically competent staff, consultants, and contractors (Pall et al. 2019). Failures that could result in project delays include: the investor's or sponsor's insufficient financial resources; the turnkey contractor's or vendor's financial crisis; the project management team's or investor's incompetent project manager; the investor's lack of management experience at an earlier stage; the project control functions' poor performance; and the team's and project organization's poor communication (Suppramaniam et al. 2018; Wadie 2020). The Contractor may occasionally provide the owner with a limited amount of information via reports and submittals. They would later assert uncertainties for which the Owner might be liable. The owner would not see the full picture, and the turnkey contractor and subcontractor's transmission of information would be delayed, as shown by the Daily Progress Reports (DPR), Requests for Inspections (RFI), and claims. A clause in the Contract that requires the contemporaneous document to be submitted during the action rather than populating the documents after the issue has occurred or at the end of the project is needed to prevent this situation (Long 2021).

The company is adaptable and covers both technology and people, but it needs to have a better understanding of the opportunities and dangers that people, as a team, and technology present so that it can take the necessary precautions. The collaborative culture is crucial when handling capital projects because, in the absence of a turnkey contractor, the owner/investor's inability to collaborate with prime contractors due to unusual contractual language may result in a varying design that deviates from the specification. The prime contractor may later make a claim for the time and money spent. Instead of relying on Prime Contractors to resolve issues among themselves, the Owner needs to take the initiative and work with the Contractors to find solutions. In the absence of a turnkey contractor, an EPCM contractor is a better choice to manage interfaces for small owners and deal with prime contractors (Doughtie 2019; Long 2021).

11.2.3 Project Manager Competency

The project is formally approved to begin by the project charter, which also gives the project manager permission to use the company's resources. According to ICB 4.0 clause 4.4.6, the project manager gives the team and support team members instructions to communicate with one another during the Forming stage, which will be completed at the Definition stage. In addition to leading, the project manager motivates, settles disputes, and maintains team cohesion during the Storming and Norming phase, which may occur at the conclusion of the Definition stage and the beginning of the Execution stage. Without a delegation from the project manager, the team must begin performing during the Execution phase in order for the project and team to be successful. The project may be ruined by a project manager's ineffective communication, poor leadership, poor planning, poor project monitoring and control, and failure to adhere to quality plans (Suppramaniam et al. 2018).

The project manager must recognise and evaluate risks, insist on prompt action on change orders, forecast the project using real-time data by involving the team early in the project, choose the best bid that is qualified to handle the project, and obtain permit approval on time (Lambert 2020; Gomarn & Pongpeng 2018; Wadie 2020). He must cultivate system thinking, which examines the project from a comprehensive perspective with interrelations, thereby encouraging self-for future thinking that would support envisaging the project trend regarding the current stage and risks that would arise in the future (Gandhi 2021). By using a common communication channel, collaborative thinking is a good way to resolve a variety of problems, both technically and commercially. The system for project organisation homogeneity should be presided over by the project manager (Manavalan 2021). The top management of each organisation looks for partnerships with organisations with similar business models in order to advance business, achieve alliance group objectives, and maintain both internal and external integrity for each firm's market viability and organisational agility (Doughtie 2019). The Project Head or Project Manager carries out the organization's goal. So too does the position of project manager fall outside the scope of the project organisation.

11.2.4 Scheduling method

The schedule's objective is to reflect the project execution strategy necessary to meet the contractual and organisational requirements. The project management methodology used in the project serves as the foundation for the scheduling technique. Due to its complexity, the Waterfall method typically predominates in capital projects. The scheduling technique mainly uses the work breakdown structure, Gantt chart, PERT diagram, critical path method, and critical chain method. This method works best when all project requirements are well known at the outset, along with the resources needed at each stage, and the interface is clearly visible (Roecker 2018). Poor scheduling generally results in an unrealistic estimate of resources, the trend of the project, and price escalation over the period due to an extended timeline (Alhajri & Alshibani 2018; Wadie 2020). These general features of poor scheduling are aggressive timelines, cutting corners in the scope due to ignorance at the beginning of the project or intentionally, poor planning and scheduling management by contractors, and nil updates of change in scope that will arise during construction.

External factors, such as local laws and permit approvals, must be taken into account during the engineering and execution phases (Alhajri & Alshibani 2018). Since some of these norms are unfamiliar at the beginning of the project, it must be introduced at each interval in the schedule. Failure to introduce could have detrimental effects on the project later on, and the investor or owner might be taken aback. A number of initiatives, including the critical chain method and advanced work packaging technique, have been put in place to prevent delays. The Engineering work package, Procurement work package, and Construction work package are a few examples of groups that make up the project's scope. These groups are organised so that each package is executed on a construction basis. By connecting these three work packages, level-2 and level-3 schedules are also established. For better outcomes, commitment planning is later carried out specifically for the construction work package with regular monitoring and team orientation (Monteiro & Jagnanan 2016; Herbst 2016). The integrated digital project delivery is encouraged by the advanced work package principle (Bullard & Roberts 2021). In order to maintain the integrity of the project, the project manager and project controller are crucial in managing the interface between the system and the work package.

The PERT/CPM schedule would not take into account the critical resource, such as the requirement for skilled labour, specialists, or large equipment. Second, the activities that reduce the project team's capacity to manage the total float conceal the activities float. The critical chain method (CCN) is thought to be preferable in these circumstances. In order to monitor the buffer rather than the total float, CCN uses a buffer for a particular network resource. The Theory of Constraints (TOC), on which CCN is based, focuses on at least one constraint. Effective resource use is achieved through the buffer, risk management, and focused oversight. In CCN, it can be difficult to level multiple resources and size buffers (Jo et al. 2018). Earlier identification of constraints will support us to implement the CCN method effectively, particularly for the downstream activities of the project.

Another well-known scheduling method is called Last Planner, which has five components that range from milestone level to weekly work plan. One of its components is phase planning, a collaborative approach that involves all parties involved in the project's execution, including the main contractor, OEM/vendor, subcontractor, and other agencies. Pull planning and scheduling are other names for it in construction projects that adhere to the lean principle. Barriers to change, human attitude, financial constraints, and organisational structure changes present challenges for implementation (Daniel et al. 2018; Gagen 2020).

11.2.5 Digitization

Similar to other industries like architecture, engineering, and construction (AEC), the infrastructure sector is currently undergoing a digital transformation. Through Building Information Modelling (BIM), the Architecture, Engineering, and Construction industry (AEC) has experienced mature digitization where the majority of their business activities from bidding to project handover are digitalized with little to no human interface (Lambert 2020). Adopting digitalization is difficult for the organisation managing the capital project because the management's business strategy requires that the entire business operation be transformed to the lowest level of the hierarchy. Within their organisation and ecosystem, it must be implemented (Leinwand & Mani 2021). When it comes to capital projects, large players can afford the costs associated with digitising their operations, but for medium- and small-sized players, the transition is difficult. However, there are so many platforms with applications serving the same purpose that it is impossible to find a solution for other aspects of business operation (Mavriqi et al. 2020). The application programming interface (API) to integrate different platforms is also still under development (Sommers et al. 2021). For instance, there are many application platforms for capital projects, including schedule software, SAP accounting and procurement software, contract lifecycle management (CLM) in mid-sized businesses, particularly vendors, etc. For these applications to produce a business decision, human analytics are frequently required. Second, because there is no real connection between these platforms, correlating the results of each application requires human effort.

A collaborative work environment is essentially needed for future business delivery. This would facilitate the simple digitalization of the business and eliminate routine tasks that occur repeatedly in each project phase, such as siloed meetings with vendors for engineering input or interface rather than collaborative meetings, updating various types of reports at the portfolio level and program/project level on the same objective, and holding repeated review meetings quickly. According to the Comptroller and Auditor General of the National Audit Office (2020), the investor/owner must identify the programme partner who is in charge of integrating components of the major programme, which is the capital project, and must grant authority. This benefits a smooth business process for integrating the participating organisation in the capital project, converting to digitization to ease the ongoing project, and providing a solid foundation for future projects. As a result of the stakeholders being in a cooperative environment and developing trust among one another, the likelihood of claims is decreased (GII Summit 2021). Automation will encourage project process agility in a collaborative work environment. The value chain automation process is still in its infancy (Macdonald n.d.).

11.2.6 Waterfall methodology

Since it serves as the foundation or platform upon which the project life cycle rests, the project management methodology is essential to the success of every project. A well-known methodology that has long been the only choice for challenging projects in the infrastructure sector is the waterfall method. There are benefits and drawbacks to this approach. This methodology is effective for projects that are repeated because the scope is symmetric with any previous projects that an organisation has completed and because it minimises customer involvement. It is based on upfront analysis, to put it simply. Additionally, the documentation task is kept up to date because the project's scope was clearly defined at the outset, making it simple to identify each team member's responsibilities (Donado n.d.).

The methodology, on the other hand, is formal, strict, and constrained. This methodology is better suited for projects that have well-defined requirements from the start (Roecker 2018; Mullaly 2021). Due to the project's previous phase's delay, it has a cascading effect on the deadline. The use of the Waterfall method is questionable in cases where the scope is ambiguous because new design or technology was incorporated into the project or because a work element that is brand-new to the market was added. This is because the rigidity of the Waterfall method's structure would prevent it from estimating any inherent uncertainties at the outset of the project.

11.3 Necessity of infusing Agile methodology

The previous section covered the characteristics of capital projects as well as their difficulties. Change orders, requests for a time extension, and claims at the project's closeout to defend the delay may result from the owner or investor's lack of experience and capabilities in the project or insufficient management team size to manage the project. The project's improper management has resulted in delays that have persisted for decades (Gomarnd & Pongpeng 2018). The team's integrity may appear strong at the beginning of the project, but as contractors grow aggressive and the owner is forced to deal with change orders and time extensions, it will deteriorate. This will result in the project running behind schedule and over budget (Long 2021). With the Waterfall methodology in place, it is necessary to keep the project on track from its inception until handover due to the frequency of the aforementioned events. The waterfall methodology generally executes each project phase in a sequential manner, whereas in practise there is overlap between project phases. The waterfall method of project management has been used for many years, but it has a lot of drawbacks that make it difficult to complete projects on time and on budget. To achieve the project goal, a different methodology, or agility, is required in place of the waterfall methodology.

As with product development, the owner or his representative should periodically intervene during the course of a project, as opposed to only occasionally (Roecker 2018). The undecomposed or ambiguous portion of the scope needs to be concentrated on while the work is distributed by consensus (Donado n.d.). Failure to act could result in outdated assumptions and ambiguous events, or the problem could arise during the execution. The risk or inherent uncertainties would have been underestimated at the project's beginning, putting the cost allocation at risk (Comptroller and Auditor General of National Audit Office 2020). The project organization's culture of collaboration would significantly cut down on delays and would encourage morality and integrity like a long-term strategic alliance (Manavalan 2021). The current model must be adaptable in order to adopt new principles, implement a new model, or re-engineer the business process of each project phase in order to foster a collaborative workplace culture and increase business agility (Stoica et al. 2016; Dachyar & Sanjiwo 2018). Each sector with thriving technology introduces a new workspace that requires a special approach to deal with in order to speed up response times within the value chain and improve customer presence (Stoica et al. 2016). As a result, the current Waterfall method needs to be modified to address the issues.

As an alternative, a methodology that emphasises ranking requirements in accordance with business values while emphasising the customer through a self-organized organisation is required. One of the options is the agile methodology. Agile methodology is a self-organized team that emphasises on people over the process by placing the requirements based on the business values. Agile methodology executes the project through miniature events called "Sprint," which are of smaller cycles in Software Engineering projects. The guiding principle is that the product's specification, or "Product Backlog," is divided up into various "Sprint Backlogs." The four stages of the cycle—the "planning" stage, dealing with the appropriate input to yield the desired outcome, timeline with budget release, and fixing the responsibilities—in which the sprint backlog is fed into the iteration cycle (sprint) are depicted in Figure 11.1 of the cycle. The agile framework is developed during the second phase, "design," which will discuss the functionality of the product with key tools. The third phase is the iterative "development & testing" phase, during which the team invests a significant amount of time and energy. Coding, hardware setup, user interface improvement, test plan design, testing, and improvement implementation up until product release. The module is dispensed into the product for client use during the "release" phase after receiving the required end-user training (Bitbytesoft 2022). The "Sponsor" designates a "Product Owner" as his representative to represent the product objective during the sprint under the guidance of the "Scrum Master," who coaches the cross-functional team known as the "Scrum team" on realising the actions by removing the barriers. Thus, the iterative cycle disperses the shippable product into the product's mainstream through the gradual growth in the desired outcome through managing the priorities, increased teamwork, and client approval with better project visibility (Alexsoft n.d.).

The agile principle, which is used in software engineering, is the best choice to incorporate into the waterfall methodology of the capital project in order to promote a collaborative work environment with agility in the value chain. The next section goes over the need for infusion at each stage of the capital project as well as the point of infusion.

11.4 Methodology

Technology is developing that forgoes improvements to the conventional system or introduces a substitute element that replaces the current system. While drafting the project charter, certain assumptions were made regarding the rough order estimate, which should be monitored during the definition and execution phases. The best project control team with the ability to separate the interface from engineering to commissioning is required for the project manager to have a comprehensive understanding of the project. Throughout the project, interface issues come up that prevent the beginning of the work or task and halt the flow of work. Due to a communication breakdown, the team would occasionally be unaware of other agencies' involvement or legal requirements. The fragmented work habits of the stakeholders prevent collaboration, which prevents the necessary knowledge transfer in the project's value stream. The waterfall method places a strong emphasis on the need for the workforce to follow the process. When there is a delay, the project manager or management may occasionally be able to move things along faster. A team of experts or specialists would be assembled for agility to speed up the procedure and eliminate the delay. Thus, with examples of each situation, this section discusses the shortcomings of the waterfall methodology and potential fixes through the agile principle. The application of the agile principle during the definition and execution phases of the project development life cycle is successful.

In order to accommodate the different working styles of each function in capital projects and produce the desired results, the sprint, which is an iteration cycle, has been modified in the proposed model compared to the iteration cycle in software engineering projects. The "planning phase" is the first phase of the sprint, during which the schedule and roles are established. The second stage involves deriving the technical features or fundamental data in accordance with standards and listing the requirements for further research or information. Expert cooperation is required to make it happen, and the assumptions must be mapped out as they brainstorm for the outcome. The term "collaborate/brainstorming" refers to this phase. The third stage is the “formulating or devising stage” where the technical specification and bill of quantities (BOQ) are drafted. The conformance stage, which concludes the project, is where the Product Owner-approved documents are sought and released for the following sprint or to the mainstream of the project outcome.

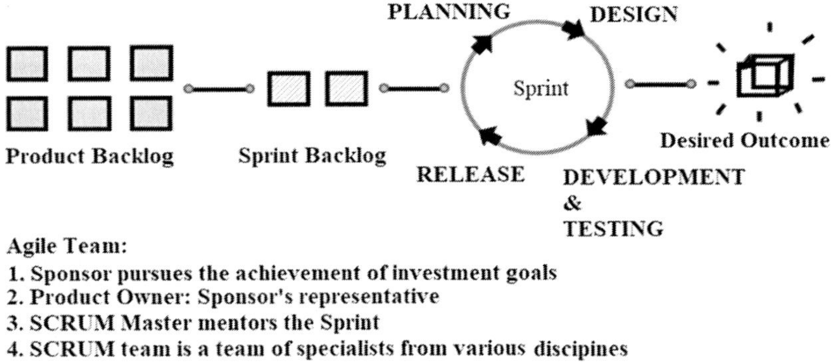

Figure 11.1 *Agile development cycle in Software Engineering*

In capital projects, different agencies, such as OEMs, vendors, or design firms, are hired directly by the client or turnkey contractor to carry out their tasks for the project in a way that offsets from the project's value chain's mainstream and eventually converges on it. Due to the task's limited scope, the team working on it will be small, and there won't be much interference from the customer or a turnkey contractor. The best option in these situations is the Scrum methodology. The task is given a priority in the sprint backlog according to the scrum methodology from the product backlog. The sprint is then completed to produce the desired result, and the Product Owner reviews it for compliance before moving on to the project's mainstream. Figure 11.4 of this paper shows a schematic representation of the scrum methodology. The suggested model includes this methodology as an optional component.

To illustrate the application of the agile principle, scenarios are chosen from each stage of the project life cycle, namely the conception stage, engineering stage, construction stage, and close-out stage. Due to a design-build agreement with FEED during the Conception phase, the timing of the intervention and the duration of each agile infusion are covered in this section.

11.4.1 Scenario-1: Conception stage

The consultants are given the go-ahead to begin Front End Engineering Design (FEED) following the feasibility study. Within a year, FEED is completed to specify the project's requirements, estimate costs, and lay out the fundamental engineering. As a result of FEED, the following outputs are produced: Process & Preliminary Design Basis Report, Preliminary Consumption Rates, Heat-mass balance Diagram, Process Flow Diagram (PFD), Preliminary Process & Instrumentation Diagram, Equipment Datasheet and Specification, Instrument Data Sheet, Line List, Equipment List, Utility Flow Distribution Drawing, Preliminary Layout, and Environmental Design Requirement. Depending on the nature of the company and the uniqueness of the project, the importance of this output will change.

The experts in the consulting firm who work logically to follow the owner's requirement perform FEED. In practise, there are a few situations where fragmented discussions make it difficult for disciplines to communicate with one another, which can lead to unexpected design interfaces and unanticipated assumptions about the lack of owner input or interference during project execution. Additionally, the owner's requirements might change or there might be a deviation from them on occasion, forcing the consultant to redo the fundamental engineering. Due to the pressure of project tendering and the FEED schedule, there may be a rush to finish FEED with little room for error.

Implementation of the suggested model is demonstrated for the scenario of determining the equipment list for the Steam Turbine-Generator building (TG building), with the goal of avoiding ambiguity in the following phase in the project life cycle. The TG building is a crucial utility building in power projects because the design must be more precise because numerous agencies, including OEM, fabricators, and equipment suppliers, require technical specifications early in the project so they can start doing detailed engineering and manufacturing after the project is awarded. Rotating machinery, electrical equipment, piping, exchangers, condensers, battery rooms, plant control rooms, utilities, structures, and HVAC are all housed in the TG building. The topographical survey that will provide guidance on the foundation type will also declare the type of soil present. The equipment list that would be provided from various agencies at a later stage of the project needs to be anticipated for an approximate TG building design. Expertise from various disciplines must be brought on board for collaboration. The structural tonnage of the building, another important result of this building, cannot be finalised until the equipment list is determined.

The best choice is the general agile principle because it calls for a variety of expertise. The sprint backlogs for subsequent sprints must be tentatively defined at the start of the initial sprint as per design priority if the headcount exceeds 11. The sponsor must designate his Subject Matter Experts (SME) or contract out for a cold eye review in order to increase productivity. Before beginning the incremental work, the roles are defined as follows: SME would act as the Product Owner to prioritise the product backlog into the sprint backlog and approve the outcome at the end of the sprint; Project Manager is in charge of planning and organising teams in a sprint; Project Controller could act as the Scrum Master to monitor the task and support the Project Manager for decisions; and a team of specialists or design team functions as a working team/scrum team. The Product Owner or SME verifies the results before dispensing them to the FEED document. The agile development cycle is illustrated in Figure 11.2.

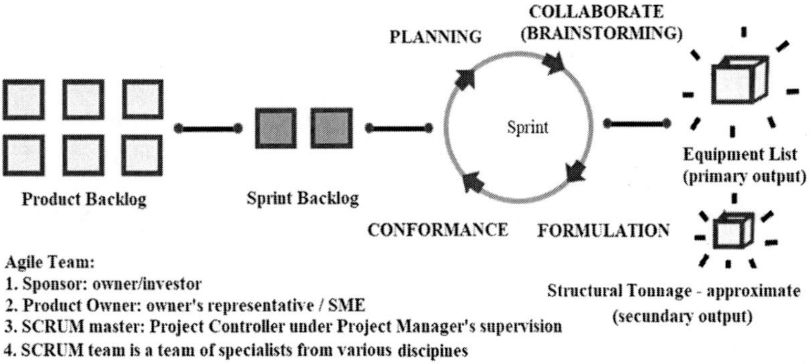

Figure 11.2 Proposed Agile development cycle in FEED

The agile development cycle, which is common in the software industry, is illustrated in Figure 11.2 in more detail. Due to the distinctive nature of the capital projects, the sprint component will vary. The planning phase is the first stage of the sprint, during which the sprint's duration, participants, and additional roles are defined. The team worked together to sketch the technical elements in the subsequent stage, using codes and standards as the primary guiding principles. The defined assumptions and constraints are logged separately. Due to the brainstorming session, this stage serves as the sprint's focal point. Formulating or devising is the third stage. Draughts have been made of the technical specification, bill of quantities (BOQ), and piping and instrumentation diagram. For final dispensation, assumption and constraint logs are reviewed once more. The conformance stage is the last step, where documents are sought out, approved by the product owner, and released for the following sprint or to FEED. As FEED contracts last for less than a year, subsequent iterations must be optimised so that the iteration cycle is limited to three or four cycles for each product or objective. The cycle time for each sprint is two to four weeks.

11.4.2 Scenario-2: Engineering phase

In order to define the system in detail during the engineering phase, the agile methodology must be used. The Distributed Control System (DCS), a control system used by all types of plants, serves as an example of how agile methodology is put into practise. The core of its design is the control logic design. The technical specifications of every plant component are used to create the control logic.

Due to the availability of vendors in capital projects, the detail design of DCS typically takes more than a year to complete using the waterfall method. Unavoidable is the staggering range of detail design. Due to the cascading effect of the Turney contactor's delayed package ordering, there is a spill over of schedule over late engineering, which delays the fed DCS vendor's receipt of technical input for logic design and additional engineering. As a result, the DCS vendor will be able to finalize the control logic from the vendors on board because modules are manufactured in sections.

As an expedition measure, the turnkey contractor can take the lead during this phase by implementing thc agile principle and working with the available vendor to hone in on the input for the detailed design. This will encourage the project team of the Turnkey Contractor to award the contract for the pending system to the fed DCS vendor for technical data and kick off the manufacturing of crucial modules at the beginning of the project. It promotes interface management with a clear identification of risk and increases value chain agility by reducing the staggering range of detail design.

Figure 11.3 depicts the agile development cycle for this case study, which is similar to the cycle shown above for the development of FEED. The Engineering Manager/Design Lead from the DCS vendor will serve as Product Owner, Project Manager or Package Manager of the turnkey contracting concern as a sponsor, and Project Controller of the turnkey contractor will serve as a scrum master to monitor the agility of the sprint and to report Project Manager for necessary action. Design engineers from various OEM/vendor will also serve as team members. To roll out the DCS module on time from engineering until component delivery, similar to the goal of the turnkey contractor, it is necessary to designate the Engineering Manager/Design Lead from the DCS vendor who serves as the Product Owner. The execution's key factor is sprint velocity, and each sprint's output must produce a required outcome along with by-products like the cable schedule, I/O list, cable vault design, room ventilation, and floor cut-out. It is essential to record the sprint activities, and the DCS vendor—the primary vendor for the iteration cycle should assign someone to play a specific role in the team. The turnkey contractor shall receive all required documents for the performance of the contract. The iteration cycle needs to be limited to 8, and the sprint implementation needs to be agreed upon mutually between the respective vendor/OEM and the turnkey contractor.

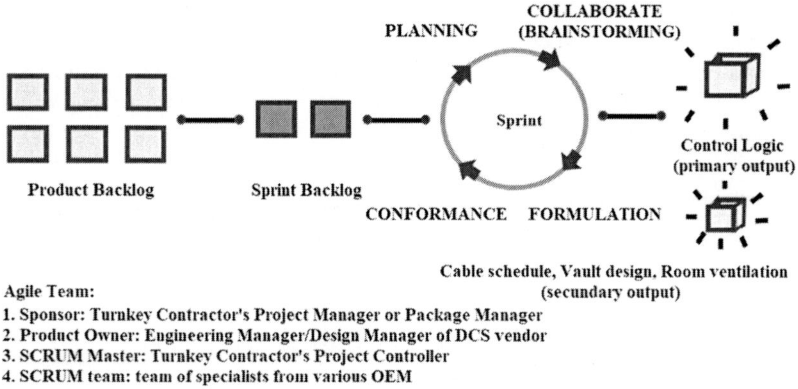

Figure 11.3 *Proposed Agile development cycle in Detail Design*

After obtaining the required technical data from other agencies, their OEM workforce completes the component's detailed design. The primary value stream of the turnkey project process is offset by this operation because the OEM/vendor facilities are where the detailed component design is done. The Engineering team will release the manufacturing drawing from the control logic and bought-out list for accessories, as is standard procedure. Delays could be the result of poor management or the team's slow processing of the control logic to the manufacturing drawing. Due to this circumstance, manufacturing drawings are being released later than expected, necessitating management decisions and additional design team guidance. In this scenario, the vendor will choose agile methodology for a quicker release of the manufacturing drawing in order to increase process agility. Given the size of the team and the skills present, the scrum methodology, one of the agile principles, would be the best option. The Product Owner will be the Engineering Manager/Design Lead of OEM, the Project Controller of OEM may serve as the Scrum Master, and designers will be team members. Due to the inclusion of technical elements, each sprint lasts anywhere from one to four weeks, so extreme caution is required. The Scrum team must order the tasks from the product backlog in the sprint backlog in order to start the iteration. At the conclusion of each iteration, each sprint that creates the manufacturing drawing and important features such as the preliminary design and schema for the following sprint is subjected to review for the release of the module to the mainstream of the project's outcome. At the start of each day, a Scrum meeting is held to discuss the backlog from the previous day and make plans for the day.

Additionally, Scrum retrospectives or reviews would take place at the end of each sprint for corrective action in the future on repeating the sprint of the same kind. The necessity of implementing scrum depicted in Figure 11.4 is optional as its implementation should not complicate the existing value stream.

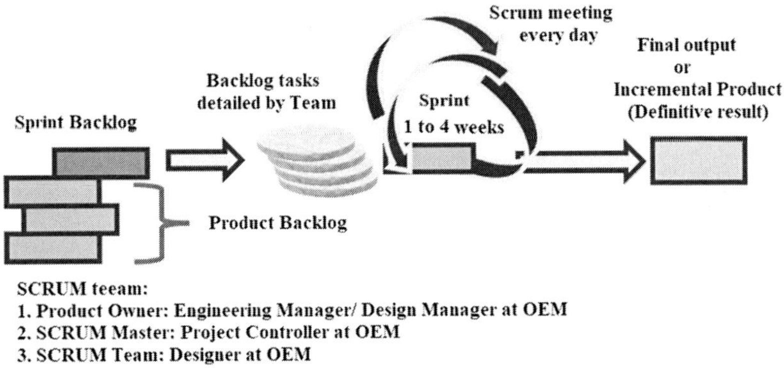

Figure 11.4 *Proposed SCRUM development cycle in Detail Design*

11.4.3 Scenario-3: Construction phase

Each area of the capital project faces more challenges during the construction phase. Let's think about adding a transmission line to the T&D project. Even though the interface's general layout is specified during the contract's award, some finer details are needed when it comes to execution. The transmission line, an overhead cable, will cross a creek, as well as existing structures, a railroad, and a highway. This line must be implemented with statutory approval, an installation window allowed by each authority, and support from the general public. As a result, the paperwork needs to be understood by the turnkey contractor's concerned departments and their installation agency.

The installation will typically start with the government authority's permit, the construction schedule, the method statement, the resource, and the installation material. There may be some unexpected events during the opening of the transmission line, such as incomplete government clearance, a longer than anticipated period for clearance, an irregular construction schedule, etc. It is essential to comprehend the assignment thoroughly before beginning it in order to prevent surprises later on.

By putting the agile principle into practise, the sponsor who demands a timely conclusion without any delays must assume the role of the product owner. At the start of the sprint, the Product Owner will prioritise the work, and at the conclusion of the sprint, the Product Owner will approve the proposals. The turnkey contractor's project manager, as the Product Owner, is responsible for organising the group's work and supervising it on a regular basis. For the work to run smoothly, the project control engineer of the turnkey contractor must act like a scrum master. An agile team must include the departmental representative from the legal department, the turnkey contractor's construction team, and installation agency engineers and subcontractors. The team must work together to complete the necessary legal requirements for the transmission line's length in the first sprint, the authorities' timetable for approving installation in the second sprint, the schedule's finalisation, and the method statement's approval in the final sprint before beginning site work. Thus, three iterations are the ideal number. This phase is covered by the agile development cycle shown in Figures 11.2 and 11.3.

11.4.4 Scenario-4: Project Closeout Phase

Each project encounters delays in completing the punch-point-related pending work. There would be a few "punch points" that required compliance from multiple disciplines, which is yet another interface issue. It is ideal for the project to close punch points at each stage of installation or commissioning work. Due to the interface between the functions, the lack of supervision, and the unorganised committee that handles the punch list, closing punch points is currently a difficult task. This would impact the schedule for the closeout phase and increase the overhead cost.

By applying the agile principle in this situation, the Field Engineering Manager/Quality Manager must assume the role of Product Owner and guide the team in place of the Project Manager. To eliminate compliance uncertainties, the Quality Manager must also play the role of Scrum Master. The required compliance could be achieved by a team of construction engineers and quality engineers from the turnkey contractor and installation agencies. For this stage, the scrum iteration model shown in Figure 11.4 is still applicable. The quality manager determines the sprint's velocity, and the three iteration cycles are perfect for a composite punch point closure.

11.5 Discussion of the Proposed Model

Above is a brief explanation of the suggestion to incorporate agile into waterfall methodology at each stage of the project. Agile is used to ensure that each task begins quickly and to thwart the slowdown of the ongoing task in each phase. Due to its linear process of publishing the design documents, engineering the equipment and parts, manufacturing the components, supply chain, installation, commissioning, and closeout with some overlap between the phases, the waterfall methodology is ideal for capital projects. In order to maintain time, cost, and quality, there is a need for agility in the process so that the quality of the work is retained without any repetition of work, either in the engineering of the component or defect identification at the work site. The point at which the agile principle is intercepted, the length of the iteration cycle, and the applicable project life cycle phases were discussed. In addition, implementing the new model must be empirical, simple to adapt to the project's stakeholders, and increase productivity in a multi-ethnic setting. The waterfall model can best be modified to incorporate the agile principle, and when to start a sprint depends on the project manager or project head's or manager's intelligence.

The hybrid model's implementation process has been described in this paper. The improved productivity in the project would be measurable after the implementation of this model.

11.6 Critical Success Factor

Agile project management methodologies are used to increase project operational agility. Agile project management would be possible with a better comprehension of the project's scope, standards, and legal requirements. The following factors must be taken into account for effective agile methodology:

a) The critical system, which would cause FEED to run behind the schedule, needs to implement the sprints. If the agile methodology makes the FEED task more difficult, it must be abandoned.
b) The project manager, owner representative, and owner engineer must decide on the sprint deployment in advance using the project document.
c) It is crucial to monitor sprints because an extended sprint will ruin the application of agile methodology. Agile is defined by the sprint's velocity.
d) By producing the necessary output and input for another system (or systems) as a byproduct, the sprint must be highly productive. Due to

the complexity of capital projects, the design of a common system or Balance of Plant (BOP) should not run out of information as the project progresses. Second, it's crucial to assign the appropriate resource to each sprint.

e) Due to the fact that sprint activities deal with technical parameters during the detailed design phase, a project member from either the main vendor or OEM will need to be delegated.
f) In order to implement agile methodology on time, the project manager and the project control team must be cautious about the project's development.

The level-2 schedule would be provided to the owner with many presumptions after the contract was awarded. A few critical concerns would be identified, and the schedule would be constructed using the waterfall method. However, some of the critical concerns would not be immediately apparent and would only be anticipated or realised later in the project. The "Group and Sort" option in the schedule allows the effective Project Control team to identify and populate the project's risk-prone areas, as well as the corresponding WBS/activities. The level-3 schedule could incorporate an agile or scrum cycle, which would have the advantage of addressing more extensive issues in order to address the risks that were noted in the level-2 schedule. Continuous use of the hybrid approach might open the door for the inclusion of an Agile tab in the scheduling tools, complete with features like roles and responsibilities, spirit length, iteration frequency, etc.

11.7 Conclusion

Every capital project has inherent uncertainties, which the team either ignores or is unaware of and which have an impact on the development later on (Comptroller and Auditor General of National Audit Office 2020). To promote a company that can adhere to a long-term strategy rather than a short-term one, the working principle needs to be changed (Hunt & Bruce 2022). The method for integrating waterfall methodology with agile methodology described in this paper must be tailored to the specifics of the project. Each stakeholder must align with the turnkey contractor's business operations as part of a gradual shift in the workplace culture to embrace the hybrid methodology. This method encourages a collaborative workplace environment. There is a chance to create a shared understanding.

In a collaborative working environment, turnkey contractors have control over a communication channel with some regulation (Manavalan 2021). The hybrid method practise speeds up the rapid turnover so that routine tasks are eliminated, which could open the door for digitising the process. Finally, a good understanding of the project scope with standards and timely triggering of appropriate agile methodology will yield a positive outcome in terms of schedule, cost, and quality.

References

Alexsoft. n.d. "Agile Project Management: Best Practice and Methodologies". Accessed February 25, 2022. https://www.altexsoft.com/whitepapers/agile-project-management-best-practices-and-methodologies/.

Alhajri, Abdullah Rasheed. Alshibani, Adel. "Critical FactBehindhind Construction Delay in Petrochemical Projects in Saudi Arabia". Energies 2018 (2018): 1-18. https://www.mdpi.com/1996-1073/11/7/1652

Alhomadi, A. A, Dehghan, R., Ruwanpura, J. Y. "The Predictability of Fast-Track_Projects". Procedia Engineering 14 (2011): 1966-1972. doi:10.1016/j.proeng.2011.07.247

Almeida, Fernando. "Challenges in Migration from Waterfall to Agile Environments". World Journal of Computer Application and Technology, 5(3) (2017): 39-49. DOI: 10.13189/wjcat.2017.050302

Al-Wadie, Saleh. 2020. "Study on the Main Causes of Project Schedule Delays". Project Management.com. May 29, 2020. https://www.projectmanagement.com/contentPages/article.cfm?ID=634519&thisPageURL=/articles/634519/--Study-on-the-Main-Causes-of-Project-Schedule-Delays&msclkid=77093ff1cf5e11ec8c10647 9621d249d&authenticated=1

Bitbytesoft. 2022. "The Phases of Agile Software Development Life Cycle & Workflow and Project Management". Accessed on April 25, 2022. https://bitbytesoft.com/phases-of-agile-software-development-life-cycle/.

Blanco, Jose Luis. Mullin, Andrew. Pandya, Kaustubh. Parsons, Matthew. Ribeirinho, Maria Joao. 2018. "Seizing opportunity in today's construction technology ecosystem". Accessed January 15, 2022.

https://www.mckinsey.com/~/media/McKinsey/Industries/Capital%20Projects%20and%20Infrastructure/Our%20Insights/Seizing%20opportunity%20in%20todays%20construction%20technology%20ecosystem/Seizing-opportunity-in-construction-technology.pdf

Bullard, Dave. Roberts, Geoff. "How implementing Construction Industry Institute (CII) best practice helps improve project delivery". Oracle Construction and Engineering Blog. November 30, 2021.

https://blogs.oracle.com/construction-engineering/post/implementing-construction-industry-institute-cii-best-practices-improve-project-delivery?msclkid=cd77fc85cf8211ec8027fa0da2ceea2b

Cheeseman, Corie. "Oracle brings a new level of intelligence to construction projects". Oracle Construction and Engineering Blog. February 10, 2021. https://www.oracle.com/ae/news/announcement/new-level-intelligence-to-construction-projects-2021-02-10/?msclkid=976574c1cec911eca811d881bb2afd2a

Comptroller and Auditor General. 2020. "Lessons learned from Major Programmes". National Audit Office, UK., November 20, 2020. https://www.nao.org.uk/insights/lessons-learned-from-major-programmes/

Dachyar, M., Sanjiwo, Z. A. H. "Business Process Re-Engineering of Engineering Procurement Construction (EPC) Project in Oil and Gas Industry in Indonesia". Indian Journal of Science and Technology, 11(9 (2018): 1-8. DOI: 10.17485/ijst/2018/v11i9/92741

Daniel, Emmanuel I. Christine, Pasquire. Dickens, Graham. Marasini, Ramesh. "Empirical study on the influence of procurement methods on last planner system implementation". Proceedings of 26th Annual Conference of the International. Group for Lean Construction (IGLC), Chennai, India (2018): 681-690. DOI: doi.org/10.24928/2018/0398

Design-Build Institute of America. 2014. "What is Design-Build? A Design-Build done right primer". Accessed January 15, 2022. https://dbia.org/wp-content/uploads/2018/05/Primers-What-is-Design-Build.pdf

Donado, Jonathan. n.d. "Waterfall vs Agile in plain English". Accessed on February 25, 2022. https://www.coursehero.com/file/82500426/Waterfall-vs-Agilepdf/?msclkid=0619faa1cf5911ec8b2e21ebb4a6df83

Doughtie, Lynne. "Agile or irrelevant: Redefining resilience." 2019 U.S. CEO Outlook. 2019. https://assets.kpmg.com/content/dam/kpmg/us/pdf/2019/06/2019-ceo-outlook.pdf

Emam, Hassan. Farrell, Peter. Abdelaal, Mohamed. A. "Causes of Delay in GCC Construction Projects". The First International Conference of the CIB Middle East & North Africa Research Network CIB-MENA 2014 (2014): 625-640.

Gagen, Alyssa. "McCarthy Building and remote Lean construction scheduling in an unpredicted environment". Oracle Construction and Engineering Blog. November 2, 2020.

https://blogs.oracle.com/construction-engineering/post/mccarthy-building-and-remote-lean-construction-scheduling-in-an-unpredictable-environment?msclkid=35363996cec911ecbfb7ae66d9539e73

Gandhi, Santhosh. 2021. "How does Systems Thinking help Futures Thinking?". Accessed February 25, 2022. https://isanthoshgandhi.medium.com/how-do-systems-thinking-help-futures-thinking-82cea75c6b90?msclkid=1ea1dfa5cf8111ecb9a9dfcb7805c032

Giffhorn, Edilson. Ensslin, Leonardo. Ensslin, Sandra Rolim., Vianna, William Barbosa. "Multicriteria Methodology for KPI Identification in Outsourced Projects". 23rd World IPMA Congress, Helsinki, Finland (2009): download from URL. https://www.academia.edu/25848932/Multicriteria_Methodology_for_KPI_Identification_in_Outsourced_Projects

GII summit. "2021 GII Summit: Project of the future". McKinsey & Company outcome report. May 2021. https://www.mckinsey.com/~/media/mckinsey/business%20functions/operations/our%20insights/2021%20gii%20summit%20project%20of%20the%20future/2021-gii-summit-recap-report_0.pdf

Gomarn, Pittayaporn. Pongpeng, Jakrapong. "Causes of construction delay from contractors and suppliers in Thailand's oil and gas platform projects". MATEC Web of Conferences 192, 02008 (2018): 1-4. http://doi.org/10.1051/matecconf/201819202008

Hatmoko, J. U. D. Khasani, R. R. "Mapping Delay Risks of EPF Projects: A Case Study of A Platform and Subsea Pipeline of An Oil and Gas Project". Annual Conference on Industrial and System Engineering (ACISE) (2019): 1-9. doi:10.1088/1757-899X/598/1/012095

Herbst, Andrew. "Integrating a Work Package Based Engineering Phase with AWP". Accessed January 10, 2022. https://vdocument.in/integrating-a-work-package-based-engineering-2016-integrating-a-work-package.html?page=1

Hunt, Vivian. Simpson, Bruce. 2022. "Putting stakeholder capitalism into practice". Interviewed by Sean Brown. Strategy & Corporate Finance Practice, McKinsey & Company discussion forum, January 2022. Transcript of discussion. https://www.mckinsey.com/capabilities/strategy-and-corporate-finance/our-insights/putting-stakeholder-capitalism-into-practice

International Project Management Association (IPMA). 2015. "4.3 Perspective". In Individual Competence Baseline for Project, Programme and Portfolio Management (ICB) version 4.0, edited by IPMA, 40-42. Switzerland: IPMA.

International Project Management Association (IPMA). 2015. "4.4 People". In Individual Competence Baseline for Project, Programme and Portfolio Management (ICB) version 4.0, edited by IPMA, 80-83. Switzerland: IPMA.

Jacob. "The Triple Constraint in Waterfall & Agile". Accessed January 10, 2022. https://www.parkingthought.com/2018-03-04-the-triple-constraint-in-waterfall-agile/?msclkid=4c880e08cf5511ec88351dbd60884a98

Jo, Sung-Hwan. Lee, Eul-Bum. Pyo, Kyoung-Youl. "Integrating a Procurement Management Process into Critical Chain Project Management (CCPM): A Case-Study on Oil and Gas Projects, the Piping Process". Sustainability 2018, 10, 1817 (2018): 1-22. https://www.mdpi.com/2071-1050/10/6/1817

Lambert, Andy. "Cost Overruns in Construction: 7 Reasons Your Project is Over Budget and What to Do About Them". Accessed January 10, 2022. https://onekeyresources.milwaukeetool.com/en/7-construction-cost-overruns?msclkid=35673180cf8011ec8f7a90385e1cd376

Leinwand, Paul. Mani, Mahadeva Matt. "Digitizing Isn't the Same as Digital Transformation". Accessed January 10, 2022. https://hbr.org/2021/03/digitizing-isnt-the-same-as-digital-transformation

Long, Richard J. ed. 2021. "In Typical Problems Leading to Delays, Cost Overruns, and Claim on Process Plant and Offshore Oil and Gas Projects". Colorado: Long International.

Macdonald, Fraser. "Five tips for successful design automation". Accessed January 10, 2022. https://www.mottmac.com/views/five-tips-for-successful-design-automation

Manavalan, Ramakrishnan. "Collaborative Work Culture to Enhance Effectiveness of Infrastructure Project Operations – Gateway for Digitalization". Proceedings of the 14th International Conference on Project Management (2021): 340-350.

Mavriqi, Ilire Hasani. Sokolovska, Natalia. Hellauer, Tony Ross. Fecher, Benedikt. "Challenges in Building Innovative, Sustainable and Open Research Infrastructures". The elephant in the lab. February 18, 2020. https://elephantinthelab.org/challenges-in-building-innovative-sustainable-and-open-research-infrastructures/

Mihăiloaie, Cristina. "KPIs vs CSFs". The KPI Institute. June 25, 2013. https://www.performancemagazine.org/kpis-vs-csfs/

Monteiro, AntonioRomero. Jagnanan, Lionel. 2016. "Advanced Work Packaging Implementation". Accessed January 10, 2022. https://documents.pub/document/advanced-work-packaging-implementation.html?page=1

Mullaly, Mulally. 2021. "Project Headway: Can Waterfall and Agile Co-exist?". Project Management.com. September 16, 2021. https://www.projectmanagement.com/videos/729277/Project-HEADWAY--Can-Waterfall-And-Agile-Co-Exist-?msclkid=ee4b68c2cf8c11ec9d146dafb52fbb07

Oracle Corporation. "The Challenges of Managing Public Infrastructure Projects". A discussion paper from Oracle. n.d. https://www.oracle.com/webfolder/s/delivery_production/docs/FY15h1/doc2/Discussion-Paper1-Challenges-MPIP.pdf?elq_mid=5737&sh=0926142616091808191326131426132605261526133105101419 35&cmid=WWPP14041323MPP006C003

Owusu, John Asare. Ofusu, Anim. "Evaluation of turnkey projects in urban water delivery in Ghana". Research Desk, Jul-Sep 2(3) (2013): 260-269. https://www.researchgate.net/publication/302907305_EVALUATION_OF_TURNKEY_PROJECTS_IN_URBAN_WATER_DELIVERY_IN_GHANA/link/57330e2e08aea45ee838ead5/download

Pall, Goutom K. Bridge, Adrian J. Gray, Jason. Skitmore, Martin. "Causes of Delay in Power Transmission Projects: An Empirical Study". Energies 2020, 13, 17 (2020): 1-29. doi:10.3390/en13010017

Prakash, Aswin. "Project Development Cycle". Slideshare. Accessed February 20, 2022. https://www.slideshare.net/ashwinprince/project-development-cycle?from_action=save

Sommers. Kaitlynn. Connaughton, Patrick. Sillanpaa, Marko. Murphy, Jim. "Critical Capabilities for Contract Life Cycle Management". Gartner Research. June 14, 2021. https://www.gartner.com/en/documents/4002482?msclkid=a2dbd1e5cf8511eca4cd178f1454c201

Stoica, Marian. Bogdan, Ghilic-Micu., Mircea, Marinela. Uscatu, Cristian. "Analyzing Agile Development – from Waterfall style to Scrumban". Informatica Economica, 20(4) (2016): 5-14.

Suppramaniam, Umesh Kumar S. Ismail, Syuhaida. Suppramaniam, Subaashnii. "Causes of delay in the construction phase of oil and gas projects in Malaysia". International Journal of Engineering & Technology, 7(2.29) (2018): 203-209.

Vassileva, Bistra. Nikolov, Mirosav. "Market entry strategies to emerging markets: a conceptual model of turnkey project development". Serbian Journal of Management, 11(2) (2016): 291-310

Zadeh, Mahsa Taghi. Dehghan, Reza. Ruwanpura, Janaka Y. Jergeas, George. "Factors Influencing Design Changes in Oil and Gas Projects". International Journal of Construction Engineering and Management, 3(4) (2014): 117-133. Doi: 10.5923/j/ijcem.20140304.03

M. Ramakrishnan has 16 years of experience in Project Planning, Risk Management, Contracts Administration, support for Forensic Schedule Delay analysis and Claim Management in the Power sector. Presently, he is working as an Owners Engineer in Planning function cum Contracts Administrator for an International Consulting firm in the Middle East. His scientific paper titled "Collaborative Work Culture to Enhance Effectiveness of Infrastructure Project Operations – Gateway for Digitalization" was published in the proceedings of the 14th International Conference on Project Management (ProMAC2021), organized by The Society of Project Management, Japan on 25-26 Nov 2021. Mr Ramakrishnan earned Bachelor's degree in Mechanical Engineering from Bharathidasan University, Tiruchirappalli, India in 2004 and a Master's degree in Production Engineering from Anna University, Chennai, India in 2006. He is a Certified Senior Project Manager from IPMA (IPMA-B) and Certified Risk Management Professional from PMI (PMI-RMP).

R. Gajanan has 18 years of experience in Project Management, Engineering Management, Quality Assurance and Control, Construction Management, Vendor Management and Plant Commissioning in various capabilities in Power, Biomass & Cogeneration, across various verticals of Oil & Gas viz Refineries, Petrochemical, LNG & FLNG and Infrastructure -Food & Chemical projects. Presently, he is working as Senior Lead Engineer in Project Management Technology Department, Overseas project division at a Leading International EPC company in Japan. Mr Gajanan earned Bachelor's degree in Mechanical Engineering from Bharathidasan University, Tiruchirappalli, India in 2004. He is a Certified QMS-Lead Auditor.

M. Naveen Kumar has 14 years of experience in various departments such as Site work execution (construction department), Project Management, Contract Management, and Project Planning in the Power and Oil & Gas sectors. Presently, he is working as Lead Planning Engineer for an International EPC company in the Middle East. Mr Naveen Kumar earned Bachelor's degree in Mechanical Engineering from Anna University in 2009 and presently pursuing a Master's degree in Manufacturing Engineering at Anna University, Chennai, India.

XII

Agile Project Management as a Multi-Level Resilience Antecedent

Igor Vrečko and Nuša Širovnik

12.1 Connecting Agile Project Management and Resilience

Organisations nowadays operate in a highly volatile, uncertain, complex, and ambiguous environment (Bennett & Lemoine 2014). Due to global competition, dynamic opportunities and the high complexity of business processes, adaptation, flexibility, and changes are inevitable for every contemporary organisation (Williams 2005). As project experts traditionally deal with this, it is no surprise that reliance on projects is increasing, and consequently, the number of project-based workers is also growing (Maylor et al. 2006). This trend is known as the phenomenon of projectification, which was initially studied as a managerial approach (e.g. Midler 1995). However, over recent years, consideration of projectification has reached far beyond the original managerial domain. Nowadays, projectification is also considered and studied as a societal trend (e.g. Jensen et al. 2017; Hubmann 2021), a human state (e.g. Cicmil et al. 2016; Jensen et al. 2017), and a philosophical issue (e.g. Jensen et al. 2016; Barondeau & Hobbs 2019). Workers in a 'projectified' environment are exposed to vulnerable situations (Cicmil et al. 2016), and projectification as a human state is often described as an oppressive discourse with extensive negative consequences for those individuals involved (Jacobsson & Jałocha 2021).

Additionally, the awareness of traditional project-based structures' shortcomings in the current dynamic landscape is becoming more present among modern managers (Williams 2005). The rise of agile practices and agile project management (APM) results from the inevitable necessity to be responsive and adaptable in managing complex and uncertain projects (Fernandez & Fernandez 2009). Agile practices emerged from the software development area, and the importance for organisations to be highly flexible and adaptive is far from limited to this specific industry.

With this in mind, the question arises: can an agile way of managing projects be an antecedent for multilevel resilience? We aim to answer this question with the help of an existing literature review, and we have structured this paper as follows. First, we introduce the phenomenon of projectification, four streams of existing projectification studies, and the impact of projectification on different levels. We establish that switching to a more project-based society is inevitable and point out potentially damaging negative consequences. Second, we summarise the existing research on resilience streams with a focus on organisational context—we examine resilience on individual, team and organisational levels and then focus on resilience antecedents. We also briefly discuss interactions between these levels and introduce a few existing studies that considered one antecedent as a source of multilevel resilience. Third, we introduce the main advantages of APM and explain how an agile approach could benefit projects outside of the software development domain. We then also point out the main challenges surrounding the agile approach in more traditional organisations and introduce the hybrid approach as a widely used way of working in practice. Fourth, we aim to connect all three concepts and discuss the possibility of APM being the antecedent for multilevel resilience. Finally, we conclude with our final thoughts and further research indications.

12.2 Projectification—its Levels and Observation Perspectives

The phenomenon of projectification was first studied in Midler's article on Renault (Midler 1995); however, the process itself was certainly not a novelty then (Maylor et al. 2006). Project-based work contributes to about one-third of all economic activities in advanced economies (Schoper et al. 2018). Consequently, business and academic interest in projectification have grown tremendously and to this day, studies go far beyond the industrial organisation field and project management discipline. Midler (1995), although cited in most projectification articles, has not provided a clear definition of the phenomenon. Nonetheless, definitions of projectification have been outlined, often based on Midler's research—for example, Bredin and Söderlund (2011) define projectification as "a change of the organisational structure, slowly moving the firm into putting more emphasis on the project dimensions of the organisational structure, from strong functional units where projects have played a subordinate role, to projects playing at centre stage with functional units acting as labour pools" (Bredin & Söderlund 2011).

Initially, projectification was studied as a managerial approach; however, recent studies investigate the phenomenon from several angles. Jacobsson and Jałocha (2021) systematically categorised existing projectification studies and identified four main streams—first, projectification as a managerial approach (e.g. Midler 1995; Wenell et al. 2017; Maylor & Turkulainen 2019), second, projectification as a societal trend (e.g. Jensen et al. 2017; Auschra et al. 2019; Mukhtar-Landgren & Fred 2019; Hubmann 2021), third, projectification as a human state (e. g. Ekstedt 2009; Jensen 2012; Packendorff & Lindgren 2014; Cicmil et al. 2016; Jensen et al. 2017), and finally, projectification as a philosophical issue (Jensen 2012; Jensen et al. 2016; Barondeau & Hobbs 2019).

The nature of projectification consequences varies depending on the level and observation perspective. On a societal (macro) level, projectification is an unavoidable direction with positive and negative consequences. On the organisational (meso) level, the phenomenon is mainly perceived positively with some possible negative consequences (Bogacz-Wojtanowska & Jałocha 2016; Henning & Wald 2019), but generally, positive consequences outweigh negative ones. Projectification as a human state is most commonly described as an oppressive discourse with extensive negative consequences for project workers (Jacobsson & Jałocha 2021). In a projectified environment, workers are exposed to vulnerable situations, both individually and collectively (Cicmil et al. 2016). Project-based work has been found to have mostly negative consequences for an individual's well-being (e.g. Bråthen & Ommundsen 2018), as it has been indicated that project-based workers are facing negative mental stress and sleeping issues (Myrmæl & Alfredsen 2018), career insecurity, inequality and unemployment (Brunila 2011; Sage 2016). Cicmil et al. (2016) argued that projectification leads individuals to inter alia, "dependence on great expectations, follies and sensations; commitment to blank sheets, fresh starts and 'professional' performance, internalisation of honour/shame and personal worthiness, exhaustion, finiteness and the end of resilience" (Cicmil et al. 2016). Both companies and individuals might be put at a certain level of risk resulting from the negative consequences, for example, in relation to a negative impact on revenues gained (Ekstedt 2009). However, to some degree, it is still possible for individuals to emancipate themselves from the oppressive conditions of projectification (Waring & Thomas 2010). The survival and effectiveness of organisations depend on the ability to withstand and adapt when faced with challenges, both from organisations and employees (Näswall et al. 2019). In other words, it depends on their resilience.

12.3 Multilevel Resilience

The interest in the resilience concept has steadily grown over the last years, especially due to challenges related to economic recessions, terrorism, natural disasters, and cyber threats (Denyer 2017), with the recent COVID-19 pandemic being an extreme example of such events (Reatze et al. 2021). Furthermore, globalisation and rapid technological advancements present new potential threats and opportunities. The awareness of the importance of organisational resilience is increasing among business leaders, as it contributes to business growth and protects continuous performance when faced with disturbing and volatile situations (Denyer 2017).

Generally, resilience is defined as "the quality of being able to return quickly to a previous good condition after problems" (Cambridge Dictionary 2022); however, we are dealing with a rather complex construct, and resilience has been a subject of different levels of analyses in past studies. In the organisational context, resilience can be defined as the organisation's ability to resist disruption and recover from consequences of adverse situations (Horne & Orr 1998) or "the ability of an organisation to anticipate, prepare for, respond and adapt to incremental change and sudden disruptions in order to survive and prosper" (Denyer 2017). Most existing literature conceptualises resilience individually; however, team-level and organisational-level resilience are common streams in resilience-related studies (Reatze et al. 2021). Most frequently, individual-level resilience is defined as a capacity, capability, or state-like ability to maintain a normal level of functioning under challenging circumstances and rapid recovery from adversity-caused setbacks (Hartmann et al. 2020). Similarly, team-level resilience is often defined as the capacity to recover from possible threats to a team's well-being, such as conflicts, setbacks, or failures (Chapman et al. 2020).

On the organisational level, resilience impacts performance, effectiveness, creativity, and innovation (Raetze et al. 2021). Strategic resilience enables organisations to respond to unexpected conditions proactively and identify opportunities within crises, further expanding their capabilities and utilising new business opportunities (Sullivan-Taylor & Wilson 2009). Resilience is not only important in terms of disruption response but also in a way of positively adapting when faced with challenging circumstances. Therefore, efforts should not only be given towards unfortunate events insurance but also towards adaptations and changes—in case of not doing so, the cost could be drastic (Denyer 2017). Outcomes of team-level resilience include team attitudes, behaviours, and performance, and similarly, individual-level resilience impacts health and well-being, employee attitudes, behaviours, performance, and success (Raetze et al. 2021). Traditionally, resilience has been described as trait-like, which would mean it is a somewhat fixed characteristic; however, it can, be developed (Masten 2001; Bonanno 2004) through different organisational (e.g. Trifoglio 2018) and HR practices (Bonanno 2004). Individuals with high confidence, hopefulness, and optimism are more likely to overcome adversities and setbacks than those without (Luthans et al. 2006).

Resilience antecedents have been a common subject of the existing research. On the organisational level, studied antecedents of resilience are financial ad material resources (e.g. Burke 2005), structural resources (e.g. Lampel et al. 2014), and human and social resources (e.g. Lengnick-Hall et al. 2011). Several studies have been focused on strategies and practices as antecedents of organisational-level resilience—for example, scenario planning (e.g. Hillmann et al. 2018), change management (e.g. Ates & Bititci 2011), and robust strategic planning (e.g. Demmer et al. 2011) have been considered as sources of organisational resilience, and a link between organisational resilience and innovation strategies has also been investigated (e.g. Wojan et al. 2018). Furthermore, corporate social responsibility practices (e.g. Ortiz-de-Mandojana & Bansal 2016), HRM practices (e.g. Bardoel et al. 2014), and certain leadership practices (e.g. Harland et al. 2005) have been analysed in relation to organisational resilience. Existing research of antecedents of individual-level resilience includes developing skills and competencies (e.g. Howard & Irving 2014), positive emotions and attitudes (e.g. Cooper et al. 2013), positive relationships (e.g. Bardoel et al. 2014), leadership and management (e.g. Ashby et al. 2013), and organisational context factors, for example, employee-orientated HR management practices (e.g. Cooke et al. 2019).

There have also been attempts to investigate multilevel resilience and how all three levels affect each other. For example, a significant positive correlation between employee and organisational resilience was observed (Prayag et al. 2020), and similarly, a strong positive correlation between individual and team resilience was also found (McEwen & Boyd 2018). Organisational resilience has also been found to be a somewhat positive predictor of employee resilience (Teng-Calleja et al. 2020), just to name a few examples. Some scholars focused specifically on cross-level resilience antecedents—for example, certain organisational factors could potentially impact team-level resilience (van der Beek & Schraagen 2015) or leadership has been considered a source of cross-level resilience (Norman et al. 2005; Hudgins 2016). However, more knowledge and research are required on cross-level antecedents and interactions of different resilience levels (Raetze et al. 2021).

It is important to note that various measures have been developed in the existing studies due to the inconsistency of resilience definitions. This results in difficulties when comparing study results, as they emerged to be heterogeneous and often conflicting. A clear conceptual foundation is required before the operationalisation of the concept, and only then can adequate measures be applied. Resilience could be studied, for example, as a stable trait, processes and mechanisms, resilience outcomes and their connections to previous findings, or the capacity to cope with adversity effectively (Raetze et al. 2021).

Resilience on all three levels can be a demanding goal in a contemporary projectified environment. We have already established that projectification causes exposure to a certain level of adversity—a state which is also a focal point of most resilience definitions. As the number of projects, project workers, and project managers increases (Maylor et al. 2006), new challenges arise, and adversity intensifies. Individuals, teams, and organisations exposed to projectification could benefit from finding a project management approach to co-enable resilience across all three levels. Additionally, various management practices have been studied as resilience antecedents. It would be reasonable to consider a certain way of managing projects as a potential source of resilience, as a project-based way of working is the centrepiece of the projectification phenomenon.

12.4 Agile Project Management as a Resilience Antecedent

Traditionally project management is a linear process based on hierarchical methods that heavily rely on plans, documents and requirement analyses conducted in early project phases (Sixsmith et al. 2014). Due to the increase of project-based work and a wider variety of types of projects, new ways of management have emerged over time. The development of agile practices, including APM, began out of the necessity to be responsive and adaptable in managing complex and uncertain projects (Fernandez & Fernandez 2009). Unsurprisingly, the agile approach emerged within the software development industry, characterised by a high degree of project-based work. The creators of so-called lightweight or agile methods, including Scrum (Schwaber & Beedle 2001; Schwaber 2004), Extreme Programming (Beck 1999), Lean Software Development (Poppendieck & Poppendieck 2003), Feature Driven Development (FDD) (Palmer & Felsing 2002), Crystal (Cockburn 2004), Adaptive Software Development (Highsmith

2000), and Dynamic System Development Method (DSDM) (Stapleton 1997), jointly published the *Agile Manifesto* in 2001 (Beck et al. 2001). The evolution of agile methods happened hand in hand with the fast growth of software products and the need to increase the efficiency of software development in order to provide customers with a product that would best fulfil their needs (Nuottila 2019).

Nowadays, the necessity of being highly flexible and adapting to the rapidly changing environment is far from limited to software development projects—organisations across all sectors face similar disruptive dynamics. Traditional project management (TPM) systems, measuring success exclusively through costs, time, quality and meeting technical requirements, have become considered ineffective. Since the agile approach has proven effective when addressing these challenges within software development, its consideration across other industries is also increasing (Ćirić & Gračanin 2017). Deliberately or not, companies are implementing some agile practices since their traditional and formalised project management approaches often fail to meet the challenges of an innovative project portfolio (Conforto et al. 2014). Even though most existing literature on APM remains within the software development domain (Fernandez & Fernandez 2009; Conforto et al. 2014), some attempts to broaden the scope have been made, and APM is now moving on to other industries. For example, APM has been studied as a possible approach to construction projects (e.g. Nowotarski & Paslawski 2015), new product development projects (e.g. Conforto et al. 2014; Stare 2014), business process management projects (e.g. Thiemich and Puhlmann, 2013), manufacturing projects (e.g. Somers et al. 2015), and services projects (e.g. Ruler 2015), just to name a few.

Positive outcomes of APM within the software industry are evident and thoroughly researched; however, the existing literature lacks empirical studies of APM benefits within other industries and projects (Ćirić & Gračanin 2017). Stare (2021) points out three key advantages of using the agile approach; first, an improved adaptation of products with the consideration of consumer demands. Second, reduced risk of failure and the possibility of monitoring the performance of specific ideas on the market. Third, reduced time to market and early usage of partial results. In a recent study, Ćirić Lalić et al. (2022) compared the efficiency of agile and traditional approaches within and beyond the software domain, considering five project success dimensions. It was found that projects that were managed more agilely achieved greater impact in two out of five categories. First, impact on the team, to enhance teamwork effectiveness and overall satisfaction of team members. This is unsurprising, as agile values and principles prioritise individuals and interactions over tools and processes (Beck et al. 2001). Second, preparation for the future, meaning that the projects contributed to the future business success by building technological and organisational capacities and infrastructure (Ćirić Lalić et al. 2022).

Matching a project with a suitable management approach is crucial for project success (Fernandez & Fernandez 2009), and a one-size-fits-all attitude is certainly not appropriate when considering using APM in different types of projects. The usefulness and benefits of the agile approach vary, depending on the project type (Ćirić & Gračanin 2017; Stare 2021). For example, Highsmith (2004) and Chin (2004) argue that agile practices, tools and techniques can be adapted when dealing with projects similar to software development projects, such as innovative and dynamic environments or experiencing constant change. Similarly, Conforto et al. (2014) suggest that the agile approach is suitable for new product development projects, as they share many characteristics with software projects, such as a high level of creativity and development through continual testing and prototyping cycles.

12.5 Challenges of APM in Non-software Industries and Hybrid Approach

Although companies in more traditional industries could benefit from adapting APM (Conforto et al. 2014), some additional issues and challenges should be considered.

First, a one-time decision to go agile could be insufficient for the organisation or even the project itself—the willingness to adapt and change needs to be present, as well as the awareness of the best management approach for a specific project situation, considering a given culture and environment (Fernandez & Fernandez 2009). For the agile approach to succeed, solely using agile methodology is insufficient. It is also important that the values, behaviours and principles of those involved align with agile methodology. For example, it would be rather difficult for a project team to successfully use the Scrum method if team members did not believe in the efficiency and appropriateness of self-organised teams (Stare 2021). The greatest challenges when implementing agile practices are the gap between organisational culture and agile values, general resistance to change, lack of leadership participation and insufficient management support.

Furthermore, inconsistent team practices and processes cause additional difficulties (Digital.ai 2021). Organisational culture dictates how people think, behave, feel, act and react; therefore, it could be considered one of the most important elements of successfully implementing the agile approach. Such transformation requires a certain change, which people usually oppose, as this means dealing with unfamiliarity and uncertainty, and change causes disturbances in people's existing routines. The severity of these challenges is much less troubling for younger organisations that have used agile practices since the beginning. However, these issues could be critical for more traditional organisations that must undergo a specific transformation to become more agile. This could also explain why some elements of the traditional non-cyclical project management approach remain in most 'agile' organisations. There could be several reasons for this—perhaps, the transition towards more agile ways of working is still ongoing. There could be difficulties due to people's general resistance to change. It is also possible that some combination of agile and traditional approaches was the most appropriate way of working for the specific organisation or the projects they manage (Stare 2021).

This brings us to our second point—the hybrid approach. Research has shown that following a 'pure' agile approach is relatively rare in practice (e.g. Stavru 2014; Špundak 2014; Stare 2021). Since the *Agile Manifesto* was created in the context of the software development industry, the entire spectrum of organisations cannot operate according to all principles fully (Gustavsson 2016). Furthermore, as already mentioned, different projects require different management approaches (Ćirić Lalić et al. 2022) and implementing the agile approach just for the sake of doing so will most probably not help to achieve the expected results (Thiemich & Puhlmann 2013). Challenges, which are not typical for software development projects, but are present in other industries, could potentially be addressed with a hybrid approach (Conforto et al. 2014); hence, different forms of hybrid practices have been developed over recent years. In fact, in many situations, a hybrid approach with elements of both agile and traditional practices may be the most appropriate way of working (Fernandez and Fernandez 2009), and the two approaches should be combined to optimise the benefits from both of them (Ćirić Lalić et al. 2022). In a study of 1500 projects across 150 organisations, Reifer (2017) found that the hybrid approach is the most common when managing large projects with multiple teams in various locations. For small projects involving one team, and medium projects, involving two to five teams at the same location, the hybrid approach was the second most common approach after Scrum and a Scrum-based derivative, which turned out to be the most popular approach by far. Stare (2021) compared the VersionOne and Digital.ai research results between 2009 and 2019 and found that the hybrid approach represented between 5% and 14% of all practices during the observed period. It is also important to note that in this case, practices were referred to as the organisation's "own", meaning organisations developed a customised approach, combining elements of both traditional and agile. One example, Agile with Discipline, was observed during a case study at the IBM Center of Excellence. It integrates elements of the waterfall model used within an agile framework (Adelakun et al. 2017). A recent study compared traditional, agile, and hybrid project management approaches and found that the effects of hybrid approaches were similar to those of pure agile. Results validate that the combination of agile and traditional, which is very common in practice, is the leading project management approach, and hybrid could be the way to go. Compared to traditional approaches, hybrid and agile approaches significantly increased stakeholders' success within the same budget, time, scope, and quality outcomes (Gemino et al. 2021). This could also explain the lack of empirical evidence indicating that hybrid approaches would represent a large portion of the studied population of projects in the earlier mentioned study by Gemino et al. (2021). Results of the study indicated that 51% of studied projects could be categorised as hybrid (Gemino et al. 2021). Interestingly, Stare (2021) found that 85% of cyclical projects already have cycles planned before the project kick-off, meaning those projects are more hybrid than agile. That being said, this is probably a result of searching for the right approach for specific situations—hands-on and not a consequence of the systematic implementation of hybrid project management (Stare 2021).

12.6 Beyond Project Management in a Resilient and Projectified World

Projectification is an unavoidable direction, and it affects us in many ways—not only as individuals but also in organisational and societal contexts. Furthermore, all organisations are nowadays exposed to a highly volatile, uncertain, complex, and ambiguous environment (Bennett & Lemoine 2014), and projectification is yet another factor that contributes to these turbulent dynamics. Organisational resilience is a strategic necessity for organisations to prosper in the ever-changing dynamic environment (Douglas 2021). Since projectification means shifting towards more project-based work, one possible solution is a more agile approach to project management, which is now considered outside of software development projects, where it first originated from. Furthermore, studies in the past have considered different strategies and practices as sources of organisational resilience. Therefore, in a projectified environment, APM could be considered as well.

A recent study comparing agile, hybrid and traditional approaches found that agile practices have a more significant positive impact on two out of five project success dimensions. First, the impact on the team enhances teamwork effectiveness and overall satisfaction (Ćirić Lalić et al. 2022). This is unsurprising, as agile values and principles prioritise individuals and interactions over tools and processes (Beck et al. 2001). Considering the main challenges of project managers today, which include communication, team and people management and increasing emotional management, such as managing frustration, stress, and disconnection (Ballesteros Sánchez 2018; Digital.ai 2021), this result is very encouraging. This is in line with other reported benefits of APM, and interestingly, many of them are connected with the first principle of the *Agile Manifesto,* "Individuals and interactions over processes and tools," such as improvement of team collaboration, increase in transparency, visibility and knowledge sharing, improvement of focus, etc. (Gustavsson 2016). Considering all of the above, it is reasonable to assume that APM could, in a way, be a possible source of individual-level and team-level resilience. Second, preparation for the future, meaning that these projects contributed to the future business success by building technological and organisational capacities and infrastructure (Ćirić Lalić et al. 2022).

Furthermore, reported beneficial outcomes of APM are also increased productivity levels, speed and quality, customer interactions, flexibility, and coping with change are beneficial reported outcomes of APM (Gustavsson 2016). APM could, therefore, also be an antecedent of organisational-level resilience. Furthermore, dependencies and connections between individual, team and organisational resilience levels should also be considered. Over recent years, multiple resilience studies across all three levels have been conducted, some researching how a single antecedent functions across all three levels simultaneously (Raetze 2021). Adaptation of the agile approach to project management could benefit the people and organisations involved. Perhaps, due to the agile adapting agile approach, even positive consequences of projectification on an individual level could be discovered, as this is the currently under-researched side of the phenomenon (Jacobsson & Jałocha 2021).

It is important to note that organisations across different sectors and projects across various areas mean that some clarification regarding the term "agile" and "agile project management" should be considered. Matching a project with an appropriate project management approach is crucial for project success (Fernandez & Fernandez 2009)—the hybrid approach, combining both agile and traditional elements, is the most appropriate in many scenarios and, unsurprisingly, also quite common in practice (Ćirić

Lalić et al. 2022). Furthermore, some TPM elements are still present in many organisations shifting towards more agile working methods (Stare 2021). Therefore, in future empirical research, we should focus on organisations and teams that use "pure" agile methods and different versions of the hybrid approach.

In the organisational context, being resilient means being prepared for adversity (Danyer 2017), which requires an improved overall capacity to act without knowing what must be done (Wildavsky 1988). In other words, being resilient requires agility. That said, being agile does not only mean using specific agile methods in project management—it is a broader notion concerning all levels of organisations.

12.7 Conclusion

Projectification, resilience and APM are all relatively new concepts, receiving much attention in academic and business areas over recent years. This is not at all surprising when considering global trends and the general characteristics of the world we currently live in. Projectification has become a widespread trend in today's business landscape, leading to an increased reliance on project-based work and adopting agile project management practices. However, this trend has also resulted in potentially negative consequences for individuals and organisations, leading to the need for resilience in uncertain and complex project environments.

In this chapter, we have explored the potential of agile project management as an antecedent for multilevel resilience. Our literature review found that while limited research explores the connections between projectification, resilience and agile project management, there is enough evidence to suggest that these three concepts are interrelated and that further investigation is needed.

One possible direction for future research is to explore how agile project management practices can enhance resilience at various levels, including the individual, team and organisational levels. For example, agile project management practices emphasise collaboration, adaptability and continuous improvement, which can help teams and organisations navigate complex and uncertain project environments more effectively.

Furthermore, the research could also explore the potential challenges and limitations of implementing agile project management practices in traditional organisations that may have more rigid structures and processes. For example, agile project management practices may require a significant cultural shift within an organisation and may not be suitable for all projects or industries.

Future research could also explore the potential role of leadership in promoting resilience in project environments. Effective leadership is critical in creating a supportive and resilient project culture where individuals and teams feel empowered to take risks and learn from their mistakes.

Finally, there is also an opportunity for practical contributions to modern organisations. This chapter suggests that agile project management practices could potentially enhance resilience in project environments, and organisations could consider implementing these practices to improve their project outcomes and mitigate potential negative consequences associated with projectification.

In conclusion, the intersection of projectification, resilience and agile project management is a complex and underexplored area of research. While our literature review has provided some insights into potential connections between these three concepts, further investigation is needed to understand their interplay fully. We hope our contribution has sparked interest in this area and encouraged future research to enhance our understanding of how organisations can effectively manage projects in today's dynamic and uncertain business environment.

References

Adelakun, Oluseyi, Rodrigo Garcia, Rami Ismail, and Tomasz Tabaka. 2017. "Hybrid Project Management: Agile with Discipline." CONF-IRM 2017 Proceedings 14:1–13.

Ashby, Suzanne E., Stephanie Ryan, Melanie Gray, and Carole James. 2013. "Factors That Influence the Professional Resilience of Occupational Therapists in Mental Health Practice." *Australian Occupational Therapy Journal* 60 (2): 110–119. doi:10.1111/1440–1630.12012.

Ates, Aylin, and Umit Bititci. 2011. "Change Process: A Key Enabler for Building Resilient SMEs." International Journal of Production Research 49 (18): 5601–5618. doi:10.1080/00207543.2011.563825.

Auschra, Christine, Timo Braun, Thomas Schmidt, and Jörg Sydow. 2019. "Patterns of Project-Based Organizing in New Venture Creation: Projectification of an Entrepreneurial Ecosystem." *International Journal of Managing Projects in Business* 12 (1): 48–70.

Ballesteros Sánchez, Luis Ignacio, Isabel Ortiz Marcos, and Rafael Rodríguez Rivero. 2018. "The Impact of Projectification on Managers: Main Challenges." In The 6th IPMA Research Conference: Project Management and Its Impact on Societies, edited by Newton Maruyama, 87–97. Río de Janeiro.

Bardoel, Elizabeth A., Timothy M. Pettit, Helen De Cieri, and Lynne McMillan. 2014. "Employee Resilience: An Emerging Challenge for HRM." *Asia Pacific Journal of Human Resources* 52 (3): 279–297. doi:10.1111/1744–7941.12033.

Barondeau, Reginald and Brian Hobbs. 2019. "A Pragmatic Sociological Examination of Projectification." International Journal of Managing Projects in Business 12 (2): 282–297.

Beck, Kent. 1999. *Extreme Programming Explained.* Reading: Addison-Wesley.

Beck, Kent, Mike Beedle, Arie van Bennekum, Alistair Cockburn, Ward Cunningham, Martin Fowler, et al. 2001. "Manifesto for Agile Software Development." Accessed 3rd March 2022. http://agilemanifesto.org/.

Bennett, Nathan, and G. James Lemoine. 2014. "What a Difference a Word Makes: Understanding Threats to Performance in a VUCA World." *Business Horizons* 57 (3): 311–317.

Bogacz-Wojtanowska, Ewa and Barbara Jałocha. 2016. "The Bright Side of Social Economy Sector's Projectification: A Study of Successful Social Enterprises." *Project Management Research and Practice* 3:1–20.

Bonanno, George A. 2004. "Loss, Trauma, and Human Resilience: Have We Underestimated the Human Capacity to Thrive After Extremely Aversive Events?" *American Psychologist* 59 (1): 20–28.

Bråthen, Cecilie and Mari Ommundsen. 2018. "The 'Dark Side' of Projectification: The Impact of Project Work on the Employees' Well-Being. A Quantitative Study of the Impact of Project Work Exposure on Employees' Work-Related Well-Being." Kristiansand: University of Agder.

Bredin, Karin and Jonas Söderlund. "Projectification on the Way." In Human Resource Management in Project-Based Organisations, edited by Karin Bredin and Jonas Söderlund, 1–22. London: Palgrave Macmillan, 2011.

Brunila, Kristiina. "The projectisation, marketisation and therapisation of education." *European Educational Research Journal* 10, no. 3 (2011): 421–432.

Burke, Ronald J. "Effects of 9/11 on individuals and organisations: Down but not out!" Disaster Prevention and Management: An International Journal 14 (2005): 629–638. doi:10.1108/09653560510634052.

Cambridge Dictionary. "Resilience." Retrieved on 15th March 2022 from *Cambridge Dictionary*:
https://dictionary.cambridge.org/dictionary/english/resilience.

Carmeli, Abraham, Avner Levi and Raffaella Peccei. "Resilience and Creative Problem-Solving Capacities in Project Teams: A Relational

View." *International Journal of Project Management* 39, no. 5 (2021): 546–556.

Chapman, Mark T., Rachel L. Lines, Matthew Crane, Karen J. Ducker, Nikos Ntoumanis, Paul Peeling, and Daniel F. Gucciardi. "Team Resilience: A Scoping Review of Conceptual and Empirical Work." *Work and Stress* 34, no. 1 (2020): 57–81.

Cicmil, Svetlana, Mats Lindgren and Jonas Packendorff. "The Project (Management) Discourse and Its Consequences: On Vulnerability and Unsustainability in Project-Based Work." *New Technology, Work and Employment* 31, no. 1 (2016): 58–76.

Conforto, Edivandro C., Fabio Salum, Daniel C. Amaral, Sergio Luis da Silva, and Luciano F. de Almeida. "Can Agile Project Management Be Adopted by Industries Other Than Software Development?" *Project Management Journal* 45, no. 3 (2014): 21–34.

Cooke, Fang Lee, Brian Cooper, Tim Bartram, Jun Wang and Hongmei Mei. "Mapping the Relationships between High-Performance Work Systems, Employee Resilience and Engagement: A Study of the Banking Industry in China." *The International Journal of Human Resource Management* 30, no. 8 (2019): 1239–1260. doi:10.1080/09585192.

Cooper, Cary, Jill Flint-Taylor and Michael Pearn. *Building Resilience for Success: A Resource for Managers and Organisations*. Basingstoke: Palgrave, 2013.

Ćirić Lalić, Danijela, Boris Lalić, Milovan Delić, Dragana Gračanin, and Dušan Stefanović. "How Project Management Approach Impact Project Success? From Traditional to Agile." *International Journal of Managing Projects in Business* 15, no. 3 (2022): 494–521.

Ćirić, Danijela and Danijela Gračanin. "Agile Project Management Beyond Software Industry." In XVII International Scientific Conference on Industrial Systems (IS'17), 332–337. Novi Sad: University of Novi Sad, Faculty of Technical Sciences, 2017.

Demmer, William A., Susan K. Vickery, and Roger Calantone. "Engendering Resilience in Small- and Medium-Sized Enterprises (SMEs): A Case Study of Demmer Corporation." *International Journal of Production Research* 49, no. 18 (2011): 5395–5413. doi:10.1080/00207543.2011.563903.

Denyer, David. Organisational Resilience: A Summary of Academic Evidence, Business Insights and New Thinking. Cranfield: BSI and Cranfield School of Management, 2017.

Digital.ai. "15th State of Agile Report." Retrieved on 5th March 2022 from Digital.ai:

https://digital.ai/resource-center/analyst-reports/state-of-agile-report.

Douglas, Sara. "Building Organisational Resilience through Human Capital Management Strategy." *Development and Learning in Organisations* 35, no. 5 (2021): 19–21. doi:10.1108/DLO-08-2020-0180.

Ekstedt, Eskil. "A New Division of Labour: The 'Projectification' of Working and Industrial Life." In *Building Anticipation of Restructuring in Europe*, edited by V. M. A. Moreau, S. Negrelli, and P. Pochet, 31–53. Bruxelles: Peter Lang Verlag, 2009.

Fernandez, Daniel J., and Jonathon D. Fernandez. "Agile Project Management—Agillism Versus Traditional Approaches." *The Journal of Computer Information Systems* 49, no. 2 (2009): 10–17.

Gemino, Andrew, Barbara Horner Reich and Paulo M. Serrador. "Agile, Traditional, and Hybrid Approaches to Project Success: Is Hybrid a Poor Second Choice?" *Project Management Journal* 52, no. 2 (2021): 161–175.

Gustavsson, Tomas. "Benefits of Agile Project Management in a Non-Software Development Context: A Literature Review." In Project Management Development—Practice and Perspectives: Fifth International Scientific Conference on Project Management in the Baltic Countries, edited by A. Katunskyte, R. Mikalsen, and J. V. Gudmundsson, 114–124. Riga: Latvijas Universitate, 2016.

Harland, Leah, William Harrison, James R. Jones, and Robin Reiter-Palmon. "Leadership Behaviors and Subordinate Resilience." Journal of Leadership and Organizational Studies 11, no. 2 (2005): 2–14. doi:10.1177/107179190501100202.

Hartmann, Sarah, Markus Weiss, Alexandra Newman, and Martin Hoegl. "Resilience in the Workplace: A Multilevel Review and Synthesis." *Applied Psychology* 69, no. 3 (2020): 913–959.

Henning, Christian H., and Andreas Wald. "Toward a Wiser Projectification: Macroeconomic Effects of Firm-Level Project Work." *International Journal of Project Management* 37, no. 6 (2019): 807–819.

Highsmith, Jim. *Adaptive Software Development: A Collaborative Approach to Managing Complex Systems*. New York: Dorset House, 2000.

Hillmann, Julia, Stephanie Duchek, Jan Meyr, and Elisabeth Guenther. "Educating Future Managers for Developing Resilient Organisations: The Role of Scenario Planning." *Journal of Management Education* 42, no. 4 (2018): 461–495. doi:10.1177/1052562918766350.

Horne, John F., and James E. Orr. "Assessing Behaviors That Create Resilient Organisations." *Employment Relations Today* 24, no. 4 (1998): 29–39.

Howard, Charles S., and J. Allen Irving. "The Impact of Obstacles Defined by Developmental Antecedents on Resilience in Leadership Formation." *Management Research Review* 37, no. 5 (2014): 466–478. doi:10.1108/MRR-03-2013-0072.

Hubmann, Maren. "Chronicity of disruptive project rhythms: The projectification of the 'post-Ebola' health system rebuilding in Sierra Leone." *Time and Society* 30, no. 3 (2021): 379–401. doi:10.1177/0961463X211005207.

Hudgins, Tiffany A. "Resilience, job satisfaction and anticipated turnover in nurse leaders." *Journal of Nursing Management* 24, no. 2 (2016): E62-E69. doi:10.1111/jonm.12289.

Jacobsson, Mattias and Bartłomiej Jałocha. "Four images of projectification: An integrative review." *International Journal of Managing Projects in Business* 14, no. 7 (2021): 1583–1604.

Jensen, Anders F. *The Project Society*. Aarhus: Aarhus Universitetsforlaget, 2012.

Jensen, Anders, Carsten Thuesen and Jonas Geraldi. "The projectification of everything: Projects as a human condition." *Project Management Journal* 47, no. 3 (2016): 21–34.

Jensen, Christian, Sara Johansson and Maja Löfström. "Projectification of the Public Human Services—Identifying Four 'Archetypical' Project Organizations Based on Time, Space and Relationship Challenges." Paper presented at the International Research Society for Public Management (IRSPM) 21st Annual Conference, Budapest, April 19–21, 2017, 1–26.

Lampel, Joseph, Ajay Bhalla and Pushkar P. Jha. "Does governance confer organisational resilience? Evidence from UK employee-owned businesses." *European Management Journal* 32, no. 1 (2014): 66–72. doi:10.1016/j.emj.2013.06.009.

Lengnick-Hall, Cynthia A., Terri E. Beck, and Mark L. Lengnick-Hall. "Developing a capacity for organisational resilience through strategic human resource management." *Human Resource Management* Review 21, no. 3 (2011): 243–255. doi:10.1016/j.hrmr.2010.07.001.

Luthans, Fred, Greg R. Vogelgesang, and Philomena B. Lester. "Developing the psychological capital of resiliency." *Human Resource Development Review* 5, no. 1 (2006): 25–44.

Masten, Ann S. "Ordinary magic: Resilience processes in development." *American Psychologist* 56, no. 3 (2001): 703–706.

Maylor, Harvey and Ville Turkulainen. "The concept of organisational projectification: past, present and beyond?" *International Journal of Managing Projects in Business* 12, no. 3 (2019): 565–577.

Maylor, Harvey, Terry Brady, Tim Cooke-Davies and Damian Hodgson. "From projectification to programmification." *International Journal of Project Management* 24, no. 8 (2006): 663–674.

McEwen, Kathryn and Carolyn M. Boyd. "A measure of team resilience: Developing the resilience at work team scale." *Journal of Occupational and Environmental Medicine* 60, no. 3 (2018): 258–272.

Midler, Christophe. "Projectification of the Firm: the Renault Case." *Scand. Journal of Management* 11, no. 4 (1995): 363–375.

Mukhtar-Landgren, Dalia and Mikael Fred. "Re-compartmentalising local policies? The translation and mediation of European structural funds in Sweden." *Critical Policy Studies* 13, no. 4 (2019): 488–506.

Myrmæl, Ingvild E., and Hanne H. Alfredsen. "The 'Dark Side' of Projectification: The Impact of Project Work on the Employees' Emotions. What Are the Negative Aspects of Project Work and its Effects on the Individual Project Worker's Emotions in a Project Life Cycle?" Kristiansand: University of Agder, 2018.

Näswall, Katharina, Susanna Malinen, Jonathan Kuntz, and Michael Hodliffe. "Employee resilience: development and validation of a measure." *Journal of Managerial Psychology* 34, no. 5 (2019): 353–367.

Norman, Shannon, Bruce Luthans and Kyle Luthans. "The proposed contagion effect of hopeful leaders on the resiliency of employees and organisations." *Journal of Leadership and Organizational Studies* (2005): 55–64. doi:10.1177/107179190501200205.

Nowotarski, Paweł and Jacek Paslawski. "Barriers in Running Construction SME—Case Study on Introduction of Agile Methodology to Electrical Subcontractor." *Procedia Engineering* 22 (2015): 47–56.

Nuottila, Jukka. "Flexibility in agile projects. Contracting practices and organisational arrangements." Oulu: University of Oulu, 2019.

Ortiz-de-Mandojana, Natalia and Pratima Bansal. "The long-term benefits of organisational resilience through sustainable business practices." *Strategic Management Journal* 37, no. 8 (2016): 1615–1631. doi:10.1002/smj.2410.

Palmer, Scott R., and John M. Felsing. 2002. A Practical Guide to Feature-Driven Development. New York: Prentice Hall PTR.

Poppendieck, Mary and Tom Poppendieck. 2003. Lean Software Development: An Agile Toolkit for Software Development Managers. Boston: Addison-Wesley Professional.

Prayag, Girish, Simon Spector, Caroline Orchiston, and Muntasir Chowdhury. 2020. "Psychological Resilience, Organisational Resilience and Life Satisfaction in Tourism Firms: Insights from the Canterbury Earthquakes." *Current Issues in Tourism* 23 (10): 1216–1233. doi:10.1080/13683500.2019.1607832.

Raetze, Sebastian, Simon Duchek, Terence M. Maynard, and Bradley L. Kirkman. 2021. "Resilience in Organisations: An Integrative Multilevel Review and Editorial Introduction." *Journal of Organizational Behavior* 46 (4): 607–656.

Reifer, Donald J. 2017. "Quantitative Analysis of Agile Methods Study (2017): Twelve Major Findings." Retrieved on 3rd April 2022 from InfoQ: https://www.infoq.com/articles/reifer-agile-study-2017/.

Ruler, Betteke van. 2015. "Agile Public Relations Planning: The Reflective Communication Scrum." *Public Relations Review* 41 (2): 187–194.

Sage, Daniel. 2016. "Professionalization, Projectification and Pressurization: Insights from Construction Project Management." In *Perspectives on Contemporary Professional Work: Challenges and Experiences*, edited by Valérie A. Wilkinson, David Hislop, and Christina Coupland, 338–361. Cheltenham: Edward Elgar Publishing.

Schoper, Yvonne-Gabriele, Andreas Wald, Thórarinn Ingi Helgi and Thorvaldur Vigfusson Fridgeirsson. 2018. "Projectification in Western Economies: A Comparative Study of Germany, Norway and Iceland." *International Journal of Project Management* 36 (1): 71–82.

Schwaber, Ken. 2004. *Agile Project Management with SCRUM*. Redmond: Microsoft Press.

Schwaber, Ken and Mike Beedle. 2001. *Agile Software Development with Scrum*. New York: Prentice Hall.

Sixsmith, Andrew, Chris Freeburn and Gerry Mooney. 2014. "Project Management in Practice: Views from the Trenches." Paper presented at the 24th International Business Information Management Association Conference.

Stapleton, Jennifer. 1997. Dynamic Systems Development Method. Boston: Addison Wesley.

Stare, Aljaž. "Agile Project Management in Product Development Projects." Procedia—Social and Behavioral Sciences 119 (2014): 295–304.

Stare, Aljaž. *Agilno!? Projekti, zaposleni, podjetja*. Ljubljana: Agencija POTI, 2021.

Stavru, Stelian. "A Critical Examination of Recent Industrial Surveys on Agile Method Usage." *Journal of Systems and Software* 94, no. 1 (2014): 87–97.

Sullivan-Taylor, Bridget and David C. Wilson. "Managing the Threat of Terrorism in British Travel and Leisure Organizations." *Organisation Studies* 30, no. 2/3 (2009): 251–276.

Špundak, Marko. "Mixed Agile/Traditional Project Management Methodology—Reality or Illusion?" Procedia—Social and Behavioral Sciences 119 (2014): 939–948.

Teng-Calleja, Marites, Ma. Regina M. Hechanova, Patricia R. Sabile, and Aleli V. Villasanta. "Building Organization and Employee Resilience in Disaster Contexts." *International Journal of Workplace Health Management* 13, no. 4 (2020): 393–411. doi:10.1108/IJWHM-09-2019-0122.

Thiemich, Christian and Florian Puhlmann. "An Agile BPM Project Methodology." In Business Process Management, edited by Frank Daniel, Jixuan Wang, and Barbara Weber, 291–306. Lecture Notes in Computer Science, vol 8094. Berlin, Heidelberg: Springer, 2013.

Trifoglio, Valentina. *Connections between Resilience, Work-Related Factors and Perceived Organizational Practices-Focus on Older Finnish Nurses*. Tampere: University of Tampere, 2018.

van der Beek, Daniëlle and Jan Maarten Schraagen. "ADAPTER: Analysing and Developing Adaptability and Performance in Teams to Enhance Resilience." *Reliability Engineering and System Safety* 141 (2015): 33–44. doi:10.1016/j.ress.2015.03.019.

Waring, Teresa and Peter Thomas. "The Insidious Growth of Societal Projectification: Emancipatory Research with Public Sector Staff in the North of England." In the 5th *Making Projects Critical Workshop*. Bristol, 2010.

Wenell, Tobias, Erik Ekstedt and Anders Lundin. "On the Road to Project Society—A Swedish Story: Managing and Working in Project Society." *PM World Journal* 6, no. 1 (2017): 1–6.

Wildavsky, Aaron. *Searching for Safety*. New Brunswick: Transaction Press, 1988.

Williams, Terry. "Assessing and Moving on from the Dominant Project Management Discourse in the Light of Project Overruns." *IEEE Transactions on Engineering Management* 52, no. 4 (2005): 497–508.

Wojan, Timothy R., Darrell Crown, and Anil Rupasingha. "Varieties of Innovation and Business Survival: Does Pursuit of Incremental or Far-Ranging Innovation Make Manufacturing Establishments More Resilient?" *Research Policy 47*, no. 9 (2018): 1801–1810. doi:10.1016/j.respol.2018.06.011.

Igor Vrečko, PhD, is an associate professor of general management and vice dean for development projects and cooperation with the environment at the University of Maribor, Faculty of Economics and Business. He is a highly interdisciplinary and transdisciplinary-orientated researcher focusing on project management and its integration with strategic, innovation and crisis management. He has published over 100 scientific and professional papers in national and international journals and books. He is also an experienced editor and reviewer, serving on national and international scientific journal editorial boards. In addition to his academic work, Vrečko has gained extensive practical experience through consultancy projects in domestic and foreign companies. He was a director of the international project management certification process for Slovenia and is currently the president of the Slovenian Project Management Association. He is the head of the Institute of Project Management at the University of Maribort.

Nuša Širovnik is pursuing a PhD at the University of Maribor, Faculty of Economics and Business. Her research focus is on the phenomenon of projectification, especially in relation to the impact on workplace and employee well-being consequences. Furthermore, she is interested in resilience and agility on individual and team levels to address projectification-related challenges. Professionally, she has experience in national and international projects, mostly across the retail industry. As a senior project associate at a large multinational company, she is a part of the Program Office, focusing on data and analytics products and building an agile organisation.